Today's women have been praying for years for a sweeping revival in our nation. As we excitedly watch and experience brush fires erupting here and there, this book gives us not only Biblical and historic evidence of God using women in past revivals, but the possibility of God doing it again. What a timely and encouraging book!

—Evelyn Christenson

Any book that models women of faith making a difference in an upside down culture must be read. Keeping lively and faithful is a full time job and one that "must" be sought by all believing women. This book helps.

—Jill Briscoe

Next to the Word of God, reading the biographies of great Christians of the past has impacted my life more than anything else. *Women of Awakenings* features many women whom God has used to inspire and challenge me to pursue Him with all my heart, soul, mind, and strength. These are ordinary women like you and me who simply walked in faith's obedience pursuing holiness, as Hebrews 12 says, without which no one will see the Lord. It is my prayer that God will use this book to revive you in these difficult days as you look beyond the temporal to the eternal, as you look to that day when we shall stand before Him to give an account of the deeds done in our flesh. Such an awareness, along with testimonies such as these in *Women of Awakenings*, should keep us in a state of revival.

—Kay Arthur

Women
of
Awakenings

Women of Awakenings: The Historic Contribution of Women to Revival Movements

Published by Kregel Publications, a division of Kregel, Inc., P.O. Box 2607, Grand Rapids, MI 49501. Kregel Publications provides trusted, biblical publications for Christian growth and service. Your comments and suggestions are valued.

Cover design: Alan G. Hartman
Book design: Nicholas G. Richardson

Library of Congress Cataloging-in-Publication Data
Drummond, Lewis A.
  Women of awakenings: the historic contribution of women to revival movements / Lewis Drummond, Betty Drummond.
      p.   cm.
  Includes bibliographical references.
    1. Women in Christianity—Biography. 2. Church renewal—Biography. 3. Revivals—Biography. I. Drummond, Betty II. Title.
BR1713.D78   1997   270'.082—dc20   95-32043
                                                                              CIP

ISBN 0-8254-2474-7

Printed in the United States of America
1 2 3 4 5 / 01 00 99 98 97

Women of Awakenings

The Historic Contribution of Women to Revival Movements

Lewis and Betty Drummond

kregel
PUBLICATIONS

Grand Rapids, MI 49501

To all godly women who desire
a spiritual awakening and
who pray that they might be
partners with the Holy Spirit
for the coming awakening in
our nation and world.

CONTENTS

FOREWORD

Whenever Dr. and Mrs. Drummond speak, I listen. Their love for Jesus Christ, their heart for the Gospel, their faith in God's Word, their joy in Christian service, their dependence in prayer, their endurance in suffering, and their patience in persecution have given them a credibility that goes beyond any degrees or positions they hold. The Drummonds dare to live out in practical experience their Christian faith.

Therefore, when they contacted me about writing a foreword to this book, I not only felt honored but eager to read what Lewis and Betty had to say about women of awakenings. Once again, their enthusiasm for the subject is supported by personal practice. Outside my own family, no one has been more encouraging and supportive of me in ministry than have Dr. and Mrs. Drummond. They are valued mentors to whom I turn for answers to doctrinal, theological, historical, and very practical questions.

As I sincerely recommend this volume, I cannot help but wonder if there would be more awakenings if there were more men and women such as Lewis and Betty who would encourage, instruct, guide, and liberate women as we seek to develop our spiritual gifts and answer God's call in our lives. I pray that this book might be used of God to encourage others either to be or to support women in ministry throughout the church in the hope that God will once again send us a great awakening.

—ANNE GRAHAM LOTZ

PREFACE

A true spiritual awakening has intrigued, challenged, and fascinated God's people throughout the ages. When those "times of refreshing . . . come from the presence of the Lord" (Acts 3:19 KJV), the entire community comes alive as the breath of God blows gently over it. Believers are revived, the church gears to new kingdom action, multitudes come to Christ, and society is transformed. Little wonder that real revival has been the heart cry of the faithful down through the annals of biblical and church history.

The incredible events that transpire during a spiritual awakening, or revival as it is variously termed, all but defy imagination. Many are brought to faith in Christ, the church moves into deep dedication, civic and social righteousness invades the land, nothing is ever quite the same again, and God gets great glory to Himself. Clearly, we stand in need of such a movement today. One should take courage; God has brought about revival myriads of times and in myriad manners. Moreover, at the immediate moment, it appears as if the Spirit of God may soon so move once again. Pockets of revival have recently broken out on several campuses and in churches across America. There is more interest, concern, and prayer for a fresh awakening than has been evident for decades. Could this be God's hour?

If an awakening does come, whom will God use in the movement? We think of the notable men whom the Holy Spirit lifted up in revival in the past—men like Girolamo Savanrolo, John Hus, Martin Luther, and in more recent times, John Wesley, George Whitefield, Jonathan Edwards, Charles Spurgeon, and many others. All were powerfully used by God. But men do not constitute the whole story; in many spiritual movements God has raised up and mightily used *women*. A look into the Scriptures makes it clear that women such as Deborah in the Old Testament and Priscilla in the New Testament have played a key role in reviving God's people. Church history abounds with the same principle—God uses women in spiritual awakenings.

The purpose of this book is to delve into the lives of a number of women of God whom the Holy Spirit has touched to foster awakenings. The relevance of this book seems obvious for three reasons. First, interest in revival abounds. Second, this book should encourage that interest and, above all, encourage prayer for revival. Finally, it is hoped that this book will inform and challenge contemporary Christians as to what constitutes a true spiritual awakening and how it comes about. If the reader is informed and challenged, the efforts of the authors will be well rewarded.

The format of this work will begin with two biblical instances of God's use of women and then chronologically travel through the pages of history viewing the lives and ministries of a number of outstanding personalities. Its purpose is more, however, than a brief historical or biographical sketch of great women; its purpose is to challenge, inform, inspire, and move the church to seek God for an awakening today.

ACKNOWLEDGMENTS

We would be remiss if we did not express gratitude and acknowledge our debt to several people who made this volume, *Women of Awakenings,* possible.

First, our appreciation goes to our able secretaries, Mrs. Debbie Morgan and Mrs. Mary Morgan. They spent many hours on the manuscript and put the chapters in final form. Also, we are grateful to Dennis Hillman of Kregel Publications for his help in this work. It was he, on hearing Betty's idea for such a book, who encouraged us to undertake the task.

Perhaps, above all, gratitude must go to several able biographers upon whose work we greatly depended for each chapter. They must be acknowledged with profound appreciation. Without their labor this book could have hardly been produced. Some of those we depended most heavily upon are

- Catherine Bromwell-Booth, *Catherine Booth* (Hodder and Stoughton);
- Eliza Clarke, *Susanna Wesley* (Roberts Brothers);
- Patricia Daniels Cornwell, *A Time for Remembering* (Harper and Row);
- Edith Dean, *Great Women of the Christian Faith* (Harper and Row);
- Peter W. Gentry, *The Countess of Huntingdon* (People Called Methodists, No. 4);
- Norman Grubb, *Mighty through God* (Lutterworth Press);
- James G. Lawson, *Deeper Experiences of Famous Christians* (Warner Press);
- Marie Monsen, *The Awakening* (China Inland Mission);
- Charles Ray, *Mrs. C. H. Spurgeon* (Passmore and Alabaster);
- Kathleen White, *Amy Carmichael* (Bethany House Publishers);

Several of these biographies are quite old, and the authors are deceased. Yet, their works remain, and we give God praise for their keeping alive great women of awakenings.

We wish to also acknowledge the following sources for the photos and illustrations used in the book.

Chapter 1, Deborah
From Harriet Beecher Stowe's *Woman in Sacred History* (New York: J. B. Ford Company, 1873), 98.

Chapter 2, Priscilla
Ibid., 366.

Chapter 3, Madam Guyon
From James Gilchrist Lawson's *Deeper Experiences of Famous Christians* (Anderson, Ind.: Warner Press, 1911), 86.

Chapter 4, Susanna Wesley
Engraving from an unknown portrait. By courtesy of The New Room, Bristol, England. Photo by Eileen Tweedy.

Chapter 5, Selina, Countess of Huntingdon
From Arnold Dallimore's *George Whitefield*, Vol. 2 (Westchester, Ill.: Cornerstone Books, 1979), 144.

Chapter 6, Susannah Spurgeon
From Lewis Drummond's *Spurgeon: Prince of Preachers* (Grand Rapids: Kregel, 1992), 176.

Chapter 7, Catherine Booth
From John Ervine's *God's Soldier: General William Booth* (London: William Heinemann, Ltd., 1934), 131.

Chapter 8, Amy Carmichael
From Frank Houghton's *Amy Carmichael of Dohnavur* (London: S.P.C.K., 1954), 52.

Chapter 9, Edith Moules
From *Mighty Through God: The Life of Edith Moules* (London: Lutterworth Press, 1951), frontispiece.

Chapter 10, Bertha Smith
From Lewis Drummond's *Miss Bertha: Woman of Revival* (Nashville: Broadman & Holman, 1996), 1.

Chapter 12, Ruth Bell Graham
From Patricia Daniels Cornwell's *A Time for Remembering: The Ruth Bell Graham Story* (New York: Harper & Row, 1986), 208.

Women of Awakenings

What was the glow
   That was on her face?
What was the glory;
   What was the grace
That brightened each mile
   Of the road she trod?
It was this:
   She walked with God.

PROLOGUE

The Essence of an Awakening

Marie Monsen, Bertha Smith, and Ola Culpepper are the so-called guilty ones. These three women are responsible! True—*blessedly responsible*—but for what? It sounds like an intriguing tale. True—*blessedly true*. What lurks behind this story?

It all began in the Chinese seaport city of Chefoo. The year was 1927. Communist political activity was stirring up serious unrest in Shantung province, the large province situated in northeast China. The United States government strongly advised all the American missionaries to leave Shantung and quarter in Chefoo until the unrest settled down. So Bertha and Ola, who were serving as Baptist missionaries from the United States, made their way to the coast. Marie, a Norwegian Lutheran missionary, would soon join them.

Over a score of missionaries soon gathered in a small mission compound of only two buildings. The Chefoo accommodations left much to be desired. The unrest that the Communists and others caused in Shantung almost found its equal in the unrest felt by the idle missionaries in their cramped quarters. What were they to do? They finally decided to make their sojourn into something of a spiritual retreat, and they asked Marie Monsen to come and share her testimony with them. Share she did. She exposed their lives to the truths of the Bible regarding godliness, which began a deep stirring—and quest—for a true touch from God.

"Are you filled with the Holy Spirit?" Marie would ask.

"You must confess and forsake all your known sins if God is to fill you with His Power," she declared. "God demands holiness," she cried.

Dr. Charles Culpepper, Ola's husband, felt particularly moved. Ola, likewise, experienced a deep probing of the Holy Spirit.

Then it happened. Ola, who suffered from optic neuritis, told Charles that she had become convinced that God wanted to heal her. She had only partial vision in the affected eye, and it caused much pain. Previously she had gone for treatment to a fine specialist, a physician from Vienna,

19

Austria, and a world authority on the malady, who was serving a temporary residency at Central Medical Hopital in China's capital city. But all he could do was change Ola's glasses and offer very little hope.

So, Ola asked Marie to gather the group to pray for her healing. Heal her? Ask for a miracle? This was quite unheard of among the Baptist missionaries in those days. They strove to get all their sins confessed "up to date," however, and they came together for prayer. Maybe God would do something unusual. Charles said that electric excitement filled the air. They all became convinced that God had something in store for them that they had never known before.

The earnest group of about twelve missionaries formed a circle around Ola as she placed her glasses on the mantle of the fireplace. Dr. Culpepper read from the Bible:

> *Is any one of you in trouble? He should pray. Is anyone happy?*
> *Let him sing songs of praise. Is any one of you sick? He should*
> *call the elders of the church to pray over him and anoint him*
> *with oil in the name of the Lord. And the prayer offered in faith*
> *will make the sick person well; the Lord will raise him up. If he*
> *has sinned, he will be forgiven. Therefore confess your sins to*
> *each other and pray for each other so that you may be healed.*
> *The prayer of a righteous man is powerful and effective (James*
> *5:13–16 NIV).*

Charles then anointed Ola with oil and asked the missionaries to place their hands on Ola's head and pray for healing.

Suddenly, Bertha Smith broke in and it all but upset the proverbial apple cart. She said,

> I had gone into that room, so far as I knew, absolutely right with the Lord. I would not have dared to go otherwise. But when I stretched my hand out to Mrs. Culpepper's head, I had to bring it back. There facing me was Miss Hartwell, a missionary with whom I had had a little trouble. In her early years, she had been teaching illiterate women to read.
>
> I had been asked to serve as principal in our boys' school while the missionary principal was on furlough. I had majored in education and by that time had had ten years' experience in teaching. I thought that I was "the last word" in education! I had recommended Miss Hartwell to lead daily worship in that school. After a few weeks, I asked another missionary to tell her that her methods for teaching old women were not appropriate for high-school boys. She was hurt, of course.

But what about my proud self? I did not have a particle of sympathy for her. Right there before everyone, I had to say, "Miss Hartwell, I did not have the proper attitude toward you about that school affair. I beg you to forgive me!" My hand then joined the others and we prayed.

Had I refused to confess that sin, and joined in the prayer with it covered, I believe that I would have hindered the prayer of the others, and the eye could not have been healed.

Now they could truly pray. And how they did pray. Then, as Bertha expressed it, "heaven came down." They did not even have to ask Ola if she had been healed. They all knew in their hearts that their prayer of faith had brought the Lord's healing power to His servant. The pain left, and Ola left her glasses on the mantle the rest of her life. God had come. Bertha said that they all walked around the room praising God. They had climbed a mountaintop of ecstasy.

That was the beginning of the great Shantung Revival of 1927–1936. What days they were. The churches filled, the Chinese believers were mightily awakened, multitudes came to new saving faith in Christ, and God was wonderfully glorified. Those three women were guilty all right— *blessedly guilty.*

But what if Marie, Ola, and Bertha had not been willing to become God's channel of revival? Where would China be had they resisted the Lord's purpose? Only God knows. But they did yield to Christ's sovereignty and became true *women of awakening.*

History abounds with stories of such women. We all know the epics of great men of revival like John Wesley, George Whitfield, Jonathan Edwards, and others. But women, also, have many times played a significant and vital role in such monumental movements. There have been many Berthas, Olas, and Maries in the course of God's dealings. This book tells the story of just some of those mighty women of revival.

All this raises a basic question that demands an answer before we delve into the fascinating lives of such women. The question is: What constitutes a true revival—that is, what really takes place when a revival, or a great awakening, in the biblical, historical sense, breaks in on a people? The answer is: Many wonderful things. Here are a few; the Isaiah experience (Isaiah 6) pictures them well. It all begins with:

A New Vision of God

In the year that King Uzziah died, [Isaiah] saw the LORD seated on a throne, high and exalted, and the train of his robe filled the temple. Above him were seraphs, each with six wings: With two wings they covered their faces, with two they covered their feet,

*and with two they were flying. And they were calling to one an-
other: "Holy, holy, holy is the LORD Almighty; the whole earth is
full of his glory."*

*At the sound of their voices the doorposts and thresholds shook
and the temple was filled with smoke (Isa. 6:1–4 NIV).*

The first foundational principle of a great awakening centers in the
fact that we will never see revival until we see God. Often that fresh
vision comes in the context of confusion and difficulty. King Uzziah had
died. He had been a good king. What would happen to Israel now? Would
they continue to be "good"—or would they go "bad"? So many of Israel's
kings had been anything but good and, consequently, led God's people
astray. Isaiah needed a new touch from heaven to face the new situation,
as we so often do in our day.

What happens when we do see God? Basically, we become vividly
conscious of one fundamental fact: God is utterly *holy*. He is love and
power, gracious and all-knowing; but above all, *He is holy*.

A New Vision of One's Own Self

Then, after we experience Holy God, we get a new vision of ourselves.

*"Woe to me!" [Isaiah] cried. "I am ruined! For I am a man of
unclean lips, and I live among a people of unclean lips, and my
eyes have seen the King, the LORD Almighty" (Isa. 6:5 NIV).*

Seeing God as perfect holiness, we inevitably see ourselves as poor sinners, undone and unclean. This truth can be a very painful experience, but
it is essential to genuine revival. Unless we can see ourselves as we *truly*
are, we will never experience a true awakening. Remember Bertha Smith.

A New Experience of Confession, Forgiveness, and Cleansing

*"Woe to me!" I cried. . . . Then one of the seraphs flew to me with
a live coal in his hand, which he had taken with tongs from the
altar. With it he touched my mouth and said, "See, this has touched
your lips; your guilt is taken away and your sin atoned for" (Isa.
6:5–7 NIV).*

Two essential issues emerge from this step in revival. First, we come
to confession of our sins as they are searched out by the Holy Spirit (Ps.
139:23), and second, we find God's gracious cleansing. John had it right
in his first epistle when he wrote: "If we claim to be without sin, we
deceive ourselves and the truth is not in us. If we confess our sins, he is

faithful and just and will forgive us our sins and purify us from all unrighteousness" (1 John 1:8–9 NIV).

We must, as Christians, confess every known sin. As the Spirit of God reveals them to us, they are to be confessed one by one, just as they were committed. Notice that Isaiah confessed a specific sin—his unclean lips. When such honesty is achieved by the searching Holy Spirit, the precious blood of Christ cleanses and deep fellowship with God emerges (1 John 1:7). Then the next step is prepared.

A New Call and Commitment

> *Then I heard the voice of the Lord saying, "Whom shall I send? And who will go for us?" And I said, "Here am I. Send me!" (Isa. 6:8 NIV).*

This principle of spiritual awakening involves several important points: First, there must be a genuine surrender of one's entire will to the will of God (Rom. 12:1–2). In a word, we make Jesus Christ what we call Him: *Lord.* Second, there must be the constant infilling of the Holy Spirit. True believers receive the Spirit at conversion; revived believers are continually filled with all His fullness (Eph. 5:18) through surrender and by faith, claiming His fullness for service and spiritual fruit-bearing (Eph. 3:14–21; Gal. 5:22–24). Third, there must be a walk with God in such depth that one can hear His voice. This demands the discipline of abiding in Christ through prayer, Scripture reading, and keeping one's sins constantly cleansed (John 15:1–4). Fourth, there must be a commitment to serve Christ faithfully and for His glory only, especially sharing one's faith with unbelievers that they might be saved. This is how multitudes come to Christ during a revival: God's revived people do evangelism (Matt. 28:18–20). Fifth, there must be a meeting of all human needs as much as possible (Matt. 25:34–40). Virtually every great social movement has grown out of spiritual awakenings. No conflict exists between evangelism and social action. Believers who have been revived simply step into people's lives and meet their needs just as Jesus did. Sixth, there must be a continuation in all these matters regardless of the sacrifice or difficulties. Isaiah asked, "LORD, how long?" God answered, "Until the cities are devestated and without inhabitant" (v. 11). In other words, we must continue until there are simply no more people with needs. That is real sacrifice. But we serve the Lord Christ (Col. 3:24), not ourselves. Finally, in it all, God's honor must be sought (1 Cor. 10:31). It is obvious that such movements do not stem from women or men. Revival breaks in on the scene from the absolute sovereignty of Holy God. He does the reviving; we just cooperate with Him. Therefore, to God be the glory, great things He has done.

There is little wonder, then, that the church flourishes when it experiences genuine revival. People, churches, society, and nations are dramatically transformed during a spiritual awakening. Obviously, a spiritual awakening stands as a desperate, contemporary need. God has done it many times before. He can do it again.

In the Bible, all the wonderful principles of revival are discovered, and often the divine revelation in the Word of God demonstrates that the Holy Spirit uses great women of faith. So, we begin the fascinating history of *Women of Awakenings* with two dramatic biblical events wherein our Lord raised up two women to bring revival to the land.

Women
of
Awakenings

Chapter One

DEBORAH

The Prophetess of Awakening

They reached the height and entered the Promised Land. But the history of the Israelite people soon slipped into one of scaling the mountain peaks only to slide down into a dark, dismal valley. This proved true not only politically, socially, and militarily, but above all, *spiritually*. Yet for Israel, all these various factors were seen as one amalgamated whole. Life was a unity in the minds of God's people, and defeat in the social, military, or economic spheres became tantamount to spiritual defeat and decline. The principle of the separation of church and state was an inconceivable concept for the Jews. They did not distinguish between the secular and the sacred. Whatever happened to them in any realm of life essentially had its roots in their spiritual experience because they saw life holistically. Although this principle is ultimately true for any nation of any time, the Israelite people realized it profoundly—and felt it keenly.

At the time of the judges (1200–1100 B.C.E.), a king had not yet been raised up in Israel and the nation had its ups and downs. The people attained spiritual heights, only to slump down into valleys of spiritual depression. Only as God periodically put His hand upon some individual to turn Israel around and bring it back to its spiritual roots were the people once again able to scale those spiritual mountains from which they had fallen.

Before the anointing of Saul as the first king of Israel, the leaders who brought Israel out of its spiritual lapses were called judges. Many judges cross the pages of Israel's history, but none stands out more clearly than does Deborah. As inconceivable as it may be for us moderns as we reflect on the twelfth century B.C.E. in the Middle East—where women were considered no more than property—the judge who brought about such an exemplary reviving work proved to be none other than a woman.

The Inevitable Slump

As the Israelites moved farther into Canaan and continued their conquest, God left among them a remnant of the nations to test their spiritual

27

commitment. He left five lords of the Philistines and all the Canaanites, Sidonites, and Hivites. These people became a formidable foe and test for Israel, who often failed. After the death of Joshua, Israel soon slipped into a spiritual "slough of despond," even to the point of serving the Baal idols. The Bible declares:

> *Then the sons of Israel did evil in the sight of the LORD, and served the Baals, and they forsook the LORD, the God of their fathers, who had brought them out of the land of Egypt and followed other gods from among the gods of the peoples who were around them, and bowed themselves down to them; thus they provoked the Lord to anger (Judg. 2:11–12).*

Israel was repetitively rebellious, and as the writer of Judges goes on to say, "They turned aside quickly from the way in which their fathers had walked in, obeying the commandments of the LORD" (Judg. 2:17). Because they did this of their own choice; "the anger of the LORD burned against Israel" (Judg. 2:14). Inevitably their idolatry led to degrading servitude in the service of the surrounding peoples. Joshua would have been mortified had he seen it. But God is a redeeming God and He sent deliverance time and again.

The Succession of Liberating Judges

After Israel had wandered about in their sin and servitude, God raised up the first judge, Othniel, Caleb's younger brother. The Spirit of the Lord came mightily upon him and he judged Israel, giving them great reprieve from their oppressors. The land had rest for forty years, then he passed off the scene. Once again, however, the old pattern reasserted itself and the Israelites fell into rebellion against God and His Word. Then the Lord in His grace raised up another judge by the name of Ehud, the son of Gera, a Bejamite. Israel returned to its spiritual heights as Ehud led them in the ways of the Lord.

Another time of deliverance came through the ministry of Shamgar, the son of Anath. He went to war with the Philistines with a message of God's liberating power. But again, the inevitable scenario asserted itself. Shamgar died, and, like a broken record, Israel did "evil in the sight of the LORD" (Judg. 4:1).

The reason that such continual spiritual decline developed was because of the lack of consistent spiritual leadership. The tribes of Israel seemingly could not unite against their enemies; and that constituted a spiritual issue. It must be realized that the Canaanites, Hivites, and the other nations who opposed Israel's conquest of Palestine were viewed by Israel as the agents of evil. Their defeat, therefore, became a spiritual conquest more than a military, economic, or political conquest. To understand that principle is to understand the Jews, even to this day.

So after Ehud and his successor, Shamgar, we again see Israel in the depths. But right at that moment, Israel was in for a real surprise: God raised up Deborah, a woman, an agent of awakening.

A New Judge

One of the startling things that Deborah accomplished, as we shall see in more detail, was not only that she became God's instrument to bring about a great military victory, but she also became the first judge to accomplish a solid coalition of most of the scattered tribes of Israel. This coalition was a tremendous political, military, and spiritual step forward. Simply put, Deborah, a woman, was mightily used of God. A new spirit invaded erring Israel. Deborah became a great woman of revival as spiritual awakening dawned in the land through her life and ministry.

The Condition of Israel: The Need of Revival

The condition that Deborah faced as she began to ascend to the role of judge and spiritual leader of the wayward nation was grave.

Concerning the need for revival and thus the ministry of Deborah, God's Word states: "Then the sons of Israel again did evil in the sight of the LORD, after Ehud died. And the LORD sold them into the hand of Jabin king of Canaan, who reigned in Hazor; and the commander of his army was Sisera, who lived in Harosheth-hagoyim" (Judg. 4:1–2).

To grasp the basic principles of true revival and renewal, we must understand the basic need for such a movement. Before Deborah began to judge, Israel had became a perfect paradigm of a nation in need of a spiritual awakening. The book of Judges makes it very clear that Israel's condition was such that they stood in dire need of divine intervention because no genuine spiritual person rose to the role of national leadership.

It seems inevitable that the absence of spiritual leaders always precipitates a people's straying from God's will; conversely, strong godly leaders can play a most significant role in keeping a people on a high spiritual plain. History is replete with this principle. A classic, more contemporary example can be found in America's Second Great Awakening. That fascinating story illustrates the principle perfectly.

The Second Great Awakening

In the late 1780s a great surge of revival power swept the newly formed United States of America. The Second Awakening, as it became known, broke over the land. It began in Methodist and Baptist circles in Virginia and soon spread to the Carolinas. Although it started as a Baptist and Methodist movement, the Presbyterians and others soon became involved.

Caught up in the awakening were two North Carolina Presbyterian ministers, James McGready and his protégé Barton Stone.

McGready and Stone were destined to be greatly used by God. Trekking through the Cumberland Gap, they took up their ministries in Kentucky. James McGready, after two or three years in Tennessee, settled in Logan County, Kentucky, and began preaching at the Red River Meeting House.

McGready was an "impassioned preacher, diligent pastor, and fervent man of prayer."[1] In June of 1800, he called on the people of south-central Kentucky to gather for an extended four-day observance of the Lord's Supper. People came in expectation of blessings, and God dramatically met their faith. The Holy Spirit fell powerfully on them. The climax came on the final day when John McGee, a Methodist minister, gave the closing exhortation. His own words describe the scene: "I . . . exhorted them to let the Lord omnipotent reign in their hearts, and submit to him, and their souls should live. . . . I turned again and losing sight of fear of man, I went through the house shouting and exhorting with all possible ecstasy and energy, and the floor was soon covered by the slain."

What an experience it must have been to witness those days! McGready tells us: "No person seemed to wish to go home—hunger and sleep seemed to affect nobody—eternal things were the vast concern. Here awakening and converting work was to be found in every part of the multitude.

The Cane Ridge Revival

Of the people at the Red River revival, none was singled out by God for more usefulness than was Barton Stone. He, invited and urged to serve by frontiersman Daniel Boone, had been preaching at the Cane Ridge Meeting House in Bourbon County, Kentucky. Stone, overwhelmed with the Red River revival, went home and in May 1801 called for a similar meeting at Cane Ridge. The meeting began and many were blessed. He called for a similar meeting in August, and to the utter astonishment of all, over twenty thousand people arrived for the six-day camp meeting. It was an incredible event, in the sparsely populated frontier.

Among the thousands converted was James B. Finley, who later became a Methodist circuit rider. He later wrote:

A strange supernatural power seemed to pervade the entire mass of mind there collected. . . . I stepped up on to a log, where I could have a better view of the surging sea of humanity. The scene that then presented itself to my mind was indescribable. At one time I saw at least five hundred swept down in a moment, as if a battery of a thousand guns had been opened upon them and then immediately followed shrieks and shouts that rent the very heavens.

The American frontier caught fire and was radically transformed for Christ.

One wonders what early America would have been without the leadership of James McGready, Barton Stone, and others who marched out in the Second Great Awakening. God used them to revolutionize the young nation and make it one of the most Christian societies that the world had seen for many years.

Leadership plays a vital role in great awakenings.

Deborah's Day

But where true spiritual leaders are not present, people and churches and societies tend to develop a deadly complacency about sin. Such complacency certainly describes the situation in Deborah's day. In the song of Deborah, recorded in Judges, chapter five, these words were sung:

"Why did you sit among the sheepfolds, to hear the piping for the flocks? Among the divisions of Reuben there were great searchings of heart" (Judg. 5:16).

"'Curse Meroz,' said the angel of the LORD, 'utterly curse its inhabitants, because they did not come to the help of the LORD, to the help of the LORD against the warriors'" (Judg. 5:23).

It must be remembered that God's essential attribute is holiness. To repeat the emphases in the prologue to this volume, the Seraphims continually hover over the throne of our great God crying, "Holy, holy, holy is the LORD of hosts; the whole earth is full of His glory" (Isa. 6:3). God, Himself being Holy, demands the same of His people. The Scriptures state, "You . . . shall be holy" (Lev. 20:7). But when no clear word of God comes from His prophets, as in the case after the death of Ehud, the people develop a deadening apathy over the quest for holiness, and this in turn develops a complacency concerning sin. The inevitable outcome is judgment.

God in His righteousness must judge His unholy people. So God sent His judgment through the surrounding nations. The Canaanites, supported by their vast armies, suppressed the Israelites. Not only that, the Canaanites' 900 iron chariots constituted a continual threat of annihilation to Israel. As Judges 4:3 states, "the Canaanites oppressed the sons of Israel severely for twenty years." Think of it—oppression for twenty long years. It produced for the Jews a life of subjection, humiliation, and dehumanization. They were virtually reduced to the status in which they had been during their Egyptian bondage: life filled with heartache, misery, and privation. They were looked upon as mere chattel in the eyes of the oppressive Canaanites.

One of the most dehumanizing things about the entire situation revolved around the fact that the surrounding peoples did not want to be "contaminated" by the erring Jews; people avoided them. They did not want to be in any way identified with the Israelites. In the song of Deborah we read: "In the days of Shamgar, the son of Anath, in the days of Jael, the highways were deserted and travelers went by roundabout ways" (Judg. 5:6).

What a tragedy. The very people whom God delivered from Egypt by mighty miracles and who saw constant victory in the conquest of the land of Canaan became repulsive to the native people. The people of Israel were seen as mere outcasts—the inevitable result of complacency over personal sins.

Not only did Israel grovel in its misery, God's judgment had fallen on their very livelihood—they had no success in farming. We read, "the peasantry ceased, they ceased in Israel" (Judg. 5:7). They were plagued not only with humiliation, but they also stood in constant want of the basic necessities of life. They were a farming and herding people. This formed their very culture. Abraham, Isaac, and Jacob, their illustrious forefathers, were men of the field. Now, the actual foundation of their society and economy was torn out from under them.

On and on go the indictments against the Israelites because of their complacency over sin, their giving themselves to the things of this world, and their failing to keep their eyes on the spiritual goal of God and His Glory. They stood in desperate need. They probably asked more than once, "Can even God get us out of this situation?" They would soon learn that nothing is too hard for the Lord (Gen. 18:14).

The Beginning of the Revival

One bright ray of hope finally began to break across the Israelites' dismal horizon. Some, but probably not very many, began to sense it. Soon others joined them until we read: "The people of Israel cried to the LORD" (Judg. 4:3 RSV). Simply put, they began to see their dire need. Moreover, they recognized their problem as essentially *spiritual*, which became their first ray of hope. One wonders why years earlier they were not brought up short. Why did they have to endure twenty years of oppression, twenty years of privation, twenty years of humiliation, twenty years of not experiencing the presence of God among them? Yet this demonstrates the deceitfulness and the deception of blinding sin. Sin clouds the eye to even stark realities, but at last, some in Israel, moved by the Holy Spirit, began to realize their real need—and they cried to the Lord. The first step to renewal always arises from conviction and fervent prayer.

In the tenth century B.C.E., Deborah and a few other leaders in Israel were moved by the Spirit of God to the place where they recognized that their only hope rested in the Lord. With the 900 iron chariots of the Canaanites against the puny bows and arrows of the Israelites, the situation seemed absolutely hopeless. But in God, hope always abounds. We have the assurance that when God acts, He acts in power that leads to triumph and victory. So the people of Israel began earnestly to cry to the Lord. May it be said that there has never been a revival until people get to the place of despair. Dispair is what makes for great praying. History teems with the principle of prayer to the sovereign God for spiritual awakening. In the warp and woof of the weaving of any great revival, the warp is the earnest prayers of God's people, and the woof is the absolute sovereignty of God.

The Recipe for Revival

The divine mix that always seems to result in revival is now clear: a desperate need, a willing God who providentially maneuvers circumstances to a climax, and a dedicated handful of prayer warriors who will intercede until the revival dawns. A spiritual prayer band and the sovereignty of God constitute the recipe that always provides bread for the hungry. As Samuel Chadwick expressed it:

> There is no power like that of prevailing prayer—of Abraham pleading for Sodom, Jacob wrestling in the stillness of the night, Moses standing in the breach, Hannah intoxicated with sorrow, David heartbroken with remorse and grief, Jesus in sweat of blood. Add to this list from the records of the church your personal observation and experience, and always there is the cost of passion unto blood. Such prayer prevails. It turns ordinary mortals into men of power. It brings power. It brings fire. It brings rain. It brings life. It brings God.

Israel Is Ready

For Israel, everything now basically fell in place. By the working of the Spirit of God, Israel finally saw its need. Furthermore, it realized, in the light of all the circumstances, that its only hope rested in the Lord. Therefore, the Israelites began to cry to the Lord in earnest intercession. Then, the last basic principle of a true revival emerged. God burst on the scene in the person of His spokesperson to turn Israel back to Himself; and wonder of wonders, especially for Israeli culture, it was a woman. The Bible says: "The peasantry ceased, they ceased in Israel, until I, Deborah, arose, a mother in Israel" (Judg. 5:7).

Who was this incredible personality whom God used to awaken the Israelites? Who was this mother in Israel?

Deborah, God's Woman of Awakening

Many unique things can be said about this fascinating woman. To begin with, she stands as the only woman in the Old Testament who was

elevated to a position of political and spiritual power by the common
consent of the people. She became one of the really great judges of Israel. Few women in the history of the human race have ascended to the
place of power, dignity, and authority among her people as did Deborah.
As one biographer put it, "She was like Joan of Ark, who twenty seven
centuries later rode in the front of the French and led them to victory."[2]

Deborah had a rather insignificant background. She became the wife
of Lapidoth, a man who apparently had little or no prominence in the
minds of the Israelites. Long before Deborah became the nation's leader,
she served as a homemaker. The Scriptures state that she lived on the
road between Ramah and Bethel. In a rather humble home in the hill
country of Ephraim, she lived out her early years. Still, her home was in
a beautiful spot. Olive and palm trees flourished in that area of Palestine.
Although Deborah probably displayed some leadership capabilities, the
average Israelite would have never seen her in the role she finally filled.
Nevertheless, she acquired some place of leadership in the spiritual life
of the nation, because as the Bible points out, she served as the keeper of
the tabernacle lamps. This was a very humble task, but significantly, it
kept her in the presence of God. In this matrix, God no doubt began to
shape Deborah into the mighty woman of the Spirit that she ultimately
became. No man had been raised up to judge Israel because God had
something very special for the nation through this homemaker, just a
humble keeper of the tabernacle lamps. She was to give the light of life to
the Israelites as she led them into a true spiritual awakening.

The Bible does not tell us how Deborah developed in both her spiritual
life and her perception concerning the people's need of renewal. Yet within
a few years, we find her judging Israel. As her predecessor, Ehud, and
others had done, she dispensed God's judgment in the various civil cases
that came before her. We must remember that civil and temporal affairs
were not compartmentalized apart from spiritual affairs in the Jewish mind-
set. The Jews understood God's will and purpose as permeating everything. So Deborah, early on, began to enlighten Israel concerning its basic
need. She became a spokesperson for God, declaring His will to the people.

Not only did Deborah sit in the seat of judgment but the people of
Israel soon began to recognize her outstanding leadership and authority.
Furthermore, she became a prophetess. This simply means that she declared God's whole truth. She no doubt had a hand in what we call the
Pentateuch, which contains the Law of Moses as well as Israel's history
up to that point in time. Thus, by the Holy Spirit's unction and the Scriptures, she began to proclaim to the people God's purpose in every area of
life. God had raised up His prophetess. And the people heard her gladly.

Deborah became a powerful preacher—although not a thundering
prophet like Amos, who cried out to the people, "Prepare to meet thy

God" (Amos 4:12), nor a highly educated, sophisticated person of the court as was Isaiah—but Deborah knew her Lord's call to give the people God's truth that convicted, changed, challenged, and converted them. She became the channel through which spiritual awakening came.

God raises up prophetesses as well as prophets. God's call to women is verified in the New Testament as well as the Old Testament. The prophet Joel, whom Peter quoted on the day of Pentecost, said:

> *And it shall be in the last days, God says, That I will pour forth of My Spirit upon all mankind; And your sons and your daughters shall prophesy, And your young men shall see visions, And your old men shall dream dreams; Even upon My bondslaves, both men and women, I will in those days pour forth of My Spirit And they shall prophesy (Acts 2:17–18).*

Remember also, Philip, the deacon, who had several daughters who prophesied (Acts 21:8–9). Moreover, as we shall see in the next chapter, Priscilla, a close worker with the apostle Paul, had an outstanding leadership role in the first century church. God truly does raise up prophetesses, and Deborah became God's spokeswoman to begin renewal in Israel.

Now the stage was set. Israel sensed the need, and hope in Yahweh burned brightly through the prophesying of Deborah. God's Word was proclaimed and this led to revival.

The Dynamics of an Awakening

Revivals often emerge in the context of the preaching of the Word of God. This has been proven true time and again. In America's first Great Awakening under the leadership of spiritual giants like George Whitfield and Jonathan Edwards, preaching, such as Jonathan Edward's famous sermon, "Sinners in the Hands of an Angry God," played a very vital role.

> O sinner! consider the fearful danger you are in. Tis a great furnace of wrath, a wide and bottomless pit, full of the fire of wrath, that you are held over in the hand of that God whose wrath is provoked and incensed as much against many of the damned in hell. You hang by a slender thread, with the flames of divine wrath flashing about it, and ready every moment to singe it and burn it asunder; and you have no interest in any Mediator, and nothing to lay hold of to save yourself, nothing to keep off the flames of wrath, nothing of your own, nothing that you ever have done, nothing that you can do, to induce God to spare you one moment.

Therefore let every one that is out of Christ now awake and fly
from the wrath to come. The wrath of Almighty God is now un-
doubtedly hanging over a great part of this congregation. Let every one fly out of Sodom. "Haste and escape for your lives, look
not behind you, escape to the mountain, lest ye be consumed."[3]

Great preaching or prophesying is mightily used by God. And Deborah
filled the role.

Deborah's Prophesying

In the Prologue we witnessed the story of Bertha Smith, Ola Culpepper,
and Marie Monsen and the absolute necessity of brokenness over sins
before a real awakening can come. We will see this in more detail as we
look into the lives of these and other great women of awakening. The
Word of God becomes the Holy Spirit's instrument to bring about that
spirit of repentance. When Deborah prophesied, the people heard. They
hung on her words as early Americans did on Jonathan Edward's
preaching. In addition, because she had also been judging Israel, they
understood the will and purpose of God for their lives. The Law came
alive. This combination of preaching and the Law no doubt led the
Israelites to genuine repentance. A true turning to God by His people
launched the movement (2 Chron. 7:14). A sweeping revival invariably
precipitates a humble heart and subsequent repentance. Israel had become
complacent about their sin and their need for a refreshing touch from
God. That had to change. Right then God raised up His prophetess so that
the erring nation might come to the place of deep repentance through her
prophesying.

Then a special word came from Deborah—this time to one person in
particular—Barak. She had a word of the Lord for him, and she was a
courageous woman to confront him. As one biographer has expressed it:

We can imagine that Deborah looked the part of a great and noble
woman. She must have had fire in her eyes, determination in her
step, and a positive ring to her voice. We can see her, a tall, handsome woman, wearing a dress of blue crash striped in red and
yellow and a yellow turban with a long, pure-white cotton veil,
lace edged, reaching to the hem of her dress. A feminine woman,
who never had the ambition to push herself forward, Deborah
better personified the homemaker in Israel than a warrior. But as
she counseled with her people and began to sense their common
danger, she kindled in them an enthusiasm for immediate action
against the enemy.

The Leadership

Deborah was moved to summon Barak, one of Israel's key military leaders (Judg. 4:6). Barak, the son of Abinoam, lived in Kedash and traveled to Deborah's side to hear the council of God for his life. Together, in collaboration before the Lord, they began to lay plans for what they sensed to be God's design for the deliverance of Israel. They felt confident that the Lord would work for them and through them.

The oppressor of Israel at that time was Sisera, a military commander in Hazor (Judg. 4:7). Yet he was merely the secondary problem. The struggle revolved around Jaban the king of Hazor or Canaan (Judg. 4:2). Recent archeological investigations have made it clear that Hazor once boasted of itself as a great kingdom in the days of Joshua (Josh. 11:10). Hazor had retained a fair vestige of power even after Israel's invasion. (Recall that God left many of the Canaanites in the land for the testing of Israel.)

Deborah and Barak brought together some ten thousand foot troops primarily from the tribes of Zebulun and Naphtali (Judg. 4:10). The Israelite forces gathered on Mount Tabor, situated northeast of the great Esdraelon Plain. Sisera, no mean military strategist, stationed his forces at Keishon on the way to "Taanach by the waters of Megiddo" (Judg. 5:19).

It is remarkable to see how God's people responded. A word going out from a woman in the Middle East, centuries before Christ, was usually totally unheeded if not laughed at. Yet ten thousand men came from across Israel, particularly from two tribes. Deborah, no doubt, had an incredibly magnetic personality. Her secret rested in the fact that she had a call and a word from God.

In fact, Deborah's compelling word so moved Barak that: "Barak said to her, 'If you will go with me, then I will go; but if you will not go with me, I will not go.' And she said, 'I will surely go with you; nevertheless, the honor shall not be yours on the journey that you are about to take, for the Lord will sell Sisera into the hands of a woman.' Then Deborah arose and went with Barak to Kedesh." (Judg. 4:8–9).

There must have been an aura about this woman that indicated the hand of God upon her life, much like Moses' aura. Simply put, Deborah lived in the Presence. Moreover, Deborah was obviously a woman utterly committed to the will of God. Judges 4:10 reads: "And Barak called Zebulun and Naphtali together to Kedesh, and ten thousand men went up with him; Deborah also went up with him." She did not shirk the battle; she went into the fray in the will of God. She exemplified what the apostle Paul said many years later: "I urge you therefore, brethren, by the mercies of God, to present your bodies a living and holy sacrifice, acceptable to God, which is your spiritual service of worship. And do not be conformed to this world, but be transformed by the renewing of your mind, that you may prove what the will of God is, that which is good and acceptable and perfect" (Rom. 12:1–2). Without deep commitment, regardless of the sacrifice—even the sacrifice of death if need be—there simply will not be a mighty movement of God upon an individual or a nation.

The Welsh Experience

The Welsh revival of 1904 paints a perfect picture of God's captivating the will of spiritual leaders before He blesses the land with an awakening. The Welsh revival was ignited in a theological school. Evangelist Seth Joshua had been invited to speak in a local church and also to the ministerial students. There is nothing unusual about that; special lectures are part and parcel of a theological education. During one of Joshua's messages in the church, the evangelist touched on the theme of doing God's will. In the course of his sermon he said, "God could mightily use any person whom he could *bend* to His will." Many were mightily moved. Involved in the service on that occasion was twenty-six-year-old Evan Roberts, a fine young student. The preacher's words fell like a bludgeoning hammer on Roberts's sensitive soul. In deep distress, he sank to his knees and from a crushed conscience cried, "O God, bend me!" And God bent him. Then lifting him up, the Holy Spirit through His bent servant began a movement for Christ and righteousness that put Wales in a spiritual spiral upward like it had never seen before—or since. The great Welsh revival of 1904–1906 came to pass through committment.

The Battle

God had certainly bent Deborah. Then another Word of God came through this woman of awakening: "Deborah said to Barak, 'Arise! For this is the day in which the LORD has given Sisera into your hands; behold, the LORD has gone out before you.' So Barak went down from Mount Tabor with ten thousand men following him" (Judg. 4:14). The battle began. The forces of light and darkness engaged. God and Satan faced each other on the battlefield. What would be the outcome? The Bible gives the account in glorious words of victory for God and the Israelites. The two chapters of Judges that comprise the Deborah and Barak victory story are compelling. Chapter 4 is purely prose, a historical account. Then chapter 5 is in the literary genre of song or poem. No doubt the people sang the account as well as read it. In the context of prose and poetry we see the wonderful victory that God achieved.

The Victory of Revival

To defeat the Canaanites was the same as saying that God had mightily awakened His people. We discover ten beautiful spiritual realities that surfaced in the victory that God achieved through Deborah, His woman of awakening. How we need to see them repeated in our day.

First, the people themselves had already faithfully responded to the Word of God, repenting of their sins and committing themselves to God even to the point of death (Judg. 4:10).

Second, in that context, God saw fit to work mightily. He bared His mighty arm. In the great victory that He accomplished, God used His miracle-working power (Judg. 4:15, 23; 5:4–5, 20–21). Barak, it seems, had been somewhat fainthearted, perhaps even weak in faith, before going into battle. He said that he would not go on the field of conflict unless Deborah was with him. "Then Barak said to her, 'If you will go with me, then I will go: but if you will not go with me, I will not go'" (Judg. 4:8). Deborah's response was:"'I will surely go with you; nevertheless, the honor shall not be yours on the journey that you are about to take, for the Lord will sell Sisera into the hands of a woman.' Then Deborah arose and went with Barak to Kadesh." (Judg. 4:9). So with Barak on the field of conflict, but with Deborah and her Presence with him, God prepared His miracle work.

The armies assembled. There stood Sisera with his 900 iron chariots and an untold number of foot soldiers. On the other side of the battle line was Deborah and Barak with their ten thousand men armed with only bows and arrows. Right then, in that unbalanced military situation, Deborah cried to Barak, "'Arise! For this is the day in which the LORD has given Sisera into your hands; behold, the LORD has gone out before you'" (Judg. 4:14).

God acted powerfully. We learn from the writings of Josephus, a first-century Jewish historian, and indirectly from the song of Deborah (Judg. 5) that a great storm of sleet and hail burst over the plain from the east. This meant that the driving rain and hail flew right in the face of Sisera, his army, and his charioteers. The slingers and the archers had a very difficult time even aiming their lethal weapons. The swordsmen no doubt slipped and slid about. Not only that, the waters of the River Kishon, near the waters of Megiddo, became raging torrents and played havoc with Sisera's chariots.

Third, the enemy suffered a sound defeat. The armies of Jabin, under the military leadership of Sisera, were routed and crushed (Judg. 4:15). God had wrought His victory. Israel was freed. Their days of slavery were over. Once again they could hold their heads high in the market-place. God had vindicated His people as He mightily revived them individually and nationally.

Fourth, God accomplished such a victory over the Canaanite armies that Sisera, the leader, was judged and killed. What a fascinating aspect of the revival story this account is. How did Sisera die? By the hands of a woman. Let the Bible speak for itself concerning this interesting event:

Now Sisera fled away on foot to the tent of Jael the wife of Heber
the Kenite, for there was peace between Jabin the king of Hazor
and the house of Heber the Kenite. And Jael went out to meet
Sisera, and said to him, "Turn aside, my master, turn aside to
me! Do not be afraid." And he turned aside to her into the tent,
and she covered him with a rug. And he said to her, "Please give
me a little water to drink, for I am thirsty." So she opened a bottle
of milk and gave him a drink; then she covered him. And he said
to her, "Stand in the doorway of the tent, and it shall be if anyone
comes and inquires of you, and says, 'Is there anyone here?' that
you shall say, 'No.'" But Jael, Heber's wife, took a tent peg and
seized a hammer in her hand, and went secretly to him and drove
the peg into his temple, and it went through into the ground; for
he was sound asleep and exhausted. So he died. And behold, as
Barak pursued Sisera, Jael came out to meet him and said to
him, "Come, and I will show you the man whom you are seek-
ing." And he entered with her, and behold Sisera was lying dead
with the tent peg in his temple (Judg. 4:17–22).

Little wonder, therefore, that the writer could say, "So God subdued
on that day Jabin the king of Canaan before the sons of Israel" (Judg.
4:23).

Fifth, not only was Sisera slain, Canaan was subdued, and Jabin with
it. The Scriptural account tells us that "the hands of the sons of Israel
pressed heavier and heavier upon Jabin, the King of Canaan, until they
had destroyed Jabin, the King of Canaan" (Judg. 4:24). When God gives
victory, He gives full victory; when God revives His people, He revives
them thoroughly; when God defeats evil, He eradicates it victoriously.
And it all came about because of this woman of awakening.

Sixth, another interesting aspect of the fascinating event rests in the
fact that not all of Israel responded. Although Deborah had done much to
unify the tribes of Israel, some simply would not commit themselves to
the plan and purpose of God. In the Song of Deborah and Barak, they are
chided.

> Why did you sit among the sheepfolds,
>   To hear the piping for the flocks?
> Among the divisions of Reuben
>   There were great resolves of heart.
> Gilead remained across the Jordan;
>   And why did Dan stay in ships?
> Asher sat at the seashore,
>   And remained by its landings.

"Curse Meroz," said the angel of the LORD,
"Utterly curse its inhabitants;
Because they did not come to the help of the LORD,
To the help of the LORD against the warriors"
(Judg. 5:16–17, 23).

Clearly, God was displeased with Gilead and Dan, as well as Meroz. They simply would not respond to God's call through this woman. Such a pattern always asserts itself in any spiritual awakening. There will always be those who are either complacent or even resistant to God; some even ridicule. How tragic it is when God's people, because of a lack of spiritual perception, cut themselves off from a great work of the Holy Spirit. The Lord's judgment rests on them for not being the yielded servants that God intends all of His people to be.

Seventh, great praise to God rose from His faithful servants. Hear the praise that Deborah raised up to God. It is a fascinating song that Deborah sang. Called by some the "Victory Song," this passage actually reflects the early stages of the Hebrew language, demonstrating its development as a Canaanite dialect. Her words resonate in the hearts of all true revived people to this day:

"That the leaders led in Israel, That the people volunteered, Bless the LORD! Hear, O kings; give ear, O rulers! I— to the LORD, I will sing, I will sing praise to the LORD, the God of Israel. LORD, when Thou didst go out from Seir, When Thou didst march from the field of Edom, The earth quaked, the heavens also dripped, Even the clouds dripped water. The mountains quaked at the presence of the LORD, This Sinai, at the presence of the LORD, the God of Israel" (Judg. 5: 2–5).

Revival is designed to bring great praise and honor to our God, who alone is the Sovereign Author of any great awakening.

Eighth, the people now found rest (Judg. 5:31). How wonderful to rest in the bosom of the Father's blessings. To know that He is pleased and to have seen Him work and accomplish great things is marvelous indeed. Restoration had come and now the fields could once again be planted. The tabernacle lights could be lit with a glow that perhaps they had not seen for some time. The name of Israel had again been vindicated among the people of the Near East. He who had brought them with the mighty hand out of the land of Egypt had now brought them from the oppression of the Canaanites. That is real revival! What a woman of awakening Deborah was.

Ninth, the Canaanites sunk in dismay. They had clearly expected victory. The last portion of Deborah's song tells us that the mother of Sisera looked through the lattice window anticipating seeing her son striding home in great triumph. But to her dismay, and that of all the Canaanites, he lay defeated and dead. The world never can quite understand God's workings and how He so miraculously saves His people.

Tenth, God vindicated and set forth the principle that He mightily uses women as well as men in these great movements that we call spiritual awakenings. This message needs to be understood and heeded today by women—and men also—that God uses women and could once again raise up a great woman of awakening. The succeeding chapters of this book clearly demonstrate that God has raised up women a multitude of times. It should be the prayer of all the church that God would raise up women like Deborah.

Conclusion

In light of all of these dynamics of revival in the life of Deborah, it is little wonder that she is called "a mother in Israel" (Judg. 5:7). To receive that designation constitutes the highest accolade that the nation could bestow upon her. It may be difficult in our contemporary culture to realize what an honor this title actually signified. It made her, in the eyes of the people, a spiritual giant and one whom history would record as a woman God could use in true revival. May God give us many Deborahs in our time.

Endnotes

1. The quotes in this chapter are taken from Mendall Taylor, *Exploring Evangelism* (Kansas City: Beacon Hill Press, 1964).
2. Edith Dean, *All the Women of the Bible* (Edison, N.J.: Book Sales, Inc., 1985), 69.
3. Jonathan Edwards, "Sinners in the Hands of an Angry God."

Chapter Two

PRISCILLA

The "House-Church" Awakening

If ever there was a time in the history of the church of Jesus Christ when God worked with absolutely overwhelming power, it was during the dynamic first century. We do not often think of the New Testament church in the terms of a great awakening. Yet, in a very real sense, it experienced revival in the most profound manner. Two reasons attest to this fact.

First, first-century Judaism had sunk into a number of disturbing, spiritually dehabilitating "isms." Israel harbored Pharaseeism, Sadduceeism, Herodianism, various abhorations of the truth of God ranging all the way from the Zealots to the apathetic. Of course, a sincere and faithful remnant remained—it always does. Nevertheless, Israel stood in great need of a deep, revolutionary movement of the Holy Spirit.

Second, in the early days of the church as recorded in Acts, the church hardly had time to fall into decline and then experience revival. The New Testament simply records the marvelous thing that God did in and through the life and ministry of our Lord Jesus Christ and the early years of church life. In that context, we see revival exemplified in its most in-depth sense. To put it simply, when a true awakening comes to the people of God, it essentially restores the church to the basic principles of spiritual life that were so clearly demonstrated in the first-century Christian assemblies. Therefore, what unfolded in the life and ministry of the apostles constitutes revival in its most dynamic form. And right in the midst of those dramatic days Priscilla came on the scene to be significantly used by God. Thus, Priscilla became a true woman of awakening because she served in the context of revival in its purest form: New Testament Christianity.

Therefore, it is wise to take what may seem a rather lengthy excursion to see what actually transpired in the New Testament era. It will be well worth it because it is important first of all, to understand those dynamics in order to understand Priscilla. Most importantly, however, it will enable us to grasp the true essence of revival. The first-century church epitomized what a genuine awakening is all about. It sets the pattern for what we shall see the Holy Spirit of God do through all of the great women of this book in fostering revival. Therefore, we move into our excursion of Acts chapters one and two.

New Testament Revival

All the essential ingredients for a great awakening unfold in a very dramatic fashion in early Acts. The book of Acts literally bursts with exciting stories. Moreover, "It is not merely a mechanical story of the journeying of Paul, or of the doings of Peter. It is intended to reveal to us the process through which Christ proceeds in new power, consequent upon the things He began to do and teach, toward the ultimate and final victory."[1]

The ultimate and final victory that God has in store for His people will gloriously unfold at the second coming of our Lord Jesus Christ. In the meantime, God intends His people to exemplify the patterns that were set forth through the ministry of the spiritual giants of the early church. So, to that beautiful story and Priscilla's place in it, we proceed.

The scenario unfolds as the early disciples gathered on the Mount of Olives just before the triumphant ascension of our Lord to glory. To catch something of the emotions of that scene becomes all but overwhelming. The life, death, and resurrection of Jesus had transpired. Now Jesus stood ready to ascend back to the Father, take His seat on the right hand of the throne of glory, send the Holy Spirit, and intercede for the saints until His glorious return. What a moment it must have been for those disciples. In that setting they asked the question: "Lord, are you at this time going to restore the kingdom to Israel?" (Acts 1:6 NIV).

It must be granted that the disciples' query does not strike one as a very perceptive question. They were still captive to the Jewish concept of an immediate earthly kingdom that would be established by their Messiah. Surely, they reasoned, this would be the moment in which Israel would be restored to the splendor of David and Solomon's reign; hence the question. They failed to realize that the kingdom is essentially a spiritual kingdom. The establishment of a visible earthly kingdom awaits the second coming of Christ. This does not mean that there would be no immediate conquests; nor does it mean that there would be no contemporary splendor. To the contrary, all of these are factors of the present manifestation of the kingdom of God. A political reign of Messiah remains, however, in the future. This they missed, so the Lord had to set the record straight. Jesus pointed out that those times and seasons rest in the Father's keeping, and it is not for them to know (Acts 1:7). Only the Father in heaven knows the day of the Lord's return in glory. Then Jesus said something of great significance. Until that day arrives—in the meantime—there remains a vital task to be done to further the present manifestation of the kingdom on earth. The Lord said in very emphatic language, "But you shall receive power when the Holy Spirit has come upon you; and you shall be My witnesses both in Jerusalem, and in all Judea and Samaria, and even to the remotest part of the earth" (Acts 1:8).

In that word, our Lord gave us our contemporary marching orders and laid out the first principle of true spiritual awakening.

When Revival Comes, the Church Acquires Proper Priorities

What makes up the church's primary task until Jesus comes? What does God desire to see happening among His people more than any other single thing? The poet properly expressed it:

> Give us a watchword for the hour,
> A thrilling word, a word of power;
> A battle-cry, a flaming breath,
> That calls to conquest or to death;
> A word to rouse the church from rest,
> To heed her Master's high behest,
> The call is given: Ye hosts arise,
> Our watchword is *Evangelize!*

That is it! That is the primary priority of God's people. We are commissioned to take the Gospel to all peoples in all the world. Global evangelization and mission makes up our primary task. This alone accomplishes the fulfilling of the Great Commission (Matt. 28:19–20). This alone will transform societies and bring the world to the foot of the cross. This alone makes Christians the "salt of the earth" and the "light of the world" (Matt. 5:13–14). We are to engage in global evangelistic outreach, "the evangelization of the world in this generation." Anything short of that demands revival among God's people.

It must be said that evangelism, the winning of unbelievers to faith in Jesus Christ, does not constitute everything that the church is required to do to fulfill the purpose of God. There are many ministries to which God's people must give themselves. The hungry are to be fed; the unclothed must have their needs met; the homeless need a roof put over their heads; the sick must be ministered to; and on and on. Wherever human need exists, God expects the church of Jesus Christ to step in and with what resources and strength it has to meet those needs. Love demands such services (1 John 3:17–18).

Evangelism, however, is the highest priority of service. The reason for this is obvious; everyone's greatest need is to come to faith in Jesus

Christ. Not only are temporal blessings at stake (the Lord said that He had come to give life and give it more abundantly [John 10:10]), but eternity rests in the balance. As the old-time preachers used to say, "There is a heaven to gain and a hell to shun." Even though that statement may not sound as attractive as it once did, it remains true. Therefore, bringing the Good News of Jesus Christ to a lost and a dying world must take the prominent place in the church's priorities of ministries. The faithfulness of the first-century believers in this regard always inspires. They went everywhere, making any sacrifice that they deemed necessary to bring the Gospel to a needy world. Hunger, shipwreck, imprisonment, displacement, suffering, and death did not deter them. They were compelled to take Christ to every person. In that dynamic setting Priscilla played a vital role.

A Motive to Evangelize

Yet what will bring the people of God into such an in-depth involvement in world evangelization? The answer is simple: the Holy Spirit must create a genuine passion for the lost. History constantly repeats the principle that when someone has a true passion, great things take place. David Brainard, a young missionary to the American Indians in the mid-seventeenth century said: "I cared not where or how I lived or what hardships I went through so that I could but gain souls for Christ. While I was asleep I dreamed of these things, and when I awoke, the first thing I thought of was this great work. All my desire was for the conversion of the heathen and my hope was in God." With that deep desire, David Brainard went out to declare the Gospel to native Americans, and revival broke out all about him. Multitudes in the American wilderness came to faith in Christ. An excerpt from his journal reads:

> The power of God seemed to descend upon the assembly "like a rushing, mighty wind," and with an astonishing energy bore down on all before it. I stood amazed at the influence that seized the audience almost universally and could compare it to nothing more aptly than the irresistible force of a mighty torrent. . . . Almost all persons of all ages were bowed down with concern together, and scarce one was able to withstand the shock of this surprising operation.[2]

That is real revival, and it had its birth in the passion of one person. Something of that spirit permeated the entire life and ministry of Priscilla. As her story unfolds, one of the startling and sterling characteristics of her service to Christ centered in her passion for the Gospel.

This now leads to the next principle:

Revival Comes When the Power of God Comes

One of the most thrilling accounts in all of the Scriptures of God's dealings with His children is found in Acts, chapter 2.

And when the day of Pentecost had come, they were all together in one place. And suddenly there came from heaven a noise like a violent, rushing wind, and it filled the whole house where they were sitting. And there appeared to them tongues as of fire distributing themselves, and they rested on each one of them. And they were all filled with the Holy Spirit and began to speak with other tongues, as the Spirit was giving them utterance (Acts 2:1–4).

An awakening, in the final analysis, is no more but no less than the outpouring of the Holy Spirit. It is vital and essential that we recognize that revivals are not conjured up by human ingenuity and programs, but by the outpouring of the Holy Spirit. True, Pentecost, in the historical sense, cannot be repeated. This occurrence culminated in the once-and-for-all giving of the Holy Spirit to the church. Since that divine moment every true believer in the Lord Jesus Christ receives the gift of the Spirit. The third person of the Trinity actually indwells the new believer and his or her body thus becomes the temple of God (1 Cor. 6:19). What an awesome reality that is—but also what an awesome responsibility. The believer's experience of the Spirit in all His fullness becomes vital. If there is no Spirit, there is no revival. That is the simplicity of it all.

The point to be emphasized rests in the fact that though all believers possess the Holy Spirit, all believers are not necessarily *filled* with the Holy Spirit. God, however, intends all Christians to experience His fullness, for that becomes the essence of true revival on the personal level. What does it mean to be "filled with the Spirit"? (Eph. 5:18).

As could well be expected, Jesus, our example in all things, lived out His entire ministry in the power of the Holy Spirit. All that He said and did flowed from the Holy Spirit's presence and power in his life. This is reiterated constantly in the four Gospels. John put it this way: "For the one whom God sent speaks authentic words of God—and there can be no measuring of the Spirit given to him" (John 3:34, PHILLIPS). Jesus was *always* full of the Holy Spirit (Luke 4:1). If Christ truly is our example in all things, as we often say, then we should attempt to emulate Him in His relationship to the Spirit of God.

Great servants of Christ have inwardly followed their Lord into the Spirit-filled life. Dr. R. A. Torrey, Bible teacher, professor, and preacher, gave his testimony in these words: "I had been a minister for some years before I came to the place where I saw that I had no right to preach until I was definitely baptized with the Holy Ghost. I went to a business friend of mine and said to him in private, "I am never going to enter my pulpit again until I have been baptized with the Holy Spirit and know it or until God tells me to go."[3]

Charles H. Spurgeon, no doubt the greatest of all Victorian preachers, on one occasion quoted in a sermon Luke 11:13: "If you then, being evil, know how to give good gifts to your children, how much more shall your heavenly Father give the Holy Spirit to those who ask Him!" Spurgeon then cried out to the eager congregation, "O, let us ask Him at once with all our hearts. Am I not so happy as to have in this audience some who will immediately ask? You that are the children of God—to you is this promise specially made. Ask God to make you all the Spirit of God can make you, not only a satisfied believer who has drunk for himself, but a useful believer who overflows his neighborhood with blessing."[4]

The emphasis of being filled with the Holy Spirit did not end with the closing of the nineteenth century. But what does it mean to our practical, everyday Christian walk?

First, the experience of being filled is vital to a healthy, growing Christian experience. This stands true for several reasons. Initially, only the Spirit-filled believer can know the constant, conscious presence of Jesus Christ. Although our Lord never leaves His people, to be conscious of His presence, one must be filled with the life of the Spirit. Griffith Thomas, a British scholar, states: "The only true immanence of God is the presence of Christ by the Holy Spirit in the heart and life of the believer. . . . It is in relation to the Holy Spirit that the Christian doctrine of God meets the deepest human need."[5] The Holy Spirit makes the divine immanence an experiential and dynamic reality.

Further, the Holy Spirit not only makes the divine presence real, He enables Christians to live a holy life. To talk about holy living may sound somewhat archaic today. Yet the Bible sets forth the concept repeatedly (e.g., 2 Cor. 7:1; 1 Thess. 4:7; and Heb. 12:14). Personal holiness should never be seen as an outmoded idea. What constitutes holy living? Holy living simply means developing a lifestyle that is pleasing to God and like God. "Be ye holy; for I am holy" (1 Pet. 1:16 KJV). All Christians recognize the inner compulsion to live like the Lord Jesus Christ. The Holy Spirit alone can effect such a lifestyle.

Therefore, in the light of all that has been said biblically, historically, and experientially, it can be summarized that God fully expects all believers to be filled with the Holy Spirit. That alone makes personal Christianity vital and alive. This is revival living at its height and must be experienced by all who would know God dynamically and make their impact on a very needy world.

The final question now becomes: How does one become filled with the Holy Spirit? Five simple principles should answer this fundamental question. They form the spiritual exercise to experience the Spirit-filled, revived life.

First, there must be an acknowledgment of need. If we satisfy ourselves with our present spiritual state, little progress will be made in the things of God. The Lord Jesus Christ said, "Blessed are those who hunger and thirst for righteousness, for they shall be satisfied" (Matt. 5:6).

After God has created something of a genuine hunger and thirst for His best, and having acknowledged our need, the next step is to abandon all *known* sins. We can hardly confess *unknown* sins, although as we mature God will step-by-step show us even these. To make a 100 percent break with all conscious sin is absolutely necessary. The confession of all known iniquities lies at the bottom of our seeking. This is not a call for sinless perfection, because we all have unconscious sin. Yet we can make a break with every *known* sin. We must strive to be able to say with Paul, "I always take pains to have a clear conscience toward God and toward men" (Acts 24:16).

The next exercise centers in abdicating the throne of one's heart. In the final analysis, we always face one basic issue: Will I control my own life or will I truly make Jesus Lord of all? We are forced to decide for one or the other. God's Word is very plain on this point. Remember, the Holy Spirit is given to "those who obey him" (Acts 5:32). Jesus must be Lord.

Fourth, after acknowledging need, abandoning sin, and abdicating control of our lives, we simply ask God to fill us with his Spirit. Jesus promised, "If you then, being evil, know how to give good gifts to your children, how much more shall your heavenly Father give the Holy Spirit to those who ask him?" (Luke 11:13). God deeply desires His hungry-hearted children to come into His presence through prayer and ask Him for the fullness of the Spirit. He waits for cleansed, yielded, Christians simply to ask Him.

Finally, having asked, we now accept the Spirit's fullness by faith and thank God for His grace. We need not necessarily pray long and agonizingly. God honors the acceptance of faith. We receive salvation by faith alone and do not ask for any sign or particular feeling that God has genuinely saved us; so, also, we claim by faith the infilling of the Holy Spirit. And what God has done for a multitude of others, He can and will do for us all. Our Lord offers the revived, Spirit-filled life to every believer who is yielded, cleansed, and filled.

When the Spirit comes, revival comes. Priscilla certainly knew the Spirit-filled life and thus God used her in spreading the awakening. The beautiful story of her recognition of those New Testament principles will be made clear as we study her revived life in the context of the Roman, Ephesian, and Corinthian churches where she and her husband ministered so effectively.

Proper Proclamation Is Vital to Revival

One of the interesting incidents in the ministry of Priscilla revolved around her leading Apollos into a full grasp of the Gospel. From the book of Acts, we learn that Apollos, a very eloquent man, did not completely understand the Gospel of Christ. Priscilla helped him tremendously. She had a firm hold on the essence of the message, a principle that shines forth as vital and essential for true revival. People are not brought to faith in Christ unless they hear the complete Gospel of Christ. Thus, to have a full knowledge of the message that Paul calls the "power of God unto salvation" (Rom. 1:16) is vital to any lasting revival. This raises the question: What is the "Good News"?

The Gospel or Good News has a definite body of biblical, theological content. It can be outlined simply as follows:

- Jesus is the long awaited, hoped-for *Messiah* (Acts 2:36).
- Jesus, God manifest in the flesh (the Incarnation), lived a perfect sinless life and engaged in teaching the truth, healing the sick, and ministering to the needs of every level, thus *revealing* God (Acts 2:22).
- Christ died vicariously upon the cross as the *Great Substitute* for the sins of all humanity. He died in our place and for us so the righteousness of God can be accounted to us (Acts 2:23).
- Jesus *rose bodily* from the grave as the Victor over sin, death, hell, and the Devil (Acts 2:24).
- Jesus demands that people fully and completely repent of their sins, placing their faith, trust, and reliance upon Him and His work of redemption alone (Acts 2:38).

Jesus promises that those who respond positively to Him will have forgiveness of sins, eternal life, and a place in the kingdom. All of these points were made very clear in Acts 2, when Peter stood up and preached on the day of Pentecost.

Peter's sermon forms the essential content of the Gospel message. The truth of the Word brings people under conviction and thus to genuine salvation (John 16:7–11). Through the years, the message has been used mightily in awakenings. When Peter finished his sermon, three thousand responded to the call to salvation. What a day of revival that turned out to be.

An Awakening Arrives on the Wings of Fervent Prayer

Acts 1:14 (KJV) reads: "These all continued with one accord in prayer." Charles Finney, the great nineteenth-century revivalist, put the proper emphasis on it when he said, "Prayer is an essential link in the chain of courses that lead to revival." That is the secret. A great revival arises from great praying, as we shall see over and again in these biographies of great women of awakenings. Search as you will through the pages of the Bible or walk through the corridors of church history, and you will discover that before revival comes, the foundation of prayer has been laid. Prayer becomes the key.

All that has been said to this point constitutes the heart of New Testament Christianity. Thus, it becomes the heart of revival living. Therefore, it is vital that we grasp these awakening principles. Every chapter in this book reflects that fact. True, it did seem a rather long run through Acts chapters one and two, but if we do not understand revival, we may never see our need for such a movement of God in our lives. Thus, we see why Priscilla lived in the center of an awakening: she was simply living out New Testament Christianity. So with this essential background of the essence of revival, we turn directly to her intriguing story.

Priscilla's Revival Ministry

All the principles of revival find a direct parallel in that which motivated and permeated Priscilla's ministry. In the first place, Priscilla was a leader.

Revivals have leaders. We have seen in Deborah's life the principle that God uses in raising up a prophet. Clearly, Priscilla emerged in the New Testament days as a leader of like stature; in her own right, she was a prophetess of the first order. Although she is never mentioned in the New Testament apart from her husband Aquila, in three of the five different recordings of her name along with Aquila, she is mentioned *first*. It is "Priscilla and Aquila" not "Aquila and Priscilla" that predominates. This may seem insignificant to our Western mind-set; but in writings from first-century Palastine, the name of the most prominent person was placed first. This was considered good Greek syntax to emphasize their position. This becomes clear, for example, in the first missionary journey of Paul and Barnabas, the narrative starts off in Acts 13 as "Barnabas and Saul." About halfway through that first missionary trek around the Mediterranean, the terminology changes from "Barnabas and Saul" to "Paul and Barnabas" and continues that way throughout the rest of the journey and into Paul's entire ministry. Paul is always mentioned first. Luke wrote that way to make a point. Bible scholars agree that this is significant, not only for Paul and Barnabas, but also for Priscilla and Aquila. The leader is mentioned first, and Priscilla had that very role.

Historical facts, information that is not directly recorded in the Scriptures, give testimony to Priscilla's prominent position and even to her fame in the early church. Tertullius, one of the early church fathers recorded, "By the holy Prisca [Priscilla], the Gospel is preached." Rome has been a Christian center for centuries, and today, no visit to Rome is complete without walking through the catacombs—the tombs where first-century Christians met to worship, safe from the emperor's persecution. One of the oldest catacombs of Rome was named for Priscilla. In her honor it was called the "Coemeterium Priscilla." There is even a church called, "Titulus Saint Prisca," erected on the Aventine in Rome. On the church is found the inscription, "Titulus Aquila at Prisca." In many places in Rome, Priscilla's name appears on monuments. Even a legendary writing emerged in the tenth century under the title, "Acts of St. Prisca." Quite obviously, she stood as an honored woman in the early days of the Christian movement.

Priscilla's Role

But it is in the New Testament that we see the significance of Prisca's leadership in revival. The first mention of her is found in Acts 18. When Paul arrived in Corinth, he met Priscilla and Aquila. It is interesting to note that Paul always called Priscilla, Prisca. That is her more formal name. Luke tended to use the name Priscilla, the diminutive of Prisca, thus, less formal and more personal and which would be used among acquaintances. Luke must have been personally acquainted with Priscilla. Aquila, her husband, had a Latin name, its meaning derived from the word *eagle*.

Some commentators believe that the husband-and-wife team, for they are always mentioned together, came from Pontus, a Roman province along the Black Sea. Some have conjectured that perhaps Aquila had Roman citizenship, but little evidence for that idea can be found. Some continually say that he was a slave at one time. Other scholars attempt to make Priscilla a Roman citizen. They base this conclusion on the fact that a patrician family by the name of Prisca lived in Rome. They also give as evidence that this was the reason for her being named before her husband in most instances. Much of this is conjecture. As a very fine Bible scholar, however, has pointed out, the fact that "she is usually mentioned before her husband is indeed remarkable for first century usage, but probably is less due to her social status than to her prominence in Christian circles. Not to detract from Aquila's ministry, but Priscilla seems to have been one of those women like Lydia whose service in the Christian community stood out."[6]

Priscilla and Aquila had been living in Corinth for some time when Paul arrived. Paul got to Corinth probably sometime around the middle of A.D. 49. The implication is that Priscilla and Aquila were there due to the persecution that had come upon Roman Christians. Claudius, the emperor, expelled all Jews from Rome, including Priscilla and Aquila. Aquila being Jewish by birth and a native of Pontus, had to leave the capital.

Priscilla and Aquila were no doubt already Christians when they entered Corinth, a city of refuge. Having been driven to this part of the Roman empire because of their faith—and carrying their faith with them—they typified many early Christians. Thus, they settled down in Corinth and there began their work of ministry.

Corinth

Corinth had gained notoriety as a very cosmopolitan city. Its key commercial location and the subsequent commerce that flowed through it made it such. Priscilla, probably a Gentile, fit into the Greek culture well. This gave her opportunities to lead in Christian witness in the sophisticated city; and Corinth certainly was in need of hearing the message. Being the political capital of southern Greece, it served as the residence of the Roman procouncil. Although a Greek city, it existed under Roman rule. A strange mixture of wealth and poverty characterized the metropolis. The life of the wealthy was one of incredible luxury and frivolous lifestyles; the poor endured the exact opposite. It has been said that Corinth, at that time, filled the roll of "the Vanity Fair of the Roman Empire, at once the London and the Paris of the first century after Christ."[7] The masses were infected with this worldly atmosphere. Multitudes lived very immoral and degraded lifestyles. The theater had sunk into vulgarity, and the ostentatious sensuality of the wealthy likewise contributed to the corruption of the city. Moral corruption even filtered down to the slaves. A phrase of derision, said when one wanted to heap insults upon others, was, "They live as they do in Corinth." To live as such became known as to "Corinthisize." The most flagrant corruption of the city could be found in the religious practices of the Corinthians. Historians called their temples a "hot bed of pollution." The worship of Aphrodite, with its shame and debauchery, polluted the city.

Yet God said to Paul that He had many people in that city, and that he should not hold peace (Acts 18:9). The foundation had been laid through the leadership of Priscilla along with her husband Aquila. When Paul began his work in Corinth, Priscilla and Aquila had already been laboring successfully, sharing their faith in the midst of much corruption and opposition. Little wonder that one New Testament scholar refers to the prominence of Priscilla in that work as showing "fervency of spirit . . . (and) ability of character."[8]

All of this indicates something of the outstanding leadership of this unusual woman. God had His hand on Prisca as a prophetess, one who shared the wonderful message of redemption through Jesus Christ. She was a "Deborah" in the New Testament sense; a true woman of awakening. She propigated dramatic Christianity, which leads to one of Priscilla's greatest accomplishments. She became instrumental in touching the life of one of the most significant preachers of the first-century church.

Priscilla Helps Apollos

The fascinating account of Priscilla's impact on Apollos is found in Acts 18:23–26:

> *And having spent some time there, he departed and passed successively through the Galatian region and Phrygia, strengthening all the disciples. Now a certain Jew named Apollos, an Alexandrian by birth, an eloquent man, came to Ephesus; and he was mighty in the Scriptures. This man had been instructed in the way of the Lord; and being fervent in spirit, he was speaking and teaching accurately the things concerning Jesus, being acquainted only with the baptism of John; and he began to speak out boldly in the synagogue. But when Priscilla and Aquila heard him, they took him aside and explained to him the way of God more accurately.*

Again we see the prominence of Priscilla in that she is mentioned before her husband Aquila in the twenty-sixth verse. Of course, this by no means implies that Aquila had nothing to do with the ministry. If anything, they were a team. So here comes Apollos, an eloquent scholarly man, but in serious need of a clearer grasp of the Gospel. He is tremendously influenced and helped by the ministry of this godly woman and her husband. Who was this needy man?

Apollos

By some set of circumstances, probably because they were traveling with Paul, Priscilla and Aquila are now in Ephesus. That summer Paul was on his third missionary journey and had left Priscilla and Aquila in Ephesus. Apollos, the Scriptures tell us, was a Jew of Alexandria, who reached Ephesus probably in the summer of A.D. 54.

Apollos was a man of sterling character. He had the reputation of being a "learned man"; moreover, he was "a man mighty in the Scriptures," and "fervent in spirit" (Acts 18:24–25). All this conveys a marvelous biblical complement to the man's spiritual experience. He had been instructed in the ways of the Lord; however, something did not quite ring true in his eloquent preaching. There seemed to be a serious lack in the message he declared—something very central to the heart of the Gospel. When Priscilla and Aquila heard him preach in the synagogue, they began to probe him, and he confessed that he had been instructed in the way of the Lord but only knew the baptism of John. John the Baptist, the forerunner of Jesus, had not presented the full Gospel as it was now crystallized in the early church. So Priscilla and Aquila proceeded to instruct Apollos more fully as to the nature of the Good News. The Bible says "They took him aside and explained to him the Way of God more accurately" (Acts 18:26).

A tribute goes to Priscilla in that she fully understood the Gospel and would share it with all who would listen. She was apparently so adept in the basic theology of the Christian experience that she ably instructed such a learned, scholarly, devout man as Apollos. Apollos deserves a tribute as well in light of the fact that he was open and receptive to hearing the Word from this woman of God, which speaks of his openness to all the truth contained in the Gospel message.

Outlined earlier in the account of the Day of Pentecost (Acts 2) the full Gospel message was presented: that the Gospel centers in the life, death, resurrection, and ascension of our Lord Jesus Christ and the call to full repentance and fervent faith in our Lord and His atoning work. Priscilla shared with all the acumen of a woman wellversed in the Scriptures. Consequently, she convinced the learned Apollos of his need to grasp fully the entire message of Christ and then to proclaim it fearlessly. We see from subsequent accounts in the New Testament that Apollos had learned well and had preached the Gospel with great effect to all who would listen. The providence of God surely worked in Priscilla's ministry at Ephesus, especially in her encounter with Apollos.

When the apostle Paul had first met Priscilla and her husband, they were working together as tentmakers in the city of Corinth. There they learned to be colaborers in the Gospel. If there was anything lacking in the spiritual experience of Priscilla at that time, it no doubt was fulfilled through the ministry of Paul. The three became so close that they began traveling together. What a trio they must have made. They eventually arrived in Ephesus where Paul stayed but a short time, leaving behind Priscilla and Aquila that they might minister to the converts that had been made. How the Holy Spirit led in those early years of the infant church shines out as a sterling example of God's amazing grace. What a contribution this woman of revival made.

The House-Church Ministry

When Paul returned to Ephesus one year later, after having left Priscilla and her husband there, he discovered that a fine house-church had been organized by this godly lady. Thus, Priscilla gained valuable experience.

In the good care of the Lord, Priscilla and Aquila finally made their way back to Rome. One of the significant works of Priscilla took place there: She again lead a house-church, a type of ministry that became very common in early Christianity. Then, it seems, the couple returned once more to Ephesus and took up the ministry. Much of Priscilla and Aquila's service centered in the house-church ministry; and in all Priscilla led.

Commentator and New Testament scholar, William Barkley, has an interesting summation of the impact of Priscilla and her house-church. He wrote:

> Prisca and Aquila lived a curiously nomadic and unsettled life. Aquila himself had been born in Pontus in Asia Minor (Acts 18:2). We find them resident first in Rome, then in Corinth, then in Ephesus, then back in Rome, and then finally back in Ephesus; but wherever we find them, we find that their home is a center of Christian fellowship and service. Every home should be a Church, for a Church is a place where Jesus dwells. From the home of Prisca and Aquila, wherever they were, there radiated friendship and fellowship and love. If anyone is a stranger in a strange town or a strange land, one of the most valuable things in the world is to have a home away from home into which to go. Such a home takes away loneliness and protects from temptation. Sometimes we think of a home as a place with a shut door, a place into which we can go and shut the door and keep the world out: but equally a home should be a place with an open door. The open door, the open hand, and the open heart are the characteristics of the Christian life.[9]

No elaborate church buildings existed in the early years of Christian history. In fact, hardly any record can be found of a church building for the first three hundred years of the Christian era. The house-church became the primary means of a settled fellowship or congregation. In the city of Corinth, for example, it may have been that there were dozens of small house-churches. So when Paul wrote his letter to the Corinthians, it would not have been just to one single house-church, but to the whole church of Jesus Christ in the city of Corinth. The letter would have been circulated around to the various smaller congregations that met in homes. Of course, there may well have been occasions when the whole church came together for purposes of worship and festivities; still, the main motif of the early years of the Christian movement in its organized sense centered around the house-church. These are very similar to what we call today "house groups." It is a time-honored method that God has used down through the centuries of the Christian movement. And right at the heart of the movement we find Priscilla making her significant contribution.

Persecutions

It should be pointed out that everything was not always easy for Priscilla and her husband as they ministered in the name of Christ. Paul goes so far as to say: "Greet Prisca and Aquila, my fellow workers in Christ Jesus, who for my life risked their own necks, to whom not only do I give thanks, but also all the churches of the Gentiles; also greet the church that is in their house. Greet Epaenetus, my beloved, who is the first convert to Christ from Asia" (Rom. 16:3–5).

The persecution that the couple felt started in Rome when Claudius' edict forced them to leave their home and their business. Paul states that they "risk their necks" for the Gospel of Christ. All that is implied in Paul's words remains unknown. Suffice it to say that they were certainly in the heat of the oppression that came upon the early church. Yet surely God even used that to aid in the spreading of the Gospel. Recall the tremendous resistance to the Gospel that Paul encountered in Ephesus by the hands of Demetrius, the idle fabricator. Priscilla and Aquila were there to give aid and encouragement.

Fortunately, the edict of Claudius that expelled all Jewish people from Rome lost its effect through the years and the dedicated husband and wife returned to their original home and business in Rome. Still, it was no easy path they trod. Persecution was the lot that fell to most early Christians virtually everywhere. But, as seen, Priscilla and Aquila were of such spiritual courage and fortitude that they were willing to risk their necks, that is to give their lives if necessary for the sake of the Gospel. No doubt the words of Paul rang in Priscilla's ears, "all who desire to live godly in Christ Jesus will be persecuted" (2 Tim. 3:12). What a sterling character our woman of awakening had. We must never forget, however, that courage and suffering forms the seedbed that causes the church to flourish. Priscilla will always stand as a model of what it means to suffer for Christ in the setting of true renewal and to do it positively and valiantly.

A Working Woman

It is further interesting to note that Priscilla served as a working woman. Along with her husband Aquila, they made tents. She probably wove tent cloth. In those days, a tent was not something people used just to camp out. Great events would often take place in tents, and, of course, for nomadic people, it became their only home. So she did have an important contribution to make to society even in her secular labors. In reality, Priscilla shouldered a threefold task. She worked to help supply the family's necessary needs. She had to maintain her own home for her husband and herself. Above all, though, she conducted her house-church and thus served as a prophetess in declaring the Gospel of Christ. Needless to say, it was full-time work to which she gave herself. With the energy that Christ supplied, and her determination to honor the Lord Jesus in all things, she stands out as a remarkable personality and an example in the marvelous awakening that rocked the first-century world.

It can be said that Priscilla left us all a great legacy. Her tremendous impact on Apollos, the significance of the house-churches that she fostered and maintained, and the revival will always be remembered.

A Last Word

In Paul's last letter of farewell, 2 Timothy, he wrote, "Greet Prisca and Aquila," (2 Tim. 4:19). The implications of this greeting centers in the reality that from the very beginning of their Christian experience, Priscilla and her husband unswervingly maintained their faith, served Christ faithfully, journeyed at great cost to themselves, risked their very lives for the Gospel, maintained house-churches wherever they went (Rom. 16:3–5), and persevered faithfully to the end. The consummation of their life was reached and the great apostle Paul remembered them in his very last letter. What a tribute to this woman of revival. In all the dynamics of the first-century church as outlined in the first portion of this chapter, she carried on a true revival ministry. Awakenings seemingly burst all around her, whether in Rome, Ephesus, Corinth, or back to Rome. Revival frames the ministry that she experienced, and that becomes our inspiration from this woman of awakening. The pattern has been set.

Endnotes

1. G. Campbell Morgan, *The Acts of the Apostles* (London: Pickering and Ingalls, Ltd., 1924), 7.
2. Journal of David Brainard.
3. R. A. Torrey, *The Holy Spirit: Who He Is and What He Does* (New York: Fleming H. Revell, 1927), 198.
4. From a sermon by C. H. Spurgeon.
5. W. H. Griffith Thomas, *The Holy Spirit of God*, 3d edition (Grand Rapids: William B. Eerdmans, 1955), 196–97.
6. John Polhill, "Acts of the Apostles," in *New American Commentary* (Nashville: Broadman Press, 1992), 382.
7. G. Campbell Morgan, *Acts of the Apostles* (London: Pickering and Ingalls, Pub., 1924), 334.
8. *Expositor's Greek Testament*, Vol. 2 (Grand Rapids: William B. Eerdmans, 1951), 384.
9. William Barkley, *The Letter to the Romans* (Philadelphia: The Westminister Press, 1955), 229.

Chapter Three

MADAM GUYON
The French Awakening

High society saw Mademoiselle de La Mothe as a stunning, vivacious young French girl. She lived in fashionable Paris during the corrupt and profligate times of Louis XIV. The reign of the opulent king precipitated perhaps the most pleasure-loving and corrupt society that France had ever seen, and the young mademoiselle fit in beautifully. She had a proud heart and the prestige and social status to go with it. She was, it must be confessed, an outstanding beauty, which made her spirit and station understandable.

Jeanne Marie Bouvieres, the damsel's given name, was born at Montargis, France, a small town approximately fifty miles north of Paris. April 13, 1648, marked her birth into the de La Mothe family. Symbolic is the fact that her birth came approximately one hundred years after the great Protestant Reformation made itself felt in Europe; later she would play a decisive roll in evangelical Christianity. In the meantime, she would live the good life.

Jeanne Marie's family boasted itself as one of the outstanding aristocratic families of France. They were highly respected and even rather religiously inclined. Her father held the title Seigneur, or Lord, de la Mothe. Despite the family's religious inclinations, though, young Jeanne Marie got caught up in the fast-paced life of Louis XIV's reign. Actually, she got quite carried away with it. Her life in high society, coupled with the ambitions harbored for her by the family, destined her for a life of worldliness, if not corruption, in Louis's court. But first, deep religious feelings stirred her childhood heart.

Early Days

Jeanne Marie had already faced and overcome some significant obstacles in her early life. While in infancy, she fell victim to an illness that caused her parents to despair for her very life. But she rallied and at the age of two and a half was sent to the Ursuline seminary in her home town to be educated by the Catholic sisters.

Young Jeanne did not settle in too well with seminary life, and after a short time, she returned home. She stayed with her parents for some time but did not find home life all that comforting or assuring either. Her mother left her chiefly in the care of the servants, and her early education became quite neglected.

In 1651, the Duchess of Montbason came to Montargis, Jeanne's home town, to reside with the Benedictine nuns in their convent. She met little Jeanne and became so taken with the young girl that the Duchess asked Jeanne's father to allow his daughter, who was then only age four, to live with her at the convent to keep her company. In that setting, Jeanne began to realize her need of a Savior even at her very early age. She had a very dramatic dream one night wherein she caught something of a glimpse of the misery of those who remain impenitent in their sins. As best she could, and as best she understood at that point in her little life, she dedicated herself to live for God. She even vowed that she would be willing to become a martyr for the Lord Jesus Christ.

As young Jeanne shared something of her spiritual struggles with the nuns, the sisters pretended that they were convinced that God truly wanted her to become a martyr. Her little heart and mind could not quite grasp it all, and in her confusion, she came to believe that the nuns were going to put her to death. She fell on her knees when that sobering, chilling thought gripped her heart, and, on her knees in prayer, she submitted herself to God in a very deep sense. Then began a mock scene. The nuns led Jeanne into a room and caused her to kneel on a cloth that they had spread out on the floor. One of the older girls of the convent, in theatrical fashion, appeared as an executioner and raised a cutlass. Little Jeanne, terrified, cried out that even though she had been willing to give herself to God as a martyr, she was not at liberty to die without her father's sanction. After the ordeal ended, the nuns rather heartlessly chided her. They said that she was not truly willing to die for Christ, and that she had just made the excuse of her father's permission to escape martyrdom.

The bizarre incident profoundly shook the girl's religious feelings. Guilt swept over her tender heart. She felt that she had denied the Lord and it brought great darkness into her very soul. Nevertheless, the Benedictines did treat her with reasonable kindness, but her health began to deteriorate once again and she had to be taken home only to be left once more in the care of the servants.

Jeanne had a half-sister who had entered the Ursuline convent. So at the age of seven, Jeanne, too, was packed off again to the Ursuline convent to be with her sister. Her half-sister took her under her wing, and the young lady soon began to excel in learning and piety.

A New Turn

At the age of eight, Jeanne's life took a significant turn. Henrietta Maria, queen of England, fled to her native land of France as a refugee from the civil war that raged in England at the time. Cromwell's armies were rapidly defeating the armies of the monarchy, and the queen had to escape. In France, Queen Henrietta Maria visited the de La Mothe family. Little Jeanne so exuded learning and beauty and piety that she captured the queen's heart. Queen Henriette begged Jeanne's father to allow her to take the child with her and make her the maid of honor to the princess. But Lord de La Mothe refused. Was this missed opportunity? Not from the spiritual perspective; God had great things in store for the child.

Two years passed and at the age of ten, Jeanne's parents placed her, this time, in a Dominican convent. This came about at the request of the prioress, who had a great affection for young Jeanne. She remained in the convent for some eight months and continued to excel in learning and piety. But her general health was still very poor and her future seemed quite uncertain. In the Dominican convent, however, another step forward in her spiritual experience took place. She found a Bible. The Scriptures were an unknown book to her, but, in the providence of God, somehow a copy had been left in her chamber. Even though she was only ten years old, she threw herself into reading the Word of God. It impacted her profoundly. She said, "I spent whole days in reading it, giving no attention to other books or other subjects from morning to night. And having great powers of recollection, I committed to memory the historical parts entirely."[1] During Jeanne's stay in the Dominican convent, she virtually saturated herself in the Scriptures. It had been her fondest wish to take the sacrament, the Roman Catholic version of the Lord's Supper.

Depression

Even though Jeanne had spent so much time with Roman Catholic nuns and in the Scriptures, she began to neglect her spiritual duties. Consequently, something of a spiritual depression and melancholy settled over her heart and mind. Her religious consciousness finally deteriorated to the point where she even gave up her religious profession and practices. It seemed a strange turn of events, but later in life she readily confessed that her religious profession at that time was merely superficial. She went through the motions for appearance. Love for God did not form the motivating dynamic of her religiosity. One day, all that would change.

Then once more, in the goodness and grace of God, Jeanne's father placed her back in the Ursuline Seminary. She again fell under the influence of her pious and prayerful half-sister. Now, as a more mature young lady, she was led to give herself to God in a more mature manner. She finally took of the sacrament, which gave her a momentary satisfaction. Yet something seemed missing. Jeanne still did not truly and fully find salvation in Jesus Christ, though she realized it not. Lasting peace evaded her. So she muddled along in her spiritual life. That inner unrest could not go on for long; as puberty began, she seemed destined to go the world's way.

The World and Its Charm

Jeanne grew tall and developed into a beautiful young lady in her early teens. The family smiled on her beauty and demeanor. Her mother especially lavished her with indulgences in dress and the things of this world. With Jeanne's lack of true saving faith and its attending peace and commitment, it is understandable that before long the world had gained full sway in young Jeanne's life. The quest for true religion and a relationship with God through Christ was laid aside and virtually forgotten as she was allured by the world. Yet, paradoxically, she was not completely devoid of religious feelings; she would grow concerned about her spiritual life one day but the next day be interested only in her beauty and dress and her growing reputation in society and this world with all its charms. Hers became a seesaw existence at best.

While the conflict continued on in Jeanne's life, a young man, a cousin of hers named de Tossi, came by the family home on his way to Cochin, China. He had dedicated his life to be a Roman Catholic missionary priest. His visit, though very short, made a deep impression on the teenager. Strangely, young Jeanne did not even see him when he visited the family; her mother and father told her of his consecration and dedication to Christ. Her heart was so touched that she wept all the rest of the day and all night. The thought of the contrast between her own worldly life and that of her pious cousin was what moved her so deeply. In this rather oblique manner, the Spirit of God spoke to Jeanne and created in her a new sense of her spiritual need. She did her very best to give up her worldliness and bring herself into a right relationship with spiritual things. She sought the forgiveness of God and those whom she had wronged in any way. She gave herself to religious service by visiting the poor, giving them food and clothing, and teaching them the catechism. Her own devotional life developed. She spent much time in private reading and prayer. Some of the great Catholic mystics moved her significantly as she read their devotional books, such as *The Life of Madam de Chantal*. The writings of Thomas à Kempis and Francis de Sales touched her also.

Another Shift

Jeanne began to give serious thought to becoming a nun, but despite her religious devotion and seeking, she had yet to find true peace and rest in the Lord Jesus Christ. Then, about a year after beginning her earnest quest for God, Jeanne fell in love with a young man, a near relative of hers. She was only fourteen years of age but extremely mature for her years. Jeanne soon became so involved with the young man that she began once again to neglect her spiritual disciplines. Her prayer life and her devotional readings by and large fell by the wayside. The pleasure that she once had in seeking the Lord she gave over for this young man. Her whole spiritual experience again became a matter of indifference. She began to read romance novels and spent an incredible amount of time just standing before the mirror admiring her own beauty. She became very vain.

As can be imagined, the worldly people of French society thought very highly of her. In 1663, the de La Mothe family moved to Paris. That certainly did not help Jeanne's spirituality and her search for peace in Christ. Paris completely wrapped itself in the pleasure-seeking reign of Louis XIV. The entire family got caught up in the social scene, which deepened young Jeanne's involvement in sheer pleasure. The whole world seemed before her, and she had one objective—to make a mark in it as a beautiful and vivacious socialite.

Along with her beauty, Jeanne possessed a keen intellect and displayed brilliant powers of conversation. She soon became a favorite in Paris society. She received invitations to all the important parties and social events. Her love for her young man quickly faded and she more and more involved herself in a whirlwind social life. Then Jeanne met her future husband, M. Jaques Guyon, a man of great wealth. Strangely enough, he was the only one who actually sought her hand in marriage.

A New Life and Its Difficulties

Jeanne had no great affection for Jaques Guyon, but her father arranged the marriage and insisted that she be wed to him. She yielded to her father's wishes and the wedding took place in 1664, just one year after the family had moved to Paris. Jeanne was only sixteen at the time and her husband was thirty-eight. She had now become Madame Guyon, but she had a long difficult road to traverse before becoming Madame Guyon, woman of awakening.

The age gap in their marriage became a problem. Even more serious, the home to which her husband took Jeanne became so-called a house of mourning. The young bride's mother-in-law was a rather crude personality with no education or refinement. She governed the whole household like a tyrant. Jaques had many good qualities and loved his young wife, but he had several physical infirmities, and because of the temper of his mother, Jeanne's life became miserable. Her hopes for earthly status and happiness crumbled about her, though later, she could gladly say that everything that had transpired in her life rested in the providence of God to call her out of her pride and worldliness. Still, at the time it all proved to be a tremendous burden.

The Trial of Faith

God was clearly allowing Jeanne to go through fiery trials so that the dross in her life could be consumed, as the Bible states: "In this you greatly rejoice, though now for a little while you may have had to suffer grief in all kinds of trials. These have come so that your faith—of greater worth than gold, which perishes even though refined by fire—may be proved genuine and may result in praise, glory and honor when Jesus Christ is revealed" (1 Peter 1:6–7 NIV). Jeanne confessed, "Such was the strength of my natural pride that nothing but some dispensation of sorrow would have broken down my spirit, and turned me to God." Later she could actually pray, "Thou hast ordered these things, O my God, for my salvation! In goodness Thou hast afflicted me. Enlightened by the result, I have since clearly seen, that these dealings of Thy providence were necessary, in order to make me die to my vain and haughty nature."

In the second year of their marriage, a son was born to the family and Jeanne devoted herself to the lad. She began to turn her eyes toward God even more sincerely as she sensed the need of bringing the child up in "the nurture and admonition of the Lord" (Eph. 6:4 KJV).

It seemed that trials and tribulations dogged Jeanne's heels every step of her life. Soon after the birth of their son, Jaques lost a major portion of his wealth. This embittered the pugnacious mother-in-law and she made Jeanne's life even more miserable. Later in the second year of her marriage, Jeanne fell seriously ill, so ill that many thought she would not survive. But this trial, like many of the others, turned her more earnestly toward God and spiritual things. Right at that point, her beloved half-sister, who had been such an inspiration to her, passed away. Then Jeanne's own mother died. Slowly, she was learning that rest and peace reside in Jesus Christ alone. She saw that all that she had been seeking was empty and vain.

A Fresh Seeking—and Finding

Once again Jeanne immersed herself in the works of Thomas à Kempis, Francis de Sales, and the life of Madam Chantal. God in His good providence at that moment caused a very devout English lady to cross her path. In their many conversations, Jeanne learned much about the essence of what it is to experience Christ in a dynamic, personal salvation experience. Then again in God's goodness, Jeanne's missionary cousin returned from Cochin, China. He helped the young mother tremendously. Not only that, a Franciscan monk visited the home often and counseled her in spiritual matters. This Franciscan, used by the Holy Spirit, opened to Jeanne the need of seeking Christ through faith and not resting on mere human works as found in the church sacraments. St. Francis, the godly founder of the Franciscan order, had learned that principle, and many of his disciples zealously shared it with others. In St. Francis' day it sparked a true revival. Madam Guyon was now clearly attaining a grasp of the simple Gospel of Jesus Christ.

Throughout all these dynamics, Jeanne began to see that a true relationship with God centered in the heart and not in a routine of ceremonial religious duties, regardless of how faithful one may be in the ceremonies. She began to realize the necessity of resting on the great principle that Paul so fearlessly defended: A person comes to know God in salvation not by the works of the Law, but by simple faith in Jesus Christ. She recognized that God's grace was the answer to her need.

After the Franciscan friar told Jeanne of the joy and thrill of salvation and forgiveness through faith in Christ, she said,

> Having said these words, the Franciscan left me. They were to me like the stroke of a dart, which pierced my heart asunder. I felt at this instant deeply wounded with the love of God—a wound so delightful that I desired it never to be healed. These words brought into my heart what I had been seeking so many years; or rather they made me discover what was there, and which I did not enjoy for want of knowing it.

Later she related,

> I told this good man, that I did not know what he had done to me; that my heart was quite changed; that God was there; for from that moment He had given me an experience of His presence in my soul—not merely as an object intellectually perceived by the application of the mind, but as a thing really possessed after the sweetest manner. I experienced those words in the Canticles: "Thy name is as a precious ointment poured forth; therefore do the virgins love Thee." For I felt in my soul an unction, which, as a salutary perfume healed in a moment all my wounds. I slept not all that night, because Thy love, O my God! flowed in me like delicious oil, and burned as a fire which was going to destroy all that was left of self in an instant. I was all of a sudden so altered, that I was hardly to be known either to myself or others.

On July 24, 1668, Jeanne passed from death unto life. Madam Guyon was only twenty years of age when she had her marvelous experience of salvation through faith in the Lord Jesus Christ. She said,

> Nothing was more easy to me now than to practice prayer. Hours passed away like moments, while I could hardly do anything else

but pray. The fervency of my love allowed me no intermission. It was a prayer of rejoicing and of possession, wherein the taste of God was so great, so pure, so unblended and uninterrupted, that it drew and absorbed the powers of the soul into a profound recollection, a state of confiding and affectionate rest in God, existing without intellectual effort.

Some time later she said to the Franciscan, "I love God far more than the most affectionate lover among men loves the object of his earthly attachment." "This love of God," she related, "occupied my heart so constantly and strongly, that it was very difficult for me to think of anything else. Nothing else seemed worth attention."[8] Before long, as she said, "I bade farewell forever to assemblies which I had visited, to plays and diversions, to dancing, to unprofitable walks, and to parties of pleasure. The amusements and pleasures which are so much prized and esteemed by the world now appeared to me dull and insipid—so much so, that I wondered how I ever could have enjoyed them." The grace of God had transformed the young socialite.

Service Begins

Jeanne and Jaques had a second son, born in 1667 a year before she came into her experience of Christ. And now with the little boys, she was able to point them to Christ and give herself to the service of her Lord in a new and fresh way. She began to devote herself to the care of needy children. She taught many poor young girls a trade to save them from a life of prostitution. She also worked with those who had already fallen into the vicious trade. Having still considerable means, she would assist poor tradesmen and mechanics to get started in business. In the setting of all of her ministry, she never neglected her spiritual life. She matured into a great woman of prayer. She said, "So strong, almost insatiable, was my desire for communion with God that I arose at four o'clock to pray." Prayer became the all-consuming pleasure of her life.

One can imagine how the social set in Paris began to view the young lady. They stood astonished that one so young and beautiful and intellectual could be so utterly given to the service of Christ. Actually, the pleasure-loving society people were so convicted by her life that they began to ridicule her. Even her own relatives did not grasp what had happened, and her avaricious mother-in-law sought to make her life even more miserable. For a period of time she even alienated Jaques.

The Family Grows—So Do Problems

In 1669, a daughter was born to Madam Guyon. The little girl served as a great comfort to her. Jeanne Guyon's spiritual life continued to deepen and broaden, as did her service for Christ. For two years she lived on the mountaintop of spiritual experience. But then, as often happens, even among the spiritually minded, she began to compromise and conform to some of the world's ways. Her devotion cooled. She began to neglect prayer and to once again look more favorably on worldly society. But the Spirit of God soon brought her up short. The conviction of the Holy Spirit humbled her, and she saw her error and immediately retreated to her sanctuary of prayer.

Being young in the Lord, Jeanne began experiencing a mountaintop-and-valley spiritual journey. Down in the valley she would slide, tempted by worldly dress and conversation. Then, as the Spirit of God spoke to her heart, she would come back to Christ in repentance. She was saved, but had not yet learned the principle of victory in Christ. She longed to have someone who could teach her more about how to maintain a consistent walk with Christ and become a victor. Her salvation was secure, but consistent sanctification eluded her. Spiritual help in Romanist France proved very meager, however, so she struggled on.

Victory at Last

Then one day as Madam Guyon was walking across one of the many beautiful bridges over the River Seine in Paris, a poor man in religious garb suddenly joined her and entered into conversation. He seemed to know all about her spiritual struggles, her strengths and her weaknesses and how God had been dealing in her life. It was quite incredible. Madam Guyon said,

> This man spoke to me in a wonderful manner of God and of divine things. He gave me to understand that God required not merely a heart of which it could only be said it is forgiven, but a heart which could properly, and in some real sense, be designated as holy, that it was not sufficient to escape hell, but that He demanded also the subjection of the evils of our nature, and the utmost purity and height of Christian attainment. The Spirit of God bare witness to what he said. The words of this remarkable man, whom I never saw before, and whom I have never seen since, penetrated my very soul. Deeply affected and overcome by what he had said, I had no sooner reached the church [she was on her way to Notre Dame] than I fainted away.

That Madam Guyon received a direct message through the miraculous grace of God is unquestionable. It impacted her life profoundly. That very day, before leaving Notre Dame, she resolved to give herself to the Lord anew and afresh. She finally realized through all her struggles the impossibility of serving both God and the world. She fully and finally resolved, in her own words, "From this day, this hour, if it be possible, I will be wholly the Lord's. The world shall have no portion in me." She later actually drew up and signed her "Covenant of Consecration," which has been a source of blessing to many as they have sought a deeper consecration to Christ. The essence of it all is simply that Madam Guyon yielded herself without reserve to the will of God. She not only dramatically found freedom from the up-and-down experiences of the past, she was thrust almost immediately into a severe testing time that destroyed all of her idols, joys, and ambitions and fixed her hope and ambitions totally on Jesus Christ. This woman of awakening was being prepared for a great ministry.

Trials

On October 4, 1670, being just a little more than twenty-two years of age, a blow came that staggered Jeanne. She fell victim to a very virulent form of smallpox. The disease by and large destroyed her beauty. But it precipitated such a dynamic relationship with Jesus Christ that she could say,

> The devastation without was counterbalanced by peace within. My soul was kept in a state of contentment, greater than can be expressed. Reminded continually of one of the causes of my religious trials and falls, I indulged the hope of regaining my inward liberty by the loss of that outward beauty which had been my grief. This view of my condition rendered my soul so well satisfied and so united to God, that I would not have exchanged its condition for that of the most happy prince in the world. As I lay in my bed, suffering the total deprivation of that which had been a snare to my pride, I experienced a joy unspeakable. I praised God with profound silence. When I was so far recovered as to be able to sit up in my bed, I ordered a mirror to be brought, and indulged my curiosity so far as to view myself in it. I was no longer what I was once. It was then I saw my heavenly Father had not been unfaithful in His work, but had ordered the sacrifice in all reality.

A blessing in disguise!

But more blows were still to come. Her youngest son, to whom she felt such love, was taken. She said, "This blow, struck me to the heart. I was overwhelmed; but God gave me strength in my weakness. I loved my young boy tenderly; but though I was greatly afflicted at his death, I saw the hand of the Lord so clearly, that I shed no tears. I offered him up to

God; and said in the language of Job, 'The Lord gave and the Lord hath taken away. Blessed be His name.'"

In 1676, Jaques, Jeanne's husband, who had become fully reconciled to her, was taken in death. So many who were dear to her were gone. Like Job, her life seemed to lay in shambles at her feet. Yet she saw so clearly the hand of God in it all that she could exclaim, "Oh, adorable conduct of my God! There must be no guide, no prop for the person whom Thou art leading into the regions of darkness and death. There must be no conductor, no support to the man whom Thou art determined to destroy to the entire destruction of the natural life."

It must be remembered that Madame Guyon was only in her mid-twenties when all these tragedies befell her. But the greatest trial of all was yet to come; as the mystics term the experience, the dark night of the soul soon came over the gracious saint. Madam Guyon fell into a state of deep spiritual depression and desolation. In 1674, she slipped into what she called her "state of privation, or desolation." This was a very common experience, especially among medieval mystics. Though they sought God earnestly and fervently, it appeared as though God remained far removed. Even in prayer the heavens seemed as brass. The sufferers cried out with the Psalmist that God would not forsake them, but still they felt utterly desolate and forsaken. This went on in Madam Guyon's life for seven long, depressing, difficult years. In that entire time there was no joy, peace, or reassuring emotions With all of her earthly props knocked out and now her spiritual emotions in shambles, she had to find an answer.

New Insight

At this stage, Jeanne began to correspond with a Roman priest by the name of Father La Combe, an eminent leader in the Barnabite order. She had earlier been used by the Spirit of God to lead Father La Combe into a genuine salvation experience through faith in Christ. Now he, in turn, became the instrument in leading her out of her darkness into a life of simple faith. He began to show Madam Guyon that the Spirit of God was crucifying the self-life in her. Slowly, gradually, but ever so beautifully, the great truths of her crucifiction with Christ and her ressurection with Him (Rom. 6:1–12) began to dawn, and her darkness began to dissipate.

Jeanne appointed a day and wrote Pastor La Combe, earnestly seeking him to fast and pray for her, that is, if the letter should reach him in time. La Combe was some distance off, but the letter did reach him and both he and Madam Guyon spent the day in prayer and fasting, though separated by many miles. God met her in a very marvelous way. The clouds of darkness lifted, and joy and glory once again filled her soul. As one author has put it, "The Holy Spirit opened her eyes to see that her afflictions were God's mercies in disguise. They were like the dark tunnels which are shortcuts through the mountains of difficulties and into the valleys of blessings beyond. They were God's chariots leading her upwards toward heaven. The vessel had been purified and fitted for His abode, and the Spirit of God, the heavenly Comforter, took up His abode in her heart." Madam Guyon herself said:

> On the 22nd of July, 1680, that happy day, my soul was delivered from all its pains. From the time of the first letter from Father La Combe I began to recover a new life. I was then indeed, only like a dead person raised up, who is in the beginning of his restoration, and raised up to a life of hope rather than of actual possession; but on this day I was restored, as it were, to perfect life, and set wholly at liberty. I was no longer depressed, no longer borne down under the burden of sorrow. I had thought God lost, and lost forever; but I found Him again. And He returned to me with unspeakable magnificence and purity.
>
> In a wonderful manner, difficult to explain, all that which had been taken from me, was not only restored, but restored with increase and new advantages. In Thee, O my God, I found it all, and more than all! The peace I now possessed was all holy, heavenly, inexpressible. What I had possessed some years before, in the period of my spiritual enjoyment, was consolation, peace—the gift of God rather than the Giver; but now, I was brought into such harmony with the will of God, that I might now be said to possess not merely consolation, but the God of consolation; not merely peace, but the God of peace. This true peace of mind was worth all that I had undergone, although it was only in its dawning.

Jeanne had made the mistake of getting her eyes off the Lord Himself and fixing them on the joy and peace she was experiencing. In the seven-year struggle, she longed to have peace and joy restored rather than simply, in faith, looking to God. Slowly she learned that the life of faith is the answer; and it is a much higher and holier life than that of one's mere religious emotion. She discovered that she must have her eyes fixed solely on the Lord and not upon herself, not even her emotional reaction to her religious experience.

A new deep peace pervaded Madame Guyon's entire life. She said that she feared nothing, and now everything was fulfilled in God. This became the beginning of her own personal revival. God never uses one of His children in revival until revival first touches her or his own heart. The new simplicity and power of revival pervaded her entire experience. She was so filled with the deep abiding peace and joy of the Holy Spirit that she immediately began to share these great truths. Awakening signs were on their way through this woman of God.

Revival Blessings

Although the coming awakening never permeated the whole nation of France, the many hundreds and ultimately thousands who were touched by Madam Guyon constituted a true revival in itself. She led multitudes into a deeper, richer, and fuller experience of God, and that is the essence of real revival.

The beautiful simplicity of Jeanne's faith in Christ led many to a similar simple faith in Christ for salvation. As is often seen, one of the hallmarks of revival centers in the conversion of multitudes. But Madam Guyon had a second revivalistic contribution to make: What she had learned through many years of trial and struggle and testing, she shared with others. She boldly declared the wonderful principle of sanctification through faith, just as salvation comes by grace through faith. She had learned what Paul meant when he said in Galatians 2:20 (NIV), "I have been crucified with Christ and I no longer live, but Christ lives in me. The life I live in the body, I live by faith in the Son of God, who loved me and gave himself for me." That, too, lies at the heart of a spiritual awakening. She shared with so many the secret of genuine victory over the self-life and the end of the struggle by taking in faith death to herself. The unction and power of the Holy Spirit mightily rested on her—and worked through her. Everywhere she went, multitudes besieged her. Spiritually hungry people constantly came to her for spiritual refreshment. As one author put it, "Revivals of religion began in almost every place visited by her, and all over France earnest Christians began to seek the deeper experience taught by her."

Not only did Madam Guyon become a channel of revival, but Father La Combe likewise shared the same message with great spiritual power. God touched many through the devoted, evangelical priest.

One of the most significant contributions that Jeanne Guyon made centered in the influence she exerted on Archbishop Fenelon. She led the young cleric into a deeper experience of Christ and he too began to spread the message all over France. Fenelon became a man of great piety and a highly gifted servant of Christ. The godliness of his life made an impact everywhere he went. He became archbishop of Cambry in France. Even though he met much opposition from the king of France and leading personalities of the day, including the Pope, his Christian spirit and intellectual genius, and above all the power of the Holy Spirit in his life, caused him to triumph over all obstacles. He became one of the most-loved men of France. Throughout the world his name still stands as a synonym for holiness and spirituality. Much of this can be attributed to Madam Guyon. In these ways the revival spread.

Opposition

Never has there been a true spiritual awakening without opposition, often with violence. Even though many French people were revived through Madame Guyon and left their worldliness and consecrated their lives holy to God, large numbers of the clergy severely criticized and condemned Madam Guyon and the revival movement. But then, history abounds with such a pattern. So often the chief opponents to revival are the clergymen. Actual persecution fell on Madam Guyon, Father La Combe, Fenelon, and others who were caught up in the new spirit. Father La Combe was even imprisoned and tortured. His suffering became so acute that he all but lost his reason.

As incredible as it may seem, Louis XIV imprisoned even Madam Guyon. The evil monarch thought he could stamp out the voice of this godly woman and her followers; but he was sadly mistaken. First of all, Jeanne Guyon had learned how to suffer. She endured the persecutions with Christian patience and grace. In reality, it strengthened her spiritual life. She spent her days in prison writing, praying, and praising.

While in prison, Madame Guyon's enemies tried to poison her. They failed, but as a consequence, she suffered for several years from the affects of the poisoning. Finally, after some eight months of imprisonment, her friends secured her release. By this time, Jeanne's writings were being read all over France and in many other parts of Europe as well. Countless thousands were brought to Christ and into a deeper depth of dedication.

In 1695, Madam Guyon once again found herself imprisoned by the devilish king. He incarcerated her in the castle of Vincennes. A year later the authorities transferred her to a prison in Vaugiard. Then in 1698, back in Paris she was thrown into the Bastile, the infamous prison of the city. She languished for four long years in that dreaded dungeon, but she could testify that her faith in God and in His goodness so abounded that the prison seemed like a palace. In 1702, Jeanne was released from the Bastile and banished to Blois. There she spent the last years of her life faithfully serving Christ and fostering the awakening movement that God had used her to launch. In 1717, at sixty-nine years of age, she went to be with her Lord in perfect peace. A life full of hopes and joys and finally glorious victories testify to her faithfulness to Christ.

Lasting Blessings

Madam Guyon became the author of sixty volumes. She also composed many great poems. Her writings bless people yet today. Many of her writings, like those of John Bunyon, were composed while in prison. The English poet, Cowper, translated several of her poetical works into English. The hymns she wrote are sung in our churches.

Beyond doubt, Madam Guyon, celebrated mystic, dedicated servant of Christ, and godly Christian leader, became to France what Savonarola, God's great spokesman for revival in Italy, became to his nation. Ultimately, she impacted people throughout the world. John Wesley, for example, confessed the debt he owed to Madam Guyon and her writings. The spiritual lessons that he learned from her ministry remained with him throughout his life.

Madam Guyon remained a Roman Catholic throughout her life, but she very much epitomized the spirit of the modern Quakers. She has actually been termed, "a Quaker born out of due time." One of the leading Quaker leaders said, "No society has been so influenced by Madam Guyon as the Quakers have been." Her spiritual movement became known as quietism, and what Madam Guyon meant by quietness centered in quiet submission to the will of God and to the leadership and instruction of the Holy Spirit. That is the kind of quietism that God honors and the kind that eventually explodes into genuine revival.

Madam Guyon never became a great organizer or promoter of revival, as one might perhaps view John Wesley or other leaders; it was simply her deeply profound Christian experience and utter dedication to God that impacted so many and led to an awakening. That reality can be expressed in her own words:

> To me remains nor place nor time;
> My country is in every clime;
> I can be calm and free from care
> On any shore since God is there.

Thus, God once again brought profound spiritual awakening through a great woman of God. The world stands indebted to Madam Guyon, woman of awakening.

Endnotes

1. The quotes in this chapter are taken from James Gilchrist Lawson, *Deeper Experiences of Famous Christians* (Anderson, Ind.: The Warner Press, 1911), 90.

Chapter Four

SUSANNA WESLEY

The Mother of Awakening

In the history of great awakenings, no stirring of the Holy Spirit shines forth more clearly and more symbolically of the essence of true revival, than the great eighteenth-century awakening that transformed Britain and America. It not only gave rebirth to the Christian movement in Great Britain, it gave birth to a new nation: the United States of America. The only way to describe this incredible work of God is to exclaim: "What days those were!"

As the movement began, spiritual giants burst on the scene—men such as George Whitfield, Jonathan Edwards, Howel Harris, Theodore Frelinghussen, the Tennents, and in one sense of the word, the figureheads of it all, John and Charles Wesley. Not only were all the major evangelical denominations of America and Britain genuinely awakened but also a movement, Methodism, that has lasted for over two hundred and fifty years, had its birth. Forever linked to the Methodist movement will be the names of John and Charles Wesley. Through their ministry, tens of thousands of churches have been started around the world, and literally millions of people have been brought to faith in Christ. Social reform also grew out of the awakening.

Biographies and monographs of these great men of God are numerous and are being written to this day. The name *Wesley* is almost synonymous with *revival*. Behind this movement—the Methodist tidal wave of revival—stood a woman: a minister's wife and mother. Being a deeply devout Christian, she instilled spiritual fervor into the hearts of her children, especially in the hearts of her famous sons, John and Charles. Her name was Susanna Wesley, and she was a spiritual giant, a mother of awakening. As one biographer has put it, "The Wesley's mother was the mother of Methodism in a religious and moral sense; for her courage, her submissiveness to authority, the high tone of her mind, its independence, and its self-control, the warmth of her devotional feelings and the practical direction given to them, came up and were visibly repeated in the character and conduct of her sons." We must meet this mother of revival.

Beginnings and Background

The church, on the march for the glory of Christ, could never have had a better commander than John Wesley. He possessed a military instinct along with a keen mind and, above all, a genius for organizing and equipping the "troops" for spiritual conquest. A born leader with a strong personality, John possessed the ability to cut through minutia and go straight to the point. So blessed of the Holy Spirit was he that the great Methodist movement carries on to this day. And all of that, in many respects, grew out of the legacy that he received from his godly mother, Susanna.

Boys often reproduce the central characteristics of their mothers, and John and Charles had a mother to model after. She was the twenty-fifth and youngest child in her family. Her father, Dr. Samuel Annesley, saw Susanna come into this world by his second wife in Spital Yard, London, January 20, 1669. From both sides of the family little Susanna inherited a noble ancestry. Her mother's father was the well-known John White of Pembrokeshire. Being a staunch Welshman and a graduate of Jesus College at the University of Oxford, he became a member of Parliament in 1640 on being elected from Southwark in London. He served as an active member of the party that opposed King Charles I.

Charles I reigned as an ardent high churchman, thus standing in staunch opposition to the Puritan movement of his day. That stance sealed his doom. His reign ended in tragedy; the Cromwells dethroned and executed him. In the mélée of the civil war that followed, the Puritans gained absolute political power under Oliver Cromwell. Supporting that movement was Susanna's father. He wrote a large manifesto entitled, *The First Century of Scandalous and Malignant Priests*. It centered in an indictment of the lack of spirituality and commitment to Christ among Anglican clergymen, and can be seen today in London's British Museum.

It must be granted that during the reign of Charles I, the Church of England's ministry had deteriorated dramatically. Some of the interesting and yet tragic facts are that many of the clergy never even saw their parish. They drew the salary of a full rector but left all the work to curates while they lived the "good life" in London or elsewhere. Many ministers never read their Bibles or preached a sermon. One observer said, "The English clergy of the day are the most remiss of their labours in private, and the least severe in their lives."

Consequently, much of society skidded down the slippery slope of moral decay—despite the recent victories of the Puritans. Philosophical deism and rationalism reigned; spiritually, scepticism and immorality dominated the scene. A saying in the pubs declared: "Get drunk for a penny, dead drunk for two pense." That attitude did not dominate just the lower classes. Lord Chesterfield, in a letter to his son, instructed him in the art of seduction as part of a polite education. They were dark days indeed. Revival stood as the paramount need.

Against all these abuses, parliamentarian John White stood tall and made his influence felt in the British Parliament. He died at the early age of fifty-four in 1644, leaving a heritage of spirituality and fortitude in his granddaughter Susanna.

Susanna's father, Dr. Annesley, had an aristocratic background, and he looked it, every inch of him. His father and the earl of Anglesey were first cousins, their fathers being brothers. As a young man, Annesley became a student at Queens College, Oxford, at the age of fifteen. He proved to be a fine student and received a Master of Arts degree. At the age of twenty-four he became an Anglican minister.

Dr. Annesley attained a notable reputation and in 1648, on a solemn national fast day, preached a sermon before the entire House of Commons. Puritanism had gained control under Cromwell, and much to the chagrin of many in the House, Annesley said that it was un-Christlike to execute the king. Not only that, he spoke against the abuses of the Cromwell government, which obviously did not endear him to many. But he was a man of conviction and spoke his mind. Nonetheless, the Parish of St. John the Evangelist on Friday Street in Cheapside, London, unanimously elected him as their pastor and minister in 1652. They saw him as a man of keen spiritual insight, who was courageous and a genuine man of God. He became a prominent "Puritan divine," even though he had not approved of the execution of Charles I.

Dr. Annesley was of presbyterian persuasion. That is to say, he believed in the Presbyterian form of church government, which stood in opposition to the Church of England's episcopacy approach. But in 1662, Parliament passed the Act of Uniformity bill. The Act of Uniformity demanded that all ministers of the Anglican communion sign the Uniformity manifesto, which demanded adherence to the traditional episcopacy Anglican views on church life and government. As a result, some two thousand clergymen of presbyterian persuasion refused to sign and forthwith were ejected from their parishes. Among those were notable names like the great Richard Baxter. Thus, Susanna's father found himself without a parish.

The dynamics of the ecclesiastical situation turned, however, and ten years later Parliament passed the Declaration of Indulgence. This reversed the Act of Uniformity. Dr. Annesley became pastor of the Meeting House in Little Saint Helens, a nonconformist congregation. There he ministered to the satisfaction and appreciation of his congregation for the rest of his life. Upon his settlement in Little Saint Helens, Susanna had just turned three years of age.

Susanna enjoyed a settled home life. Her godly father now had a secure ministry until the day of his death. The very spiritual home in which
Susanna grew up also became her legacy. She was christened in the Anglican tradition by the notable puritan, Thomas Manton.

As has been seen, the Annesleys had a large brood. At Susanna's christening, Thomas Manton was asked how many "olive branches" Dr.
Annesley had. The great puritan preacher replied that it was either a couple
of dozen or a quarter of a hundred. Of course, there were probably several infant deaths among the many children, because infant mortality in
those days was appallingly high. Still, his "quiver was very full indeed."

Early Youth and Marriage

Susanna, with her fine background, grew into a very mature young
lady. She had a ready flow of words along with an abundance of common
sense. One could say that she was also a gifted letter writer. The correspondence that she left is quite remarkable. She had an acquaintance with
the French language and had immersed herself into a serious study of the
religious issues of the day. But her personal Christian faith captured her
attention the most. Moreover, she inherited her father's strong will. She
deliberately chose to follow the traditional Church of England rather than
remain among the nonconformists like her father. Susanna broke ranks
and identified herself with the Anglican Church. Yet, to the end of his
life, she was her father's favorite child, and her sterling qualities stood
out to all.

During those early days, Samuel Wesley, who himself could boast of a
long family line of gentlemen and scholars, made several visits to the
Annesley home.

Father Samuel

Samuel Wesley was a son of the Reverend John Wesley, the vicar of
Interborn, Whitchurch in Dorsetshire. John Wesley, like Susanna's father, became one of the ejected clergymen, a victim of the Act of Uniformity. He too had his unbending convictions; it was that sort of time.

Samuel Wesley, John's son, had many positive character traits due to
his favored background. At college he became a very able student with an
exceptional gift for writing. But he also had his problems. He loved
involving himself in controversies. Coming from a nonconforming
background, he took the same church stance as did the girl whom he
would marry, Susanna. At the age of twenty-one he forsook his
nonconforming connections and joined the Church of England.
Furthermore, he made up his mind to go to Oxford University. In August
1683, with only forty-five shillings in his pocket, he went to Oxford and
entered Exeter College as a servitor. That means he matriculated as a

full-fledged student but had to serve the other more wealthy students. He would polish their boots, bring them their meals, clean their rooms, and do general menial chores. Nevertheless, he received an excellent education. He also helped maintain himself by teaching and writing papers for the more wealthy undergraduates. He probably ought not to have done the latter because it was not academically correct, but he did get himself through college. He passed his examinations and in June 1688 he received his Bachelor of Arts degree.

Samuel Wesley left Oxford at the time that the first Declaration of Indulgence was declared under James II. Samuel received "deacon's orders" through Dr. Sprat, the bishop of Rochester, which gave him the right to be a curate under the leadership of a minister in the Church of England. Today he would be called an assistant pastor. His stipend was twenty-eight pounds a year, a very scant living even in those frugal days. He remained in that post some twelve months, after which he received ordination as a priest of the Church of England. Dr. Compton, the bishop of London at Saint Andrews, Holborn, officiated the ceremony on February 24, 1689. That was exactly twelve days after William and Mary had been declared the new sovereigns of Great Britain.

Samuel's first position, after becoming a full-fledged ordained priest of the Anglican Church, was an appointment as chaplain on board a naval man-of-war. He received seventy pounds a year in that position, which made him comparatively well off. Further, this position gave him time to develop his writing skills because the demands on a naval chaplain were not heavy. He developed into a very able writer.

After a time Samuel resigned his chaplaincy and again became a curate in London, with an income of thirty pounds, which he doubled with his writings. In that setting, he and Susanna Annesley met, fell in love, and were married in the spring of 1689. It is not known what church they were married in or who officiated, but the wedding sealed their hearts, and their hands were joined in Christian ministry.

Married Life

Susanna, somewhat younger than her husband Samuel, possessed a quite different temperament. She was very economical and a good housekeeper. Samuel's handling of money left something to be desired—as we shall see.

The new couple lived for two years in London, during which time their eldest son, Samuel Jr., was born. Susanna's husband united in a small business with a Mr. Dunton to supplement his ministerial work. They established the *Athenian Gazette,* a weekly publication that continued for some years. Samuel, being now an able writer and a respected minister of the Gospel, prompted one admirer to say:

He, Samuel, was a man of profound knowledge, not only of the
Holy Scriptures, of the Councils, and of the Fathers, but also of
every other art that comes within those called liberal. His zeal
and ability in giving spiritual directions were great. With invin-
cible power he confirmed the wavering and confuted heretics.
Beneath the genial warmth of his wit the most barren subject
became fertile and divertive. His style was sweet and manly, soft
without satiety, and learned without pedantry. . . . His compassion for the sufferings of his fellow-creatures was as great as his
learning.[1]

Samuel Wesley truly had become a quite learned theologian along with
possessing a real gift of expressing theology. But he loved controversy
and enjoyed writing on controversial theological ideas. Yet he really was
a good thinker and a respected pastor.

Leaving London

Before the Wesley's final settlement in Epworth—a small community
tucked away in a corner of Lincolnshire, a town that has now become
famous because of the fact that the Wesleys spent the major portion of
their lives and raised their very large family there—a call came from the
little country parish church of South Ornsby. Procured for them in 1690
by the marquis of Normanby, it proved to be a happy ministry. Samuel,
only twenty-eight years of age at that time and Susanna a mere twenty-
two, packed up with little four-month-old Samuel Jr. and left London for
the country ministry. There were only thirty-six houses and about two
hundred and sixty citizens in the ancient parish, but the work went well
and the family began to grow.

In 1693, the Reverend Samuel Wesley published a major ten-volume
work, *The Life of Our Blessed Lord and Savior Jesus Christ.* He dedicated it to Queen Mary. In it he gave a very gracious word to his wife to
whom he had now been married for four years. It reads as follows:

> She graced my humble roof and blest my life,
> Blest me by a far greater name than wife;
> Yet still I bore an undisputed sway,
> Nor wasn't her task, but pleasure to obey:
> Scarce thought, much less could act, what I denied.
> In our low house there was no room for pride;
> Nor need I e'er direct what still was right,
> She studied my convenience and delight.
> Nor did I for her care ungrateful prove,
> But only used my power to show my love:

Whate'er she asked I gave without reproach or grudge,
For still she reason asked, and I was judge.
All my commands requests at her fair hands,
And her requests to me were all commands.
To other thresholds rarely she'd incline:
Her house her pleasure was, and she was mine;
Rarely abroad, or never but with me,
Or when by pity called, or charity.

Queen Mary, duly impressed, after a short time became the instrument in seeing to the Wesley's move to Epworth.

To Epworth

The move to Epworth proved to be most significant. It came with a bit of grief, however, because just as the Wesleys were leaving South Ornsby, Dr. Annesley went to be with the Lord on the last day of 1696. Susanna, only twenty-seven, was expecting her eighth child.

So, in 1697, the Wesleys moved to Epworth on the opposite side of the county from Lincoln. Epworth, being a small market town, could only boast of two thousand inhabitants. It rests on something of a peninsula called the Isle of Axholme, a district that is about ten miles long and four miles broad. It is surrounded by the rivers Trent, Don, and Idle.

The parish church itself was a very old structure in Wesley's days, and it had been dedicated to Saint Andrew. The home that was provided for the ministering family really looked like something of a palace in comparison to what they called their mud hut at South Ornsby. It stood three stories tall with five gables and timber and plaster walls. It had a thatched roof of straw and contained a kitchen, hall, parlor, buttery, and three large upper rooms with others for more common use. A beautiful garden also surrounded it. Samuel and Susannah were thrilled with their new home, but problems soon arose.

For some reason, Samuel Wesley never seemed able to handle his finances, putting the family in debt continually. This was a real hardship for Susanna, causing many an anxious hour and considerable struggle for her. But God's blessings rested on them, and their needs seemingly always were met one way or another. The family continued to grow, though several of the children died in infancy. Into this matrix, John and Charles were born; and history was soon to be written. At about the turn of the eighteenth century, Samuel Wesley's aged mother came to live with them at Epworth. She no doubt became a tremendous help to the young wife with the large growing family, because Susanna always had a difficult time during pregnancy and would many times be virtually confined to bed for months at a stretch.

In May 1701, circumstances had become very difficult financially for the young couple. They needed coal because it was still very cold in that part of England. After putting all their coins together, six shillings was all they had. Fortunately, the countess of Northhampton somehow heard of their predicament, and she gave them ten pounds to alleviate the pressure they were under. The money actually arrived on a morning that found them completely penniless, and it did not arrive one moment too soon, for that very evening twins were born to Susanna—a boy and a girl. A year later, the twins had passed away, as had a little boy who was born before the twins. Such a heart wrenching time it was! Yet sorrow and hardship were building spiritual steel into Susanna's backbone as the Spirit of God molded her into a true mother of revival.

Susanna's Schooling

Susanna is well-known for the time she spent instructing her children in spiritual matters, despite her incredible responsibilities and hardships. In reality, she did far more than just instruct them in the things of the Lord. She conducted a regular school for her family, six hours every day. She kept to this routine for twenty years with very few interruptions.

In this schooling, Susanna instilled in her children not only good learning but also the basic principles of the Christian faith. She exercised great patience with her children (some of them were slow learners). One day her husband sat in on the group and he counted the times she repeated one particular fact to one child twenty times. "I wonder at your patience," said Samuel. "You have told that child twenty times the same things." Susanna replied, "If I had satisfied myself by mentioning it only nineteen times, I should have lost all my labor. It was the twentieth time that crowned it." Little question can be raised that John and Charles were not tremendously influenced by their mother's faithfulness. Later in life, John realized and deeply appreciated her sacrifice. He would often ask his mother to write down in full detail all that she had done in educating the family. Susanna's reluctance to tell her story comes out in a letter dated February 12, 1732:

> The writing of anything about my way of education I am much averse to. It cannot, I think, be of service to any one to know how I, who have lived such a retired life for so many years, used to employ my time and care in bringing up my children. No one can, without renouncing the world in the most literal sense, observe my method; and there are few, if any, that would entirely devote above twenty years of the prime of life in hopes to save the souls of their children, which they think may be saved without so much ado; for that was my principal intention, however unskillfully and unsuccessfully managed.

John, however, kept after her, and Susanna finally relented and allowed herself to be persuaded. She outlined to John her methodology, writing from Epworth on July 24, 1732:

Dear Son,—According to your desire, I have collected the principal rules I observed in educating my family.

First, it had been observed that cowardice and fear of punishment often lead children into lying till they get a custom of it which they cannot leave. To prevent this, a law was made that whoever was charged with a fault of which they were guilty, if they would ingenuously confess it and promise to amend should not be beaten. This rule prevented a great deal of lying.

Second, that no sinful action, as lying, pilfering at church or on the Lord's Day, disobedience, quarreling, etc., should ever pass unpunished.

Third, that no child should be ever chid or beat twice for the same fault, and that if they amended they should never be upbraided with it afterwards.

Fourth, that every signal act of obedience, especially when it crossed upon their own inclinations, should be always commended, and frequently rewarded according to the merits of the case.

Fifth, that if ever any child performed an act of obedience, or did anything with an intention to please, though the performance was not well, yet the obedience and intention should be kindly accepted, and the child with sweetness directed how to do better for the future.

Sixth, that propriety [the rights of property] be invariably preserved, and none suffered to invade the property of another in the smallest matter.

Seventh, that promises be strictly observed; and a gift once bestowed, and so the right passed away from the donor, be not resumed, but left to the disposal of him to whom it was given, unless it were conditional, and the condition of the obligation not performed.

Eighth, that no girl be taught to work till she can read very well; and that she be kept to her work with the same application and for the same time that she was held to in reading. This rule also is much to be observed, for the putting children to learn sewing before they can read perfectly is the very reason why so few women can read fit to be heard, and never to be well understood.

Susanna Wesley

It may seem a long quote, but it is important in laying the foundation for the revival in and through the ministry of John and Charles Wesley. For a mother to take the kind of time and effort that Susanna did with her many children is really quite phenomenal. Although we have home schools today, mothers are not nearly as pressed as was this mother. With a host of children, no modern conveniences, constant debt with financial constraints that were almost incredible, the continual absence of her husband (which shall be discussed in a moment) coupled with her own illnesses makes one wonder how she ever accomplished the task. But God's hand rested powerfully on her. Revival waited in the wings, to be brought center stage through her children. Susanna's sacrifice paid off wonderfully.

Samuel's Absences

Through Samuel Wesley's writings, his image grew in stature among Anglican ecclesiastical circles. As a consequence, he became a member of the convocation. This group of Anglican clergymen sat governing much of the life of the Church of England. The honor, however, involved Samuel's being in London at the denominational headquarters for weeks and months at a time. Susanna almost seemed a widow. During these absences, Mrs. Wesley had the entire responsibility of the home on her hands. She became responsible not only for the family but virtually for the parish and church as well. She kept the church records along with seeing to it that all congregational needs were met. Furthermore, the Wesley's maintained a small farm. The farm assured that they would never starve, but it involved considerable work. Yet, in the midst of it all, she kept things going on the home front and the family did well—a remarkable feat.

Samuel had written a very fine work entitled, *History of the Old and New Testament, Attempted in Verse, and Adorned with Three Hundred and Thirty Scriptures*. The royalties from that production would help the family financially. He also traveled to the capital and made a financial appeal to various acquaintances and friends. They responded, recognizing something of the financial difficulties and importance of his ministry. The dean of Exeter gave him ten pounds; the archbishop of Canterbury, ten guineas; the marquis of Normanby, twenty; the marchioness, five. With a few other contributions he raised the sum of sixty pounds. As can be imagined, when he came home and told the family that he had raised sixty pounds, they all rejoiced. This would pay off some of the debts entirely and a portion of the others, still leaving them ten pounds for immediate expenses.

Difficulties were far from over, however. The very next summer proved to be terribly hot and dry. The thatched roof of the parsonage became incredibly dry. Probably from the kitchen chimney that needed sweeping, sparks fell on the roof and the thatch caught fire. Fortunately, the house did not burn down, but a great deal of damage had been done. Wesley's response was, "He that is born to be a poet must, I'm afraid, live and die poor."

In this general time frame, war broke out. The duke of Marlborough engaged in a campaign to break the power of France. Susanna's attitude toward conflict surfaced. She wrote:

> Since I am not satisfied of the lawfulness of the war, I cannot beg a blessing on our arms till I can have the opinion of one wiser, and a more competent judge than myself, in this point, namely, whether a private person that had no hand in the beginning of the war, but did always disapprove of it, may, notwithstanding, implore God's blessing on it, and pray for the good success of those arms which were taken up, I think, unlawfully. In the meantime, I think it my duty, since I cannot join in public worship, to spend the time others take in that, in humbling myself before God for my own and the nation's sins.

Right at that juncture John was born. He came into the world a rather delicate child. His father baptized him when only a few hours old lest he die unbaptized. The parents christened him John Benjamin, named after two baby boys, the tenth and the eleventh Wesley children, who had died in infancy.

In 1704, the oldest Wesley boy, Samuel, matriculated into Westminster School—a real achievement. Samuel always seemed something of a favorite of Susanna, at least her correspondence indicates such. She wrote him often, and on August 4, 1704 she penned the following letter:

> Dear Sammy,—I have been ill a great while, but am now, I thank God, well recovered. I thought to have been with you ere this, but I doubt if I shall see you this summer; therefore send me word particularly what you want.
>
> I would ere now have finished my discourse begun so long ago, if I had enjoyed more health; but I hope I shall be able to finish it quickly, and then have you transcribe all your letters; for they may be more useful to you than they are now, because you will be better able to understand them. I shall be employing my thoughts on useful subjects for you when I have time, for I desire nothing in this world so much as to have my children well instructed in the principles of religion, that they may walk in the narrow way which alone leads to happiness. Particularly I am

concerned for you, who were, even before your birth, dedicated to the service of the sanctuary, that you may be an ornament of that Church of which you are a member, and be instrumental (if God shall spare your life) in bringing many souls to Heaven. Take heed, therefore, in the first place, of your own, lest you yourself should be a castaway.

A little later she wrote her son again and said, "Dear Sammy,—Let your light so shine before men that they may see your good works and glorify your Father which is in Heaven." Susannah was always vitally concerned about the spiritual well-being of her children.

In that same year, August (1704), the duke of Marlborough became the hero of the hour in Britain. At the Battle of Blenhiem he defeated the French. Father Samuel wrote a ninety-four-line poem entitled, *Marlborough, or the Fate of Europe*. The duke of Marlborough, quite pleased with the work, granted to Wesley the chaplaincy of Colonel Lepelle's regiment. Nothing really came of it, however. Because of Wesley's stand on particular political issues, the Whig party deprived him of the chaplaincy. This was a disappointment, but in the overall plan of God, perhaps it proved best for the family. The worst trial still stood in the wings, soon to come center stage.

Wesley's Imprisonment

Samuel Wesley, never reticent in expressing himself on political issues, which cost him the chaplaincy to Colonel Lepelle's regiment, further commented on a recent election, which angered one of his debtors. As a consequence, the man demanded immediate payment. Wesley did not have any funds and so was arrested and sent to Lincoln jail. He gave an account of the event in his own hand, writing to the archbishop of York:

My Lord,—Now I am at rest, for I am come to the haven where I've long expected to be. On Friday last (June 23), when I had been, in christening a child, at Epworth, I was arrested in my churchyard by one who had been my servant, and gathered my tithe last year, at the suit of one of Mr. Whichcott's relations and zealous friends (M. Pinder), according to their promise when they were in the Isle before the Election. The sum was not thirty pounds, but it was as good as five hundred. Now they knew the burning of my flax, (roof), my London journey, and their throwing me out of my regiment had both sunk my credit and exhausted my money. My adversary was sent to where I was on the road, to meet me, that I might make some proposals to him. But all his answer (which I have by me) was, that I must immediately pay the whole sum or go to prison. Thither I went with no great concern for myself, and find much more civility and satisfaction here than in Brevibus gyaris of my own Epworth. I thank God my wife was pretty well recovered, and churched some days before I was taken from her; and hope she'll be able to look to my family, if they don't turn them out of doors, as they have often threatened to do. One of my biggest concerns was my being forced to leave my poor lambs in the midst of so many wolves. But the great Shepherd is able to provide for them and to preserve them. My wife bears it with that courage which becomes her, and which I expected from her.

Wesley's wife, our Susanna, bore it remarkably well as Samuel himself acknowledged. Still, it must have been a trial to this dear woman. The embarrassment was bad enough, let alone the financial strain. Apparently, Wesley simply did not know how to handle his money, and his imprisonment became a very trying time. The archbishop of York asked Mrs. Wesley about her actual situation. She replied, "My Lord, I will freely own to your Grace that, strictly speaking, I never did want bread. But then I had so much care to get it before it was eat, and to pay for it after, as has often made it very unpleasant to me. And I think to have bread on such terms is the next degree of wretchedness to having none at all." The Archbishop replied, "You are certainly right." He gave Susannah a large sum of money that greatly relieved the situation. After three months in jail, Samuel Wesley, assisted by friends, payed off about half of his debts and was released from prison. Samuel wrote his oldest son, away in school at Westminster, "Now on both these accounts you know what you owe to one of the best of mothers." How true.

Another Son Is Born

On December 18, 1707, the "sweet singer of Methodism" came into the world permaturely. Charles became the eighteenth child. His health was so fragile that he could not even be dressed, and he had to be wrapped up in wool for some time. Although he had a very difficult start in life, he lived to a good old age and became the companion in revival with his older brother John.

The Fire

John Wesley always said that he saw himself "a brand plucked out of the fire" (Zech. 3:2). While Charles was still an infant, on February 19, 1704, the Wesley's house burned down. It became a very graphic, unforgettable drama that deeply impacted John. The first fire had only consumed a portion of the thatched roof. This conflagration gutted the house completely, and John barely escaped with his life. Susanna wrote a very graphic portrayal of the event to her son Samuel Jr. A few days later, Samuel wrote a more detailed account to the duke of Buckingham. A vivid picture emerged:

> On Wednesday last, at half an hour after eleven at night, in a quarter of an hour's time or less, my house at Epworth was burnt down to the ground—I hope, by accident, but God knows all. We had been brewing, but had done all; every spark of fire quenched before five o'clock that evening,—at least six hours before the house was on fire. Perhaps the chimney above might take fire (though it had been swept not long since) and break through into the thatch. Yet it is strange I should neither see nor smell anything of it, having been in my study in that part of the house till above half an hour after ten. Then I locked the doors of that part of the house where my wheat and other corn lay, which was threshed, and went to bed.
>
> The servants had not been in bed a quarter of an hour when the fire began. My wife being near her time, and very weak, lay in the next chamber. A little after eleven I heard "Fire!" cried in the street, next to which I lay. If I had been in my own chamber as usual, we had all been lost. I threw myself out of bed, got on my waistcoat and nightgown, and looked out of the window; saw the reflection of the flame, but knew not where it was; ran to my wife's chamber with one stocking on, and my breeches in my hand; would have broken open the door, which was bolted within, but could not. My two eldest children (Susanna and Emilia) were with her. They rose, and ran towards the staircase, to raise the rest of the house. Then I saw it was our own house, all in a light blaze, and nothing but a door between the flame and the staircase.
>
> I ran back to my wife, who by this time had got out of bed naked and opened the door. I bade her fly for her life. We had a little silver and some gold,—about £20. She would have stayed for it, but I pushed her out; got her and my two eldest children downstairs (where two of the servants were now got) and asked for the keys. They knew nothing of them. I ran upstairs and found them, came down and opened the street door. The thatch was fallen in all on fire. The northeast wind drove all the sheets of flame in my face, as if reverberated in a lamp. I got twice on the steps, and was drove down again. I ran to the garden door and opened it. The fire was there more moderate. I bade them all follow, but found only two with me, and the maid with another (Charles) in her arms that cannot go, but all naked. I ran with

them to my house of office in the garden, out of the reach of the flames; put the least in the other's lap; and, not finding my wife follow me, ran back into the house to seek her. The servants and two of the children were got out at a window. In the kitchen I found my eldest daughter, naked, and asked her for her mother. She could not tell me where she was. I took her up and carried her to the rest in the garden; came in the second time and ran upstairs, the flame breaking through the wall at the staircase; thought all my children were safe, and hoped my wife was some way got out. I then remembered my books, and felt in my pocket for the key of the chamber which led to my study. I could not find the key, though I searched a second time. Had I opened that door I must have perished.

I ran down, and went to my children in the garden, to help them over the wall. When I was without, I heard one of my poor lambs, left still above stairs, about six years old, cry out dismally, "Help me!" I ran in again to go upstairs, but the staircase was now all afire. I tried to force up through it a second time, holding my breeches over my head, but the stream of fire beat me down. I thought I had done my duty; went out of the house to that part of my family I had saved, in the garden, with the killing cry of my child in my ears. I made them all kneel down, and we prayed God to receive his soul.

I tried to break down the pales and get my children over into the street, but could not; then went under the flame, and got them over the wall. Now I put on my breeches and leaped after them. One of my maid-servants that had brought out the least child got out much at the same time. She was saluted with a hearty curse by one of the neighbors, and told that we had fired the house ourselves, the second time, on purpose. I ran about inquiring for my wife and other children; met the chief man and chief constable of the town going from my house, not towards it to help me. I took him by the hand and said, "God's will be done!" His answer was: "Will you never have done your tricks? You fired your house once before; did you not get enough by it then, that you have done it again?" This was cold comfort. I said, "God forgive you! I find you are chief man still." But I had a little better soon after, hearing that my wife was saved, and then I fell on mother earth and blessed God. I went to her. She was alive, and could just speak. She thought I had perished, and so did all the rest, not having seen me nor any share of eight children for a quarter of an hour; and by this time all the chambers and everything was reduced to ashes, for the fire was stronger than a furnace, the

violent wind beating it down on the house. She told me afterwards
how she escaped. When I went first to open the back door she
endeavored to force through the fire at the fore door, but was
struck back twice to the ground. She thought to have died there,
but prayed to Christ to help her. She found new strength, got up
alone, and waded through two or three yards of flame, the fire on
the ground being up to her knees. She had nothing on but her
shoes and a wrapping gown and one coat on her arm. This she
wrapped about her breast, and got safe through into the yard, but
no soul yet to help her. She never looked up or spake till I came,
only when they brought her last child to her bade them lay it on
the bed. This was the lad whom I heard cry in the house, but God
saved him almost by a miracle. He only was forgot by the servants
in a hurry. He ran to the window towards the yard, stood upon a
chair, and cried for help. There were not a few people gathered
one of whom, who loves me, helped up another to the window.
The child seeing a man come into the window was frightened,
and ran away to get to his mother's chamber. He could not open
the door, so ran back again. The man was fallen down from the
window, and all the bed and hangings in the room where he was
were blazing. They helped up the man the second time, and poor
Jacky (John) leaped into his arms and was saved. I could not
believe it till I had kissed him two or three times. My wife then
said unto me, "Are your books safe?" I told her it was not much
now she and all the rest were preserved, for we lost not one soul,
though I escaped with the skin of my teeth. A little lumber was
saved below stairs, but not one rag or leaf above. We found some
of the silver in a lump, which I shall send up to Mr. Hoar to sell
for me.

Mr. Smith of Gainsborough, and others, have sent for some of
my children. I have left my wife at Epworth, trembling; but hope
God will preserve her, and fear not but He will provide for us. I
want nothing, having above half my barley saved in my barns
unthreshed. I had finished my alterations in the "Life of Christ" a
little while since, and transcribed three copies of it; but all is lost.
God be praised!

. . . I hope my wife will recover and not miscarry, but God will
give me my nineteenth child. She has burnt her legs, but they
mend. When I came to her, her lips were black. I did not know
her. Some of the children are a little burnt, but not hurt or disfig-
ured. I only got a small blister on my hand. The neighbors send
us clothes, for it is cold without them.

The family lost everything. All of the books, letters, and literary work went up in smoke and flame. They even lost the papers of the Annesley family. The only thing to survive was a poem by Samuel Wesley that had been set to music. The Methodist hymnbook still contains it under the title "Behold the Savior of Mankind." In March, just about a month after the fire, Kezia was born. She became the nineteenth, and last, child of Mrs. Wesley.

John's own account of the fire paints a very graphic description. When the building went up in flames, the parents thought that young John was in the burning house unable to escape. Samuel had bowed his head and had given John's spirit to God, who had given it. At that moment John awoke. In his own words he said:

> I did not cry, as they imagined, unless it was afterwards. I remember all the circumstance as distinctly as though it were but yesterday. Seeing the room was very light, I called to the maid to take me up. But none answering, I put my head out of the curtains and saw streaks of fire on the top of the room. I got up and ran to the door, but could get no farther, all beyond it being in a blaze. I then climbed up on the chest which stood near the window; one in the yard saw me, and proposed running to fetch a ladder. Another answered, "There will not be time; but I have thought of another experiment. Here, I will fix myself against the wall, lift a light man and set him upon my shoulders." They did so, and he took me out of the window. Just then the whole roof fell in; but it fell inward, or we had all been crushed at once. When they brought me into the house where my father was he cried out: "Come, neighbors, let us kneel down; let us give thanks to God! He has given me all my eight children; let the house go. I am rich enough."

The Wesleys not only suffered the loss of many material things, some of the children had to be sent to relatives and friends. The tragedy broke up the solidarity of the family. Through it all, Susanna was primarily concerned about the spiritual life of her children. In writing to her oldest boy, she concluded a letter with these words: "I cannot tell whether you have ever seriously considered the lost and miserable condition you are in by nature. If you have not, it is high time to begin to do it; and I shall earnestly beseech the Almighty to enlighten your mind, to renew and sanctify you by His Holy Spirit, that you may be His child by adoption here, and an heir of His blessed kingdom hereafter."

Above all, Susanna desired to see her children embrace living, vibrant faith in the Lord Jesus Christ. That is a true mother's heart and the essence of real revival, which would one day come, with Susanna seeing it.

The Home Rebuilt

The Wesleys' home—the Rectory, in Anglican terminology—was rebuilt in typical Queen Anne style—a red brick. The new home compared quite favorably to the old. However, Samuel had to be away a good part of the year, and so his wife and children were in the new home by themselves. In spite of her own physical weakness and weariness, Susanna struggled on to keep the family together and well-educated. In that setting, daughter Emilia discovered a book on the Danish mission to Tranquebar. Susanna wrote to her husband in London, "When after you went to London, Emilia found in your study the account of the Danish Missionaries, which, having never seen, I desired her to read to me. I was never, I think, more affected with anything than with the relation of their travels, and was exceedingly pleased with the noble design they were engaged in." This must have given Mother Susanna something of a world-wide vision for the work of Christ. Although it may be conjecture, perhaps this became the instrument in instilling in John the principle of the global dimension of the Gospel. At any rate, that principle permeated the mind-sets of sons John and Charles. They not only sailed to Georgia in the American Colonies as missionaries themselves, but made John Wesley's famous statement, "the world is my parish" the guiding philosophy of Methodism.

New Problems

Difficulties continued to plague the family. In the spring of 1712, while Samuel Wesley once again had to be in London for convocation, five of the children came down with smallpox. Susanna said of John, who was afflicted, "Jack bore his disease bravely, like a man, and indeed a Christian, without any complaint." To his mother and father, John had become "Jack," and at times, his mother calling him "Jacky." The Wesleys were an affectionate family.

In this same year, with Samuel Wesley away, the curate, Wesley's assistant, did the preaching and carried on the basic duties of the church. He was a dry, dull preacher and not too popular with the parishioners. Also, at this time, Mrs. Wesley began to hold a service every Sunday evening in the rectory kitchen for the benefit of her own children and the servants. One of the servants told his parents about Mrs. Wesley's informal service. The parents asked permission to come. Of course it was granted, and before long, others began to come, until forty or fifty assembled every Sunday afternoon to hear Susanna teach the Bible. The group finally grew into about two hundred. Susanna had become a very effective leader and teacher of the Word of God.

As can be imagined, this caused difficulties. The reverend Inman, the curate, sent a letter to Wesley in London requesting that he stop his wife's meetings, saying that more people were attending them than actually came to the church. It seemed as though jealously had a grip on the young curate. Wesley responded and requested his wife to stop the meetings. The Wesleys had their detractors in the parish as it was, and Samuel felt that they did not need further division. Susanna wrote back and said quite bluntly,

> I shall not inquire how it was possible that you should be prevailed on by the senseless clamor of two or three of the worst of your parish to condemn what you so lately approved . . . or do you think that what they say is of sufficient reason to forebear a thing that has already done so much good, and may, by the blessing of God, do much more? . . . I need not tell you the consequences if you determine to put an end to our meeting. You may easily perceive what prejudice it may raise in the minds of these people against Inman, especially, who has had so little wit as to speak publicly against it. . . . If you do, after all, think fit to dissolve this assembly, and do not tell me that you desire me to do it, for that will not satisfy my conscience; but send me your positive command, in such full and expressed terms as may absolve me from all guilt and punishment for neglecting this opportunity of doing good, when you and I shall appear before the great and awful tribunal of our Lord Jesus Christ."

Susanna was not reticent about being frank with her husband over a matter that she felt so deeply about. Fortunately, the matter was resolved when convocation in London ended and Wesley himself came home and took up his regular pastoral ministry and preaching services; thus making it unnecessary for Mrs. Wesley to hold services. That resolved the conflict and ended the meetings; nevertheless, it presents an insight into something of the forthrightness, tenacity, spiritual perception, and ability of this great woman.

Ghosts?

In those days, considerable superstition and emphasis on the occult abounded. It would have been hard to find a Britisher at that time who did not believe in ghosts. Some felt that they had a spiritual justification for para-normal phenomenon because of the one phrase in the Apostle's Creed: "I believe in the communion of saints." After Samuel's death, Susanna herself fully believed that she could sense her deceased husband's presence on many occasions. Susanna was clearly a confirmed Christian and spiritually-minded woman, yet she must also be seen in the context of eighteenth-century England. John and Charles, to some extent, were caught up in this idea as well. John invariably preached on the subject on All Saints Day and did so with much enthusiasm. Something of the same idea is implicitly involved in some of Charles' great hymns.

One of Susanna's first experiences with "ghosts" came about because of some extraordinary noises that were heard at the Epworth rectory. In December 1716, strange sounds erupted in the house, which Susanna immediately interpreted as signifying that some impending tragedy hovered over the family. Nothing happened to any of her children, herself, or her husband. But afterward she attributed the noises to the disappearance of her brother, who lived in India and had vanished without a word. The sounds continued for many years and were heard by all the members of the family. Susanna wrote her oldest son on one occasion and said:

> One night it made such a noise in the room over our heads, as if several people were walking, then ran up and down stairs, and was so outrageous that we thought the children would be frightened; so your father and I rose and went down in the dark to light a candle. Just as we came to the bottom of the broad stairs, having hold of each other, on my side there seemed as if somebody had emptied a bag of money at my feet; and on his, as if all the bottles under the stairs (which were many) had been dashed in a thousand pieces. We passed through the hall into the kitchen, and got a candle, and went to see the children, whom we found asleep. . . . One night, about six o'clock, he went into the nursery in the dark, and at first heard several deep groans, then knocking. He adjured it to speak, if it had power, and tell him why it troubled his house; but no voice was heard, but it knocked thrice aloud.

Not only were there strange noises in the rectory, but objects would move about at times. It seemed as though the noises would always be the loudest when the family was at prayers, especially when they were praying for King George and the prince. Samuel even said that he had three times been pushed by an invisible power, once against the corner of his desk in his study, the second time against the door of the chamber, and the third time against the right side of the frame of the door casing; strange happenings.

A very curious situation arose a hundred years after the Wesleys had been gone from the Epworth rectory. Strange noises were heard by the then incumbent; yet no trace or account could be made of them.

It must also be remembered that this was the eighteenth century, and these kinds of situations were reported regularly. Can a reasonable answer be found? Some attribute such happenings to mere superstition or see them as purely psychological. Others view them as demonic forces. Some say that God was giving some sort of warning. Whatever the case, these so-called ghosts certainly appeared to be very real and cannot be gainsayed purely on the basis of eighteenth-century superstition, because the situations had all the earmarks of having actually happened, whatever the source may have been. One cannot help but feel that the noises were probably more demonic than anything else. Occult practices, witchcraft, and séances abounded in those times. In the following century, even Sir Arthur Conan Doyle, the famous author of the Sherlock Holmes mysteries, got caught up in the spiritism of the day. So even the Wesleys had their encounter with strange happenings of the age.

Serious Problems

A proverb from the seventeenth century says: When poverty comes in at the door, love flies out the window. To some extent this proved true in the case of the Wesleys. On one occasion, Susanna wrote to one of her sons and confessed that unfortunately she and Samuel had never seen many situations alike. To compound it all, as Emilia one time said, "The situation in the home was best described as 'intolerable want and affliction.'" She went on to say that there were many times "scandalous want of necessaries." Susanna suffered frequent illnesses and on occasion the family fully expected her to die. The only solution that some of the children saw was to marry and get out. Unfortunately, several of the marriages, especially those of the daughters, did not have happy endings. John, who married later, also experienced a marital tragedy.

Yet, in the face of it all, Susanna's deep faith and concern about the spiritual welfare of her children grew. On February 23, 1725, she wrote to her son John:

> Dear Jacky,—The alteration of your temper has occasioned me much speculation. I, who am apt to be sanguine, hope it may proceed from the operation of God's Holy Spirit, that, by taking away your relish of sensual enjoyments, He may prepare and dispose your mind for a more serious and close application to things of a more sublime and spiritual nature. . . . I heartily wish you would enter upon a serious examination of yourself, that you may know whether you have a reasonable hope of salvation; that is, whether you are in a state of faith and repentance or not, which you know are the conditions of the gospel covenant on our part.

Susanna's fervency that people come into a true saving relationship with Jesus Christ, especially her children, is most evident. Writing to her husband on one occasion she penned:

> As I am a woman, so I am also mistress of a large family. And though the superior charge of the souls contained in it, lies upon you; yet, in your absence, I cannot but look upon every soul you leave under my care, as a talent committed to me under a trust, by the great Lord of all the families, both of heaven and earth. And if I am unfaithful to him or you, in neglecting to improve these talents, how shall I answer unto him, when he shall command me to render an account of my stewardship?
>
> As these, and other such like thoughts, made me at first take a more than ordinary care of the souls of my children and servants.[2]

In her own right, Susanna became something of an evangelist. That spirit eventually gripped her sons John and Charles and, as a consequence, made a tremendous contribution to the revival.

Moreover, Susanna felt a deep concern that her children keep a proper balance between theology and experience—one of the areas in which she disagreed with her pastor husband. In writing to John she once said, "Mr. Wesley [the father] differs from me, and would engage you, I believe, in critical learning, which, though accidentally of use, is in no wise preferable to the other. I earnestly pray God to avert that great evil from you engaging in trifling studies to neglect of such things as are absolutely necessary."[3] John deeply appreciated his mother's advice and on many occasions sought her mind on matters. While a student at Oxford University he kept constant correspondence with her. For example, in 1725, several years before his "conversion" experience at Altersgate, which shall be discussed later, he wrote Susanna, asking the following questions:

> You have so well satisfied me as to the tenets of Thomas à Kempis, that I have ventured to trouble you once more on a more dubious subject. I have heard one I take to be a person of good judgment say, that she would advise no one very young to read Dr. Taylor on Holy Living and Dying. She added, that he almost put her out of her senses when she was fifteen or sixteen years old; because he seemed to exclude all from being in a way of salvation who did not come up to his rules, some of which are altogether impracticable.[4]

Jeremy Taylor's *Holy Living and Wholly Dying* is a classic. In John's early years, however, it apparently did not make the impression on John that the great Puritan author would have wished.

Susanna, always quick to reply to her children's questions, gave her judgment of Thomas à Kempis: "I take à Kempis to have been an honest weak man, with more zeal than knowledge, by his condemning all mirth or pleasure as sinful or useless, in opposition to so many and plain texts of scripture."[5]

John continued with his studies and took his master's degree at Oxford. Upon graduation he was ordained by Bishop Potter and preached his first sermon at South Leigh near Oxford. He then went back to Lincolnshire and served as his father's assistant. A short time later, he received the honor of being elected as a fellow of Lincoln College. The family felt duly proud. John's father wrote a letter in which he addressed him as "Dear Mr. Fellow-elect of Lincoln." When John went to Oxford to take up his fellowship in September 1725, he became a lecturer in Greek and the moderator of the classes. His brother Charles had become a student at Christ Church, Oxford, and John proved to be of considerable help to him.

A New Venture

The pastorate of the small church at Wroote, some four or five miles from Epworth, became vacant. It was under the general parish and leadership of the Epworth rector, Samuel Wesley. So Samuel took up this responsibility in addition to the Epworth church. This gave him an extra fifty pounds a year, which helped the family's financial situation. Wesley also continued to write, as did many of the other Wesleys who proved very capable with the pen. Of course, this gift shone most clearly in Charles.

In this general time frame an unusal opportunity came to Charles. Garrett Wesley of Dangan Castle in Ireland, wrote to Samuel Wesley to ask if he had a son named Charles. He went on to say that he would very much appreciate Charles' being permitted to become his heir. Garrett Wesley was a quite wealthy man and this would obviously assure a secure financial future for young Charles, not to mention the help it could mean for the family. But Charles refused the offer and a more distant relative was chosen as heir. It may seem a strange decision, but it made Charles something of a hero to his brother John, who said that Charles had engineered "a fair escape" from worldly temptations. Later Methodist writers likened Charles to Moses "who esteem[ed] the reproach of Christ greater riches than the treasures of Egypt" (Heb. 11:26 kjv). So the die was cast; the family would remain in financial straits.

While John served his fellowship at Lincoln College, he fell in love with a young lady in Worcestershire, Betty Kirkham by name. John experienced his first love but nothing came of the situation, and it was some years before he did marry. That marriage, as pointed out, ended in disaster. Humanly speaking, John would have been better off to have married Betty, but all that rests in the providence of God.

A Near Tragedy

Some five or six years later, Susanna and Samuel were in a wagon making a short trip to Low Millwood. Samuel sat in a chair at the rear of the wagon and Susanna settled in at the other end. Daughter Mattie was between them and the maid seated herself behind Susanna. Just as they reached the crest of a small hill, the horses were suddenly startled and took off in a gallop. It flung Samuel and his chair out onto the roadway. The maid grabbed Susanna's chair and held her in. Susanna cried out to stop the horses for fear Samuel had been killed. He did suffer rather serious injuries and was so shaken by the accident that he never quite fully recovered. It caused him, probably for the first time, to think seriously what would become of his wife and unmarried daughters if he were to die, but he carried on for years, the injuries not seriously inhibiting his ministry.

Susanna and Samuel dearly loved their daughter Mary, or Moll, as all affectionately called her, who unfortunately suffered from a deformity. John Whitelamb, a very poor, but very fine Christian young man fell in love with Mary. They married and were extremely happy, and Whitelamb became the curate at the little church at Wroote, Samuel having now left that particular work to others. The young pastor enjoyed a very fruitful ministry. Tragically, Mary died about one year after they were married, and with her baby (both apparently died during childbirth), was buried at the Wroote church. The Wesleys felt the loss tremendously. They had cared for their daughter for so long and she seemed so happily married; but it was all cut so short. The grieving husband, John Whitelamb, stayed at Wroote the rest of his ministerial life. He served the church some thirty years, before going to be with the Lord and joining his dear Moll in 1769.

Partings

Sickness seemed to be the lot of virtually the entire family. So many of the nineteen children had died in infancy, and now Samuel Wesley was not well at all. It did grieve Susanna that her husband's health seemed to increasingly fail. Samuel, though, still had to make his periodic journeys to London for convocation and to see his publications through to success. His last journey to London was to facilitate the publishing of his work, *Dissertations on Job*. He printed 500 copies at the first edition since more than 300 had already been subscribed for. But the end drew near.

Samuel went to be with the Lord on February 14, 1735. Susanna was deeply grieved, and as one author expressed it, "thoroughly broken down." Even before Samuel's departure, as he lay upon his death bed, Susanna was devastated. She walked into his bedroom but fainted and had to be carried out, because she saw her husband quickly slipping away. When the trumpet call came and Samuel drew his last breath, John stood by the bedside and committed his father to the Lord. Death had come to an incredibly gifted, controversial, problem-ladened, dedicated man of God. He was an enigmatic character, but God used him in many wonderful respects despite all of the problems he engendered. Above all else, he was the father of two spiritual giants who were soon to be used of God in great revival. Susanna and Samuel had been married for forty-six years, thirty-nine of which were spent at Epworth. Now Susanna faced widowhood.

Upon Samuel's death, Susanna settled his affairs and went to stay for a short time with her eldest daughter Emilia. The move proved a great comfort. To be with Emilia brought some peace because the attachment between them had been strong throughout the years.

Off to Georgia

Shortly after the death of their father, John and Charles Wesley prepared to fulfill their commitment to travel to Georgia. General James Oglethorpe, the founder of the colony of Georgia, had been in correspondence with the Wesley brothers' father. In 1732, Oglethorpe returned to England to enlist recruits to populate the area and do missionary work among the native Americans. The venture proved successful in that he enlisted 130 Highlanders and 170 Germans to travel with him to Georgia. He also got a commitment from John Wesley that John would serve as a chaplain and missionary, with Charles going along as his private secretary. At first John did not warm up to the idea but later consented. His reluctance centered in the fact that he could not feel peace in leaving England while his aged and infirmed mother still lived. Yet his mother, quite content with Emilia, insisted that he go. She said, "Had I twenty sons, I should rejoice that they were all so employed, though I should never see them more." The decision was made, and Charles at once took ordination and deacon's and priest's orders. The Wesley men were now ready to sail to Georgia. They embarked at Graves End on the ship, *Symmonds*, on October 14, 1735. In September of the next year, Susanna moved to reside with her eldest son at Tiverton. Samuel, named after his father, and his wife welcomed her with open arms.

Before long, some rather disturbing news came from Georgia. John and Charles felt a real unease in what they were experiencing there. Charles returned after only one year in the Colonies, reaching England on December 3, 1736. The next summer, Susanna took up residency with her daughter Martha Hall and son-in-law in London. The family later moved to Fisherton, near Salisbury, where Susanna also lived with them.

While Susanna resided in Fisherton, she had the joy of seeing John return from Georgia. From what she gathered, both John and Charles had no desire to ever go back and they never did. It was at this time that John began to have deep stirrings in his own spiritual life.

While Susanna resided in London, she had written something of profound significance to her son. The letter is dated Thursday, March 8, 1737:

> You have heard, I suppose, that Mr. Whitfield is taking a progress through these parts to make a collection for a house in Georgia for orphans and such of the natives' children as they will part with, to learn our language and religion. He came hither to see me, and we talked about your brothers. I told him I did not like their way of living, wished them in some place of their own, wherein they might regularly preach, etc. He replied, "I could not conceive the good they did in London; that the greatest part of our clergy were asleep, and that there never was a greater need of itinerant preachers than now;" upon which a gentleman that came with him said that my son Charles had converted him, and that my sons spent all their time in doing good. I then asked Mr. Whitfield if my sons were not for making some innovations in the Church, which I much feared. He assured me they were so far from it that they endeavored all they could to reconcile Dissenters to our communion; that my son John had baptized five adult Presbyterians in our own way on St. Paul's Day, and, he believed, would bring over many to our communion. His stay was short, so I could not talk with him so much as I desired. He seems to be a very good man, and one who truly desires the salvation of mankind. God grant that the wisdom of the serpent may be joined to the innocence of the dove![6]

As one historian termed it, "One of the most important events in modern religious history"[7] was about to burst on the British—and American—scene.

The Beginnings of the Revival

It will be remembered that Jeremy Taylor's *Holy Living and Wholly Dying* had not impressed John earlier on, though later it meant much more to him. Also, William Law's works significantly influenced John. In America, John crossed paths with a Moravian bishop by the name of Spangenberg. The following conversation took place:

> Spangenberg: "Do you know Jesus Christ?"
> John: "I know He is the Savior of the world."
> Spangenberg: "True, but do you know that He has saved you?"
> John: "I hope He has died to save me."

Later Spangenberg said, "I fear they were vain words."

John, though he served as an ordained Anglican priest, had his master's degree from Oxford University in religious studies, had become a practicing clergyman, and had even gone to Georgia as a missionary, had still not come into a the full assurance of salvation. But then neither had his brother Charles. Charles had returned to London, disturbed in heart and mind. Eighteen months later, John returned saying, "I went to America to convert the Indians, but oh, who will convert me?"

The stirrings in John's heart seemingly started through an incident that occurred while he and Charles were on their way to America. A terrible storm swept over their small ship. John and Charles were beside themselves with fear and anxiety. On the ship were several Moravian missionaries who had come out of the great awakening that had gripped their communion at the estate of Ludwig Von Zinzendorf. The Moravian brethren came from what we know as modern-day Prague in Eastern Europe. They had great missionary zeal, but what proved so disturbing to the Wesleys was not only the terrible storm, but also the fact that the Moravians were calm and peaceful, which shook them even more. It helped them to see more vividly than before how uncertain they were about their own salvation. Back in London, John and Charles met another Moravian leader by the name of Peter Bohler, who deeply influenced the brothers. They began to worship regularly with the Moravian fellowship that met on Aldersgate Street in London. Peter Bohler became instrumental in the conversion of both of these men.

John and Charles struggled before they came into a living, vibrant, saving faith in the Lord Jesus Christ. Yet their entire background resounded with the Gospel, delivered at the hands of their godly mother. James Burns, an eminent historian on spiritual awakenings, gives a graphic account of Charles' conversion, which occurred on May 21, 1738:

> A plain, ordinary woman, but of a deeply devout character, and to her there came an intense conviction that she ought to speak some words of comfort to him [Charles]. Long she struggled against it, but at length, overpowered, she entered his room, and with an intense voice said: "In the name of Jesus of Nazareth, arise! Thou shalt be healed of all thy infirmities." Wesley was, according to his own confession, composing himself to sleep. Suddenly the words, breaking in upon the silence around him, fell upon his ears with startling effect. "They struck me to the heart," he says. "I never heard words uttered with like solemnity." I sighed within myself, and said, "Oh that Christ would thus speak to me!" Suddenly the light dawned, his whole being seemed to be caught in a transport. From the lips of a woman without education, and driven by a mysterious and uncontrollable impulse, the message of deliverance came.[8]

Then, a short time later, John came to living faith in Christ. The Moravians, along with their friend George Whitefield, who two years earlier had come into a deep experience of assuring grace, touched John. Burns also gives the account of John's experience, which took place on May 24, 1738:

> When he [John] opened his Bible at five o'clock in the morning his eyes were caught by these great words: "There are given unto us exceeding great and precious promises that we should be partakers of the divine nature." A little later, as he left the room, he opened his Bible again, and there came a mighty rush of hope to his heart as he read this sentence:—"Thou art not far from the Kingdom of God." Throughout the day he was kept in a constant state of agitation; everything around him seemed to be vocal, heralding some coming event. What followed had best be read in his own words. "In the evening," he says, "I went very unwillingly to a Society in Aldersgate Street, where one was reading Luther's preface to the Epistle to the Romans. About a quarter before nine, while he was describing the change wrought by God in the heart through faith in Christ, I felt my heart strangely warmed. I felt I did trust Christ, Christ alone, for salvation; and an assurance was given me that He had taken away my sins, even mine, and saved me from the law of sin and death. I began to pray with all my might for those who had in a more especial manner despitefully used me and persecuted me. I then testified openly to all there what I now first felt in my heart."[9]

So at last, after a long pilgrimage, the saving light of Christ flooded the brothers' hearts.

John still had his struggles, however. He had his days of doubts. He said, "It was not long, before the enemy suggested, 'This cannot be faith; for where is thy joy?'" But then he came to realize that peace and victory over sin are brought about by simple faith in the indwelling Christ. The battle ended, the war was won.

The real breaking of revival came on New Year's Day, 1739, very early in the morning. In his journal, John Wesley gives the following account:

> Monday, January 1, 1739. Mr. Hall, Kinchin, Ingham, Whitefield, Hutchins, and my brother Charles were present at our love-feast in Fette Lane, with about sixty of our brethren. About three in the morning, as we were continuing instant in prayer, the power of God came mightily upon us, insomuch that many cried out for exceeding joy, and many fell to the ground. As soon as we

recovered a little from the awe and amazement at the presence of His majesty, we broke out with one voice, "We praise Thee, O God, we acknowledge Thee to be Lord."[10]

God had now completed the circle. John and Charles could join hands with George Whitefield and permit the Holy Spirit to use them in a genuine awakening. His grace had done its beautiful work. Susanna, of course, rejoiced in the experience of her children. She wrote Charles and said:

> Blessed be God, who showed you the necessity you were in of a Savior to deliver you from the power of sin and Satan (for Christ will be no Savior to such as seeing not their need of one), and directed you by faith to lay hold of that stupendous mercy offered us by redeeming love. Jesus is the only physician of soul; His blood, the only salve that can heal a wounded conscience. . . . No, there is none but Christ, none but Christ, who is sufficient for these things. Blessed be God, He is an all sufficient Savior; blessed be His holy name, that thou hast found him a Savior to thee, my son! Oh, let us love Him much, for we have much forgiven.[11]

She wrote again to Charles. It seems she did not quite fully understand all that the boys had experienced; yet she rejoiced, and wrote:

> I heartily rejoice that you have now attained to a strong and lively hope in God's mercy through Christ. Not that I can think you were totally without saving faith before; but it is one thing to have faith, and another thing to be sensible we have it. Faith is the fruit of the Spirit and the gift of God, but to feel or be inwardly sensible that we have true faith, requires a further operation of God's Holy Spirit. You say you have peace, but not joy in believing. Blessed be God for peace! May this peace rest with you. Joy will follow, perhaps not very closely, but it will follow faith and love. God's promises are sealed to us but not dated, therefore patiently attend His pleasure. He will give you joy in believing. Amen.[12]

Susanna herself soon acquired her real assurance of salvation. John wrote:

> She had scarce heard such a thing mentioned as having God's Spirit bear witness with our spirit: much less did she imagine that this was the common privilege of all true believers.

"Therefore," she said, "I never durst ask it for myself. But two or three weeks ago, while my son Hall [the family with whom she was staying] was pronouncing these words in delivering the cup to me [in communion], "The blood of our Lord Jesus Christ, which was given for thee," the words struck through my heart, and I knew God for Christ's sake had forgiven me all my sins."[13]

Thus, Susanna moved into the spirit of assurance as had her sons. Now all things seemed in place and the revival began to sweep the land but not without problems for the Wesleys themselves.

A Brother in Opposition

The oldest son of the family, Samuel Jr., felt that the emphases of John and Charles, and even his own mother Susanna, were not right. He seemingly opposed the evangelism of John and Charles and George Whitefield. Probably his "high churchmanship" became the obstacle that kept him from joining in the movement. But Susanna took her stand with Charles and John and though her oldest son Samuel was very dear to her, she felt him to be wrong in this matter. God clearly worked powerfully in revival through John and Charles. Strangely, yet in the providence of God, on November 5 of that year (1739) Samuel was taken very ill when seemingly in good health. At three o'clock in the morning, he died after only four hours of suffering. He was only forty-nine years of age. Although Samuel's death deeply grieved the family, they carried on as the awakening broke across all England, Wales, and Scotland, not to mention the American Colonies.

New Methods

New innovations characterized the revival movement—especially one. John, at the behest of George Whitefield, began preaching in the open air. George had been at it for three or four years—and with great success, speaking at times to twenty thousand. This shocked John at first. He said, "I could scarce reconcile myself at first to this strange way of preaching in the fields, of which he [Whitefield] gave me an example on Sunday; having been all of my life 'til very lately so tenacious of every point relating to decency and order, that I should have thought the saving of souls almost sacrilege, if it had not been done in a church." John himself was something of a high churchman, but he soon realized that the new method of declaring the Gospel was mightily blessed of God. So, he gave himself to it, and multitudes came to hear. Deep conviction fell on the people. Some of the accounts of his preaching are quite remarkable:

As soon as he [John] got upon the stand he stroked back his hair and turned his face towards where I stood, and, I thought, fixed his eyes upon me. His countenance fixed such an awful dread upon me, before I heard him speak, that it made my heart beat like the pendulum of a clock; and when he did speak, I thought his whole discourse was aimed at me. When he had done, I said, "This man can tell the secrets of my heart; he hath not left me there; for he hath showed me the remedy, even the blood of Jesus." I thought he spoke to no one but me, and I durst not look up, for I thought all the people were looking at me. But before Mr. Wesley concluded his sermon, he cried out, "Let the wicked forsake his way, and the unrighteous man his thoughts; and let him return to the Lord, and He will have mercy upon him; and to our God, for He will abundantly pardon." I said, "If that be true, I will turn to God today."[14]

In it all, John said, "It is the Lord, let Him do what seemeth Him good. What am I, that I should withstand God?"[15] Susanna was in full agreement with her son's ministry, even if it was "outside" the church. Further, lay people began preaching. Susanna sanctioned lay preaching too and praised the Lord for the great work that was being accomplished in the awakening. The fact that Susanna experienced a personal revival is indicated by a letter she wrote to Charles on October 2, 1740:

I am not one of those who have never been enlightened, or made partaker of the heavenly gift, or of the Holy Ghost, but have many years since been fully awakened, and am deeply sensible of sin, both original and actual. . . . I do, I will believe; and though I am the greatest of sinners, that does not discourage me; for all my transgressions are the sins of a finite person, but the merits of our Lord's sufferings and righteousness are infinite! If I do want anything without which I cannot be saved (of which I am not at present sensible), then I believe I shall not die before that want is supplied.

By this time America had felt the same touch of revival, especially through the ministry of the Wesleys' friend and fellow revivalist, George Whitefield.

The revival movement had its home base at what became known as the "Foundry." In Moorfields, London, there was a large park boardered by and filled with elm trees. On the east side of the park an old tiled building stood. It had been a foundry originally and had been used for manufacturing guns that were cast in metal. In 1716, a terrible explosion took place in the foundry, blowing off the roof and killing and maiming many people. It left the old foundry vacant and in virtual ruins. Through the benevolence of concerned friends, the sight was purchased, and the building underwent a complete renovation, becoming the headquarters for Wesley as well as a worship center. The blessings that were found and experienced there thrilled London. Moreover, it became something of a home for the Wesleys.

A Mother of Revival

When John and Charles settled in London, their mother left the Halls and came to live with them. She had been their strength through the years. She must now be their strength in her last years. And what glorious years they were: a great awakening was afoot, and her sons served as the vanguard. In March 1741, daughter Kezia died at Bexley at the age of thirty-two. She died in the faith. Her brother Charles and the family rejoiced in that assurance. Susanna's last years were profoundly blessed of God as she witnessed her life being lived out in revival through her boys. She indeed had become a mother of revival.

The End Draws Near

Mrs. Wesley suffered from chronic gout, which was hereditary. Her strength seemed to quickly ebb away, and she fell quite ill. She had served Christ faithfully through many struggles. The end of her days had come. Her children were aware of it, to their great sorrow. Charles had an obligation out of the city, but he thought that surely she would linger until he returned, and in almost typical, tenacious fashion she did. John was also away preaching at Bristol. On hearing that his beloved mother was failing fast, he rode off on Sunday evening, July 18, 1742, after he had preached to a large congregation. He reached the Foundry on the twentieth. Seeing his beloved mother on her bed, John penned these words in his journal: "I found my mother on the borders of eternity: but she has no doubt or fear, nor any desire but, as soon as God should call her, to depart and be with Christ."

The following Friday afternoon it became obvious that the call had come. Susanna lay speechless, but conscious. Charles read a prayer as he had done seven years previously for his beloved father.

At four o'clock in the afternoon, Charles left his mother's side for a moment to have a cup of tea. Suddenly, one of his sisters called him back. Susanna opened her eyes wide, and fixed them upward for a moment. Then her eyelids dropped and she was ushered into the presence of Christ without a struggle or a sigh. The children stood around the bed and fulfilled her last request, which she had uttered a little before she lost her speech; "Children, as soon as I am released, sing a psalm of praise to

God." Susanna had gone to be with the Lord very peacefully and in the full assurance of faith. Just before her death she had uttered the prayer: "My dear Savior, are you come to help me in my extremity at last?" The answer: "Yes." And Jesus helped her home.

The tearful family buried Susanna on Sunday, August 1, in Bunhill Fields. John conducted the funeral service in the Church of England liturgy. A large number of friends had also gathered and they sang a hymn of praise. John preached a beautiful sermon to the multitudes; it is considered one of the most eloquent and passionate of all of his messages.

A simple stone was placed at the head of Susannah's resting place. The epitaph had been penned by her beloved son, Charles. It reads:

Here lies the Body
of
Mrs. Susanna Wesley,
Youngest and last surviving daughter of
Dr. Samuel Annesley.

In sure and steadfast hope to rise,
And claim her mansion in the skies,
A Christian here her flesh laid down,
The cross exchanging for a crown.
True daughter of affliction, she,
Inured to pain and misery,
Mourned a long night of grief and fears,
A legal night of seventy years.
The Father then revealed His Son,
Him in the broken bread made known;
She knew and felt her sins forgiven,
And found the earnest of her heaven.
Meet for the fellowship above,
She heard the call "Arise, my love."
"I come," her dying looks replied,
And lamb-like, as her Lord, she died.

A spiritual giant, a woman highly esteemed, had gone to be with her Lord. But the revival flourished. The Wesley brothers labors alone were incredible. And where did John and Charles get such commitment? Largely from the commitment of their dear mother.

Thus ends the saga of a mother of awakening. What an example to mothers today of what a godly woman can see accomplished by the grace of Christ in the life of her children. May God raise up many Susanna Wesleys that we might see revival in our time.

Endnotes
 1. Eliza Clark, *Famous Women, Susanna Wesley* (Boston: Roberts Brothers, 1891), 30.
 2. Correspondence of Susanna Wesley.
 3. Clark, *Famous Women*, 182.
 4. Correspondence of Susanna Wesley.
 5. Clark, *Famous Women*, 184.
 6. Ibid., 239.
 7. James Burns, *Revivals and Their Leaders* (Grand Rapids: Baker Book House, 1960), 283.
 8. Ibid., 299–300.
 9. Ibid., 301.
10. Mendall Taylor, *Exploring Evangelism* (Kansas City: Beacon Hill Press, 1964), 254.
11. Clarke, *Famous Women*, 240–41.
12. Ibid., 242.
13. Ibid., 245–46.
14. Burns, *Revivals*, 329–30.
15. The following quotes are taken from Clarke, *Famous Women*.

Chapter Five

SELINA, COUNTESS OF HUNTINGDON

The Patroness of Awakening

Royalty framed her background. Eighteenth-century England dictated her social consciousness. Religion drove her heart. Revival became her experience. Such statements summarize the life of a beautiful lady, Selina, the Countess of Huntingdon.

Selina's Heritage

In one of the remote corners of Leicestershire, in the wooded valley close to Charnwood Forest, England, a lovely stone church that was erected by Sir Robert Shirley stands. Although he professed Protestantism, he did not support the Cromwells in the civil war that dominated British politics in those days. He was an active advocate for the restoration of the monarchy. Over the door of Holy Trinity Church, the building Sir Robert was responsible for erecting, this inscription stands out in bold relief:

> In the years 1653 when all things sacred were throughout ye nation either demolished or profaned, Sir Robert Shirley Baronet founded this church, whose singular praise it is to have done ye best things in ye worst times. And hoped them in the most calamitous. The righteous shall be had in everlasting remembrance.[1]

Sir Robert paid heavily for his advocacy of the Restoration. It landed him in the Tower of London, and there he died in 1656. Actually, historians see his death as one of the great tragedies of the period. Being a very able and devout man, he also could trace his descent back to Edward the Confessor. But such were the crosscurrents of that time of deep civil unrest in British life.

Sir Robert had a son, who, in 1677, received the title of Baron Ferrers, later to become the first Earl Ferrers in 1711. On the Earl's death, the

115

Honorable Washington Shirley succeeded him in that noble royal position. Washington Shirley's mother was of the Washington family who were the ancestors of George Washington, the first president of the United States. Washington Shirley became the father of three lovely daughters. The middle offspring, named Selina, was born August 24, 1707.

The Early Years

Little Selina grew up at Staunton Harold. She was a quiet little girl and had days of melancholy. Her seriousness and rather somber approach to life developed into a deep religious consciousness, even during her early years. That which probably precipitated her early religious feelings was the death of a child about her own age in the community. Somehow little Selina felt the blow deeply. She followed the funeral cortege to the churchyard and stood there throughout the service of burial. She would often return to the cemetery and spend time with her thoughts about her friend who had passed on in death. She continually wondered what it would be like in eternity.

Those early days of childhood melancholy, even the serious religiosity it spawned, began to wane as Selina entered puberty. She became a very gracious, vivacious young woman. Lady Selina, as she became known, moved into a life of royal society and aristocratic gaiety, and the rather frivolous lifestyle of the landed gentry made itself felt in her life. She developed a very charming personality, and in the circles in which she moved, she soon made many friends.

Lady Fanny Shirley became one of Selina's closet companions. Lady Shirley had a very enviable position in the court, which Selina found most attractive. She often visited her friend at Twickenham where Lady Fanny lived. There she met many of the celebrities of British aristocracy. The earl of Chesterfield, Viscount Bolingbroke, and other well-known names in eighteenth-century England became her acquaintances. At the same time, however, deep stirrings of the Spirit of God still nagged at her. Ultimately, the rather superficial life of high society with all of its frivolity began to lose its charm. She would actually pray that she might escape her lifestyle by marrying into a family who was serious about the things of God. The Lord heard that prayer, and she soon found herself being courted by a young earl.

Selina Meets Her Husband-to-Be

The House of Hastings has boasted many notable names throughout centuries of British history. It was the family name for the various earls of Huntingdon created by King Henry VIII in 1529. Many noble men found their places in that prestigious line. They could trace their ancestry back to medieval times to the Duke of Clarence, the brother of King Edward IV. Royal blood flowed in their veins and they revelled in it.

The ninth earl of Huntingdon was born November 12, 1696, at Donington Park. His parents named him Theophilus, after his father. The eighth earl, Theophilus' father, had served in the military in the Somerset Light Infantry. But military life had not appealed to young Theophilus. Although his father had acquired some renown in the very last battle ever fought on English soil, the Monmouth Rebellion, young Theophilus was more academically inclined. So off to Oxford to study classical literature he went.

Theophilus received his title as the ninth earl in 1705. Although he never served as an official member of the royal court, at the coronation of George II he bore the Sword of State—a high honor. A biographer said of him that he was "capable of excelling in every form of public life, yet chose to appear in none." Theophilus and Selina became acquainted when she had visited the earl's sisters at Donington Park. The sparks flew and they became greatly attracted to each other. A typical British courtship followed, and, according to protocol, the earl of Huntingdon asked Lady Selina to be his bride. They were genuinely and deeply in love with one another. After the traditional period of engagement, they united their hands in marriage on June 3, 1728. A wonderful union and a very happy home emerged and was blessed of God.

Life Together

Theophilus and Selina were matched for each other. Both involved themselves deeply in the Church of England and its ministry, and thus the foundations were laid for a fruitful life together. The new couple moved to Theophilus' estate, Donington Hall. Selina had by this time become a very mature young woman, and all appreciated and loved her—the servants thought highly of her as did the entire community. A wonderful family—four sons and three daughters—came along. Selina became a caring and gracious mother. Tragically, as so often happened in those days, only one of her daughters lived a relatively long life. The eldest child, Elizabeth, outlived her mother, but all the other children died before Selina went to her eternal reward. Elizabeth later became the Countess of Moira and was a well-known personality in her circle.

The young couple raised their family in the lovely Donington Hall, which had been built by George Hastings the fourth earl of Huntingdon. Erected in 1595, it stood on an extensive plot of land. Architect William Wilkins, who had served as a chief architect of the National Gallery in London that still graces Trafalgar Square, built the manor house in Gothic style. The Huntingdons also had a town house on Downing Street, Westminster, London—No. 12, next door to the famous No. 10 Downing Street, the home of Britain's prime minister. Quite obviously, the family enjoyed wealth and were highly regarded and accepted in the upper circles of eighteenth-century British life.

Theophilus and Selina found court life interesting and rewarding. Selina herself became a regular attender at court. All of the courtiers held her in high regard, yet Selina always found it a joy to get back home to Donington with her precious family.

The young countess had a real commitment to the Church of England; still, something caused a cloud to hover over her relationship with Christ. She had many doubts and could not seem to get a spiritual perspective that would bring her true peace. She struggled on for some time.

A New Venture of Faith

Lord Huntingdon had four unmarried sisters. All were radiant Christians. His oldest half-sister, Lady Betty Hastings, was an especially devout believer. She enjoyed a rich, daily experience of Christ. She involved herself significantly in the beginnings of the revival that became known as the "Methodist Movement," actually helping finance George Whitefield's study at Oxford University. John and Charles Wesley had already traveled to Georgia in October of 1735 in the hopes of ministering to the native Americans and to do benevolent work. Whitefield and the Wesley brothers were destined to become the spark that would ignite the Methodist fire.

But what about Selina? Why the cloud of doubt?

The youngest of Theophilus' sisters, Lady Margaret, had previously experienced a glorious conversion experience. Benjamin Ingham had been used to lead her to Christ, and her life glowed with the presence of the Lord. Selina longed to have the full assurance of faith that her sister-in-law enjoyed. Although a devout church member, Selina simply did not have the confidence that she had truly been born again. Her faith rested in her good works—and she did work hard in church and civil affairs. She had made the mistake, however, of going about to establish her own righteousness. The apostle Paul warned about that, especially in his letters to the Romans and Galatians. But the countess simply did not grasp it all, and consequently, the cloud of doubt deepened daily. The Spirit of God probed her heart with deep conviction. She had to find an answer.

Right at that time Selina became quite ill. Her anxiety would not subside, but what was she to do? God in His grace soon provided the answer. Lady Margaret came to visit Selina in her illness, and it happened. Margaret shared that since she had simply put her entire faith and trust in Jesus Christ because of what He had done on the cross and in His glorious resurrection, she had become "as happy as an angel." Margaret's testimony spoke profoundly to the countess. For several days and weeks, the spiritual struggle raged on, until in July 1739 she finally just surrendered her all—her sin, herself, her future—to Jesus Christ. Peace flooded Selina's soul. The change was dramatic—her health improved, and she became a new woman in Christ. Now she could be a woman of awakening.

The Foundations of the Revival: The Moravians

One of the men who had traveled with the Wesleys to the colonies was Benjamin Ingham. He stayed in Georgia, but a short time before he journeyed back to London to enlist more men for the Georgia mission. While in London, some Moravian Brethren crossed his path. Through the ministry of the Moravians, Ingham came into a dynamic evangelical experience of Christ. This eventually opened the great door of God's providence for Selina.

The Moravian movement is a fascinating story of revival in itself. Count Ludwig Von Zinzendorf, a young man of royal heritage, studied theology in Germany. He sat at the feet of Herman August Francke at Halle University in Saxony. Francke had been the protégé of the great German Pietist, Pastor Philip Spenner. The Pietist movement was anything but a superficial, emotional piety, as it has sometimes been understood. The Pietists were in many respects the continental counterpart of the Puritans of Britain. They stood for several very important evangelical realities. The cornerstone of the faith and experience of the Puritan-pietist movement revolved around the following:

- The central thrust of the movement centered in the new birth. They believed that people are saved by grace through faith and that no one comes into a right relationship apart from being born again.
- They believed in religious enthusiasm in the good sense. They always "tested the spirits" by the objective Scriptures. They believed that there was a genuine emotional content in one's experience of Christ, but the emotions did not take ascent over the intellect or vise versa. They were a balanced people.
- The Pietists strongly advocated "felicity." Felicity is the "joy of the Lord," which, as Nehemiah said, "is our strength" (Neh. 8:10).
- They were committed to the Holy Spirit's effecting holiness of life. They believed that sanctification was not only a position in Christ but also a process wherein the believer is molded into the image of the Lord Jesus. They considered perfectionism a heresy, but they believed that godliness was a vital experience.
- The Puritans and the Pietists were biblicists. They believed that all truth comes from God and that truth is revealed in the person of the Lord Jesus Christ as He is seen in the Holy Scriptures. The Reformed doctrine of *sola scriptura* became their hallmark.

- The Puritan-Pietist movement, therefore, had a deep commitment to higher education. They were an intellectual people, and a deep-feeling people. Their whole life revolved around faith in Jesus Christ and an understanding of the Christian life through the Bible.

If all that sounds very much like revival, *it is*. These principles were deeply ingrained into the spiritual fiber of Count Zinzendorf. After he received his education, he went back to the estate that he had named *Herrenhut,* which literally means "the Lord's watch," where he began to give refuge to oppressed Moravian Brethren. The people had been converted under the legacy of John Hus, the great pre-Reformation Reformer of Prague, in the Czech Republic. As they traveled west to escape persecution, Zinzendorf gave them asylum on his land. One Sunday morning, while observing the Lord's Supper, God opened the heavens and a great revival broke out in their midst. They had been praying earnestly for such an awakening and God heard and answered. The Moravian Revival thrust a significant missionary zeal into the Reformation movement that impacted the whole Western world.

Many Moravian missionaries came to North and South America. For example, Bethlehem, Pennsylvania; Winston-Salem, North Carolina; and other notable American communities were first established as Moravian settlements. The Moravians profoundly impacted the Whitefield-Wesley movement. One of the first instances of this was Benjamin Ingham's fellowship with the London Moravians where he found a new living faith in Christ. Later, God's Spirit used him to bring Lady Margaret to Christ, and a spiritual chain reaction began.

God's Providence

In November 1741, Lady Margaret and Benjamin Ingham married. Of course, some of the rather snobbish aristocracy turned up their noses. Lady Mary Worthly Montague said, "The news I have from London is that Lady Margaret Hastings has disposed of herself to a poor wandering Methodist." But God surely engineered in the affair; they had a beautiful, happy home. Most important to the revival, by Divine Providence's working through Benjamin Ingham, Selina met the Wesley brothers, John and Charles. Then in May 1742, a few months after her conversion, the countess invited John to come to Donington Hall and preach. That was four years after Wesley's well-known Aldersgate experience. A friendship developed also with Charles Wesley. Thus, along with a friendship with George Whitefield that had developed, she began to involve herself in the awakening which was now already well in progress. Selina would soon be known as the "Patroness of Awakening."

The Revival Moves over Britain

In the chapter on John Wesley's mother, Susanna Wesley, much of the dynamics of the eighteenth-century revival have been presented. The story of John's conversion after coming home from Georgia is well-known in all of evangelical life. John and Charles along with George Whitefield were preaching with great effect across the country—most of the time in the open air or at the Foundry, the building in London that John Wesley had been able to acquire as a permanent place from which the Gospel could go forth unhindered.

Selina had a clear grasp, even as a young Christian, of how God was at work in her country. She realized that a true awakening had come. She began to speak about revival to everyone as she had opportunity, and her word of witness spread widely, especially in court circles. Of course, she did her best to share her new, living faith with her husband, the earl. Yet somehow the message did not seem to grip him. He seemed quite good natured about it all and expressed appreciation for her concern, but made no personal commitment to Christ himself. He did nothing to inhibit Selina's devotion to the Lord and would even, on occasion, accompany her to Methodist services. Still, he had apprehensions about his wife's being so zealous.

Dr. Benson, the one-time bishop of Gloucester, had been Lord Huntingdon's professor during university days. Huntingdon felt that Selina needed to have a good talk with the doctor to cool her down a bit. They met and the bishop found himself almost at a loss as how to cope with this devout young Christian. He gave her every argument that he could muster concerning the problem with the Methodists, but she countered him with well-reasoned rebuttals. She quite convincingly argued that the Methodists fit well within the Church of England's articles. Thus, the bishop found himself very much on the defensive.

Bishop Benson had actually been the one who ordained George Whitefield, though he later expressed regret over having ordained the young evangelist. He now felt that Whitefield was responsible for Selina's excessive enthusiasm (she had become a close friend to Whitefield by this time), but she settled the whole matter when she said, "My Lord, mark my words, when you are on your dying bed, that will be one of the few ordinations you will reflect upon with complacence." It is to be said to the good bishop's benefit that Selina's prophesy was fulfilled. Not long before the bishop faced death, he sent Whitefield a gift of ten guineas and earnestly sought the prayers of the revivalist.

A Courtly Ministry

Selina served as a woman of the court, thus finding herself constantly surrounded by the highest echelon of British society. This gave her an incredible opportunity to share her faith in the most unusual places. Her zeal knew no bounds—she would witness to all people in every situation. Her friends were amazed. She had such a vibrant testimony that she made a profound impression on countless people. Many of the lords and ladies of the land accompanied her to hear the Methodist preachers—they were especially attracted to Whitefield's tabernacle in London. The multitudes who came to Christ under the preaching of the Wesleys and Whitefield are all but incalculable. The revival spread all over the land like a tidal wave, and at the crest of many a wave stood Selina, the faithful witness. Support, influence, and the opening of doors became Lady Huntingdon's most significant contributions to the movement that transformed Britain.

On October 13, 1746, as a relatively young man, Selina's husband, Lord Huntingdon, died. The countess, as can be imagined, was deeply grieved. She loved him dearly. But sadly, he had never made a real profession of faith in Christ. He did say, "I greatly admire the morality of the Bible, but the doctrine of the atonement I cannot comprehend." What a tragedy! And what a heartache for this woman of awakening. Lord Huntingdon was an admirable man from a human perspective and had many great qualities, but how it broke Selina's heart that he did not have a vibrant faith in the accomplished work of Christ. She built a beautiful memorial to him in St. Helen's Church, Ashby-de-la-Zouch, but life could never quite be the same again.

Selina had now become the dowager countess. She left Donington Hall, and her son, Lord Francis Hastings, received the earldom. Selina made her home in Ashby Place, not far from Donington, where she could be close to the family. She actually administered the family estates for her son before he came of age and could accept the full responsibilities as the new lord of Huntingdon. She also served her son for years as his administrator when he traveled abroad on extended business trips. But now, after her husband's death, she felt free to give herself unreservedly to the great eighteenth-century awakening. Being a very wealthy woman, she not only gave of her time unstintingly, she also gave an incredible fortune to the movement.

Howel Harris, the renowned Welsh evangelist, opened the doors of revival in Wales. Selina heard him preach for the first time at Trevecca in Breconshire. A fiery preacher, Harris had a powerful anointing of the Spirit of God. His name should be classified with John and Charles Wesley and George Whitefield.

Some years earlier Howel Harris had introduced Selina to George Whitefield, which is how they first became acquainted. God's providence worked beautifully in the situation. After the introduction, Selina invited George to her Chelsea home in London. She gathered several of her friends of the court, and there Whitefield spoke twice. George Whitefield was an incredibly effective preacher. In many respects he served as the spark of the revival, whereas John Wesley became the organizer of the movement. Whitefield had a deep rich resonant voice that could be heard by tens of thousands in the open air. He is considered, along with Charles Spurgeon, one of the greatest English-speaking preachers to have ever declared the Gospel. Aspects of his life have been touched upon in other chapters, but it is worthwhile to note here that the relationship that developed between Whitefield and the countess became tremendously significant to the eighteenth-century awakening. Through George Whitefield's ministry, Selina probably made her greatest contribution to the movement.

History records an interesting, rather humorous, footnote on Whitefield. As a lad, George had contracted a serious case of measles that left him with one eye severely crossed. His hecklers called him "Dr. Squintom." But his physical unattractiveness did not detract from his tremendous preaching. So moved was the countess by her first real encounter with Whitefield at her Chelsea home, that she immediately made him her chaplain.

When Selina offered the post to Whitefield, as one biographer put it, "It almost took George's breath away." After all, he was just a pub keeper's son who had spent his youth serving beer and ale to the loud patrons of his parents' public house. After something of the shock of the offer wore off, George said, "I am ashamed to think your ladyship will admit me under your roof." He did not even feel worthy to be there, let alone be the chaplain of Huntingdon's countess. This speaks of something of the mindset of eighteenth-century British life wherein the aristocracy and the courtiers were considered to be in a world of their own. But of course, Whitefield gladly accepted the countess's offer, and much to his credit, he never let his position create any sense of spiritual pride.

A New Thrust

Whitefield's move into high society brought a new aspect to the Wesley-Whitefield Revival. Not only did "Dr. Squintom" preach to the working masses—along with the hecklers—in the open air, he now had an open door to the courtiers and the highest echelon of British society. Lady Huntingdon's drawing room became a chapel for Whitefield, and he measured up to the task, because he had set his sights on the sharing of the Gospel of Christ to all who would listen. He preached to the nobility just as he preached to the masses of London at Kennington Common (park), where the Londoners would gather by the thousands to hear him declare the Gospel. He served as a faithful preacher of the full Christian message and would not water down his sermons one iota simply because royalty was present. He was an orator, and with the eloquence of Shakespeare and the dynamic of a fervent preacher, he impacted countless lives across the entirety of the British spectrum. Lady Huntingdon's ability to open doors proved most fruitful.

It is amazing how well Whitefield was received by the aristocracy. One day the duchess of Marlborough, who was in her eighties, wrote to the countess of Huntingdon: "God knows, we all need mending, none more than myself; women of wit, beauty and quality cannot bear too many humiliating truths." But they did bear them and hung onto George Whitefield's preaching as did the masses of the lower classes. Of course, there were exceptions. The duchess of Buckingham proved to be of a different ilk. Her husband, the marquess of Normandy, had built a beautiful house in St. James Park in the heart of London. It is now known as Buckingham Palace. She wrote in a letter to Lady Huntingdon these vindictive words concerning revival preaching: "It is monstrous to be told that you have a heart as sinful as the common wretches that crawl on the earth. This is highly offensive and insulting. . . ." Yet, as paradoxical as it may seem, she ended her letter by saying, "I shall be most happy to come and hear your favorite preacher."

One interesting anecdote in Whitefield's preaching to the nobility came from the duchess of Suffolk. She had become the mistress of George II. When she heard Whitefield preach, she was insulted and absolutely convinced that someone had told him all about her. She cried that Whitefield had deliberately directed his sermon at her sin. She actually went into a rage and accosted Lady Huntingdon face-to-face. The Holy Spirit does convict of "sin, righteousness and judgement" (John 16:8). The Gospel becomes a divider of people.

As can be imagined, Lady Huntingdon began to receive considerable criticism for her work in the revival, some even poked fun at her. Horace Walpole said to a friend, "Methodism is more fashionable than anything but brag; the women play very deep at both." But this slander made it evident that God was using women significantly in the eighteenth-century awakening. Never has there been a real revival movement without slander and opposition. It serves as an indicator of God's probing work—actually, it is a good sign of the working of the Holy Spirit.

Selina's Tenacity

Selina, caught up in the revival spirit, proved to be anything but reticent in addressing spiritual problems. On one occasion she forthrightly rebuked the archbishop of Canterbury because of a practice he engaged in—holding very questionable parties at Lambeth Palace, his London residence. He brushed the criticism aside in a very flippant manner, though. Consequently, Selina went to the king himself and revealed the situation. The king in turn called in the archbishop, whose name was Cornwallis, and gave him a royal reprimand. Selina had influence and power and did not hesitate to use it for the good of the revival.

George II died and George III came to the throne. He was the king who was ultimately responsible for the American Revolution. In his earlier years, before he began to become somewhat demented, he had very high regard for the countess of Huntingdon. On one occasion he said to her, "I have been told so many odd stories about your Ladyship that I felt a great degree of curiosity to see if you were at all like other women; and I am happy in having an opportunity of assuring your Ladyship of the very good opinion of you and how highly I estimate your character, your zeal and abilities, which cannot be consecrated to a more noble purpose." Selina had revival clout.

David Garrick, the proprietor of the famous Drury Lane Theater, which still stands in London, was a notable man of the stage. He admired Whitefield profoundly and once said that the great preacher could reduce an audience to tears by merely repeating the word, *Mesopotamia*. On one occasion, Garrick produced a play that unfairly ridiculed Whitefield. The countess went to Garrick and urged him to drop the play. He did. She then went on to petition the various legal authorities to put a stop to those who were persecuting the Methodists because a degree of persecution was beginning to develop, as it always does in spiritual awakenings. One wonders what would have become of the awakening had it not been for the influence of the countess in situations like these.

In those days, virtually all the stately homes had their own private chapels for family worship. The chaplains of the chapels were appointed and supported by the wealthy noble families. When Whitefield became Lady Huntingdon's chaplain in 1748, he soon became the most attractive chaplain of any manor house. Although he spent much of his time in itinerant ministry, and several years in America, he still held his chaplaincy post. But because of Whitefield's wide travels, many different preachers were invited to share the Gospel in Lady Huntingdon's chapel services. She had become familiar with practically all the great Methodist preachers, so she would invite friends and neighbors to come hear them. Notable people such as John and Charles Wesley, William Grimshaw, Augustus Toplady, Henry Venn, and many others preached in Selina's home. Those were wonderful days. Whitefield himself described it: "We have the sacrament every morning, heavenly conversation all day, and preach at night. This is to live at Court!" Not many courts in England were like hers, but the Countess of Huntingdon, through that means, did much to further the revival in the upper circles of nobility and society.

Selina's Travels and Developing Work

The countess would travel from her country estate to her London home in Chelsea. Later, she moved from Chelsea to Portland Road in Cavendish Square because her new home gave her more room for her evangelistic work. She opened her kitchen doors so the servants could hear the Gospel while the noble people listened to the Word in another part of the house. She also had residences in the west country and held meetings there as well. Her home in Bath, in the west of England, is still standing.

Further, Selina supported many evangelical revivalists in addition to George Whitefield. Martin Madan became a recipient of her money and support as did William Romaine. Madan had been converted under John Wesley's preaching and served as the first chaplain to the Lock Hospital. John Berridge also received aid from Lady Huntingdon. The well-known Roland Hill, pastor of the famous Surrey Chapel and considered by Lady Huntingdon as "the second Whitefield," preached for Selina. A breach, however, occurred between Hill and the countess that never really healed, because he was a very outspoken man—probably too much so. As can be imagined, all of the chaplains whom Selina supported and helped, and the number was obviously significant, were not always appreciated by the regular clergymen of the Church of England. Despite this, she carried on the noble work.

The Building of Chapels

The countess of Huntingdon threw herself ever more extensively into the revival work as the years passed. She would tour the country visiting the preachers whom she supported. She would see to it that they were given the opportunities to preach in churches or in the open air, her influence being widely respected.

The countess began to build chapels for the Methodist preachers in various parts of Britain. She opened the first building in Brighton, on the English Channel some fifty miles south of London. She called it Brighthelmstone. Built in 1761, it still stands. Selina built her third chapel in the county of Sussex at Lewes in 1765. Lewes is a town some ten or fifteen miles outside of Brighton. These chapels made a tremendous contribution as they gave a more secure venue for the declaration of the Gospel than was always possible in the open air. On one occasion, Selina had the opportunity to acquire property to build yet another chapel. She raised seven hundred pounds (£700) by selling some of her own jewelry. Martin Madden preached the dedication sermon and soon people were brought to Christ.

A large mansion in Sussex, near Wivelsfield, became available for lease. Selina immediately stepped in, leased the property, and made one of the large rooms a place of worship. Many were brought to faith in Christ in that building, which became known as Otehall Chapel. Her work did much to evangelize that part of South England. Three years later, in 1768, the countess built and opened a chapel in Tombridge Wells. This is a very well-known town in Kent, southeast of London. Being a spa, it drew people, especially of the aristocracy, for the baths.

As mentioned, Lady Huntingdon had an estate in the west of England. In the Bath chapel on one occasion, the well-known Horace Walpole came to hear John Wesley preach. Walpole wrote about Wesley: "Wesley is a clean, elderly man, fresh-colored, his hair smoothly combed, but with a little soupcon of curl at the ends." He went on to say that he was "wondrous clever, but as evidently an actor as Garrick." Walpole said that Wesley preached with such a rapid-fire barrage of words with little or no accent that he was not sure that he had really heard what was uttered. Yet he granted there were "parts of eloquence in it!"[16] Needless to say, Wesley was an effective preacher.

Selina's chapel work can be summed up in Whitefield's words: "Her house is a Bethel; to us in the ministry it looks like a college."

The College

Something rather prophetic lurked in Whitefield's words when he said that Selina's home looked like a college. She had always been a devotee of good education, especially from a Christian perspective. Back in 1742, she had actually been responsible for the development of a school for children at Ashby. For several years, between 1749 and 1758, she had done all she could in helping Whitefield raise funds for the Bethesda Orphanage in Savannah, Georgia, and a new college in New Jersey. Whitefield had a very significant benevolent ministry in America as well as an itinerant preaching ministry. Because of Selina's closeness to Whitefield, she had an indirect hand in the development of Princeton University and Dartmouth College in America along with the Repton School in Britain. Her commitment to higher education was obvious, seeing it as another aspect of the expanding work of the revival.

Selina developed a regular program of sponsoring young men who were training for the ministry. She normally sent them to Oxford University. Tragically, in 1768, six students were dismissed from Oxford because of their Methodist approach to Christian service and ministry, but the tragedy turned into something very positive. This expulsion galvanized the countess to start a theological college of her own. Because of her relationship with Howel Harris in Wales, who had set up a Moravian-style Christian community in his home, she cast her eyes on Trevecca, Harris' community. The locale seemed to provide the ideal spot where she could develop a college, and Harris would be there to give it direction. She acquired a twenty-five-year lease on an old sixteenth-century house. She renovated and opened it on August 24, 1768, her birthday. George Whitefield preached the opening ceremony, and Trevecca College was born.

John Fletcher of Madeley became the honorary president and Thomas Easterbrook served as the headmaster, or as we would say in America,

the dean of the school. The college prospered, and at the first anniversary
of its founding, John Wesley preached.

The school never had a large enrollment; that was not the intent. It did
have the normal full curriculum of Latin, philosophy, Greek, church history, systematic theology, biblical studies, and so forth. The zealous students were trained to further the revival. The countess herself provided
for each student all their housing and board along with tuition plus one
new suit of clothing each year. She took a personal interest in them all
and was a tremendous inspiration.

The Connection

In reality, the countess had almost developed something of a
"minidenomination" in itself. The chapels that she had built across the
country, the chapels in her homes, and the many chaplains that she supported, all developed into a very tight-knit "Connection," as it came to
be called. Actually, a small denomination, as it were, came into being.
Yet it must be made clear that she remained firmly committed to the
Church of England. As significant as the Connection became for Selina,
she stayed in the established church. She always worshiped with the
Church of England prayer book in all of her chapels. The students at
Trevecca College, of course, often went to different communions; some
to the Anglican; some to dissenting churches; and some to her Connection. She did not insist on their use of Anglican liturgy, though she was
devoted to it herself. She was an ecumenically minded person, yet at
the same time committed to the established church. She did insist upon
one thing, however. Her students had to be fully committed to the evangelical faith.

In 1794, a certain student by the name of Hawkesworth received ordination in Whitefield's tabernacle in Plymouth. In some senses, this
ordination foreshadowed Wesley's beginning to ordain ministers exclu-
sively for the Methodist ministry. A new step in the Connection was
taken.

In the 1790s, the lease on the Trevecca property expired. This forced
the college to move, and Selina relocated it at Cheshunt in Herts. It occupied that spot until 1905 when again it moved, this time to Cambridge
under the name of Cheshunt College. It continued on in the Cambridge
context until it merged with the Presbyterian Westminster College in 1968.
It now provides theological education for many ministers in the Church
of England. It is also interesting to note that Huntingdon College in Mont-
gomery, Alabama, was influenced to some extent by Selina, the countess
of Huntingdon. She had befriended and supported the early Methodist
movement in the United States and hence, the naming of the college after
her in the state of Alabama.

Tragic Divisions Come

It is common knowledge that John Wesley, from the purely theological perspective, committed himself to Armenian theology. That is to say, he rejected at least some of the basic tenants of the so-called five points of the Synod of Dort. The five points read as follows:

- *T*otal depravity of a person outside of Christ
- *U*nconditional election and predestination
- *L*imited atonement, limited to the elect only
- *I*rresistible grace of God
- *P*erseverance of the saints

These five points form the well-known tulip acrostic, and they became the rallying cry to which Armenians protested. Those of a more Calvinistic persuasion adhered to every point in the acrostic. Much discussion—even wrangling—ensued over this during the seventeenth and eighteenth centuries, and continues today in some circles. The theology of the Calvinists and the adherents of Dort (some hold that there is a difference between the two) became what is commonly called Reformed theology because John Calvin and Martin Luther and a host of other Reformers basically embraced those views. Armenians did not, and hence a serious division over these issues erupted among the Methodists. Wesley was a convinced Armenian, and the issue threw him, to a degree, in opposition to Howel Harris and George Whitefield and most of the evangelicals in the Church of England. Whitefield and Harris were Reformed in theology. Still, they worked on together hand in hand with the Wesley brothers for several years. The simple preaching of the Gospel bound them together and this formed the heart and essence of the evangelical thrust.

At one junction in the various theological discussions that took place, John Wesley preached a vehement sermon against the Calvinist position, especially that of predestination. He entertained very strong feelings in this respect and did not hesitate to make them known. Then he began to toy with the idea that perhaps he should publish the anti-Calvinist sermon. Virtually everyone in the Methodist movement urged him not to do so for fear that it would cause a serious division if it was published. So Wesley decided to cast lots to see whether or not he should publish—a rather strange way to seek God's leadership on such a questionable issue. But he plunged ahead, and strangely enough the lot came up that he should publish his sermon. Again, against the earnest urgings of his friends not to do so, he dug in his heals and published the sermon, which indeed did split the Methodist movement. Throughout the following years, George Whitfield and even Charles Wesley did all they could to reconcile the issue and restore harmony, but seemingly to no avail. That publication delivered a serious blow to the great eighteenth-century revival. Lady Huntingdon inevitably was drawn into the conflict. Over this issue she had serious questions, however, because her close friend Whitefield was Reformed in theology.

Other conflicts began to appear on the horizon. As has already been pointed out, Selina, in her earlier years, had a close relationship with John and Charles Wesley. During those days she gave them much support and opened many doors for them. Before her husband died, she and the earl would attend the Fetter Lane Moravian Meeting House in London with the brothers. In the context of the Fetter Lane meetings a conflict surfaced between John Wesley and the Moravians over a certain point. The issue that had arisen among the Fetter Lane group centered in the doctrine of spiritual "stillness." This approach to spirituality was actually a throwback to medieval mysticism. The adherents to stillness advocated that those seeking salvation in Christ should just wait for assurance to overcome them without prayer or even without reading the Scriptures. This purely emotional approach was very questionable. As a consequence, all the Methodists withdrew from the Moravian society in July 1740. Lady Huntingdon had supported the Wesleys in this conflict, and she admired Wesley despite the Calvinistic-Armenian question. She particularly appreciated John's doctrine of "perfect love." Selina said that it was "the doctrine I hope to live and die by; it is absolutely the most complete thing I know."

But as great as was Selina's admiration for John and Charles, her appreciation for Whitefield superseded it. Before long the countess, no doubt under the influence of George Whitefield's powerful preaching, began to move toward the Calvinistic persuasion. Selina's contact with Howel Harris also deepened her commitment to Reformed theology. By the time she made Whitefield her chaplain in 1748, she had settled quite firmly in the Calvinistic camp. This did not precipitate any break with Wesley, but their association began to cool off. Conflict can do that, even in great revival times.

George Whitefield and John Wesley developed something of a different attitude toward Lady Huntingdon as well. George Whitefield admired her profoundly and always had a complimentary word for her. One biographer stated that he flattered the countess rather extravagantly. Wesley took a quite opposite view. He would not even keep a special place for her if she were late to a Foundry service, which was just not done to nobility in those days. Wesley's strong-minded ways would simply not let him give preference. Yet it is only fair to say that Wesley did truly admire the countess. He said that she was "much devoted to God, having a thousand valuable and amiable qualities." But he would have also said this about others. She no doubt sensed something of the difference in attitude between Wesley and Whitfield, and this may possibly have been somewhat influential in her choosing Calvinist theology. But that is pure conjecture.

In September 1748, Wesley engaged Selina in a long theological discussion on the issues. In describing the interview later he said, "I trust I delivered my own soul. And she received it well, the tears standing in her eyes." But as her influence and the Connection grew, she more and more moved to the Reformed side and friction began to develop between the two.

The London Conference

The London Conference of 1770 saw the publication of *The Large Minutes*, a document that outlined Methodist theology and doctrinal positions. The Methodists with Wesley in the forefront argued from the Armenian perspective that Calvinism lent itself to antinomianism, a heresy that has been condemned by church councils throughout the years. Antinomianism advocated that a person, who was saved by grace and kept secure in grace, would not be motivated to high moral standards. The antinomians argued if one is kept in grace through no human effort, why worry about living a holy life. Clearly this constituted a real departure from the New Testament. God demands holiness of life, and Calvinism certainly had not implied anything to the contrary. Calvin himself was revolted by such a thought. Nonetheless, this criticism was aimed at the Calvinists. Lady Huntingdon became deeply disturbed over the issue. She urged Walter Shirley to send a circular letter to all her supporters to raise a protest at the next conference of the Connection to be held in Bristol. Wesley did recant somewhat and admitted that there had been a misunderstanding, but the whole affair did not help the relationship between the countess and the Wesleyan Methodists.

The next barb in the relationship occurred when Wesley published a vindication of the *Minutes*. This pushed the countess over the brink, and thereafter she insisted that everyone who served her in the chapels had to be Calvinistic. This precipitated the resignation of Joseph Benson and John Fletcher from Trevecca College. Whitefield had always tried to be something of a mediator in such a conflict, but he had died in America just before the controversy over the *Minutes* erupted. So the countess and John Wesley came to a parting of the ways.

The tragedy is that both the Armenians and the Calvinists preached the simple Gospel and were blessed of God in seeing many saved. Nothing in their conflicting views precluded that. One could be committed to either approach and preach Christ with no compromise. How sad it is that the preachers did not reconcile. Wesley's friends were probably right in urging John not to publish the sermon that ignited the explosion.

There is a more positive end to the story, however. When John Wesley died on March 2, 1791, in his final hours he made his well-known declaration: "The best is yet to come." But Joseph Bradford, who had been at Wesley's bedside when he died, reports John Wesley as also saying, "I the Chief of Sinners am, but Jesus died for me." When the countess of Huntingdon heard that, she asked Bradford if it was true; he assured her that those were Wesley's own words. Bradford went on to say that this was the message that Wesley had preached all through his life. The countess realized that John Wesley did faithfully preach the Gospel, even though she had at times thought otherwise. She literally burst into tears that the misunderstanding had gone on for so many years. So at least something of a reconciliation of spirit came to the countess.

Despite all the difficulties and dissension that came to the revival movement, the Spirit of God overruled and the awakening continued.

The Spa Fields Incident

In the north of London, there was a large area known as London Spa, or Spa Fields. It had been used as a recreational area but was definitely on the rowdy side. A large building had been erected on the site called the Pantheon, constructed on the plan of the well-known building in Rome. Designed for public entertainment and other recreational activities, its doors were closed at the time. Lady Huntingdon thought this might be a good place to further evangelistic work in that particular section of London. The work would demand heavy expenses, however, and she already found herself quite committed financially to her other works. So she reluctantly decided against taking on the project.

A group of evangelical Christians, however, felt it to be an opportunity that must be taken. So in 1777, they renovated and opened the building for worship. They had no sooner opened the doors, when a clergyman of the Church of England brought a lawsuit against them. He contended that he had the right to appoint the preachers who were using the building and receive a portion of the offerings. Of course, the evangelical churchmen refused, and he took the case to the consistory court. The court ruled in his favor and shut the chapel down. When the countess heard of this situation she was appalled. The evangelical churchman who had started the work had been persuaded that her privileged position and the use of her own chaplains could avoid the court ruling. Consequently, she took lease of the building and appointed two men to officiate in the Spa Fields Chapel.

Yet once again the Anglican clergyman took the case to court and the judge again upheld his suit. This was a devastating decision, because it not only closed the London Spa Fields Chapel, but by implications, the enemies of the revival could make a case and perhaps close all of Selina's chapels. Actually, she had been advised incorrectly. Lawyers had told her that her ministry in any premises she operated, as long as it constituted her property, would be viewed by the court as a "domestic" chaplaincy. Therefore, she would have charge of the opening of any chapel and could choose the clergyman. But now the court had ruled otherwise. She faced a serious dilemma of having to face the possibility of continual court cases or register her chapels as dissenting meeting houses under the Toleration Act of 1689, which would consequently make her, at least technically, a dissenter. The affair caused her much inner conflict. She had been a faithful Anglican all her life, but the issue had to be resolved. Very reluctantly, but seeing this as her only course of action, she took the step and became a dissenter. The affair caused a real wrench in her heart. She said, "I am to be cast out of the Church of England, only for what I have been doing these forty years—speaking and living for Jesus Christ." Thus, in 1781, the sixty-seven chapels that she had established were no longer societies within the Church of England. They became commonly known as the "Societies in the secession patronized by Lady Huntingdon," now officially called the "Countess of Huntingdon's Connection."

This move deeply disturbed the chaplains who saw themselves as faithful Anglicans. All but two of her many chaplains resigned. Those leaving feared that if they did not sever their Huntingdon ties, they would jeopardize their "orders in the Church." They simply did not wish to become dissenters. The two who stayed were Thomas Wills (a relative) and Dr. Thomas Haweis. This thrust the countess into absolute dependence upon her college to supply preachers for the Connection churches. Yet she, though left the Anglican communion, continued to use the Church of England's liturgy in all of her chapels. Eventually, however, the chapels did become more like the free churches in liturgy and worship style.

This problem, though it fostered a very difficult time for Lady Huntingdon, really did not sap the strength of the work. The chapels carried on and flourished. The preaching of the Gospel did not diminish, and many continually came to saving faith in Jesus Christ. But her Connection churches began to do their own ordinations as the work progressed, becoming a full-fledged dissenting denomination.

The Years Pass

As the last decade of the eighteenth century dawned, the countess had reached eighty-four years of age—a ripe old age for those days. The question arose as to what would happen to the work after the Lord called her home. She herself felt much in favor of the ecclesiastical structures of the General Association, a group quite similar to the Welsh-Calvinistic Methodists. Up to this time, the countess had made all the appointments of ministers and had overseen the work virtually by herself. But she realized that the years were passing, so she decided to develop local trustees and divide the work into associations. This would hopefully spread the responsibilities over a number of people. The plan did not set well at all with several, and she felt constrained to drop the entire idea. She very much regretted this move that had been thrust upon her. Still, something had to be done to carry on the work when she was unable. Finally, she bequeathed all her chapels and houses to four persons to maintain the work at their discretion. In the end, Lady Erskine, who had been one of the four, took on the bulk of the management of the Connection. She had been working with the countess for many years and shared the same spirit and approach as Selina.

Through the years, the Connection slowly diminished as chapels closed and the movement began to merge into Congregationalism. There are, at the present time, some twenty-five chapels in the Connection, but they are mostly situated in northeast and south-central England.

The End of a Woman of Awakening, But Not the End of Revival

During her last days, Selina, woman of awakening, lived in a house next to the Spa Fields Chapel. She had suffered a severe ruptured blood vessel in November 1790, and her health steadily deteriorated thereafter. She became increasingly weaker, though her mind stayed as alert as ever. Near the end she said, "My work is done. I have nothing to do but to go to my Heavenly Father." When the sun rose on June 17, 1791, Lady Huntingdon was translated into the presence of her Lord whom she loved with all her heart. The curtain dropped on a great woman of awakening. She was buried in the chancel of St. Helen's Church in Ashby-de-la-Zouch.

A great woman had gone to her reward, and what a reward it no doubt was. A woman of nobility who gave a fortune to the spreading of the Gospel, she humbly served as one who simply touched lives with the compassionate spirit of her Lord. Symbolic of Selina's spirit and at great risk to herself, the countess went to Sarah Wesley's bedside and spent three weeks nursing her smallpox. Two of Selina's own sons had died with smallpox; one can thus appreciate her commitment to overcome fear so as to help one needy person. During Handel's last days, she spent time with him, giving him encouragement in his last illness. She was always on the alert to be of help, service, and consolation to anyone in need, and these qualities typified her life.

In 1770, when George Whitefield died, the countess was virtually inconsolable. At Whitefield's death she became the sole proprietor of the Bethesda Orphanage in Savannah, Georgia. She rose to the occasion. It became the impetus for her to send missionaries to the Colonies. When she put out a call to volunteers at her Trevecca College, seven students responded, were appointed, and sent to America. Bethesda Orphanage exists and functions to this day in Savannah, Georgia. Throughout the years it has been a tremendous haven of spiritual and physical comfort to many homeless children.

The countess also made a wonderful contribution to Sierra Leone in Africa. John Marrant, a young black man, came to faith in Christ under Whitefield's ministry in Charleston, South Carolina. He moved to England and was ordained in the countess' chapel at Bath in 1785. After his ordination he traveled to Nova Scotia and there worked as a missionary among the African-Americans. Many blacks from America had escaped from the crosscurrents of America's slavery problems to Nova Scotia. In Nova Scotia, Marrant established a church and, in 1792, led eleven hundred of his converts to establish a new West African colony. There the work progressed and churches were planted. They became known as "her ladyship's churches in Sierra Leone." Eleven of the countess' black churches with thirteen hundred members are still in existence in West Africa. That constitutes something of the impact that the countess of Huntingdon had through George Whitefield.

Not only did the countess influence lives individually, but the amount of finances that she expended in the work grew to gigantic proportions. Some have estimated that she gave over a hundred thousand pounds in her lifetime. By contemporary standards, that would be many millions of dollars. Although she was extremely wealthy, she lived a quite sacrificial lifestyle. Henry Venn, a deep admirer, said of her, "No equipage, no livery servants, no house, all these given up, that perishing sinners might hear the life-giving sound and be enriched with all spiritual blessings."

As one biographer said, Selina did not fill the role of a preacher or theologian but was a devoted leader who believed in total commitment for herself and no less than that from others. She played a central role in the evangelical revival by being a link among the Wesleys, Whitefield, the Welsh-Calvinistic Methodists, the Moravians, and the Anglican evangelicals. Through her friendship with Isaac Watts and Philip Doddridge, she helped carry Christ's message to the dissenting cause as well. Little wonder that Horace Walpole called her "Queen of the Methodists." Selina was a great lady, an incredibly dedicated Christian, and a true woman of God.

A fitting end to this beautiful story of a great woman of awakening came from the pen of biographer Peter Gentry. He wrote:

> Her [Selina's] increasing absence [from Court] was noticed and led the Prince [of Wales] to inquire of one of the other ladies present as to the reason for this. "I suppose she is busy praying with her beggars," she replied with a sneer. "Lady Charlotte," said the Prince, "when I am dying, I think I shall be happy to seize the skirt of Lady Huntingdon's mantle, to lift me up with her to heaven."

Woman of the court, woman of generosity, woman of awakening—this is Selina, the Countess of Huntingdon, one of God's great gifts to spiritual awakening.

Endnotes
1. The quotes in this chapter are taken from Peter W. Gentry, *The Countess of Huntingdon* (Number 4 in the series, "People Called Methodists," 1994).

Chapter Six

SUSANNAH SPURGEON

The Pastor's Wife of Awakening

The old cliché is correct: Behind every great man there stands a great woman. There may be a few exceptions, but the saying certainly rings true for the great Victorian preacher, Charles Haddon Spurgeon. Known as the "Prince of Preachers," the Spirit of God used him to build the largest evangelical church in the world during his thirty-seven-year ministry in London. Behind him in love, support, and prayer stood his lovely wife, Susannah. In reality she stood *beside* him more than *behind* him. If ever there was a pastor's wife who took a stalwart stand with her husband, Susannah filled the role. In the revival that broke out in the context of their shared ministry, she played a most significant part. Susannah Thompson Spurgeon's life unfolds as the story of a pastor's wife in true spiritual awakening.

The London Revival of the Mid-Nineteenth Century

England languished in dire need of spiritual awakening. The impact of the Wesley-Whitfield Revival had spent its force and Britain once again longed for a fresh touch from heaven. Few thought that it would begin with the rather brash nineteen-year-old preacher who received a call to become pastor of New Park Street Baptist Church of London, England, in 1854.

The eloquent preaching of the young man from Cambridgeshire had audiences sitting on the edges of their seats. When Spurgeon preached, "the spellbound audiences must have thought that John Bunyan II was speaking to them." But could a mere lad be God's instrument in revival? Other great preachers were on the scene in the mid-nineteenth century, men such as Joseph Parker, R. W. Dale, and Alexander Maclaren. Surely God would choose one of that stature to foster a spiritual awakening. Yet, Spurgeon seemed to have that indefinable something that superseded all human factors. A new atmosphere had begun to settle on London. What was going on? Spurgeon himself sensed it as did a few others. The answer is quite simple: Spurgeon came to the pastorate of the New Park Street Baptist Church as a spiritual revival emerged on the scene.

Few biographers, it seems, have understood the revival principle that was operative in the early ministry of Charles and Susannah Spurgeon. He was a great preacher, she, a great wife for a pastor, but that does not explain it all. Charles himself said, "The times of refreshing from the presence of the Lord have at last dawned upon our land. Everywhere there are signs of aroused activity and increased earnestness. A spirit of prayer is visiting our churches, and its paths are dropping fatness. The first breath of the rushing mighty wind is already discerned, while on rising evangelists the tongues of fire have evidently descended." Revival began to dawn and it deeply influenced the Spurgeons' ministry, which explains it all.

The Spurgeons knew well the principles of revival. The Wesley-Whitefield awakening had occurred in the previous century. Charles admired Whitefield, no doubt patterning aspects of his ministry after him. Out of the eighteenth-century awakening, the British Baptists received a significant touch. As historian Ernest A. Payne put it:

> The English Baptists are generally accorded the distinction of being the first in modern times to found a society deliberately and exclusively aimed at the evangelization of the non-Christian world, and there is no doubt at all about the important repercussions which their action had in other branches of the Church. The founders of the London Missionary Society and the Church Missionary Society, and those who sought to awaken the conscience of the Church of Scotland in regard to world-evangelization, confessed that they had been challenged and inspired by what the Baptists had done.[1]

In that spirit, there arose on the scene missionary giants like William Carey and Andrew Fuller. The great Thomas Chalmers also emerged in that context.

Some of the more strict British Baptists expressed displeasure with the revival movement, but the Wesley-Whitefield Revival did much to break the grip of hyper-Calvinism, thus paving the way for an evangelistic thrust to enter the Baptist movement. The revival that broke out in Spurgeon's ministry epitomized the new spirit. When Spurgeon spoke of the "times of refreshing," he referred to the Prayer Revival that had moved over the British scene from 1859–1860. That significant work had its conception in supplication, had gestated in intercession, and had given birth to revival in America during the winter of 1857–1858.

The revival set America ablaze. In Chicago, two thousand gathered

daily in the Metropolitan Theater just to pray. Revivals broke out in secular schools. For example, in a Cleveland, Ohio, high school, all but two
boys were converted. New social programs were launched. Praying
laypeople, both men and women, became the spearheads of the movement. God in His sovereignty had been pleased to visit the nation with
His glory. For two years, fifty thousand people a month joined the churches
in America, and there were only thirty million people in the United States
at that time.

A revival of such magnitude always encompasses vast areas. The spirit
of prayer moved across the Atlantic and touched the British Isles.

England began to be warmed by the fire of revival. A united prayer
meeting was held in the throne room of Cosby Hall, London in 1859.
Soon attendance reached one hundred at the noon hour service. By the
end of the year, twenty-four prayer meetings were being held daily and
sixty prayer meetings were being held weekly in the London area. In a
short while, the number of prayer meetings grew to 120, then multiplied
thoughout the land. From London, the revival spirit spread to the coun-
ties of Surrey and Kent, then to Sussex and Hampshire on to the Isle of
Wight. Berkshire, Bristol, Gloucester, and Wiltshire also experienced the
reviving power of God.

As 1860 was ushered in, the Fortune, the Garrick, and the Sadler and
Wells theaters opened their doors for Sunday evangelistic services. Even
the staid Saint Paul's Cathedral and Westminster Abbey conducted special revival services. The ministry of Spurgeon sprang into full bloom as
the new five-thousand-seat Metropolitan Tabernacle became the home of
his growing congregation. People in Dorset flocked to hear Evan Hopkins
of later Keswick Convention notoriety. Charles Finney, the great American revivalist, preached with great effect in Bolton, England, as the revival spread and deepened over the land. As Charles Spurgeon put it:

> It were well . . . that the Divine life would break forth everywhere—
> in the parlor, the workshop, counting house, the market and streets.
> We are far too ready to confine it to the channel of Sunday services
> and religious meetings; it deserves a broader floodway and must
> have it if we are to see gladder times. It must burst out upon men
> who do not care for it, and invade chambers where it will be regarded
> as an intrusion; it must be seen by wayfaring men streaming down
> the places of traffic and concourse, *hindering the progress of sinful
> trades*, and surrounding all, whether they will or no. Would to God
> that religion were more vital and forceful among us, so as to create
> *a powerful public opinion on behalf of truth, justice and holiness*
> . . . A lie which would *purify the age*. It is much to be desired that
> the Christian church may yet have *more power and influence* all

over the world for *righteousness . . . social reform and moral progress.*[2]

That constituted revival for Charles and Susannah, and all Britain experienced it in 1860, especially in Charles and Susannah's ministry. The prayer revival became the last great spiritual awakening experienced by all of the British Isles. True, significant blessings came to Britain in the Welsh revival of 1904–1906, but that movement did not impact all of the United Kingdom to the same degree as did the Prayer Revival. The dynamics of the American aspects of the movement will be seen in the next chapter on Catherine Booth.

Spurgeon and Revival

The Spurgeons had actually bathed in the blessings of a real revival at the New Park Street Church for several years before the British Prayer Revival of 1860. The history of the church demonstrates that reality. A brief copy of the church's history was placed in the cornerstone of Metropolitan Tabernacle at its dedication. A passage from that document reads:

> From the day he (Spurgeon) commenced his labors in our midst, it pleased the Lord our God to grant us a revival *which has steadily progressed ever* since. . . . So did the Holy Ghost accompany the preaching of the Gospel with divine power that almost every sermon proved the means of awakening and regeneration to some who were hitherto "dead in trespasses and sins."

The New Park Street Chapel had been built in 1833, but the numbers had deteriorated to a small number in the years preceding C. H. Spurgeon's arrival in 1854. Yet, said Spurgeon, there were those "who never ceased to pray for a gracious revival . . . they hoped on, and hoped ever," as did the hopeful Spurgeons. Spurgeon described those early days when God's people interceded for awakening:

> When I came to New Park Street Chapel, it was but a mere handful of people to whom I first preached, yet I could never forget how earnestly they prayed. Sometimes they seemed to plead as though they could really see the Angel of the Covenant present with them, and as if they must have a blessing from him. More than once we were all so awe-struck with the solemnity of the meeting that we sat silent for some moments while the Lord's Power appeared to overshadow us; and all I could do on such occasions was to pronounce the benediction, and say "Dear friends, we have had the Spirit of God here very manifestly tonight; let us go home

and take care not to lose His gracious influence." Then down came the blessing; the house was filled with hearers, and many souls were saved.

Charles went on to say, "For six years the dew has never ceased to fall, and the rain has never been held. At this time the converts are more numerous than hither-to-fore, and the zeal of the church groweth exceedingly." The full revival then came in 1860.

The awakening work surrounding the Spurgeons so dramatically deepened that for three years up to one thousand people every Sunday were turned away from the Surrey Gardens Music Hall where Charles preached at the time because there was no room left for the worshipers— and the Music Hall seated ten thousand. How many were converted is incalculable.

Some quite amazing occurrences took place in those early revival days. For example, one Sunday in the Music Hall a man sat listening intently to Spurgeon preach. In his sermon Charles said, "There is a man sitting here, who is a shoemaker; he keeps his shop open on Sundays, and it was open last Sunday morning; he took in nine pence and there was a four pence profit; he sold his soul to Satan for four pence." The man, so intently listening, felt cut to the heart. He actually was a shoemaker and he had kept his shop open the previous Sunday and had taken in nine pence and he did make a profit of four pence. He immediately came to Christ. Dozens were saved in similar dramatic circumstances and joined the great Baptist church.

One question immediately thrusts itself to the fore: What laid behind this profound spiritual awakening under Charles and Susannah Spurgeon? If revival constitutes the answer to the staggering success, why did it happen at that time? Eric Hayden, later a pastor of the Metropolitan Tabernacle, saw three dominant factors. First, the primary foundation stone rested on the sacrificial, fervent prayers of the New Park Street people. They were a faithful group of interceding Christians. Young Spurgeon inherited that blessed legacy. Moreover, that spirit of prayer continued through the years of the Metropolitan Tabernacle ministry. The anecdote of Charles Haddon Spurgeon's taking visitors through the Metropolitan Tabernacle and showing them the prayer room in the basement and remarking, "Here is our power house," has often been repeated. That anecdote is probably apocryphal; the real story is that the prayer meetings were held upstairs on Monday night, with some three thousand people attending.

A second central feature in the Spurgeon Revival is expressed in Charles' words: "Sound doctrine and loving invitation make a good basis of material, which, when modeled by the hand of prayer and faith, will form sermons of far more value in the saving of souls than the most philosophic essays prepared elaborately, and delivered with eloquence and propriety." The revival had its birth and development in "sound doctrine" that was presented with "loving invitation." Biblical doctrine that is preached in love cannot be divorced from revival. Spurgeon believed that a lasting revival comes only through the power and sovereignty of God when His people use prayer and the plain declaration of the essential truths of orthodox, biblical theology, with loving appeal. God will move in His set time and on the wings of biblical truth. This we have seen and emphasized many times.

But there is a third dimension that Charles and Susannah Spurgeon themselves may not have fully realized. Simply stated, they were God's instruments of the hour, and rarely does one recognize how profoundly the Holy Spirit may be using one, at least at the moment. Spurgeon realized it to a point, as he said, "We must stoop before God that we may conquer amongst men." Still, Charles and Susannah probably did not realize how effective their ministry truly was. God, in sovereign grace, raises up His choice servants at the right moment to be prophets of a great movement, whether they know it or not.

So through prayer, sound doctrine with loving invitation, and a genuine man and woman of God at the New Park Street Baptist Church, revival flamed to life. The spiritual atmosphere of London crackled with excitement as hundreds of thousands thronged to hear the young man of God. Behind it all, and despite the fame and popularity that focused on Charles, stood Susannah, pastor's wife, faithful supporter, prayer warrior, and a great woman of awakening. And it is a delightful story how God brought this unusual couple together.

United in Ministry

Only God can bring together two different personalities and blend them into one in Christ, which probably demands more of the wife than the husband. The position of the wife of a great man, and especially of a great pastor, has its challenges to say the least. It requires absolute unselfishness, especially when revival comes and the husband finds himself in such demand. She must be utterly unselfish and willing to let God use her husband, and herself, as He sees fit. In a very real sense, she must see herself as a part of her husband's ministry, even if she must often remain at home. But a wife's role should certainly never be seen as a secondary role. What Charles would have been without Susannah, one could only venture to guess; but she filled the position of that unselfish, loving, committed wife who aided the revival that pervaded their ministry. As Solomon said, "Whoso findeth a wife, findeth a good thing and obtaineth favor of the Lord" (Proverbs 18:22 KJV).

Charles certainly found Solomon's statement true of Susannah. As her biographer put it, "Never did woman fulfill the marriage vow more faithfully. In sickness and in health, through good report and evil, she was ever his support and it would be difficult to find anywhere another woman, in spite of adverse circumstances and conditions, ill health and infirmity, who did such monumental work for God and man as Susannah Spurgeon."[3] The biographer went on to say, "Her life is a brilliant example of what can be done by a weak woman who devotes herself to the service of the Master and not only as the wife of Charles Haddon Spurgeon, will Mrs. Spurgeon live green in the memory of all Christians, but as herself, as a woman who found solace and suffering by ministering to the needs of others, she will stand out through all time." This is high praise for this woman of awakening, but praise truly deserved. Into every aspect of the reviving work, she threw herself—heart and soul. She not only filled the roll of a significant supporter of her famous husband, she herself was used of God to develop a most significant ministry in her own stead.

Susannah's Early Years

Susannah came into the world on January 15, 1832. She spent her early years in the southern suburbs of London in the home of her father and mother, Mr. and Mrs. R. B. Thompson. London officially encompasses only one square mile, is dominated by the Tower of London, but has throughout the centuries spilled over for many miles to become one of the great metropolitan centers of the world. The family later moved to the city of London itself.

The early nineteenth century witnessed a turbulent, revolutionary time in England. The Industrial Revolution had exploded over the land. Colonialism ran rampant. Moreover, the general culture was in great flux, with many aspects of it quite different from today. For example, as strange as it may seem in our contemporary society, well-brought-up English girls were not allowed to read the morning and evening newspapers. Susannah, therefore, grew up rather oblivious to many of the dynamics that emerged during the Victorian era. Colonial expansion and the sweeping social revolution by and large passed her by.

The family had great faith, however. Her father and mother often attended the New Park Street Chapel. The church itself sat at the southern foot of Southwark Bridge, which spanned the Thames in the heart of London's metropolitan area. As a young girl, Susannah would accompany her parents to the chapel and she always enjoyed the ministry of the pastor, the Reverend James Smith. Susannah Spurgeon later described him as a "quaint and rugged preacher, but one well versed in the blessed art of bringing souls to Christ." She went on to write, "Often had I seen him administer the Ordinance of Baptism to the candidates, wondering with a tearful longing whether I should ever be able thus to confess my faith in the Lord Jesus." She had a tender heart for God and deeply longed for the day when she herself would find a vibrant living faith in the saving grace of Christ. That day would come, under the ministry of the man whom she would marry. She said, "It was certainly somewhat singular that, in the very pulpit which had exercised such a charm over me, I should have my first glimpse of the one who was to be the love of my heart, and the light of my earthly life." In that pulpit, she herself being only twenty-two, Susannah heard the "boy preacher from the Fens." Charles, nineteen when he first preached at New Park Street Chapel and three years younger than his wife to be, soon sensed a bond growing between them.

Susannah had not yet become an actual member of the New Park Street Baptist Church. Two dear friends of the Thompson family, Mr. and Mrs. Olney, were very fond of Susannah and often invited her to visit with them. Mr. Olney served as a leading deacon of New Park Street, and when Susannah visited the Olney family on a Sunday they would invite her to the church. She always very happily accompanied them.

Spiritual Stirrings

Susannah, brought up by her godly parents, had a genuine openness to the Christian faith. On one occasion she worshiped at the old Poultry Chapel where the Reverend S. B. Bergne served as pastor. The good man of God preached from Romans 10:8, "The Word is nigh thee, even in thy mouth, and in thy heart" (KJV). The Spirit of God spoke profoundly to Susannah's heart. This became the moment when, as she said, "From that service, I date the dawning of the true light in my soul. The Lord said to me, through His servant, 'give Me thy heart,' and, constrained by His love, that night witnessed my solemn resolution of entire surrender to Himself." Actually, as Susannah reflected back on the occasion years later, this became the moment of her true conversion to Christ.

But all did not go well in Susannah's spiritual life. She soon slipped into a state of apathy and indifference. By her own confessions, "seasons of darkness" and accompanying doubt gripped her heart. Moreover, she seemed unwilling to open up to others and be helped concerning her spiritual state. So she muddled along until meeting Charles.

Charles' Call to the New Park Street Baptist Church

On a brisk Sunday morning, December 18, 1853, Charles Spurgeon preached his first sermon at New Park Street Chapel. When Charles walked up the pulpit steps of New Park Street that December morning, with a view to becoming the church's ninth pastor, the congregation did not quite know what to think. He looked a mere boy with a round baby face that made him look even younger. As he warmed up in his message, he would pull out a bright blue polka-dot handkerchief from his coat pocket and flourish it about as he made a point. Actually, he looked a bit comical, but how he did preach! With enthusiastic vigor and spiritual power he swayed the people. The people of New Park Street scooted up to the edges of their seats with excitement before Charles had traversed halfway through his sermon. Rarely had they heard such powerful preaching. His pungent, colloquial Anglo-Saxon vocabulary had them enthralled. Spurgeon would have concurred wholeheartedly with Sir Winston Churchill who said centuries later, "There is nothing more noble than an Anglo-Saxon sentence."

The service ended and the impressed congregation—only eighty in number—filed out. That afternoon the good members fanned out over south London inviting friends to the evening service. A large congregation gathered in the evening. Mrs. Unity Olney, Thomas' wife, a deeply devout Christian, suffered as an invalid and was confined to her home most of the time. Her deacon husband managed, however, to get her to church that night. After hearing Charles she simply said, "He will do! He will do!" She expressed what virtually all felt.

But there was one significant exception to the general affirmation of the many worshipers that first Sunday night. That evening a sophisticated young lady named Miss Susannah Thompson attended the service. She became the exception; she did not think much of the sermon, or the preacher. She thought him rather a country bumpkin.

Most of the people, however, were moved by the sermon, actually refusing to leave the old building until the deacons assured them that they would do their best to induce Spurgeon to come again.

The Call to the Pastorate

The Baptist's have a congregational church government. That is to say, each congregation stands autonomous and calls its own pastor at its own discretion.

Up to this point, no prospective preacher had been invited back a second time to New Park Street, but the deacons urged Charles to preach on the first, third, and fifth Sundays in January 1854. Charles, being so enthusiastically received on January 29, was offered by the decons the challenge to preach for a full six months with a view to becoming their permanent pastor. The members exuded excitement, all in anticipation that he would accept. He did. He cast the die; to London he would go if only on probation.

Susannah's Reaction

It must be confessed that Susannah did not go to the New Park Street Baptist Church from any sense of deep spiritual need that first

Sunday night that Charles preached; she only wanted to please the Olneys. As pointed out, she considered the sermon, and the preacher in particular, far from what she had envisioned in a great preacher of the Gospel. Charles' clothes had the obvious mark of a village tailor. With the great stock of black satin and the blue polka-dot handkerchief, she was almost amused. But later she had to write, "Ah! How little I then thought that my eyes looked on him who was to be my life's beloved; how little I dreamed of the honor God was preparing for me in the near future!"

After Charles accepted the pastorate of New Park Street Chapel, Susannah often met him at the home of Mr. and Mrs. Olney; thus their friendship deepened and grew. Before long, as can be surmised, his preaching and his personal witness aroused her and she realized how indifferent she had become in her spiritual life. She began to recognize how displeasing this must be to the Lord who had saved her. She openly confessed:

> Gradually I became alarmed at my back-sliding state and then, by a great effort, I sought spiritual help and guidance from Mr. William Olney (Father Olney's second son, and my cousin by marriage), who was an active worker in the Sunday School at New Park Street, and a true Mr. Greatheart and comforter of young pilgrims. He may have told the new Pastor about me,—I cannot say;—but one day I was greatly surprised to receive from Mr. Spurgeon an illustrated copy of *The Pilgrim's Progress*, in which he had written the inscription "Miss Thompson, with desires for her progress in the blessed pilgrimage, from C. H. Spurgeon, April 20, 1854."

As Charles' ministry gained momentum, so did Susannah's spiritual development. She began regularly to hear the young man preach. She said, "By a great effort, I sought spiritual help and guidance." Charles' gift to Susannah of a copy of *Pilgrim's Progress* helped her significantly. She in turn gave Charles her first gift—a complete set of the writings of theologian-Reformer John Calvin. That surely pleased him well. At that stage, spiritual concern dominated their interest. Susannah later said, speaking of Charles, "I don't think my beloved had at that time any other thought concerning me than to help a struggling soul heavenward . . . by degrees, though with much trembling, I told him of my state before God; and he gently led me, by his preaching, and by his conversations, through the power of the Holy Spirit to the cross of Christ for the peace and pardon my weary soul was longing for." The relationship rapidly moved into a wider interest.

Love Deepens

The Olneys became the human factor in the developing relationship between Susannah and Charles, by first pointing out Susannah's social and spiritual qualities to Charles. But even Charles could see she that was an attractive, slightly built young lady: "Had she weighed a pound more, she might have been a bit heavy; had she weighed a pound less, some might have thought her too slender." Beautiful, long chestnut curls framed her oval face. Her fingers were slender and tapering, almost symbolic of her Victorian grace. A sweet smile lit up her bright hazel eyes. Early pictures show Susannah to be a lovely young lady. Charles noticed. A more intimate friendship soon developed, and they began to see each other on a social level.

On June 10, 1854, the young couple attended the opening of the gigantic Crystal Palace exhibition building at Sydenham. The Crystal Palace had been moved from its original site in Hyde Park. They sat side by side in the grandstand, chaperoned of course. The Victorians would have expected that. As usual, Charles sat reading a book. How Susannah liked that is unrecorded, but one can imagine. Still, the outing took a most pleasant turn. The volume, surprisingly not one of Charles' usual heavy Puritan works, was Martin Tupper's *Proverbial Philosophy,* a book of poetry on love and marriage. He leaned over to Susannah and had her read one or two lines: "Seek a good wife from thy God, for she is the best gift of His providence. . . . Therefore think of her, and pray for her weal." Charles then looked at her affectionately and asked in a low, soft voice, "Do you pray for him who is to be your husband?" Susannah blushed and dropped her eyes as her heart beat faster—probably Charles' pulse quickened somewhat, too. He asked again softly, "Will you come and walk around the Palace with me?" They slipped away alone to stroll through the palms and flowers and exhibits of the beautiful Crystal Palace. Love began to blossom. Susannah said, "During that walk on that memorable day in June, I believe God Himself united our hearts in indissoluble bonds of true affection, and, though we knew it not, gave us to each other forever."

Charles and Susannah found many occasions to be together. Both purchased season tickets to the Crystal Palace and romantically strolled there often. But the displays were not all idyllic. In the 1850s a British scientist created a large display at the Crystal Palace of how he thought the dinosaurs looked. One wonders how Susannah, a Victorian lass, reacted to that startling sight. Still, the Crystal Palace became the place for their courtship. Susannah said in August, "Loving looks, and tender tones and clasping hands, gave way to verbal confession!" Very Victorian! Two months later, on August 2, 1854, in the garden of her grandfather's house, Charles asked Susannah to be his wife. Her answer was "Yes!" The bride to be wrote of the beautiful moment: "To me, it was a time as *solemn* as it was sweet; and with great awe in my heart I left my beloved, and hastening to the house and to an upper room I knelt before God and praised and thanked Him with happy tears for His great mercy in giving me the love of so good a man."

Susannah wrote again of that day in her diary, "It is impossible to write down all that occurred this morning. I can only adore in silence the wonder of my God, and praise Him for all his benefits."

Charles, as his correspondence with Susannah shows, proved as eloquent in expressing love in letters as expressing the Gospel in preaching. They are charming epistles, as were Susannah's to him. He once wrote her from Pompeii in Italy and said, "I send tons of love to you, hot as fresh lava." The Victorians certainly had a way of putting such things.

Shortly thereafter Susannah applied for church membership at New Park Street. She wrote out her testimony of faith to Charles, and he wrote back: "Oh! I could weep for joy (as I certainly am doing now) to think that my beloved can so well testify to a work of grace in her soul. . . . Whatever befall us, trouble and adversity, sickness or death, we need not fear a final separation, either from each other or our God. . . . I feel so deeply that I could only throw my arms around you and weep." Charles baptized Miss Thompson, his "beloved," on February 1, 1855.

Susannah learned early on that her future husband, as God's servant, put Christ's service first and was quickly becoming a famous man. Their life together would be very different from most nineteenth-century families. Even before they married, Charles would visit Susie, his pet name for Susannah, every Monday and edit his Sunday sermon while she sat there in silence. His sermons were now being published every week. Theirs was a different sort of courtship! But Miss Thompson proved to be a remarkable young lady; she took it all very well. In April 1855, Susie accompanied Charles to Colchester to meet his parents. During the happy holiday, the parents "welcomed and petted" their future daughter-in-law.

Susannah now began to spend much time in the activities of New Park Street Chapel, and not only because of her interest in Charles. She had truly come into a real relationship with Jesus Christ. She learned to love the service of the Lord. The Spirit moved in reviving many, Susannah being no exception. And love deepened in like proportion for the famous young preacher. Susannah quite naturally thrilled at Charles' popularity. Her heart went out to him as he labored in the pulpit, speaking now to very large crowds. Often she wanted to reach out to him. She said:

> Oh, how my heart ached for him! What self-control I had to exercise to appear calm and collected and keep quietly in my seat up in that little side gallery! How I longed to have the right to go and

comfort and cheer him when the service was over! But I had to walk away, as other people did,—I who belonged to him and was closer to his heart than anyone there! It was a severe discipline for a young and loving spirit.

Charles faithfully corresponded with Susie when he traveled away from London. Spurgeon undertook a preaching mission to Scotland in July 1855, his first long journey by train. In loving terms, he wrote to Susie:

I have had daydreams of you while driving along. I thought you were very near me. It is not long, dearest, before I shall again enjoy your sweet society, if the providence of God permits. I knew I loved you very much before, but now I feel how necessary you are to me; and you will not lose much by my absence, if you find me, on my return, more attentive to your feelings, as well as equally affectionate. . . . My darling, accept love of the deepest and purest kind from one who is not prone to exaggerate, but who feels that there is no room for hyperbole.

The courtship progressed happily along for nearly another year. On December 22, 1855, Charles sent Susannah a copy of his first full volume of published sermons, *The Pulpit Library*. He inscribed it saying, "In a few days it will be out of my power to present anything to Miss Thompson. Let this be a remembrance of our happy meetings and sweet conversations." In a few days they married.

The Wedding

Everyone agreed, the wedding was beautiful and was a deep spiritual experience for all. Dr. Alexander Fletcher of Finsbury Chapel solemnized the ceremony on Tuesday, January 8, 1856, at the New Park Street Chapel. The day dawned dark, damp, and cold, but by 8:00 A.M. people started streaming into the chapel. The streets clogged up as happy guests made their way to Park Street. Special police from M-Division had to be sent to control the flow of the crowds. Within half an hour the chapel filled, while the two thousand who had been turned away remained on the street to see the newlyweds depart.

During the joyous service, the attendants sang the hymn "Salvation, O the Joyful Sound." Psalm 100 was read, followed by a short sermon. The couple repeated their vows and the pronouncement was made; Charles and Susannah became husband and wife. As they left the chapel, the crowds outside cheered loudly as the smiling couple drove away in their carriage. On that day, God established one of the happiest homes in Victorian England. As Mrs. Charles Haddon Spurgeon expressed it, "God

Himself united our hearts in indissoluble bonds of true affection and gave us to each other forever." She said she felt "happy beyond words."

The young couple made their way across the English Channel for twelve delightful honeymoon days in Paris, staying in the Hotel Meurue. They visited historic palaces, churches, and museums. Susie spoke French very well, so no language problem hindered them. She coined a term of endearment for her Charles: *Tirshatha*. The term is an ancient Persian word meaning "Your Reverence." She loved Charles deeply and always cherished a spiritual reverence for her preacher husband. Likewise, Susie was always to Charles: "Our angel and delight." He often addressed her as *Wifey*, one of his terms of endearment. Susie and her Tirshatha enjoyed a most happy honeymoon. The short days were soon over, but never forgotten. On the channel crossing back home, she whispered to Charles, "O Tirshatha, often before have I been in Paris, but this time it has been ten times as charming in my eyes, because you were with me." Their romance resembled the traditional Victorian tale of lavender and old lace, reminiscent of the Brownings of Wimpole Street.

When the happy couple returned to London from their honeymoon— the call of duty had to be answered—they enjoyed a public welcome by their church members. They moved into 217 New Kent Road, their first home, and Charles immediately took up his pulpit responsibilities. A few years later they moved into their second home on Nightingale Lane near Clapham Common, southwest of New Park Street Chapel. A year-and-a-half later, on September 20, 1857, their twin boys were born. Both boys became Baptist ministers; Thomas followed in his father's footsteps and became pastor of the Metropolitan Tabernacle at Charles' death.

Home Life for the Spurgeons

Susie missed her husband as he carried on his itinerant ministries, but as a woman of awakening she bore that burden. Still, Spurgeon's constant absences from the home proved a bit of a trial to his young wife. Many times she would sit up late at night waiting for Charles. A thrill of joy always shot through her heart when she heard him coming to the door.

Only once did she really break down when Charles left for a distant preaching engagement. She just could not keep back the tears. Charles said, "Wifey, do you think that when any of the children of Israel brought a lamb to the Lord's altar as an offering to Him, they stood and wept over it when they had seen it laid there?" Susie replied, "Of course not." Charles went on tenderly, "Well, don't you see, you are giving me to God in letting me go to preach the Gospel to poor sinners, and do you think he likes to see you cry over your sacrifice?" Susie commented later, "Could ever a rebuke have been more sweetly given? It sank deep into my heart, carrying comfort; and thence-forward when I part with him, the tears were scarcely ever allowed to show themselves, or if a stray one or two dared to run over the boundaries, he would say, 'What! Crying over your lamb, Wifey!' And this reminder would quickly dry them up and put a smile in their place."

Finances proved a problem at times for the couple. Their own generosity to meet other's needs at times exceeded their resources. Once funds were needed to pay some taxes and they had no money. With great faith they prayed, and at the right moment an anonymous letter arrived containing £20. God honored their faith and their needs were met.

Susannah tells of an interesting event that occurred later in their life. Spurgeon did much of his sermon preparation for Sunday morning on Saturday evening. One particular Saturday night he just could not seemingly put his text and his thoughts together. He read the commentaries, but things simply did not come together. And he had to stand before thousands in a few hours. It was a real dilemma!

He sat up very late and was utterly worn out and dispirited, for all his efforts to get at the heart of the text were unavailing. I advised him to retire to rest and soothed him by suggesting that if he would try to sleep then he would probably in the morning feel quite refreshed and be able to study to better purpose. "If I go to sleep now, Wifey, will you wake me very early so that I may have plenty of time to prepare?" With my loving assurance that I would watch the time for him and call him soon enough he was satisfied; and like a trusting, tired child, he laid his head upon the pillow and slept silently and sweetly at once.

By-and-by a wonderful thing happened. During the first opening hours of the Sabbath, I heard him talking in his sleep, and aroused myself to listen attentively. Soon I realized that he was going over the subject of the verse which had been so obscure to him, and was giving a clear and distinct exposition of its meaning with much force and freshness. I set myself with almost trembling joy to understand and follow all that he was saying, for I knew that if I could but seize and remember the salient points of the discourse he would have no difficulty in developing and enlarging upon them. Never a preacher had a more eager and anxious hearer! But what if I should let the precious word slip? I had no means at hand of "taking notes"; so, like Nehemiah, "I prayed to the God of heaven," and asked that I might receive and retain the thoughts which he had given to his servant in his sleep, and which were so singularly entrusted into my keeping. As I lay repeating over and over again the chief points I wished to remember, my happiness was very great in an anticipation of his surprise and delight on awakening; but I had kept vigil so long, cherishing my joy, that I must have been overcome with slumber just when the usual time for rising came, for he awoke with a frightened start, and seeing the telltale clock, said, "Oh, Wifey, you said you would wake me very early, and now see the time! Oh, why did you let me sleep? What shall I do? What shall I do?" "Listen, beloved," I answered; and I told him all I had heard. "Why! That's just what I wanted," he exclaimed; "that is the true explanation of the whole verse! And you say I preached it in my sleep?" "It is wonderful," he repeated again and again, and we both praised the Lord for so remarkable a manifestation of His power and love.

Many such happy anecdotes are recorded in the marriage of Charles and Susie. She did stand beside him, even in his preaching.

The Spurgeons' second home on Nightingale Lane in Clapham was a very modest home. They demolished it in 1869 to make way for a larger home on the same spot, which can still be seen today. The contented couple named both their Nightingale Lane houses "Helensburgh House."

The happy couple delighted in their Helensburgh House. Mrs. Spurgeon described its beautiful garden and yard:

Oh, what a delightsome place we thought it, though it was a very wilderness through long neglect,—the blackberry bushes impertinently asserting themselves to be trees, and the fruit trees running wild for want of the pruning knife! It was all the more interesting to us in this sweet confusion and artlessness because we had the happy task of bringing it gradually into accord with our ideas of what a garden should be. I must admit that we made many absurd mistakes both in house and garden management, in those young days of ours; but what did that matter? No two birds ever felt more exquisite joy in building their nest in the fork of a tree-branch, than did we in planning and placing, altering and rearranging our pretty country home.[4]

The couple loved animals, as do most Britishers. Charles had a huge cat named "Dick" that weighed twenty-one pounds. Their faithful dog they called "Punch." Later, the Spurgeons moved to a lovely, large home in Norwood, South London. They named it "Westwood." The beautiful structure is demolished now, but the street on which it sat is called Spurgeon Street.

The Spurgeons had some fascinating guests in their home, whose visits constitute intriguing stories in themselves. John Ruskin, the famous author, visited them. In those days, Ruskin often worshiped at the Surrey Gardens Music Hall where Spurgeon preached, and Ruskin had become a very close friend of the great preacher. The sum of it is, the delightfully happy family maintained a happy, open home.

At times serious difficulties arose for our woman of awakening. Still, she served as a stabilizing force to Charles when difficult days did come. She always stood strong at his side. One case in point was the so-called Surrey Music Hall tragedy.

The Music Hall Tragedy

The crowds attending the New Park Street facility became overwhelming. Consequently, the church set out to construct the great Metropolitan Tabernacle that would seat up to six thousand. While the large tabernacle was under construction, Charles preached in the ten-thousand-seat Surrey Garden Music Hall. Revival rested upon the listeners, and multitudes flocked to hear the word every Sunday afternoon. Just prior to the opening day of the Music Hall Ministry, Spurgeon had a strange, subtle uneasiness. He said, "I felt over-weighted with a sense of responsibility, and filled with a mysterious premonition of some great trial shortly to befall me."[5] When the first Sunday-afternoon service came, the streets near the Surrey Gardens Music Hall soon filled with people. Ten to twelve thousand eager worshipers squeezed into the hall when the doors opened at 6:00 P.M. Another ten thousand milled about outside unable to get in. The entire area looked like a surging sea of faces. When Spurgeon arrived, the sight of the mass of humanity at first unnerved him. The largest crowd ever gathered under a roof to hear a nonconformist preacher had assembled. Spurgeon took the pulpit ten minutes before the stated hour, composed himself, and began the service.

After a few words of greeting came a prayer and a hymn. Then, in his usual style, Spurgeon read the Scriptures with a running commentary. He always did this in his New Park Street services—a common procedure in many nonconformist churches. The congregation sang another hymn and Spurgeon began his long prayer. After the "Amen" it happened. "Fire! Fire! Fire! The galleries are giving way! The place is falling! The place is falling!" came shouts from several areas in the vast crowd. Pandemonium broke loose. A terrible panic ensued as people fled from all over the building. They trod upon each other, crushed one another, jumped over the rail of the galleries. The banisters of one of the stairs gave way and many were trampled over. An eye-witness described the mad scene:

> The cries and shrieks at this period were truly terrific, to which was added the already pent-up excitement of those who had not

been able to make their exit. They pressed on, treading furiously over the dead and dying, tearing frantically at each other. Hundreds had their clothes torn from their backs in their endeavors to escape; masses of men and women were driven down and trodden over heedless of their cries and lamentations.[6]

As people in panic exploded from the hall, the thousands outside struggled to get in. A wild scene erupted.

Spurgeon sprang to his feet attempting to quell the crowds. There was no fire, no collapsing galleries, or any real problem at all. "Please be seated," he cried. "There is no cause for alarm! Please be seated!" His resonant voice boomed over the din and almost miraculously the people composed themselves and began to settle down as they sang a hymn. Pickpockets had started the uproar. There was no fire at all. Spurgeon wanted to dismiss the service immediately, even though he did not know that a real tragedy had occurred. The remaining people shouted, "Preach! Preach!" Charles attempted to do so; he did not realize anyone had been seriously injured in the pandemonium. Then a second series of cries went up. This time order was restored quickly and Charles took his text from Proverbs 3:33, "The curse of the LORD is in the house of the wicked: but he blesseth the habitation of the just" (KJV). He probably thought the new text would help the general situation and speak directly to it. But it proved to be a blunder, for now some panicked anew at the thought of judgment and joined the mob at the rear still fighting to get out, or in. He spoke a few words, the hymn "His Sovereign Power without Our Aid" was sung, and he dismissed the crowd. There were shouts until the service concluded. Charles said to the crowd, "My brain is in a whirl, and I scarcely know where I am, so great are my apprehensions that many persons must have been injured by reaching out. I would rather that you retired gradually and may God Almighty dismiss you with His blessings and carry you in safety to your home!" Sensing now that something serious must have happened, although he knew nothing of the extent of the tragedy, Charles was hurried out by friends almost in a faint.

Something truly terrible had happened. Seven people were dead and twenty-eight seriously injured, and had been taken to a local hospital. With care, friends led Charles out through a back passage so he would not see the seven corpses laid out on the ground. He did not realize anyone had died. Retiring to a friend's house in Croydon, South London, friends hoped he might escape the volcanic furor bound to erupt over him. The papers—what would they say? Later, the grisly facts were revealed to Charles and upon hearing the devastating news, he virtually collapsed. It looked like a permanent collapse. Emotionally prostrated, he pined away in deep depression.

The next day, a man saw Spurgeon being helped from a carriage at Croydon and said, "It's Mr. Spurgeon, isn't it? It must be his ghost, for last night I saw him carried out dead from The Surrey Gardens Music Hall."[7] Rumors of that nature spread all over London. The news media was cruel and critical.

Charles became so seriously depressed over the tragedy that he almost wished himself dead. The thought that he had in some sense occasioned the death and injury of several people absolutely devastated him. In Spurgeon's first book, *The Saint and His Savior*, he described his agony:

> Strong amid danger, I battled against the storm; . . . I refused to be comforted; tears were my meat by day, and dreams my terror by night. I felt as I had never felt before. "My thoughts were all a case of knives," cutting my heart in pieces, until a kind of stupor of grief ministered a mournful medicine to me. I could have truly said, "I am not mad, but surely I have had enough to madden me, if I should indulge in meditation on it." I sought and found a solitude which seemed congenial to me. I could tell my griefs to the flowers, and the dew could weep with me. Here my mind lay, like a wreck upon the sand, incapable of its usual motion. I was in a strange land, and a stranger in it. My Bible, once my daily food, was but a hand to lift the sluices of my woe. Prayer yielded no balm to me; in fact, my soul was like an infant's soul, and I could not rise to the dignity of supplication. "Broke in pieces all asunder," my thoughts which had been to me a cup of delights, were like pieces of broken glass, the piercing and cutting miseries of my pilgrimage. . . . There came the "slander of many"— bare faced fabrications, libelous slanders, and barbarous accusations. These alone might have scooped out the last drop of consolation from my cup of happiness, but the worst had come to the worst, and the utmost knowledge of the enemy could do no more.[8]

Yet, he was alive; but what the tragedy itself did not do to prostrate him emotionally, as he himself said, the press finished. The newspapers went after him unmercifully. And his new twin boys were only one month old.

Susie stood beside Charles and became of tremendous strength. She deeply empathized and stayed in fervent prayer, supporting her distraught husband. After an agonizing period the mist cleared; the sunshine of God's grace shown into the very depth of Charles' heart and mind. He saw, perhaps as never before, that it mattered not what happened to Charles Haddon Spurgeon—and even to his wife, Susie—as long as Jesus Christ was exalted. Thus, with only an interval of one Sunday out of his pulpit, Charles went back to preaching at the Surrey Hall, and the anointing rested on the Spurgeons once again.

Despite the Surrey Garden tragedy, very positive experiences gathered about Susannah's husband's preaching ministry. And what a help she was! As pointed out earlier, Spurgeon prepared his Sunday morning sermon on Saturday night and his Sunday night sermon on Sunday afternoon. He was such a genius in sermonizing, that this was all the preparation he needed, though he studied broadly all through the week. After Charles settled on his text, Susie would read to him the commentaries on the verses. Then the eloquence flowed. It all proved most remarkable.

The Press Attacks

The newspapers were merciless in their criticism of Charles. The traditional, rather stilted British press simply could not bring themselves to acknowledge the great things that were happening in the ministry of Charles and Susannah—they were so young and "inexperienced." The fact that God was bringing revival to the Spurgeons' ministry seemed to pass by the reporters without their recognition. They attacked continually for many years. But then, that often happens when true revival occurs. One cannot expect the world to understand, let alone appreciate a deep work of the Holy Spirit.

The press's attacks caused consternation on the part of the faithful gospel preacher, but Susannah, once again in her faithful support of her beloved husband, struck upon a great idea. She had printed on a large placard the beautiful promise of our Lord recorded in Matthew 5:11–12: "Blessed are ye when men shall revile you and persecute you and shall say all manner of evil against you falsely for My sake. Rejoice and be exceeding glad; for great is your reward in heaven; for so persecuted they the prophets which were before you" (KJV). She had it produced in Old English type and framed with a pretty oxford frame. She hung it on their bedroom wall. It proved a great comfort to Charles when every morning he could wake up to see God's great promise. So they travailed in patience through the early years of criticism and defamation. Finally, it became evident to virtually all that the young Spurgeon's ministry was greatly honored by God, so the newspapers backed off and actually began to praise the young couple. At that juncture the Prayer Revival of 1860 burst over the land. The new Metropolitan Tabernacle was almost ready to be occupied. New Park Street had grown from the eighty who had attended when Charles preached his first sermon to thousands who were coming every Sunday to hear him, the precursors of the great Prayer Revival. Now the whole country enjoyed the fruits of the Great Awakening.

Spurgeon was God's chosen man for that crucial moment in history—

and by his side was Susie. A new pilgrim whose name was Hopeful had arrived on the scene in Southwark, London, and the progress was phenomenal. The hoped-for awakening had come. The spiritual atmosphere of London crackled with excitement as hundreds of thousands thronged to hear the man of God.

Susannah took a very active part in every aspect of Charles' work at New Park Street Chapel and afterward at the Metropolitan Tabernacle. Dr. Campbell, one of the leading evangelical ministers of England, described a baptismal service at the Spurgeons' church:

> There was the young orator, the idol of the assembly, in the water with a countenance radiant as the light, and there, on the pathway, was Mrs. Spurgeon, a most prepossessing young lady—the admiration of all who beheld her—with courtly dignity and inimitable modesty, kindly leading forward the trembling sisters in succession to her husband, who gently and gracefully took and immersed them with varied remark and honied phrase, all kind, pertinent to the occasion, and greatly fitted to strengthen, encourage and cheer.[9]

That about says it all. Susie indeed had become a woman of awakening.

Susannah's Illness

Then, just as everything seemed to be so bright with a new day dawning, unfortunately, Susannah's health began to deteriorate quite extensively. Her poor health did not allow her to do all that she longed to do. Still she was always a very gracious hostess when people would come to visit; always supporting Charles in every aspect as ably as possible. Charles himself, far from well many times, suffered from the inherited malady, rheumatic gout. Still, in her own weakened condition, Susie stood by his side. She said:

> I deemed it my joy and privilege to be ever at his side, accompanying him on many of his preaching journeys, nursing him in his occasional illnesses, his delighted companion during his holiday trips, always watching over and attending him with the enthusiasm and sympathy which my great love for him inspired. I mention this, not to suggest any sort of merit on my part, but simply that I may here record my heartfelt gratitude to God that, for a period of ten blessed years, I was permitted to encircle him with all the comforting care and tender affection which it was in a wife's power to bestow. Afterwards God ordered it otherwise. He saw fit to reverse our position to each other; and

for a long season, suffering instead of service became my daily portion, and the care of comforting a sick wife fell upon my beloved.[10]

Charles Spurgeon fully understood all the implications of their labors and illnesses. Of her health Susannah said, "For many years I was a prisoner in a sick-chamber, and my beloved had to leave me when the strain of his many labors and responsibilities compelled him to seek rest far away from home. These separations were very painful to hearts so tenderly united as were ours, but we each bore our share of the sorrow as heroically as we could and softened it as far as possible by constant correspondence."[11]

Charles' health declined over the years also. At times he would have to retreat for convalescence to the south of France, escaping London's horrid climate. Susannah would be left as a semi-invalid back in London. What a wrench for the young couple, but still the work flourished. In the midst of illness, labors, opposition, separation, and everything the world and Satan could throw across their paths to thwart the reviving work, the progress of the kingdom of God through the ministry of Charles and Susannah grew.

When the Spurgeon's new home, described earlier, was being built, Mrs. Spurgeon was convalescing in Brighton on England's south coast, unable to do anything concerning the supervision of the building or even the decorating. She had undergone surgery under a skillful physician, Sir James Y. Simpson of Edinburgh. It helped her somewhat, but still she found it impossible to take upon herself the duty of refurbishing and preparing the new house. Right there Charles stepped in and did a lovely thing for his wife. Spurgeon wrote to his beloved Susie describing what he had done:

> My Own Dear Sufferer,—I am pained indeed to learn from T's kind note that you are still in so sad a condition. Oh, may the ever merciful God be pleased to give you ease!
>
> I have been quite a long round today,—if a "round" can be "long." First to Finsbury to buy the wardrobe,—a beauty. I hope you will live long to hang your garments in it, every thread of them precious to me for your dear sake. Next to Hewlett's for a chandelier for the dining-room. Found one quite to my taste and yours. Then to Negretti and Zambra's to buy a barometer for my own very fancy, for I have long promised to treat myself to one. On the road I obtained the Presburg biscuits, and within their box I send this note, hoping it may reach you the more quickly. They are sweetened with my love and prayers.

The bedroom will look well with the wardrobe in it; at least, so I hope. It is well made, and, I believe, as nearly as I could tell, precisely all you wished for. Joe [Mr. Joseph Passmore had given this as a present] is very good, and should have a wee note whenever darling feels she could write it without too much fatigue; but not yet. I bought also a table for you in case you should have to keep your bed. It rises or falls by a screw, and also winds sideways, so as to go over the bed, and then it has a flap for a book or paper, so that my dear one may read or write in comfort while lying down. I could not resist the pleasure of making this little gift to my poor suffering wifey, only hoping it might not often be in requisition, but might be a help when there was a needs-be for it. Remember, all I buy, I pay for. I have paid for everything as yet with the earnings of my pen, graciously sent me in time of need. It is my ambition to leave nothing for you to be anxious about. I shall find the money for the curtains, etc., and you will amuse yourself by giving orders for them after your own delightful taste.

I must not write more; and, indeed, matter runs short except the old, old story of a love which grieves over you and would fain work a miracle and raise you up to perfect health. I fear the heat afflicts you. Well did the elder say to John in Patmos concerning those who are before the throne of God, "Neither shall the sun light on them nor any heat."—Yours to love in life and death, and eternally, C.H.S.[12]

Charles Spurgeon was a loving, helpful husband to his dear wife.

In the midst of all of their difficulties, God one day did a very beautiful thing for Charles' and Susie's encouragement. Charles asked his beloved on an occasion if there was anything that she would like him to get for her. In a half-joking way, she said, "I should like an opal ring and a piping bullfinch!" Charles replied, "Ah, you know I cannot get those for you!" For several days thereafter they laughed about the event. Then Mrs. Spurgeon relates a thrilling sequel to the story:

One Thursday evening, on his return from the Tabernacle, he [the preacher] came into my room with such a beaming face and such love-lighted eyes, that I knew something had delighted him very much. In his hand he held a tiny box, and I am sure his pleasure exceeded mine as he took from it a beautiful little ring and placed it on my finger. "There is your opal ring, my darling," he said, and then he told me of the strange way in which it had come. An old lady, whom he had once seen when she was ill, sent a note to the Tabernacle to say she desired to give Mrs. Spurgeon a small present, and could someone be sent to her to receive it. Mr. Spurgeon's private secretary went accordingly and brought the little parcel, which, when opened, was found to contain this opal ring. How we talked of the Lord's tender love for His stricken child and of His condescension in thus stooping to supply an unnecessary gratification to His dear servant's sick one, I must leave my readers to imagine; but I can remember feeling that the Lord was very near to us.

Not long after that I was moved to Brighton, there to pass a crisis in my life, the result of which would be a restoration to better health, or death. One evening, when my dear husband came from London, he brought a large package with him, and, uncovering it, disclosed a cage containing a lovely piping bullfinch! My astonishment was great, my joy unbounded, and these emotions were intensified as he related the way in which he became possessed of the coveted treasure. He had been to see a dear friend of ours, whose husband was sick unto death, and after commending the sufferer to God in prayer, Mrs. T said to him, "I want you to take my pet bird to Mrs. Spurgeon; I would give him to none but her; his songs are too much for my poor husband in his weak state, and I know that Bully will interest and amuse Mrs. Spurgeon in her loneliness while you are so much away from her." Mr. Spurgeon then told her of my desire for such a companion, and together they rejoiced over the care of the loving Heavenly Father, who had so wondrously provided the very gift His child had longed for. With that cage beside him the journey to Brighton was a very short one, and when Bully piped his pretty song and took a hemp seed as a reward from the lips of his new mistress, there were eyes with joyful tears in them and hearts overflowing with praise to God in the little room by the sea that night, and the dear Pastor's comment was, "I think you are one of your Heavenly Father's spoiled children, and He just gives you whatever you ask for."[13]

"Does anyone doubt that this bird was a direct love-gift from the pitiful Father?" asks Mrs. Spurgeon. "Do I hear someone say, 'Oh! it was all "chance" that brought about such coincidences as these'?" Ah, dear friends, those of you who have been similarly indulged by Him know of a certainty that it is not so. He who cares for all the works of His hand cares with infinite tenderness for the children of His love and thinks nothing which concerns them too small or too trivial to notice. If our faith were stronger and our love more perfect, we should see far greater marvels than these in our daily lives.

The Children

One of the great thrills in the midst of the revival centered in the conversion of the twin boys. Although Susannah was weak and ailing and largely confined to her bedroom, she faithfully ministered to her boys. Her son, Thomas, as pointed out, became Charles' successor at the Metropolitan Tabernacle. He said,

> I trace my early conversion directly to her [Susannah] earnest pleading and bright example. She denied herself the pleasure of attending Sunday evening services that she might minister the Word of Life to her household. . . . My dear brother [Charles Jr.], was brought to Christ through the pointed word of a missionary; but he, too, gladly owns that mother's influence and teaching had their part in the matter. By these, the soil was made ready for a later sowing."[14]

It reminds one of another woman of awakening, Susannah Wesley—John and Charles' mother.

On September 21, 1874, the sons were baptized by their father into the fellowship of the Metropolitan Tabernacle. As mentioned previously, they both became great ministers of the Gospel of Christ. Charles Jr. served as pastor of a great Baptist church in Greenwich while Thomas ministered in New Zealand and later at the Tabernacle in London.

At this stage God began to do a new and fresh thing through this woman of awakening.

The Book Fund

For long periods Susie would have to sit in an easy chair, hoping that the day might come when she could again engage in some activities of the church, or at least care for the domestic duties of the home. However, as the years came and went, she remained confined at home. She longed to be of more use in the Lord's service and to be of help in the many labors of her husband. Fervently praying for some opportunity to serve Christ, the Lord directed her to establish what became a very central and important aspect of the Metropolitan Tabernacle ministry: the Book Fund.

The Book Fund had a providential beginning, as did most of the Tabernacle's benevolent enterprises. In the summer of 1875, Spurgeon completed his first volume of *Lectures to my Students*: a book of lectures on the Christian ministry. He handed a proof copy to his wife and asked her what she thought of the book. After reading it carefully, Mrs. Spurgeon declared that she wished she could place a copy in the hands of every minister in England. Quite casually Spurgeon said, "Then why not do so?" Without a moment's hesitation she replied, "How much will you give?" It sparked an idea, and she prayed much about it to see if God might lead in the matter. Suddenly it dawned on her that the money that was needed to launch such a project was already at hand. Susannah had a little habit of putting away in a drawer every crown piece that came into her hands. She counted enough money for 100 copies of the *Lectures.* "In that moment," she tells us, "though I knew it not, the Book Fund was inaugurated."[15]

In July 1875, Spurgeon published a note in *The Sword and the Trowel* (his monthly Christian periodical) stating that a copy of the recently issued *Lectures to My Students* would be sent free to a hundred Baptist ministers. The demand grew so great that Mrs. Spurgeon felt obligated to send out an additional 100 copies. But they had no funds. So, in the next edition of *The Sword and the Trowel,* Charles set forth the need, and asked if something could be done to provide poor ministers with much-needed books for their study and preparation of sermons. Spurgeon said that, "Some of the applicants had not been able to buy a new book for the last ten years." Immediately contributions began to roll in, the first being a gift of five shillings in stamps sent anonymously. Within two months, Mrs. Spurgeon was sending out parcels of books, not only the *Lectures* but other more extensive theological and biblical works. After that initial beginning, Mrs. Spurgeon said she never needed to ask for a shilling. The entire undertaking was quite simple. She secured gifts of books and money from Christian donors with which she then would supply the scant libraries of poor preachers.

Those grants of books extended not only to Baptist ministers but to pastors of all denominations. Moreover, Susannah distributed books other than those authored by her husband; although as could be expected, a large portion came from his pen. A myriad of letters began to flood in from the poor ministers who had benefited from the Book Fund. The letters revealed the poverty of the pastors of the smaller congregations. Spurgeon little dreamed of the dire circumstances in many pastors' homes. Even in the Church of England, particularly among the curates, the need was great. They all benefited tremendously from the Book Fund. Spurgeon called the fund "a fountain in the desert."

The expenditures for the Book Fund reached approximately twelve hundred pounds per year. At the end of Spurgeon's life, close to 150,000 volumes had been distributed among pastors. The work received wide acclaim.

Articles about the Book Fund ministry constantly appeared. For example, the *National Baptist,* March 1, 1883, wrote, "Again, Mrs. Spurgeon has made the Christian world her debtor." Even one or two poems were written about the work. Much in the spirit of Bunyan's *Pilgrim's Progress,* and, of course, her husband, she wrote in her last book:

I can see two pilgrims treading this highway of life together, hand in hand,—heart linked to heart. True, they have had rivers to ford, and mountains to cross and fierce enemies to fight, and many dangers to go through; but their Guide was watchful, their Deliverer unfailing, and of them it might truly be said, "In all their affliction He was afflicted, and the Angel of His preserve saved them; in His love and in His pity He redeemed them; and He bare them, and carried them all the days of old.". . . But, at last, they came to a place on the road where two ways met; and here, amidst the terms of a storm such as they had never before encountered, they parted company,—the one being caught up to the invisible glory,—the other, battered, and bruised by the awful tempest, henceforth toiling along the road,—alone. But the "goodness and mercy" which, for so many years, had followed the two travelers, did not leave the solitary one; rather did the tenderness of the Lord, "lead on softly," and those green pastures for the tired feet, and still waters for the solace and refreshment of His trembling child.[16]

Spurgeon's personal library consisted of up to thirty thousand volumes. When William Jewell College of Liberty, Missouri, acquired Spurgeon's personal books at the turn of the twentieth century, only five to six thousand volumes remained. Although it cannot be verified, it can probably be assumed that after the death of the pastor, his widow sent many of his own books to poor pastors through the agency of the Book Fund. Moreover, Spurgeon himself gave away some five thousand volumes to students of the Pastor's College. The ministry tremendously aided in the spread of effective preaching of the Gospel throughout Britain.

The Book Fund work seemed to help restore Susannah's health. At any rate, she became well enough in 1882 to become president of the Tabernacle Auxiliary for Zenana Mission Work. Spurgeon said: "I gratefully adore the goodness of our heavenly Father in directing my beloved wife to a work which has been to her fruitful in unutterable happiness. That it has cost her more pain than it would be fitting to reveal is most true; but that it has brought her a boundless joy is equally certain."[17]

The Book Fund was clearly a most noble work. It actually precipitated Susannah's writing a book under the title *Ten Years of My Life in the Ministry of the Book Fund*. Later she wrote *Ten Years After*. The Book Fund grew through the years. She had been well-trained in the school of faith, and this enabled her not only to carry on in the midst of her illness, but to trust God for the funding of this most important work. Only eternity will be able to tell of the blessing and the spread of the revival that grew out of this sacrificial and noble work.

The Expanding Work and Serious Illness

The work that Mrs. Spurgeon had undertaken in the Book Fund began to ramify into other areas of need. In 1877, a friend gave her a sum of money that she could draw on for the relief of poor ministers in their financial problems. Others contributed to the fund and soon the Pastors' Aid Fund was founded. This too became an exceedingly helpful work. Ministers were so lowly paid that they scarcely could put food on the table. The graciousness and generosity of the Spurgeons and others who stepped in helped many a needy ministerial family. The fund distributed many pounds annually.

Much to her husband's concern, Mrs. Spurgeon's malady developed into a very acute illness. The serious prognosis forced her son Thomas, who served a church in Australia, to come home at once. The family despaired of her life. But Susannah, with faith as strong as ever, knew her Lord was all powerful. She placed her life and all her work into the hands of her gracious Lord; God brought her through. She wrote insightfully about this time of crisis:

> At the close of a very dark and gloomy day I lay resting on my couch as the deeper night drew on, and though all was bright within my cozy little room, some of the external darkness seemed to have entered into my soul and obscured its spiritual vision. Vainly I tried to see the hand which I knew held mine and guided my fog-enveloped feet along a steep and slippery path of suffering. In sorrow of heart I asked, "Why does my Lord thus deal with His child? Why does he so often send sharp and bitter pain to visit me? Why does he permit lingering weakness to hinder the sweet service I long to render to His poor servants?" These fretful questions were quickly answered, and though in a strange language, no interpreter was needed save the conscious whisper of my own heart.
>
> For a while silence reigned in the little room, broken only by the crackling of an oak log burning on the hearth. Suddenly I heard a sweet, soft sound, a little, clear, musical note, like the tender trill of a robin beneath my window. "What can it be?" I said to my companion, who was dozing in the firelight; "surely no bird can be singing out there at this time of the year and night!" We listened, and again heard the faint plaintive notes, so sweet, so melodious, yet mysterious enough to provoke for a moment our undisguised wonder. Presently my friend exclaimed, "It comes from the log on the fire!" and we soon ascertained that her surprised assertion was correct. The fire was letting loose the imprisoned music from the old oak's inmost heart. Perchance he

had garnered up this song in the days when all went well with him, when birds twittered merrily on his branches, and the soft sunlight flecked his tender leaves with gold; but he had grown old since then and hardened; ring after ring of knotty growth had sealed up the long-forgotten melody until the fierce tongues of the flames came to consume his callousness and the vehement heat of the fire wrung from him at once a song and a sacrifice.

Oh! thought I, when the fire of affliction draws songs of praise from us, then indeed are we purified and our God is glorified! Perhaps some of us are like this old oak log—cold, hard and insensible; we should give forth no melodious sounds were it not for the fire which kindles round us, and releases tender notes of trust in Him, and cheerful compliance with His will. As I mused the fire burned and my soul found sweet comfort in the parable so strangely set forth before me. Singing in the fire! Yes, God helping us if that is the only way to get harmony out of these hard, apathetic hearts, let the furnace be heated seven times hotter than before.[18]

After Susie's comparative recovery from her crisis situation, Charles fell quite ill again in 1879. His rheumatic gout began to claim more of his strength and energy. He traveled to the south of France again to recuperate away from London's cold winters. God was faithful to Susie back home, and Charles regained strength year after year to carry on the revival ministry that he and Susannah were still enjoying at the Metropolitan Tabernacle.

The Book Fund continued to develop through those trying years. Charles wrote, thanking the heavenly Father, "By this means He called her away from her personal griefs, gave tone and concentration to her life, led her to continual dealings with Himself, and raised her nearer the center of that region where other than earthly joys and sorrows reign supreme."[19]

Other Works

Such delight did Susannah find in her ministry that she founded other works as well as the Book Fund and the Poor Pastor's Fund. She established the Westwood Clothing Society. This organization distributed clothing to needy people. She was responsible for the development of the Home Distribution of Sermons Ministry, which soon materialized into the circulation of sermons abroad. She also developed the Auxiliary Book Fund, which furthered the ministry as well. It seems incredible that a woman so plagued with physical limitations could have been used so significantly and profoundly of the Holy Spirit. But that is a result of real revival when it grips a heart and anoints a ministry.

In the midst of all these labors, it soon became evident to Susie, as her husband's illness deepened, that the end was not too far away for him, and perhaps not even for herself.

Serious Illness Again for Charles

In the winter of 1891–92, Spurgeon fell seriously ill and was just barely able to travel down to Mentone, the small resort town on the south coast of France, for recuperation where he so often had retreated. There he labored under his serious illness, the rheumatic gout that had in turn precipitated Bright's disease, the irreversible deterioration of his kidneys. By God's grace, Susie was able to travel with him—her first trip to the south of France. After several trying days, Charles seemed to improve somewhat. They were all elated.

There did appear to be some reason for the optimism; Charles began ministering to those who would gather in the Beau Revage Hotel where he and Susie and some friends stayed. On New Year's Eve of 1891, and on the New Year's Day morning of 1892, he spoke to the people, sharing the great truths of God's promises from the Bible. Susannah played the piano for the short services. The title of Charles' message was "Breaking the Long Silence." He also sent a letter and a contribution to Archibald Brown of the East London Tabernacle on the celebration of twenty-five years of ministry, saying, "You have long been dear to me, but in protest against deadly error, we have become more than ever one." On Sunday evenings, January 10 and 17, he conducted brief services in his room, reading some of his own writings. On the seventeenth they all sang the hymn, "The Sands of Time Are Sinking, the Dawn of Heaven Breaks." Little did they know how true that would prove to be. That short service became the end of all worship services for Charles on earth. January 15 had been Mrs. Spurgeon's birthday, and the same day the duke of Clarence died.

Spurgeon continued to be hopeful that in a short time he could return to his beloved people and pick up his London ministry. On January 10 he wrote home: "The steady and solid progress which had begun is continued and will continue." But that became the last written communication by his own hand to the Metropolitan Tabernacle. It was read before the people on Sunday, January 24. It continued, "The sun shines at length, and now I hope to get on." That bright, hopeful message encouraged the people. Then suddenly and unexpectedly a telegram came telling of a serious relapse. On January 25, the *Daily News* published the telegram from Mentone: "Pastor been very ill; cannot write; kept his bed three days. . . . Pray earnestly." All the papers began a diligent watch on Charles' condition. The *Times* recorded on January 28, "Mr. Spurgeon's condition still continues critical." That same day a telegram came from Mentone stating that Spurgeon had had an attack of gout in the head and hands, and was confined to his bed. Charles himself had been able to declare on January 22, "Whether I live or die, I would say, in the words of Israel to Joseph 'God shall be with you.'" That was recorded in *The Ross-Shue Journal*. Then on the twenty-ninth the *Daily News* reported: "The critical condition of Mr. Spurgeon is again awakening anxious feelings." At 3:43 P.M. on the thrity-first a telegram was sent, saying, "There is no hope." Yet, people held on to hope.

The Approaching End

Charles himself, however, seemed to realize that God was drawing the curtain on his work. He had once said in a sermon,

In a little while, there will be a concourse of persons in the streets.
Methinks I hear some one enquiring:—
What are all these people waiting for?
Do you not know? He is to be buried to-day.
And who is that?
It is Spurgeon.
What! the man that preached at the Tabernacle?
Yes; he is to be buried to-day.
That will happen very soon. And when you see my coffin carried to the silent grave, I should like every one of you, whether converted or not, to be constrained to say, 'He did earnestly urge us, in plain and simple language, not to put off the consideration of eternal things; he did entreat us to look to Christ. Now he is gone, our blood is not at his door if we perish.'[20]

It was coming to pass; the great drama had reached its finale.

Near the end, Charles said to his Susie, "Oh Wifey, I have had such a blessed time with my Lord." As he sensed earth receding and heaven opening, he said in hushed tones, "My work is done." The last verse of Scripture he was heard to recite was from Paul: "I have fought a good fight, I have finished my course, I have kept the faith" (2 Tim. 4:7 KJV). He seemed to recognize Susannah once or twice, but shortly after that he slipped quietly into sleep and became totally unconscious. Beloved Susie and dear friends sat about his bedside praying, weeping, hoping.

Bulletins started being received in London through Reuter's News, all signed by Dr. Fitzhenry, the physician in Mentone. They read:

Mentone January 31 11 A.M.
Rev. C. H. S. has had another restless night, and his condition this morning gives cause for the greatest anxiety . . .

3:30 P.M.
The Rev. C. H. Spurgeon is now insensible, and much weaker than he was this morning.
6:30 P.M.
Mr. Spurgeon's condition this evening is extremely critical. . . .
10:00 P.M.
Mr. Spurgeon is sinking fast, and all hope of his recovery has been abandoned. He is quite unconscious and suffers no pain.

Charles remained unconscious, breathing heavier and heavier. Friends shed a few tears. The hour had come. Then, at five minutes past eleven on the Sabbath night, January 31, 1892, in the words of *Pilgrim's Progress,*

After this it was noised abroad that Mr. Valiant-for-truth was taken with a summons by the same post as the other, and had this for a token that the summons was true, that his pitcher was broken at the fountain. When he understood it, he called for his friends, and told them of it. Then said he—I am going to my Father's; and though with great difficulty I have go hither, yet now I do not repent me of all the trouble I have been at to arrive where I am. My sword I give to him that shall succeed me in my pilgrimage, and my courage and skill to him that can get it. My marks and scars I carry with me, to be a witness for me that I have fought His battles, who will be my rewarder. When the day that he must go hence was come, many accompanied him to the river-side; into which as he went, he said—"Death where is thy sting?" and he said—"Grave where is thy victory?" So he passed over, and all the trumpets sounded for him on the other side."[21]

The Pilgrim had arrived home.
The five who were standing by his bedside, who "accompanied him to the riverside," were Susannah; Miss Thorne; Mr. Harrald, his secretary; Mr. Allison, a deacon at the Metropolitan Tabernacle; and Mr. Samuel. When Charles passed over, Mr. Harrald offered prayer and Mrs. Spurgeon "thanked the Lord for the previous treasure so long left to her, and sought, at the throne of grace, strength and guidance for all the future."[22] She praised God for the "unspeakable joy" she had had with her beloved. She must have found comfort in Charles' words when he said, "How blessed not to be afraid to die." Susannah sent a short telegram to Thomas in Australia. It simply stated, "Father in Heaven, Mother resigned." Mr. Harrald wired a telegram to the Metropolitan Tabernacle. It read: "Mentone 11:50—Spurgeon's Tab. London—Our beloved pastor entered Heaven 11:05 Sunday night—Harrald." When Charles' father John received the

news he said, "What a happy meeting there has been between Charles and his mother."

The news flashed all over the globe. Every part of the world heard the message and a veritable flood tide of sympathy and encouragement swept into Mentone. The telegraph wires in Mentone were blocked with the multitudes of messages to Mrs. Spurgeon. The Prince and Princess of Wales were among the first to express their deep sympathy with her in her great sorrow. The whole world mourned for the loss of the pulpit giant and devout man of God. Papers everywhere recorded the "sad day." Typical was the *Freeman,* which wrote: "A Prince has fallen in Israel." The *Baptist* recorded (February 5, 1892): "At last the blow has fallen! . . . One of England's bravest, noblest, holiest hearts lies still in death." So many eulogies were written, they almost make a book. A host of personal words were also given. "The greatest preacher of his time," declared F. B. Meyer. John Clifford said, "The enthusiasm of the great evangelical revival reappeared in him; and the passion for 'saving souls,' characteristic of Whitefield, was supreme." The great American preacher and educator, B. H. Carroll said, "Last Sunday night at Mentone, France, there died the greatest man of modern times. If every crowned head in Europe had died that night, the event would not be so momentous as the death of this one man."

The Beau Revage Hotel put a notice on its door reading, "Mr. Spurgeon fell asleep in Jesus at 11:05 P.M." Because of local French laws, it was mandatory that the body be removed from the hotel within twenty-four hours. So it was embalmed, removed, and prepared to be sent to London. Friends covered with flowers the hotel bed in which Spurgeon lay at the time of his death. The "precious body," as Susannah expressed it, rested sealed in a lead shell in a beautiful olive-wood casket. On the casket the following inscription was inscribed:

In ever-loving memory of
CHARLES HADDON SPURGEON,
Born at Kelvedon, June 19, 1834;
Fell asleep in Jesus at Mentone, January 31, 1892
"I have fought a good fight, I have finished my course,
I have kept the faith."

The Scottish Presbyterian Church of Mentone held a memorial service at 10:00 A.M.; Pastor Delapierre spoke and prayed in French. Back in London, on the next Sunday, the entire front of the Tabernacle was draped in black. The people mourned deeply. The church filled as Dr. Murray Mitchel and the Rev. Somerville, along with Mr. Harrald, conducted the service.

In the meantime, Spurgeon's remains were removed and sent back to London by train. The body reached London's Victoria Station, Platform 3, on the morning of Monday, February 8. A large crowd of over a thousand had gathered in the station. A procession of friends formed and bore his body directly to Pastors' College, which Charles had founded. There, in the common room, the massive olive-wood casket lay in state for the day. Two private services were held that Monday at the college. That same night the students lovingly carried the body into the Tabernacle and placed it on a platform just below the pulpit from which Charles had preached for so many years. On both sides of the coffin were palm branches that had been sent from the south of France by Mrs. Spurgeon. On the top of the casket lay Spurgeon's Bible that he had used at the Metropolitan Tabernacle. It was opened to the text Isaiah 14:22, "Look unto me, and be ye saved, all the ends of the earth" (KJV), the very verse that God had used to bring about Charles' conversion more than forty years earlier.

In London a huge funeral was held. People lined the road along the several-mile route from the Metropolitan Tabernacle to the South Norwood Cemetery. It was a day of national mourning when the pulpit orator was interred.

The deacons erected a simple monument over the vault that contained the remains of the great preacher. On the front of the monument a medallion of Charles and a carved likeness of the open Bible on a cushion was placed alongside a short inscription:

> HERE LIES THE BODY
> OF
> CHARLES HADDON SPURGEON
> WAITING FOR THE APPEARING OF HIS
> LORD AND SAVIOUR
> JESUS CHRIST.

On the right side of the tomb were the two verses from C. H. Spurgeon's favorite hymn,

> E'er since by faith I saw the stream
> Thy flowing wounds supply,
> Redeeming love has been my theme,
> And shall be till I die;
>
> Then in a nobler, sweeter song,
> I'll sing Thy power to save,
> When this poor lisping, stammering tongue
> Lies silent in the grave.

The tomb remains the same to the present hour. Although bombs fell on the South Norwood Cemetery during the second World War and destroyed many of the graves of the deacons and church leaders who either proceeded or later followed Spurgeon in death, there was scarcely a scratch on Spurgeon's tomb. It seemed almost a token to the continuing witness of the pulpit giant and revivalist.

God's pilgrim had reached God's Celestial City, and what a reception he must have had; for "they that be wise shall shine as the brightness of the firmament; and they that turn many to righteousness as the stars for ever and ever" (Daniel 12:3). So we say:

Farewell, O mighty "Prince of God,"
Defender of the faith once given;
By the "old paths" the martyrs trod,
Thou, too, hast gained the courts of heaven;
Fought the good fight, the victory won,
Crowned with the warrior's crown—Well done!

Spurgeon was gone. The revival in many senses of the word died with him. Yet, not really, for the legacy lived on. Susannah's widowhood lasted close to another twelve years. In many senses of the word, notwithstanding her growing age and infirmity, they were the busiest of her life. She wrote her magnum opus, *C. H. Spurgeon's Autobiography, compiled from his Diary, Letters and Records.* Although Charles himself had considered writing an autobiography and had compiled many letters, documents, and anecdotes, he was never able to find time to compose it, though he was the author of some one hundred and fifty books. It just seemed that it was not in the providence of God for Charles to write such a volume. But Mr. Harrald, Charles' secretary, and Susannah, set themselves to the task. They actually spent several years in preparation, and it was finally produced in four beautiful volumes and has been reprinted in abridged form since. Susannah had a gift for writing, and the autobiography remains a tribute, not only to Charles, but also to her great supportive work of the revival ministry of the nineteenth century.

The End Comes
In the summer of 1903, Mrs. Spurgeon had a severe attack of pneumonia. It put her in the sick bed once again. From this onslaught, she never recovered. Each day seemed to see her life slowly ebbing away. During the first week of September, it appeared as though the end had arrived. Then, through her strong faith in God and her clinging to the promise, "Though He slay me, yet will I trust Him" (Job 13:15 KJV), she regained some strength. Yet she was never able to be up again, and week after

week as she lingered on, her strength slowly slipped away. On October 7 she gave her parting blessing to her son Thomas. She said:

"The blessing, the double blessing of your father's God be upon you and upon your brother. Good-bye, Tom; the Lord bless you for ever and ever! Amen."

At the very end she clasped her feeble hands together and with a face that glowed with the light of heaven upon it, she exclaimed: "Blessed Jesus! Blessed Jesus! I can see the King in His Glory!" God peacefully took her to Himself, to His own bosom, at half-past eight on the morning of Thursday, October 22, 1903. She was interred at her husband's side at the South Norwood Cemetery where Pastor Archibald Brown, a dear friend of the family for many years, spoke the final words.

The great pastor's wife and woman of awakening joined her husband in the glories of the eternal kingdom of God. The legacy and the revival lingers on. Thank God for a faithful pastor's wife, who stood by her husband while the revival fires burned and who made her contribution to the spiritual fires that ultimately reached multitudes for the Lord Jesus Christ.

Endnotes

1. Ernest A. Payne, *The Congregational Quarterly*, "The Evangelical Revival and the Beginnings of the Modern Missionary Movement," July 1943.
2. Lewis A. Drummond, *Spurgeon: Prince of Preachers* (Grand Rapids: Kregel Publications, 1992), 263.
3. Charles Ray, *Mrs. C. H. Spurgeon* (London: Passmore and Alabaster, 1903), 3.
4. *C. H. Spurgeon Autobiography*, *Compiled by His Wife* (London: Passmore and Alabaster, 1897). A full description of the home is found on 286–87.
5. Charles Ray, *The Life of Charles Haddon Spurgeon*, 203–4.
6. G. Holden Pike, *The Life and Works of Charles Haddon Spurgeon*, Vol. II (London, Cassell and Company, Ltd.), 240.
7. W. Y. Fullerston, *C. H. Spurgeon: A Biography* (London: Williams and Norgate, Ltd., 1920), 92.
8. C. H. Spurgeon, *The Saint and His Savior* (London: Hodder and Stoughton, 1880), 371–73.
9. Ray, *Mrs. C. H. Spurgeon*, 49–50.
10. Ibid., 47–48.
11. Ibid., 51.
12. Personal letter.
13. Ray, *Mrs. C. H. Spurgeon*, 62–64.
14. Ibid., 65.
15. Ray, *The Life of Charles Haddon Spurgeon*, 357.

16. James T. Ellis, *Charles Haddon Spurgeon* (London: James Nesbett & Co.), 90.
17. Ray, *The Life of Charles Haddon Spurgeon*, 361–62.
18. Ray, *Mrs. C. H. Spurgeon*, 81–83.
19. Ibid., 93.
20. Archives, Spurgeon's College, London.
21. John Bunyon, *Pilgrim's Progress* (Glasgow: William MacKenzie), 438.
22. *Autobiography* Vol. IV, 371.

Chapter Seven

CATHERINE BOOTH

The "Army" Awakening

When wonderful revival times arrive, the land is never the same again. Such was the British scene as the 1860s began to unfold. The great Prayer Revival of 1858, as it has been termed, had touched British shores. As seen in the chapter on Susannah Spurgeon, that significant work had its birth in North America during the winter of 1857–1858. Although the developing movement centered primarily in the United States, there had been some early harbingers of coming blessings in Canada. As the mid-century decade drew to a close, the needs in the United States as far as the spiritual as well as the social and economic perspective were concerned, cried for a solution. Moreover, the dramatic devastation of the American Civil War loomed ominously on the horizon. The Second Evangelical Awakening that had swept early America beginning in 1792 had spent its force. Even though the extensive revival ministry of Charles Finney had moved many, spiritual decay had set in. A myriad of problems eroded the very foundations of society. The churches languished for want of new life and vitality, seemingly inept to influence the needy nation. The country found itself on a course of spiritual destruction.

Into that setting, in the autumn of 1857, Jeremiah Lamphier, a lay missionary of the Dutch Reform Church on Fulton Street in the heart of New York City, called for a noonday prayer service. He had diligently tried every available means to see the church revitalized and people brought to Christ, but all to no avail. Almost in despair, he thought perhaps there would be some businessmen who would be willing to gather over the noon hour and at least pray. He invited any who would attend to meet in the consistory building of the church to give themselves to an hour of prayer. A burden weighed heavily on his heart for a fresh movement from God. Convinced that revival must come, he recognized that awakenings always begin in prayer. At the same time, a quest for revival had begun at Amherst, Yale, and Williams Colleges in eastern America. Could New York City also be touched?

The stated day for prayer, September 23, 1857, arrived, but at twelve o'clock no one had come. By 12:25 no one had shown, and the depressed missionary almost decided to write it all off as a lost project. However, around 12:30, six men straggled in. Those who prayed manifested the genuine spirit of concern, so Lamphier scheduled another meeting for the next week. The following week saw the attendance double at the noon-day prayer service. Then at the next meeting there were even more on their knees beseeching God for revival. It was then decided that they should meet every day for prayer.

On October 7, just three weeks after the prayer services began, the stock market crashed. Unemployment skyrocketed. This no doubt caused many others to begin to look to God in prayer. By midwinter, the Dutch Reform church overflowed with praying people. Prayer meetings soon spread to the Methodist Church on John Street and then to the Trinity Episcopal Church on Broadway and Wall Streets. In February and March 1858, every church and public hall in central New York filled to absolute capacity with folks earnestly praying during the noon hour. The famous New York newspaper editor, Horace Greely, sent a reporter on horse and buggy to the various prayer meetings to see how many people were actually attending. He wanted to be sure that the enthusiasm had not caused an exaggeration of numbers. New York seemed abuzz with it all. The reporter raced around from meeting to meeting and in one hour (he could only get to twelve meetings), he counted 6,100 men in fervent interces-sion for revival. During that same period, reporter James Bennet of the *Herald* started a series of articles on the revival. Then the landslide came. Churches across the country began overflowing with praying people. Not only that, many conversions started taking place in the prayer services, and various evangelistic meetings were held in conjunction with the prayer effort. In one week, New York alone saw ten thousand people converted. Soon all the Hudson and Mohawk valleys were brought to fervent inter-cession. Throughout New England, church bells rang regularly at eight in the morning, at noon, and at six in the evening calling people to prayer. Charles Finney of Oberland College received a fresh blessing on his min-istry. The revival set America ablaze.

The Prayer Revival moved into the British Isles in an interesting fash-ion. It actually had all begun in Ireland. In 1856, two or three years prior to the Irish phase of the movement, a Baptist lady named Mrs. Colville had exercised an effective witness for Christ in her community. She pro-foundly influenced a young man, James McQuilkin of Ballymena. He, along with a friend, began to pray for revival in Ireland. God heard their prayers, and in 1858, the Presbyterian Church of Ireland dispatched ob-servers to the United States to investigate the Prayer Revival that had vitally gripped the country. They returned to Ireland thrilled. One of them wrote a book that God used in a significant way to put the Irish Christians to prayer for a similar movement in their land. Soon Belfast, Dublin, Cork, and much of the countryside fell under the impact of the Prayer Revival. The nation bent its knees.

As the continuing news and thrilling stories of the American awakening spread through the British Isles, Scotland began praying. Prayer meetings sprang up in Glasgow, Edinborough, and virtually all the cities and towns of the country. By 1859, the United Presbyterian Church reported that one-forth of its members regularly attended a prayer meeting for spiritual awakening. The revival broke first in Aberdeen, Glasgow, and across the few miles of water to the Isle of Butte, and then finally throughout the land. The loyal Scots experienced God's reviving power, an evangelist named Brownlow North being especially useful in those significant days. Furthermore, the news of the Irish awakening deepened the Scottish work even more.

Wales also came under the power of God—almost simultaneously with Ireland. A young Welshman, Humphrey Rowland Jones, had been studying for the ministry in America. Being caught up in the beginning of the revival in 1857, he returned home in 1858 and began preaching the necessity of revival for Wales. Together with a more seasoned minister, David Morgan, they joined hands as the awakening began in Wales. Morgan and Jones worked together most effectively. Jones, however, grew rather extreme and faded out of the picture. But Morgan moved from strength to strength as the revival gained momentum. Before long all Wales caught the fire.

Finally, England got caught up—as previously seen in the Spurgeon ministry. In this matrix William and Catherine Booth, originators of the Salvation Army, began ministering with fresh power. By the middle of the next decade, the Salvation Army launched its revolutionary thrust in Britain that eventually circled the globe. Right in the heart of that great revival of prayer, a new movement was born that has touched millions of lives for over one hundred and fifty years and continues to do so today.

Although many people know the name of William Booth and his Salvation Army, few people know of the tremendous impact of the woman of awakening behind the Army: William Booth's wonderful wife, Catherine. She is due a place in the realm of the great women of awakening. Her story is a fascinating one. It all began to unfold at Ashbourne in Derbyshire, when on January 17, 1829, little Catherine came into the world to bless the Mumford family.

Catherine's Early Life

A biographer described little Catherine Mumford as having "a sweet little face, all eyes, dark eyes now blue like her mother."[1] Yet she really favored Father Mumford more than Mother. But most important, she was blessed to be born into a dedicated Christian home that honored God. The parents kept the Lord's work and truth constantly before their children.

Early in life, Catherine had to face the death of her little sister. Even sixty years later she said, "I was scarcely more than two years old but I can remember to this day, the feeling of awe and solemnity with which the sight of death impressed my baby mind . . . the effect has lasted to this very hour." Like so often in the earlier part of the nineteenth century, many children did not survive infancy; the mortality rate was appalling. The Mumfords lost three sons in infancy and only Catherine and a son, John, born in 1833, survived.

Early in life Catherine became very conscious of God's love. She sensed the heavenly Father's care in her lovely home. From her very earliest years, Catherine's mother shared the things of Christ with her little daughter. Later Catherine was to say, "The longer I live, the more I appreciate my mother's character. She was one of the Puritan type. A woman of sternest principles and yet the embodiment of tenderness. To her, right was right, no matter what it might entail. She had an intense realization of spiritual things. Heaven seemed quite near, instead of being a far-off unreality."

Catherine, being a precocious child, could read quite well as a little girl. She loved to stand and read aloud to those who would listen, and much of what she read came from the Bible. She had already familiarized herself with many of the stories of the Scriptures and she developed a deep love for the Word of God. The Bible, along with her mother's teaching, created in her a strong moral sense. Catherine told of how as a child of three years of age, many times at night she would confess with tears before God what in her childish thoughts she considered wrong. She could not go to sleep until all was forgiven and she felt the peace of God's love and forgiveness. She developed a very sensitive conscience. This aided her as she realized that she must be absolutely yielded to the Lord and anything that displeased Him must be brought before Him in confession for the cleansing of the blood of Christ. Not only did these early experiences ingrain a spiritual sensitivity into the very fiber of her spiritual life, she also recognized the importance of training children in the things of God. This was to become a central part of her Christian service as her life unfolded in the Salvation Army ministry.

Catherine had a very intense nature. Even as a child her play seemed most serious. She cared for her dolls very conscientiously, even as a mother would care for a real child. Not introverted or unbalanced in her seriousness, she was simply a sensitive, conscientious little girl. Later her own daughter would say that Catherine was "serious, living was to her a very serious thing, she felt things so deeply."

Even though Catherine was rather shy and quite reserved, she did have a boldness about her. On occasion, when circumstances were right, she would speak out most forthrightly. This quality changed her from a lamb to a lion.

One of the beautiful things in little Catherine's life was her incredible compassion for any person in need. She had a deeply compassionate heart for those who were oppressed and suffering, even as young as she was. This love for the downcast became so ingrained in the little girl's spirit and mind that she often had to pay in physical and nervous exhaustion for her "lavish compassions." Her compassion even extended to animals. Once she saw a sheep goaded in the street. It so upset her that she ran home and flung herself on a couch in tears. She would often get into encounters with people who would ill-treat animals. But above all, her compassion centered on needy people. Even if she saw a policeman arrest a drunk, she would be there at his side because no one would intercede for him. This beautiful quality, though perhaps extreme and immature in such a small child, God used powerfully when she matured. The Holy Spirit was fashioning her with a heart to meet the needs of outcast people, those to whom the Salvation Army ministered. Something of her compassion permeates the whole approach of the Salvationists, as is common knowledge.

Other Gifts

Little Catherine was equally sensitive in the moral and spiritual sphere, much of which was ingrained in the little girl by her mother. She also acquired a very open and fertile mind, probably inherited from her father who himself was a very practical and innovative thinker. For example, he became one of the first community leaders to help bring in the streetcar. He even experimented in the making of perambulators. Everyone saw Father John as an attractive personality and a jovial, good-looking, intelligent man. His profession was coach building, and he developed a very fine business. When Catherine turned five he moved the family to his hometown of Boston in Lincolnshire, the county of the Wesleys.

John also had deep spiritual convictions. In Boston, he threw himself into helping develop the temperance movement, and he did it with real zeal. He gave lectures, and his home became something of the center of the temperance movement in that area. Catherine, much like him, shared his zeal. The two talked together constantly and the child's mind quickly grasped the sterling qualities of her Christian father.

Catherine loved her father dearly, yet, on one occasion he caused her deep grief. She had a beloved dog named Waterford. They were inseparable. As Catherine had few close personal friends, the dog virtually became that to her. And the animal watched over her like she was his own property. While outside one day Catherine stumbled and struck her foot against something and cried out in pain. Waterford, who was inside, heard her and without one moment's hesitation, literally jumped through the large glass window to come to little Catherine's rescue. The father, greatly upset at the damage the dog had caused, immediately had the animal shot. Catherine said, "For months I suffered intolerably, especially in realizing it was in an effort to alleviate my sufferings that the beautiful creature had lost its life. Days passed before I could speak to my father, although he afterwards greatly regretted his hasty action, and strove to console me as best he could." Little Catherine never really felt quite the same toward her father after that. For a time he became a stranger to her. But even that rather sad incident helped to develop something of an innate sense of justice in the girl that held her in good stead in the years to come. Catherine's mother was temperamentally different from her father. She had a deep fear of harmful temptations that little Catherine might experience outside the home. Consequently, Catherine had very few acquaintances and hardly any friends her own age. But her father, a good healthy counterpart to her mother, helped the child develop into a balanced young lady.

A New World

At this stage Catherine's mother began to feel that Catherine needed broadening; perhaps there had even been too much praying and spiritual instruction in the home. So she sent her daughter off to boarding school. In the good providence of God, the principal of the school was a sincere Christian. Catherine, twelve at the time, saw a whole new world open up. New friends and new impressions rapidly began to mature the child. History became her favorite subject and she especially excelled in writing. She enjoyed geography very much as well. She threw herself into her studies and became an avid reader, indulging herself in the serious works of various writers. It gave her a good foundation in the truth of the Christian faith and helped her in her decision-making and leadership roles. She impressed her teachers so, that soon she became a tutor to some of those who were not quite as adept in their studies.

Catherine enjoyed a happy time at the school, but not every event suited her liking. Her intense nature, which at times precipitated outbursts of temper as she entered puberty, caused some difficult times. But she was growing and learning nonetheless.

From the ages of fourteen to sixteen, Catherine gave herself to Christian doctrine, philosophy, and general theology. Being still quite young, these subjects completely consumed her. However, during her fifteenth year, she faced a deep spiritual crisis. Catherine felt that perhaps she was losing her grip on her Christian experience. Contradictory theories and concepts were presented to her and it precipitated serious inner conflict for the young lady. Again, her godly mother stepped in and helped her tremendously, and she came through the crisis successfully. In it all, she never lost her love for spiritual things; her delight was to go to chapel. She really was a most unusual young woman.

A New Love

Being a typical Victorian teenager in many respects, Catherine became very attracted to a handsome young man. He had a quick mind and was a fine conversationalist. This suited both of them well; however, he had little interest in religious things—a serious problem for Catherine. She had hoped that she would be able to win him for Christ because she realized that the Bible plainly states that a Christian is not to be "unequally yoked together with unbelievers" (2 Cor. 6:14 KJV). He resisted Catherine's witness, and though she felt drawn to the young man, she knew that she must eventually break off the relationship. She certainly did not want to drift into any kind of disobedience to God. What probably saved the day was the family's move from Boston to make their home in London in the Brixton area, which removed Catherine from the situation.

The move to London afforded Catherine the opportunity of seeing some of the great sights of London that she had always heard about, such as St. Paul's Cathedral, Westminster Abbey, the National Gallery, and all of the wonderful attractions of the capital city. She loved the metropolis. As the famous writer Samuel Johnson said, "When a man is tired of London, he is tired of life; for there is in London all that life can afford."

The Crises of Faith

As Catherine's seventeenth year rolled around, she entered another crisis in her personal religious experience. She knew much about God and was sensitive to the call of the Lord upon her life for obedience and spiritual discipline. But—it may seem rather strange—the question came before the young lady: Did she know God personally? The conflicting theologies that she encountered no longer disturbed her. The question was not, is there a God or what is He like; but did she know Him by a personal revelation of Himself in her own spiritual experience? She came to realize that knowledge merely *about* God and the practice of spiritual discipline would, in the final analysis, fail her. Catherine saw that "the Law" could not meet her need. Her cry became, "I must know, I must find." She even became uncertain whether or not she had a true saving relationship with Jesus Christ. She said, "I was terribly afraid of being self-deceived. I said, 'No, my heart is as bad as other people's, and if I have not sinned outwardly I have inwardly.' I will never rest 'til I am thoroughly and truly changed . . . faith is not logic, but logic may help faith . . . It seemed unreasonable to suppose that I could be saved and not know it." She could not really remember any time or place in her life where she definitely by simple faith received Christ in her life for her own personal salvation. Now she set herself to praying earnestly for this. She would pace about the room many nights until early morning trying to find peace. She said, "I will never rest 'til I am thoroughly and truly changed, and know it as any thief or great outward sinner . . . I refuse to be saved by logic." She determined to settle the question once and for all.

One night, absolutely exhausted from her spiritual struggle, Catherine put the Bible and hymnbook under her pillow. She tried to sleep but could not. She cried that God might give her assurance. Out of the struggle, that very night, she confessed, "I cried for nothing on earth or in heaven, but that I might find Him whom my soul panteth after. And I did find Him . . . I knew Him, I can't tell how, but I knew Him. I knew He was well pleased with me." When she awoke the next morning, she opened her hymnbook and the hymn verse struck her:

> My God, I am Thine,
> What a comfort divine,
> What a blessing to know that my Jesus is mine!

She said,

> The words came to my inmost soul with a force and illumination that they had never before possessed. It was as impossible for me to doubt, as it had been before for me to exercise faith. The assurance of my salvation seemed to fill my soul. I jumped out of bed and without waiting to dress ran into my mother's room and told her what had happened. Til then I had been very backward in speaking, even to her, upon spiritual matters. I could not open my heart to her. I was so happy I felt as if walking on air.

Personal salvation had come and God now had His servant basically ready for a great worldwide ministry, to become a woman of awakening.

The early months after her conversion Catherine described as the happiest she had ever known. She felt an inner harmony with herself and all of nature. She became a member of the Brickston Methodist Church. She submerged herself into the life of the congregation and joined the weekly Bible study. This helped her tremendously in her spiritual growth now that she had her feet planted firmly on the Rock. In those days, Mrs. Leay, the wife of a retired Methodist minister, helped her greatly. Catherine, at the age of eighteen, called her "my mother in Christ." Catherine began to speak to her acquaintances about Jesus Christ, because immediately on her conversion she became an effective witness. Her prayer life deepened and her whole countenance radiated the Lord Jesus.

A Sad Turn of Events

Catherine now had a new relationship with her parents, especially her mother. Catherine helped her mother tremendously as she had become a rather lonely old woman. There was a reason for her loneliness, a sad reason. Father John, in his early days, was a zealous and an eloquent lay Methodist preacher. He had hoped to be an ordained minister, but gradually got caught up into making money. Consequently, his spiritual life suffered and he stopped preaching. Finally, he even gave up his profession and fell by the wayside. John began to "brace himself" with a glass of wine—he who had been a temperance leader. Catherine's mother felt the anguish of all this. Moreover, she was not in good health, and it all mitigated against her well-being.

Catherine became her mother's confidant and comfort. Of course, Father John deeply grieved Catherine also. Her own intense nature, which made her predisposed towards illness, brought about a severe inflammation of the lungs. For a time, Catherine was actually in danger of dying. The doctor confined her to her room all winter.

By May, however, Catherine's health began to improve and she felt well enough to travel to the south coast to the lovely city of Brighton. The fresh air there, so much better than the pollution of London, restored her and she began to recover her strength rapidly. Still, her confinement and her father's waywardness proved very difficult. Her childhood timidity reasserted itself and she lost something of her freedom to witness for Christ. Even the glow of her salvation began to cool. But God, always gracious, restored her and she got back on her spiritual feet. She wrote in her journal, "A day of inward peace, I feel more resignation to the will of my Lord . . . I think I can say with truth and sincerity 'Thy will be done.'" On June 3, she penned,

> This morning I was much blessed in prayer. I rose earlier and went out on the level and sat down on a seat to read. . . . I felt a sweet calm overspread my spirit. The beautiful scenery around, the tranquility that reigned seemed well to suit me. . . . I have had pain in my shoulder today in my back. Although the ways of God are mysterious and past finding out . . . I know not what He is about to do with me, but I have given myself entirely into His hands.

She knew the peace and joy that only Christ can give.

Life in Christ

Catherine's health improved considerably as she experienced a vibrant walk with Christ. The Bible became increasingly real to her. She appropriated the promises of God in a far more personal sense than ever before. She learned the joy of answered prayer as God continually shed His grace in her life.

At that time another crisis arose, this time in Catherine's church. A dispute erupted in the Wesleyan Church, which led to a rupture of the entire body. A strong reform movement emerged in her denomination and it precipitated deep-seated problems that ultimately caused the split. The reform group was intent on restoring the original spiritual fervor that the Wesleyan Church had enjoyed in its early years. Catherine agreed; she felt strongly that they needed a revival. She cast her lot with the reformers, and this put her in a difficult position. Some of the members and leaders of the church had been expelled for their reforming views, and Catherine, feeling that they were in the right and the authorities wrong, let it be known, since she was never reticent in speaking out on what she felt. As a consequence, she was expelled from the Wesleyan Church. Catherine had been schooled in Methodism, and this proved a tremendous blow to her sensitive spirit. She said, "I loved it [the church] with the love which has altogether gone out of fashion among Protestants for their church. Separation from it was one of the first great troubles of my life." Thus Methodism lost one of its greatest potential members, but life in Christ has its rocky roads as well as its smooth paths.

Other Positions of Belief

Catherine was a strong advocate of equal rights and a legitimate place in Christian ministry for women. This became a very important part of her understanding of herself and the Christian experience. She said, "Never 'til woman is estimated and educated as man's equal—the literal 'she-man' of the Hebrew—will the foundation of human influence become pure or the biased of mind noble and lofty." Of course, this approach, whether all agreed or not, made her the effective Christian servant and minister that she became.

By the time Catherine reached the age of twenty-three, she enjoyed much better health. Her mother seemed to be better as well. "Prepare me for all," she had prayed. And God was surely doing that. Through her unusual childhood and adolescence, God kept leading and preparing her to be, as one has expressed it:

> A transcendent lover;
> A exquisitely affectionate wife;
> A mother of adoring sons and daughters;

A preacher of "irresistible eloquence";
One of the great figures of religious history;
A lawgiver to a new company of the redeemed on earth;
Mother of The Salvation Army.

It all can be summed up in her own words, "I give myself afresh into the hands of God, to do and to suffer, all His will."

When Catherine was just a young girl, she said, "I made up my mind. He [the man I marry] must be a sincere Christian; not a nominal one, or a mere church member, but truly converted to God." God led her to just such a man.

Catherine's "Intended"

William Booth was born in Nottingham in 1829, the same year as Catherine's birth. His early spiritual background unfolded in the Church of England. His father Samuel Booth, a builder, worked in the speculative aspects of construction. He had made and lost a fortune by the time little William turned twelve years of age. This dramatically influenced the young boy's life. He had to be taken from school and apprenticed to a pawn broker. His father gave only one reason for putting him under a pawn broker: There was money in it. Not long after, however, Samuel Booth died leaving the family in virtual poverty.

When young William turned fifteen, he found Christ in a Wesley chapel in Nottingham. Almost immediately he began to preach in street services with some Christian friends in the slum area of the city. He not only engaged in street meetings, he also held cottage prayer meetings. He powerfully witnessed for Christ, especially to the street people. When William turned twenty he moved to London hoping to find better opportunities for a livelihood and ministry as well. He hated the pawn-broker business, but felt he must stay in it—at least for awhile. He lived in his employer's home and had only Sunday as free time. He used that free time to continue his lay preaching.

Providentially, the Wesleyan Church eliminated William from their fellowship in something of the same manner as his future wife Catherine had been, but for another reason. Catherine had involved herself in the reformation agitation; William became suspect because of his street preaching. Some felt him to be a secret sympathizer with the reformation party. When the reformers discovered his excommunication, they passed a resolution inviting Booth to join them. In June 1851, he accepted the invitation and continued on as a lay preacher.

A certain Mr. Rabbits became acquainted with William Booth when he heard him preach in Walworth Chapel. He thrilled at the young man's preaching and gave him moral support in his ministry. They became close friends, Mr. Rabbits felt a godly pride in his young protégé.

The Call

Early in 1852, Mr. Rabbits urged William to leave his pawn-broker business and devote himself totally to the preaching of the Gospel. William said that there was just no way this could be done. He felt nobody really wanted him to be their pastor, and he had to live. "Yes," Mr. Rabbits replied, "but you could certainly be an evangelist." Rabbits kept insisting. William retorted that he did not have any financial support. Mr. Rabbits replied that that was pure nonsense and asked him how much he would actually need. William said, he could survive on twenty shillings a week, but where would that come from? "I will supply it, for the first three months at least," Mr. Rabbits pledged, and the deal was struck.

William found new quarters in the Walworth district in a two-room apartment, and God launched his full-time ministry in that simple way. In the setting of the Walworth Chapel, William and Catherine became acquainted; she heard William preach. Mr. Rabbits asked Catherine what she thought of the sermon. She replied, "One of the best I have heard in this chapel." Catherine got to know William better at the Rabbits' house during afternoon tea. Although at that stage it was nothing more than a casual meeting, God destined the relationship to deepen.

On Good Friday, April 10, 1852, William's twenty-third birthday became a day long remembered. He met his good friend, Mr. Rabbits, who inquired where he was going. William replied that he was on his way to make a visit. "Nonsense," again replied Mr. Rabbits. He said William must accompany him to the services at Kowper Street. "I insist," said Mr. Rabbits. William went along.

A "Chance" Encounter

As the service at Kowper Street was about to begin, in walked Catherine. She was not feeling too well after the service, so someone asked William to escort her home. They left together and were alone for the first time. Catherine and William sat side by side as the carriage rumbled over the rough east London streets. It seemed as if a light from heaven radiated in both of their hearts. They knew, just knew, that God had brought them together. Catherine wrote later,

> That little journey will never be forgotten by either of us. . . . As William expressed it, it seemed as if God flashed simultaneously into our hearts that affection which . . . none of the changing vicissitudes with which our lives have been so crowded has been able to efface . . . We struck in at once in such wonderful harmony of view and aim and feeling on various matters that passed rapidly before us, that it seemed as though, we had intimately known and loved each other for years and suddenly, after some

temporary absence, had been brought together again. Before we reached my home we both . . . felt as though we had been made for each other.

She knew that this chance meeting came from God and that they were destined to spend their lives together in Christian ministry.

Love Letters

William was soon traveling considerably in his evangelistic-preaching ministry. Consequently, much of their early courtship had to be carried on by correspondence, but they were beautiful letter writers. Theirs were Victorian love letters; and the Victorians knew how to write them. They began writing each other about once a week, but as the relationship developed, they found themselves writing to each other daily. When William was up north in Spalding, one of his letters started, "My dearest earthly treasure, bless you a thousand times for your very kind letter just received; it has done my heart good . . . I have thought about you very much and very affectionately the last few days . . . I do not doubt our future oneness." Catherine, equally responsive, wrote, "Our home . . . if we live in love, as Christ hath loved us—what a little heaven below . . ." She often addressed William as "my dearest William."

In some respects, Catherine almost assumed a mothering approach to William. His health being not too well, he would complain in his letters, and Catherine would always comfort and admonish him. She was also quite anxious that he study. In almost every letter she coaxed William to stay in the study of the Word of God and in good literature. On one occasion she asked, "Could you not rise, say by six o'clock every morning and convert your bedroom into a study 'til breakfast time? After breakfast and family devotions, could you not again retire to your room and determinately apply yourself to it 'til dinner?" That may sound rather bossy but they were in love and Catherine only wanted the best for her William. She said, "There is no letter for me, dearest, this morning. I have got so used to receiving one every morning that I feel lost without it." A deep and abiding tie was made for the future of their ministry together.

The Congregational Possibility

During the engagement period, Catherine urged William to offer himself as a candidate for the ministry in the Congregational church. In reply to her urging, William went to see the Reverend Dr. John Campbell, a well-known Congregational minister and editor of the official periodical of the Congregational union. His application for the post, however, posed something of a problem for William. Congregational theology had a strong

Calvinistic element and Booth definitely did not see himself as a Calvinist. His Wesleyan background dictated against that.

At the same time, however, William had been assured that he would never be required to preach in the Congregational church anything that he did not fully believe. Nonetheless, on his way home from an interview with Dr. Campbell, he bought the book *The Rule of Grace*. He had been instructed to study the volume. He had not read but thirty pages when he literally threw it across the room absolutely convinced that he could never adopt this teaching. Catherine had set her heart on William's being a Congregationalist, but she had to agree with him that, on questions of doctrine, he could not yield his convictions. He was, theologically speaking, a thoroughgoing Arminian, as were all the Wesleyan Methodists. It must be said that he probably did not really understand Calvinism in some of its aspects. Calvinistic doctrine does not preclude a fervent evangelism. The ministry of George Whitefield and Selina, the Countess of Huntingdon, has made that clear. But William did not see that, and so in a rather frustrated manner, he completely dropped the idea of becoming a Congregational minister. Had he gone that route, he would also have been required to enroll in college. Catherine really wanted to see her William in college, but when he dismissed the idea of becoming a Congregationalist, he likewise gave up college. Catherine became somewhat upset that William had given up the idea, but she acquiesced, saying that he could not compromise his convictions or what he understood to be God's will for his life.

The New Connection

In May 1853, rumors had it that the Wesleyan reformers would perhaps unite with the so-called Methodist New Connection. Catherine and William were very positive toward the possibility. They began to consider affiliating themselves with this new thrust and William's becoming a minister in the New Connection. However, as William made overtures to join as a preacher, they put a restriction on him. William would have to go through a four-year probation period before he could marry. The Victorians were different.

As William and Catherine considered their relationship with the New Connection, she wrote the following letter, "My dear love . . . I want to give you my thoughts and conclusions. Listen to me and then act as your judgment dictates." Then she went on to give her opinion about various aspects of the policy of the New Connection. Clearly she was becoming an advisor and a strong influence in William's life even before their marriage.

The upshot of it all was that William wrote to Dr. Cooke, a leader in the movement, and offered himself as a candidate for the ministry in the

New Connection, a four-year wait for marriage or not. But immediately he felt an uncertainty as to whether he had done the right thing. First of all, he did not have a great deal of confidence in his ability to preach. Catherine to the contrary was absolutely convinced that he could be all that the New Connection would ever want in a minister. She said to him, "Spalding will not be your final destination." (William served for a protracted time in Spalding.)

One day Catherine wrote a letter that William did not like. He wrote back admonishing her gently that at times she appeared much too inflexible when she thought she was right. They did not always see eye to eye. But disagreements did not dampen William and Catherine's love, even though they had a few rough spots to overcome.

In the midst of it all, as William still pondered whether or not to take an appointment with the New Connection, an opportunity came for him to return from Spalding to the capital and assume the responsibility at what Londoners called the Hinde Street Circuit. This involved preaching and leading several groups of believers. They offered him a salary of one hundred pounds a year. This threw both William and Catherine into more confusion. What would God have them do? In that setting Catherine said something of great significance concerning her whole approach to what would be the essence of her life in the years ahead. She said, "I believe in revivalism with all my soul. I believe that it is God's idea of the success of the gospel. Of course, you know what I mean by revivalism: The genuine work of the Spirit, and I believe these are such." She truly was a woman of awakening even in her early days before her marriage to William. Then God opened a new door.

In February 1854, Booth, still seeking God's will, went to London and stayed with Dr. Cooke. As Cooke watched him and heard him preach, he recognized something of the native intelligence and the zeal to win people to Christ that William Booth possessed. Dr. Cooke, seeing the potential in William, suggested to the New Connection Conference in June 1854, that William be made superintendent of a large London circuit. William declared himself too young for the responsibilities and suggested that he might best be appointed as an assistant to an older minister rather than being appointed as full superintendent. The assistantship suggestion was accepted. Mr. Rabbits once again stepped in and offered to pay the salary. Furthermore, as the result of Dr. Cooke's positive report on Booth to the Conference, they decided that he and Catherine should be given permission to marry in twelve-months time. Both of these eventualities thrilled William and Catherine. The future looked bright.

William went to work with an older superintendent. All things were not too pleasing, however. The older man seemed rather stiff and formal; William was the exact opposite. Nonetheless, through it all, William

Booth's reputation as a preacher spread and he began to be widely known in the New Connection circuit.

Soon a plan unfolded that offered a greater ministry. When William and Catherine married, he would be appointed to a circuit on his own and they could thus minister together.

Marriage at Last

As the wedding approached, the New Connection Conference gave William £100 a year for his preaching and traveling. The days ahead appeared very positive for the young couple. So on the morning of June 16, 1855, in a large chapel, Catherine and William were united in marriage. Only Catherine's father, William's sister, and the caretaker attended the simple ceremony. Dr. Thomas performed the vows. The happy couple left the chapel and traveled to Ryde on the Isle of Wight for a one-week honeymoon. It was not a long honeymoon nor a very affluent one, like a trip to the continent that was the dream of most Victorian young married couples. But they had a happy time, and God blessed their days.

When the week's honeymoon ended, they left for the island of Guernsey in the English Channel. William had become quite well-known on the island, and a crowd awaited them at the pier. He preached for them and then moved on to the other British Channel isle of Jersey. There William conducted a series of meetings. Their happy married life and shared ministry had begun.

Voluminous correspondence kept them close as their love deepened and as William was constantly on the move preaching. In the letters that ensued between the two, Catherine addressed William as not her "beloved" as before, but now as "my precious husband." God granted them a most happy home.

Catherine at times traveled with William in his itinerant ministry on the circuit. On one such trip they journeyed from Hull to Sheffield and throughout the area. Catherine wrote to her mother, "I never was so happy before. My precious William grows every day more in my mind and heart."

A New Joy and Responsibility

A new responsibility came to the young couple; Catherine was expecting her first baby. She no longer concerned herself about technical theological discourses, at least to the degree that she had earlier. Now she had to worry about providing clothes and the necessities for her new little one. Of course, her mind never lost its focus on the things of Christ, but she also had to busy her hands with the more mundane things of life.

While William and Catherine served in the north of England, Catherine met William's mother for the first time. She was an amicable old lady.

Catherine said that she was a "very nice looking old lady." They seemed to strike it off well. The couple much enjoyed their time up north. For example, one day they planned to see Chatsworth House, one of the great manor houses in the Sheffield area. Then some friends came and they decided to go on a hike up into the hill country. They had a great time. In many respects, they were a wholesome, fun-loving family. In the setting of all of the anticipated joys of family life and ministry with a new child, Catherine could say, "I know nothing of real unhappiness now. Underneath all temporary and surface trials, there is a deep calm flow of satisfaction and comfort." The depth of Catherine's spirituality and the work of God in her heart became obvious to all. She had truly grasped the spirit of Christ in her own personal life. God was fashioning this lovely young woman to be an effective instrument of the Lord in the great prayer revival that would soon break in on the land—and would do much to develop the fantastic movement that we know today as the Salvation Army.

The heart of William and Catherine's New Connection circuit ministry at this time revolved around, in today's vocabulary, "itinerant evangelism." They traveled far and wide in Britain. While visiting in Chester in Halifax, Catherine's time came for their first child to be born. She gave birth to a fine bouncing baby boy on March 8, 1856. Catherine picked up the baby in her arms and she and William in prayer dedicated their son to God and His service. They prayed that he would become a great preacher of the Gospel. They named him William Bramwell. Catherine penciled on a scrap of paper to her mother, "Now I know what it is to be a mother, and I feel I never loved you half as well as I ought to have done. Forgive all my shortcoming . . . my precious babe is a beauty."

A Sudden Disappointment

Soon Catherine felt able to take up their itinerant ministry once again, this time the three of them traveling together. However, when the Conference met in Nottingham early in June 1857, by a vote of forty in favor to forty-five against, the Conference unexpectedly terminated William's work as a traveling evangelist and appointed him to a permanent settlement in Brighouse. Catherine was not only shocked but deeply disappointed. She said, "I have felt it far more keenly than I thought I should, the manner in which our mission has been put down." But her deep faith and commitment to the providence of God always prevailed. She said, "I believe He will order all for the best. I have no fears for the future. I have confidence in my husband's devotion and capacity for something greater yet." Apparently a certain amount of jealousy over William's becoming so prominent a young man precipitated the Conference's decision. So it was back to London and a more settled ministry.

And Catherine proved to be right. The future did hold wonderful things for this dedicated couple. Their love for one another and their new son, whom they called by his middle name, Bramwell, was only exceeded by their love for God. Neither jealousy or anything else can defeat one who loves God supremely. Catherine's deep commitment to winning people to Christ, made her, as many called her, a "mother in Israel." The new saga began opening up for this Deborah of the nineteenth century, this woman of awakening.

A Mother in Israel

As a young lady, it will be remembered that Catherine had prayed, *Lord prepare me for all.* She did not realize at that time what "all" would mean. She felt that God had his hand upon her and wanted to use her, but she knew not how. Therefore, she attempted to prepare herself as best as she could. She studied diligently and became quite well-versed in theology and church history. When William proposed, and she saw herself as a minister's wife, she readily recognized that, as she said in her own words, "I could occupy the highest possible sphere of Christian usefulness." Quite correct; it is a high and holy calling to be a minister's wife. When children came along she realized this was also a very real part of her usefulness. So she prepared herself well for motherhood and homemaking. She could cook, bake, and sew and knew how to make a little go a long way, each a necessity in most minister's homes in those days.

Catherine's Service

Catherine had no dream of ever being a preacher herself. Before she and William married, she said, "I do want to be useful, but it must be in retirement and quietness." Being small of frame and not particularly impressive in her physical appearance, she nonetheless carried her head high and her glowing personality made her most attractive to people. She assumed the role of a minister's wife beautifully. Although home duties restricted excessive activity, she became a true prayer warrior. She prayed fervently for her husband's ministry as well as interceded for many people she knew who needed to come to faith in Christ. She became an effective counselor for those who under William's preaching would "come forward" to profess Christ as Savior and Lord. Catherine had a profound sensitivity to their need and wanted them to experience genuine salvation in Christ. She would talk with the penitent and pray with them as she poured out her heart for their complete yielding to Christ.

In all this, Catherine had not the faintest hint of a call to preach herself. But the Spirit of God was schooling her for an unusual ministry. Those who came to her were significantly touched by her words.

Probably that which prepared Catherine more than anything else for the greater ministry that soon began to unfold was the way she dealt with those who were coming to faith in Christ. Her approach to women in service no doubt also accounts for the fact that when the Salvation Army came to full bloom, all of the officers' wives received the same training as did single women officers. They were taught to deal with souls, visit in people's homes, lead meetings, and even conduct marriages and funerals.

William saw clearly, in the early days of their marriage, Catherine's gift of communication and counsel. One of the most endearing things about William centered in his utter confidence in his wife's ability to be used of the Spirit of God in evangelism. He would say, "I know you can do it, Kate." Therefore, before long he insisted that she take the leadership of a class of women members who attended their Bible studies. Twenty-nine women regularly attended.

At that juncture William urged Catherine to give some lectures. They had a little joke over the word *lecture*, but the upshot of it was that she would give a temperance talk to the Band of Hope at the chapel where they ministered. Catherine set herself to prepare. She asked her father for help in preparing her address. By this time, Mr. Mumford had once again moved back into fellowship with the Lord. He was thus able to tell her from first-hand experience some of the things that would help those who were in the grips of alcohol. The address met with such success that many invitations to lecture rolled in. The first week in January 1858, she was involved in some sort of ministry every night. That was the very year that the great Prayer Revival broke out in America. Little did Catherine and William know how this movement would give impetus to their ministry in a very short time.

The faithful couple continued to minister in the London mission in Brighouse. A new daughter, Katie, came into the world in 1858. This brought the family to two boys and a girl. A brother had joined Bramwell some time earlier. After Catherine regained her strength, she started a door-to-door ministry, talking with people and urging them to attend their services. They conducted open-air meetings as God did beautiful and unusual things. For example, a man whose life revolved around a public house (a tavern) came to Christ. He was jubilant about his new-found faith. Some of his friends actually carried him on their shoulders to celebrate his conversion. He became a very staunch member of Booth's Brighouse chapel. The harbingers of what the Salvation Army would become in the not-too-distant future was already manifesting itself. Catherine moved among these people with complete freedom and made a tremendous impact in the whole area.

A New Venture

While they were serving in this setting, Catherine took another important step. One Sunday while walking to the service in their chapel, she saw many women who just loitered about or sat in their little homes peering out the windows. It came to her that perhaps she would be doing God more service if she would minister to these people on Sunday morning rather than going to the service to enjoy it herself. She made the decision, and as she described it: "I went to the first group of women sitting on a door step . . . then I went on to the next group standing at the entrance of a low dirty court. . . . I began to realize that my Master's feet went before me, smoothing my path and preparing my way." God did wonderful things through her. Many an alcoholic and an oppressed wife were touched. She actually became the first of many a Salvation Army lassie who would do a similar work. The way was being paved for the Army to have its birth.

Another New Course for Catherine

As the Conference still insisted that the Booths stay in a settled ministry rather than being a traveling evangelistic team, they acquiesced and stayed for another year while William served as superintendent of the circuit. In William's first year at Brighouse, the chapel membership had risen from thirty-nine to three hundred. All the debts had been paid and the circuit found itself able to engage three ministers instead of two.

In those days, the couple's two boys and their sister Katie were looking for the birth of another sibling. Catherine's family was certainly growing. Right then Catherine received an invitation from the Leaders Meeting to give an address to a special prayer meeting. She immediately declined and dismissed it. She did not visualize herself as capable of doing such a thing. Catherine had no conviction whatsoever against women speaking or preaching. Actually, some time earlier the well-known American evangelist and his wife, Dr. and Mrs. Palmer, had come to Newcastle for a series of meetings. Mrs. Palmer became the principle figure in the meetings. A pastor, the Reverend Arthur Rees, attacked Mrs. Palmer by writing a pamphlet, *A Woman's Right to Preach*. He held the conviction that women should not preach; it was a man's job. Catherine took offense at this. She determined that the Reverend Authur Reese should not go unanswered. She wrote a pamphlet to defend the right of women to minister as they were led by the Spirit of God. She entitled the pamphlet: *Female Ministry*. It later became the basis of the Salvation Army's teaching on the subject. Catherine approached the subject on a broad-based level, and with good insight. She dealt with the sociological aspects of the novelty of women ministers. Then she did a biblical study of the opening chapters of the Acts of the Apostles. She wrote, "These passages expressly told that the women were assembled with the Disciples on the day of Pentecost and . . . that a cloven tongue sat upon them each, and the Holy Ghost filled them all, and they spoke as the Spirit gave them utterance. . . .

We think it a matter worthy of . . . consideration whether . . . fear [of] women's religious labors may . . . not have something to do with the comparative non-success of the gospel in these later days." She made a very forceful defense for a woman's right to preach the Gospel.

A few day after the pamphlet came off the press, on June 8, 1860, baby Emma was born just as Catherine prepared to celebrate her thirty-first birthday.

A New Step

After Catherine's refusal to speak to the class leaders, she began to realize that she no doubt had been too swift in her refusal when the unanimous invitation to speak had been given. Not only that, William urged her to speak. It looked as if a new ministry was opening. She had committed herself to the principle of women's ministry, and if God was calling her, she must not say "no." She finally got to the place where she could honestly pray, *Lord, if Thou wilt return unto me, as in the days of old and revisit me with those urgings of Thy Spirit, which I used to have, I will obey, if I die in the attempt!*

Catherine still felt somewhat reticent, however, about preaching herself. But then on Whit Sunday the crunch came. A company of over a thousand people assembled in the chapel. What actually happened should really be told in Catherine's own words:

> I was in the minister's pew with my eldest boy, then four years old . . . and not expecting anything particular. . . . I felt the Spirit come upon me. You alone who have felt it know what it means. It cannot be described. . . . It seemed as if a voice said to me, "Now, if you were to go and testify, you know I would bless it to your own soul as well as to the souls of the people." I gasped again and I said in my soul . . . "I cannot do it." I had forgotten my vow! It did not occur to me at all. All in a moment after I had said that to the Lord, I seemed to see the bedroom where I had lain, and to see myself . . . and then the Voice seemed to say to me, "Is this consistent with that promise?" And I almost jumped up and said, "No, Lord, it is the old thing over again, but I cannot do it." . . . And then the devil said, "Besides, you are not prepared, to speak. You will look like a fool and have nothing to say." He made a mistake! He overdid himself for once! It was that word that settled it. I said, "Ah! This is just the point. I have never yet been willing to be a fool for Christ, now I will be one." And without stopping for another moment, I rose up in the seat, and walked up the chapel. My dear husband was just going to conclude. He thought something had happened to me, and so did the people. We had

been there two years, and they knew my timid bashful nature. He stepped down from the pulpit to ask me, "What is the matter, my dear?" I said, "I want to say a word." He was so taken by surprise, he could only say, "My dear wife wants to say a word," and sat down. . . . I got up—God only knows how—and if any mortal ever did hang on the arm of Omnipotence, I did. I just told the people how it came about. I said, "I daresay many of you have been looking upon me as a very devoted woman, and one who has been living faithfully to God, but I have come to know that I have been living in disobedience . . . but I promised the Lord three or four months ago, and I dare not disobey."

By the time Catherine finished speaking, the whole congregation had been deeply moved. Many wept audibly and a holy hush fell over the entire congregation. All that could be heard were the sobs. At that very moment, William jumped to his feet. He startled everyone by announcing that his wife would preach in the evening service.

The whole affair unfolded, as all fully felt, in the will of God. This little diminutive life, making her confession to a Sunday morning congregation, became the great turning point. It was not just an emotional outburst. William felt absolutely persuaded in his own heart and mind that he had been prompted by the Holy Spirit and that Catherine must respond. And respond she did. Catherine, thirty-one years old at the time, moved into a new venture for Christ. And she had another thirty years to fulfill it. But how different those three decades were to be.

As can well be imagined, on that Whit Sunday evening, the chapel soon filled to capacity. People were standing in the aisles and around the walls and on the stairs. On the front pew the chapel elders took their seats alongside William. From the pulpit, Catherine stood up, small as she was, and forthrightly announced her text, "Be ye be filled with the Spirit" (taken from Eph. 5:18). Someone described her preaching as "a certain winsomeness which drew, touched, melted, fascinated." Her son, Bramwell, later described her in the pulpit as:

a slightly built woman . . . extremely gentle and refined in appearance, suggesting even timidity . . . and in her countenance such strength and intensity as made it, especially when animated, almost mesomeric in its power to hold the attention even of the indifferent and casual. . . . Her head, which was small, was well set on her shoulders, its poise and movement conveying great personal force and dignity. . . . Her eyes were wide open, rather than large . . . in the pulpit she arrested attention . . . by the modesty and simplicity of her manner.

So on that Whit Sunday evening in 1860, Catherine entered a whole new phase in her life of service. The Prayer Revival was already gripping Britain by this time, and she arose as a woman of awakening.

The Course Set

Catherine had always hoped for a permanently settled home with a study for William. They were reasonably settled in at Brighouse, but a subtle uneasiness came over William and Catherine. When Catherine realized that hundreds had been brought to Christ in just their first year of marriage through their itinerant ministry, she knew that such things as a permanent home and settlement were not the most meaningful things. More and more they both began to see the importance of William's itinerant ministry. But that ministry had been terminated by the Conference in 1857. What would God have them do? The uneasiness ended in William's divesting himself of the restraints of the Conference. He resigned his commission in 1861. In the meantime Catherine's speaking ministry grew.

Catherine's Speaking Ministry

In many respects, Catherine's early life undergirded her expanding ministry. Through her study of the Bible as a young person, and with her grasp of church history and doctrine, it all came together in a new unfolding revival ministry. After she had stood in the pulpit and had spoken so effectively, the news of her speaking gifts spread rapidly. Invitations began to come in from all quarters. In the New Castle circuit, at the Leaders Meeting on June 6, 1860, Catherine preached and all were duly impressed. It indicated their acceptance of her as a preacher.

Of course, the issue was raised, as it is today, as to whether or not women can preach and not be violating the Scriptures. Catherine became convinced in her own mind that no warrant could be found in the Bible for her not ministering as she did. Whether one called it teaching, speaking, bringing addresses, or preaching, she found the terminology irrelevant. When she stood to speak, as do many Spirit-filled women of God, her message had great effect. Moreover, the Acts of the Apostles makes it clear that women spoke in the first century. In Acts 2, we read:

In the last days, God says, I will pour out my Spirit on all people. Your sons and daughters will prophesy, your young men will see visions, your old men will dream dreams. Even on my servants, both men and women, I will pour out my Spirit in those days, and they will prophesy (Acts 2:17–18 NIV).

Acts also points out that Philip had four daughters who prophesied (Acts 21:8–9). Moreover, as we have seen, Priscilla had something of the key role in the house-church that she and her husband Aquila conducted. The alleged prohibition on women speaking in church is found in 1 Timothy 2:11–12. In the view of many Bible scholars, Paul's word here referred to the unique situation where Timothy was ministering and was not a general restriction against all women speaking. Others, of course, disagree. Be that as it may, and as controversial as it is, Catherine did have a very effective speaking ministry. As a consequence, many hundreds—even thousands—came to faith in the Lord Jesus Christ. That is exceedingly hard to deny. And it is important to notice that she never spoke except under the authority of another. This seemed to fill the basic scriptural mandate for the place of men and women in ministry. She went only to those who had specifically invited her. This was true whether she spoke in chapels, churches, or in open-air meetings.

This practice became the pattern in Salvation Army circles and persists today. Moreover, most contemporary evangelical churches allow opportunities for testimony and sharing by women. After all, the Spirit of God has fallen on sons and *daughters*. Seemingly the only prohibition against women that the New Testament presents is that normally it is a man who is to serve as the chief elder in a local church. At least one never finds a deviation from this pattern in the New Testament era. But then, disagreement surrounds this interpretation. Regardless of the controversy, God certainly used this woman in a powerful way in revival, as He clearly has in many women's lives. This holds true in various denominations as varied as Roman Catholic, Baptists, Methodists, and Pentecostal. May God give us more women of awakening of such spirit and power as Catherine Booth to bring people to Jesus Christ.

This new move into a preaching ministry is not to say that Catherine gave up her responsibility as a mother, wife, and housekeeper for her now quite-large family. Moreover, she continually kept up her work of visiting the drunkards of the locality. But a new ministry had opened. She wrote to her mother, "I have been quite as successful as I expected and have met with nothing but the greatest civility and attention. I have visited two evenings this week and attended two cottage prayer meetings at which I have given addresses and had four penitents."

Catherine often had her hands full with the constant illness that plagued the family. At one time all four children had whooping cough. Then William came down sick. Catherine said, "I felt as though I must do what I can. If I can only get a stronger body I would not mind." But God's provision, always sufficient, enabled her to carry on.

Catherine's fame grew—as she was well aware—but in genuine humility she neither feared nor courted any kind of publicity. To her, fame simply did not matter. In response to all the notoriety, she wrote:

My name is getting trumpeted round the world, I suppose. Mr. Crow informs me that it is getting into the foreign papers now, and in one of them I am represented as having my husband's clothes on! They would require to be considerably shortened before such a phenomenon could occur, would they not? Well, notwithstanding all I have heard about the papers, I have never had sufficient curiosity to buy one, nor have I ever seen my name in print except on the bills on the walls, and then I had some difficulty to believe that it really meant me. However, I suppose it did, and now I think I shall never deem anything impossible any more . . ."

So the ministry continued to grow and develop.

Catherine and William were both well-steeped in Wesleyan theology, particularly in the doctrine of holiness. They resonated with the essence of John Wesley's book, *A Practical Treatise on Christian Perfection.* Wesley's theme centered on people's experiencing full salvation, a clean heart, and perfect love. When the official *Articles for The Salvation Army* were written, in the Wesleyan spirit these words are found, "We believe that it is the privilege of all God's people to be 'wholly sanctified,' and that their 'whole spirit and soul and body' may 'be preserved blameless unto the coming of our Lord Jesus Christ' (1 Thes. 5:23 KJV)." As can be imagined, this particular doctrine created considerable criticism, both of the Booths and of the Army. Religious leaders, especially from the Church of England with their strong Reformed theology, took exception. In some sense of the word, the old conflict between Calvinism and Arminianism arose. As best can be discerned, the Booths did not teach the complete eradication of the sinful nature and hence slip into an unbiblical perfectionism. They were simply on a sincere honest quest for holiness in life. Their heart cry was, "Not my will, but Thine be done." That is most legitimate.

Moreover, the Holy Spirit honored Catherine's teaching on the subject. She said on one occasion, "I spoke a fortnight [ago] . . . on holiness, and a precious time we had. William has preached on it twice, and there is a glorious quickening amongst the people. Pray for me. I only want perfect consecration and Christ as my all, and then I might be very useful, not of myself, the most unworthy of all, but of His great and boundless love."

A Fresh Leading

As Catherine's quest for godly living and sacrificial serving deepened, both she and William look longingly at the life of an itinerant ministry. They made an appeal to the Conference that they be granted the status of traveling evangelists. After much discussion (and one would suppose wrangling), the Conference refused to appoint them to such a ministry. The Conference did grant them a leave of absence to do itinerant work because so many invitations were coming from so many sources. Still they refused the Booth's request, and this in spite of the fact of the tremendous impact of their itinerant work. As a case in point, William preached in a large Wesleyan chapel; the people, some eighteen hundred, crammed the building out to the street. The entire neighborhood was stirred, but some people had walked twenty miles to the meetings. Converts abounded.

In the light of all these circumstances, a decision had to be made. As mentioned briefly earlier, the Booths felt that they really had no alternative but to resign their position. Their traveling ministry was so blessed. So, at the annual Conference in 1861, the Booths severed their relationship with the denomination. The Conference reacted quite vehemently; no longer would the Booth's be permitted to preach in any New Connection chapels. The primitive Methodists followed suit and passed a similar resolution the same year. Further, the annual Conference of the Wesleyans met, and they too passed a resolution forbidding the use of their buildings to Mr. and Mrs. Booth. It all seems incredible, actually, rather ridiculous. But it constituted a serious blow to the ministry and a deep personal disappointment. But once again, William and Catherine knew that God's good providence would see them through. All this happened while Catherine was awaiting the birth of her fifth child. In a few weeks a new baby boy, whom they named Herbert Howard, arrived. The Booths were encouraged when a Free Methodist Chapel in Cornwall opened its doors and invited William to preach a series of meetings. The spirit of revival so moved in the ministry of Booth, that the Cornwall meeting saw more than seven thousand people over fourteen years of age come to faith in Jesus Christ. God had put His seal on the Booth's decision. Even more important, the wonderful results were indicative of how the Prayer Revival was impacting the entire British Isles. God was certainly far from through with Catherine and William, despite the action of the New Connection Conference.

The Foundation of the Army Begins to Be Laid

Both William and Catherine continued to minister in various places where the Conference vetoes did not operate. Catherine herself preached in one of the large Baptist chapels. Their fame spread far and wide over the Isles. They traveled from Cardiff to Newport to Walsall, then on to Leeds; it seemed like the entire country opened its hearts and doors. Catherine's preaching, personal work, and counseling in many respects became as significant to the work as did William's preaching. They had found their niche.

Although they did not realize it at that immediate moment, what God was doing in their lives led to the founding of the Salvation Army. On one occasion during those revival days, William conducted a campaign in Hammersmith, in the eastern part of London. He had been asked by the East London Special Service Committee to undertake one week's services—which lengthened into six. He preached in a tent on an old Quaker burial ground in White Chapel. This work necessitated his walking some distance through the White Chapel area. There he saw masses of people in dire straits, physically and spiritually. Drunkenness, prostitution, dog fights, gambling, and every other conceivable evil ran rampant through the section. God profoundly spoke to William. As he saw the squaller of east London, he realized that this was where God would have him to plant his life. No place in the British Isles stood in more need of the Gospel and a caring ministry than London's east end. He said, "Why should I be looking for work? There's my work looking for me." He recognized his destiny. That night he told Catherine, and she rejoiced. Catherine and William Booth had found their sphere of service—for life.

Six weeks after the meeting in the tent on the old burial ground, the tent itself collapsed. Whether it had actually blown down or some rogues of the area had destroyed it, is not known. William, however, trusted God for a place to preach. He found a dance hall that he could rent on Sunday. With the help of some new converts, they cleaned it up after the dancing had stopped at midnight on Saturday, and William preached on the Lord's day. Three hundred and fifty seats were carried in, and the work went on. William said, "I saw multitudes of my fellow creatures not only without God and hope, but sunk in the most desperate forms of wickedness and misery." Many found Christ.

Catherine's Expanding Impact

Catherine's ministry continued on also, but the physical strain proved almost overwhelming on both of them, and Catherine fell ill to dysentery. The sickness did not respond to medication. She lost considerable weight and the doctors prescribed that she should leave the heart of London and get out into some fresh country air. Accommodations were acquired near Turnbridge Wells, southwest of London. There she went for convalescence. One day in Turnbridge Wells as William visited Catherine, they met a Mr. Reed, a wealthy businessman. Reed asked William to speak on Sunday afternoon; he was unable to do so as he had been scheduled to speak in White Chapel. So Reed turned to Catherine and insisted that she speak. Her health somewhat restored by this time, she consented. Reed told Catherine that the meeting always closed exactly at four o'clock in the afternoon and she must not speak beyond that hour. Catherine replied with a smile, "You must be my time-keeper, for when once I am started,

I am apt to forget myself." When Catherine stood up to speak the hall was full, and the Spirit of God anointed the meeting powerfully. When four o'clock ticked off, she turned to Mr. Reed and asked, "Ought I to stop now?" Mr. Reed, in tears, raised his hand and waved her onward. He said, "Go on, go on, never mind the time." Such was the impact of her speaking.

In St. John's Wood in London, Catherine spoke with tremendous effect. At the close of the St. John Wood's meeting, a deputation of laymen offered to build her a church larger than Charles Haddon Spurgeon's great Metropolitan Tabernacle. She graciously declined, but her ministry obviously had gained the people's deep admiration. Believers would come from many parts of Britain to hear her. Journalists, businessmen, and ministers would flock in to listen to this anointed woman of God. A Mr. Knight, a member of a publishing company, said that he felt that Catherine's messages were of such importance that there ought to be a record of them. He offered to publish them. Again, she graciously refused. She said her messages were not worthy of print. She was not only a great woman of God and a great speaker but she also had a true spirit of humility.

As the Booth's work continued to grow, three years after the decision to plant their lives in east London, thirteen preaching stations had been developed. That is revival in itself.

Catherine and Revival

Catherine had become well aware of the real meaning of revival. Some years prior to the expansion of her own ministry, she had written to William on the subject. She said, "I should not have troubled you with my views on the subject. . . . If not, you will find them exactly in Finney's lectures on revivals, which I consider the most beautiful and common sense work on the subject I ever read." Finney had given the revival lectures at his church, the Chatham Street Chapel in New York City, some years before and they were published in the *New York Evangelist*, a weekly evangelical periodical. When the series was completed, the articles were put together in book form and published. The work made a tremendous impression in many parts of the world, actually spawning revivals. Finney was one of America's great evangelists of the Second Great Awakening. Catherine derived much of her theology from Charles Finney's writings. His autobiography and his lectures on theology in particular influenced her life. Catherine wrote on one occasion that she wished that she could have an hour's talk with the American evangelist. She felt that he would be able to advise her well. Finney had ministered in England, but apparently they never met. She summarized her feelings of appreciation for Finney when she wrote one of the children, "If you would read Finney, it would do more for you than anything I know of, and you could understand and appreciate him." And as well could be imagined, Finney made a similar impact on William.

Catherine did not restrict her views to just the theology and approach of Finney, however. She had a deep appreciation, as did William, for a great preacher who stood at the other end of the spectrum in general evangelical theology: Charles Haddon Spurgeon. Booth was Arminian and Spurgeon, Calvinistic. One time in London with some friends, Catherine and William went to hear Spurgeon. William recorded in his diary that he heard "a truly simple, faithful and earnest sermon. I doubt not that he is doing a very great work." It was not unusual for some of Catherine's converts to become members of Spurgeon's Tabernacle, and she did not object at all. This was indicative of the breadth of her spiritual life and her appreciation for whomever preached the Gospel faithfully and powerfully.

Catherine's ministry became so influential that she even made a very positive impression on Father Ignatius, a monk of the Roman Catholic Benedictine Order. He heard Catherine for the first time when she preached in Brighton. Taken with Catherine's message, he wrote her a letter expressing his gratitude. Her appeal certainly covered a broad area of the evangelical spectrum. In time, her itinerant preaching ministry almost paralleled that of her husband.

By 1870, the Salvation Army had virtually become a reality in almost every aspect except in name and formal structure, at least in the personal ministry of Catherine and William. In the spring of that year, the Booths purchased the People's Market building in White Chapel. They renamed it The People's Mission Hall. It was the first property owned by the Booth's evangelistic mission. From the very beginning of the work, the mission hall opened its doors every night to minister to people. By 1881, Bramwell Booth, Catherine's oldest son, was preaching with great effect. In the White Chapel building he held weeknight meetings that drew people from over Europe and even America.

Serious Illness

During these jubilant times many trials and tribulations still came. William fell victim to typhoid. When he returned to work, he did so far too soon and experienced a relapse. Once again he desperately needed Catherine's help. She would go from mission point to mission point to further the work. One of the doctors prescribed a complete year's rest away from all work and anxiety for William. Another doctor even said that William would never be able to resume charge of the mission. They actually feared for his life.

While William still struggled under his illness, Lord Shaftsbury, an outstanding Christian layman and great benevolent philanthropist, invited

him to attend a conference to consider the amalgamation of all nonde-
nominational religious organizations in London. William was still too
sick to go, so Catherine went in his place and spoke on behalf of the
Christian mission. Lord Shaftsbury expressed genuine appreciation for
the work that they were doing. That constituted a high honor because
Lord Shaftsbury was a notable London figure.

William actually had to absent himself from the work until October
1872. But by God's grace he got back on his feet. Catherine then felt free
to travel, and went to Portsmouth on the English Channel to conduct
evangelistic services. It was said that "hundreds of notorious sinners were
converted in her meetings." From there she went to campaigns in London, Wellingsborough, and Kettering. Kettering was famous as the place
where the great missionary William Carey had ministered.

By 1874, the Booths had established a number of mission stations. On
the twentieth of June 1874, leaders of the Booth's mission stations gathered in White Chapel for a conference. This particular gathering took on
prime significance; it broke ground in that women were present and took
part as delegates. Catherine's influence obviously had its impact throughout the entirety of the work. William announced at the meeting that during the previous twelve-month period gospel halls had been built or
purchased at Plaistow, Portsmouth, and Bethnal Green. Naturally, all this
acquisition of new property brought additional burdens. The work grew
so rapidly that it became evident that the enterprise had to be institution-
alized. That would firm it up and establish it for the future.

All the decisions that were made for the work were mutual decisions.
William and Catherine would always talk everything over. William called
Catherine "a counselor who in hours of perplexity and amazement" has
never failed. She had the wisdom of the Spirit upon her.

In reality, and virtually unnoticed by casual observers, the mission
continued to take on the final shape of the Salvation Army. During those
days, leaders and others in the mission would march from one place to
another led by a single cornet player. This became the forerunner of the
well-known Salvation Army bands. As they would walk through the streets
of London and play on street corners, they gathered a hearing for very
effective evangelistic street services. They would carry banners during
their marches and sing in their processions on the way to church. One of
the best known hymns goes:

> Oh I'm happy all the day
> Since He washed my sins away
> I shall never grieve Him anymore.

With the banners flying and the people marching, they almost became known as the "Halleluyah Army." In one of the great rallies at Whitby, for the first time in public, William Booth was introduced as "General." One of the reports read, "We had a review at 7:00 P.M. marching through the streets in good order singing. . . . We halted at the market place . . . and listened to a powerful address by the General." Quite obviously, the Salvation Army was soon ready for its official name and formal structure. The foundation had been wisely laid.

The Army Is Officially Formed

As the Christian Mission Report and Appeals of 1878 was being prepared, someone raised the issue of what actually constituted the Christian mission. "We are a volunteer army," was the reply. But William said that he was not a "volunteer," that he enlisted as a "regular," and came up with the word "salvation" in the place of "volunteer." Then he said, "We are a Salvation Army." This became their crucial moment. Eventually the new title came into general use among the constituency and the general public. In August 1878, the leaders proposed a new deed of constitution and incorporation. General William Booth spoke to the assembled group: "We are sent to war. We are not sent to minister to a congregation and be content if we keep things going. We are sent to make war . . . and to stop short of nothing but the subjugation of the world to the sway of the Lord Jesus."

Things now moved rapidly. The Salvation Army prepared for its full-fledged debut. A flag, a crest, and a uniform were accepted as their weapons of warfare. By the end of 1878 everything fell in place. Catherine wrote to Mrs. Phillips, a friend, "We have changed the name of the mission into The Salvation Army, and truly it is fast assuming the force and spirit of an army of the living God. I see no bounds to its extension, and if God will own and use such simple men and women . . . as we are sending out now, we can compass the whole country." How right she was. The Salvation Army not only swept the entire country, it ultimately covered the world. Hardly a country today has not felt its influence.

Some questioned William Booth's right to such authority in the new Army. But it must be realized that the organization was built entirely on voluntary adherence. The critics failed to realize that it existed as a thoroughly Christian movement with all the liberty and freedom that the Spirit of God allows His people. Of course, there were disciplines. Certain decrees state:

> Every "member" of The Salvation Army, must give clear testimony to, and evidence of, conversion through faith in the Savior, Jesus Christ, and be ready to testify to that experience. He must declare his belief in the doctrines set forth in the Deed of Constitution, and promise to do all on his part to win others to salvation. In the world,

but no longer of it, worldly amusements, companionships, dress, and indulgences must end. He must foreswear intoxicating drinks, drugs (except on Doctor's orders) and gambling; and if he aspires to play in a band, or take part in an activity for the young, or hold any office whatsoever (all unpaid services), he must also forgo tobacco smoking and taking snuff, wear a uniform when on duty; and hold himself ready to speak and pray in public."

Such rigid requirements did not tend to swell the membership of the Army, but it constituted a faithful stand for Christ on the part of the troops. Moreover, William and Catherine Booth stood as the epitome of those commitments. So the movement was established.

Catherine Carries On

Catherine's ministry continued to grow. In a visit to New Castle, she wrote about the glorious time she had. On one Sunday she spoke at the circus. Nearly four thousand people attended. On Saturday afternoon at New Castle, May 7, 1879, she presented flags to nine newly formed Army corps serving in that district.

Since all the Salvationists wore uniforms, the red jersey and typical uniform soon could be seen all over the country. The marches to church, the bands, the street services, the singing—what an impression they did make. The "Mother of the Army" traveled continuously. How she kept her stamina with the incredible demands made upon her amazed all who knew her. It can only be attributed to the strength that Christ gives (Isa. 40:31).

The Army had now grown so large that Catherine and William were rarely able to minister together. They had to go separate ways much of the time to keep the work going. Needless to say, there were those who criticized. Yet, as is so often the case, the criticism did nothing but increase interest, and God used the movement even more. Not only did the persecution and criticism open people up to investigate what the Salvation Army was all about, it gave the Salvationists themselves added zeal. The enthusiasm grew; it became a beautiful upward spiral. Revival covered the land and the Salvation Army, with Catherine and William at the forefront, was riding the crest of the beautiful awakening wave. Even the very critical *Saturday Review*, which maligned Spurgeon's ministry and most evangelical movements, had to confess, "Those must have been very dull and unsympathetic persons who could resist the pious jollity of the meeting."

In a relatively short time, much of the persecution died down. The tide began to turn in the Booth's favor. People began to realize that this was a true work of God. When criticism did come, usually from the clergy, Catherine in her gracious spirit said,

I have no desire to retaliate . . . though I might do so! All I have to say in respect to the Bishop [a critic] is that I feel quite certain that if his lordship . . . had himself attended those meetings on which he founded his remarks, he would have come to a very different conclusion. . . . I wish he had been here! . . . I shall appeal to reason and understanding—that the measures of the Salvation Army are neither foolish nor unscriptural, nor irrational.

The average person realized Catherine had spoken rightly, and thus deeply appreciated her conciliatory spirit.

A New Step

In this general mileau, Catherine became convicted that the lassies who were working so faithfully with the people needed some kind of formal training. But how could they be trained? Where would they find the resources? Catherine felt that somewhere money could be found to develop a training home for the women cadets. She prayed, and God answered. She found a house on Gore Road, London, near to where daughter Emma's family had moved in Clapton Common. They put Emma in charge. Clapton Common became famous for its large open park area where in the previous century George Whitefield had preached in the open air to the masses. The great eighteenth-century revival had transformed the country, and now Catherine like Selina, Countess of Huntingdon, was experiencing a similar movement—the establishment of a training school for the lassies. Then the Army founded a similar school for men under the leadership of Ballington, the Booth's son. Training for Salvation Army officers was begun because of Catherine's influence. Through her daughter and son she made her contribution in the Army's vital training program. She and son, Bramwell, visited the training homes regularly. A large training complex still exists in London today. This became a most significant step forward. Catherine's sense of her personal responsibility to the volunteers motivated it.

The World Before Them

It has been mentioned several times in this brief look at Catherine Booth's fascinating, productive life that the movement became worldwide. One of the exciting stories overseas occurred when the Booth's eldest daughter Katie went to France in 1881 to begin the work in that country. Katie was only twenty-two years of age at the time, but she had a good knowledge of French. It was painful for Catherine to see her go. Catherine said that Katie's departure for Paris "made me shudder." Still, she recognized that the move had been motivated by God, and in this she rejoiced. Thus, the work opened on the Continent.

The Foundation

The Bible, God's inspired Word, formed the foundation of all that Catherine and the Army believed and taught. She said, "I love this Word and regard it as the Standard of all faith, and practice, and our guide to live by." The philosophy became: The Salvation Army must conquer the world with the Gospel as the Bible says. The sword of the Spirit serves as the primary weapon in defeating sin and Satan.

As the work reached out to different cultures, it was permeated with liberty and freedom that made it welcome and effective. This approach too was largely inspired by Catherine. Probably very few Christian bodies issued more orders and regulations than did the Salvation Army, but as Catherine said, "Let us keep the message itself unadulterated . . . but in our modes of bringing it to bear on man, we are left free as air and sunlight." With that basic approach, they could adapt to the different ethnic needs of different peoples worldwide and the work took solid root wherever the Army went.

A Wonderful Spin-off

So influential did the Salvation Army become that the question arose in the established church, the Church of England, whether they should do something of the same order. Unknown to many people, the Church of England organized a similar organization called the Church Army. They too wear uniforms and do a similar work through the Church of England. This Army has made a significant contribution to the cause of Christ. It all demonstrates the tremendous impact that William and Catherine were making by this time. With the state-established Church of England copying them in methodology, Catherine and William had certainly ascended to the height of their influence. A well-known writer said of Catherine,

> Her beautiful spirit impressed itself alike upon the most exacting of her intellectual contemporaries and upon the masses of the poor. . . . The growth of her spiritual powers seems to me like one of the miracles of religious history. In her frail body the spirit of womanhood manifested its power and the Spirit of God its beauty. It is a tribute to the age in which she lived that this power and beauty were acknowledged by the world during her lifetime. She exercised a spell over many nations.

In spite of all of the difficulties and problems that they continually faced, the Salvationists grew by tens of thousands. Victory after victory became theirs. The essence of revival carried them from height to height.

The Family

The family began slipping away from the home, but all to Spirit-led Christian ministry. Bramwell married, and daughter Evangeline was becoming increasingly effective as a servant of Christ. Evangeline eventually became the director of the work in the United States and ministered in America for over thirty years, as the work spread from coast to coast in the States.

The Booths undertook a new venture in helping homeless girls. So many roamed the streets and the only place of shelter would be houses of prostitution. Some of the girls were mere children, and something had to be done, so the Salvation Army stepped in. Under the leadership of son Bramwell, an investigation was made into the pitiful condition of these young women. This precipitated Catherine's stepping into the political life of the country to do something through legislation for the protection of the girls. She addressed Prime Minister Gladstone and later his successor, Lord Salisbury. And they listened.

The Salvation Army demanded that a bill be passed that had four provisions:

- that there be protection for children, boys and girls, to the end of their seventeenth year;
- that it be made a criminal act to procure young persons for immoral purposes;
- that parents or guardians be given the right of a search warrant to recover children from brothels;
- that there be equality of men and women before the law, that is, that it should be an offence for men to solicit women.

Parliament responded. The bill, the Criminal Law Amendment Act, was passed by the House of Commons and the Army's demands were fully met. Few women could have such an influence, but Catherine was that kind of a woman.

As the latter part of the 1880s began to unfold, Catherine's work went on apace, but she was beginning to do battle with the last enemy. As Paul said, "The last enemy that shall be destroyed is death" (1 Cor. 15:26). Many years before, Catherine had written in her journal, "Thy Will be done; only let me be Thine, whether suffering or in health, whether living or dying." She had certainly gone through it all. Amidst the joy of a most happy marriage and the birth of many wonderful children who were all involved in the Lord's work, and in the face of much persecution and criticism, she had ascended the hill of revival ministry that made her one of the most respected women in the world.

The End Approaches

Catherine's health began to deteriorate. She found herself increasingly unable to do much work. Still, she summoned strength to accept an invitation to speak at the great City Temple of London. Dr. Joseph Parker, one of the most famous preachers of the nineteenth century, invited her to speak, and even as a frail little woman, she brought a tremendous message. Catherine made such an impression that a distinguished religious teacher and author from Holland wrote: "Above them all, to my mind, stands Catherine Booth. I cannot exactly describe the secret of the extraordinary, captivating power of her words, but her address remains unforgettable. Right from the beginning to the end she brought me into the personal presence of Jesus Christ."

Catherine's condition continued to worsen. The illness finally was diagnosed: terminal cancer. In May 1889, Catherine underwent a series of "electric treatments." They were given to her under anesthetic. The electric treatments had been called "a successful remedy for cancer," but such was far from the case. The slight improvement they brought about proved very temporary indeed.

By December Catherine's strength had all but failed. Congestive heart failure threatened. She had a serious hemorrhage and the doctor summoned the family. On December 15, 1889, William wrote in his diary: "My darling had a night of agony. When I went into her room at 2 A.M. . . . they were endeavoring to staunch a fresh hemorrhage. . . . After a slight improvement another difficulty set in. . . . After several painful struggles there was a great calm, and we felt the end had come." Catherine did linger on for a few more days. On December 19 she sent a brief message to the many she called her "Army Children" in all the nations. The message read: "The waters are rising, but so am I. I am not going under, but over. Don't be concerned about your dying: only go on living well, and the dying will be all right."

A Short Reprieve

The little lady was stronger than anyone would have believed. To everyone's amazement, she even regained a bit of strength. By the end of January 1890, she had rallied. Much to her delight she still lingered when the Army celebrated its twenty-fifth anniversary.

But now Catherine's life was truly coming to an end. Her strength ebbed away. On Saturday, October 4, at 9 A.M., the doctor found her a bit stronger than the night before. But it became obvious that the time had come. By noon her life was gently slipping away. Her hand lay on William's. Each of the family kissed her brow, her lips moved as her eyes searched out Bramwell's. Beloved William, with tears in his eyes, led them as they all sang, kneeling around her bed the song:

My mistakes His free grace doth cover,
My sins He doth wash away:
These feet which shrink and falter
Shall enter the Gates of Day.

Once more, as he had done before when they thought the end had come, William gave her up to the Lord. Suddenly a "gleam of joyful recognition passed over the brightening countenance," and she spoke William's name. Their eyes met and they had one parting kiss. Catherine was gone. As one writer put it, "Catherine Booth, William's little wife— Mother of his eight beauties, Mother of The Salvation Army, Mother of Nations—had gone Home. She had faced the last enemy and proved that in life and in death God is enough for us."

The revival, of course, did not end with Catherine nor did the Salvation Army. The work goes on and grows around the world to this day. But ever if there was a woman of revival, it was this little giant who conquered all, and through Jesus Christ conquered death. Praise be to God for such a woman of awakening!

Endnotes

1. The quotes in this chapter are taken from Catherine Bramwell Booth, *Catherine Booth* (London: Hodder and Stoughton, 1970).

Chapter Eight

AMY CARMICHAEL

The Indian Awakening

Ten days before Christmas, 1867, David and Catherine Carmichael had the delight of welcoming the arrival of their first child. Six wonderful children were to follow the birth of the little girl, but God had designed a fantastic future for this new infant. Her name was Amy.

David Carmichael had not married until his thirty-seventh year. A hard working man, he and his brother William labored side by side running two mills. The Carmichaels were a rather affluent family, living close to the sea at Millisle County Down, in northern Ireland. Both brothers were deeply devoted to Christ, and their devotion showed itself in very practical ways. On one occasion, the two men gave £500 to build a church-owned schoolhouse, a tidy sum in those days. The purpose for the building was for teaching during the day, then holding evening classes and church services on Sunday. John Beatty, the local Presbyterian minister, gladly received the gift and set to work on the project. The Carmichaels were committed Presbyterians.

Brother William and his wife boasted of five lovely children. Quite clearly, little Amy had no lack of playmates; she enjoyed the cadre of cousins. In those early days she stood out as a leader among the group. She failed to fill the role of a typical, prim little Victorian girl. Actually, she was something of a tomboy. Perhaps the cousins had something to do with that.

Amy's Early Life

Amy had brown eyes, which did not please her at all. She felt that brown eyes simply were not attractive. But then she remembered her mother had told her that if she sincerely asked God for anything, He would surely grant her prayers. Even at an early age, she had some spiritual stirrings. So little three-year-old Amy went to the Lord in childish fashion but in genuine sincerity, asking God to change the color of her eyes. Much to her disappointment, her eyes remained brown. She did not realize at the time that God also answers "no" as well as "yes" to prayers, and when He does answer "no," there is a very real reason. In the years that unfolded in her missionary revival ministry, those brown eyes served her very well. During her service in India, as she would search out the terribly abused temple children in India, those brown eyes, rather than the blue that she had so desired, found a glad reception among the benighted brown-eyed Indian children. God had begun preparing a vessel "fit for the Master's use."

Amy Carmichael's Formative Years

Amy developed into a very determined and well-disciplined girl. Her father taught her to be tough. He gave her swimming lessons by tying a rope around a safety belt that girdled her waist. He instructed her in how to ride a very lively pony. Amy mastered both skills. Later in life she said, "I am grateful to my father for teaching me never to give in to a difficulty."[1] Perhaps the father also contributed to Amy's tomboy spirit.

Through those early experiences, Amy learned to deal with physical stress and strain. She developed a tenacity and an obedience to spiritual principles that gave her the stamina to endure the many years of heartache and hardship she would face ministering to the poor, rejected children of India.

Not only did Amy become a very self-sufficient little lady, she developed a tender sensitivity to the needs of others. Perhaps because of her large family, this sterling quality imbedded itself deeply in the young lady. From early childhood, she would go down to the village with soup for the poor and destitute of the town. It developed in her that kind of selflessness that God so significantly blesses. Actually, Amy's benevolence was no mere childish gesture; it provided a vital service as relatively insignificant as it may seem. There were no state-run social agencies in those days, and such simple acts of charity saved many a life.

Amy's parents, being deeply devout evangelical Christians, longed to see Amy acquire a vital personal faith and commitment to the Lord Jesus Christ. They admired her charity, but they knew that she needed Christ above all. The local minister had become a close friend of the Carmichael's and his faithfulness in presenting the Gospel to the children began to impact Amy. She began to grow conscious of God's love and the wonderful salvation that He graciously grants to people of faith. Amy's religious experience was never imposed on her by her parents; thus, she developed a genuine sensitivity to the centrality of personal faith in the Lord Jesus Christ. Strangely enough, though, her actual conversion did not take place until some years later. So Amy lived out her childhood days as a happy-go-lucky, yet sensitive little girl.

Christian visitors who came to the Carmichael home from time to time—they were a hospitable family—often touched Amy's life. One such welcome visitor was the brother of the Reverend John Beatty, their minister. He served as a missionary in India. On Sunday afternoons, while home on furlough, he and his wife would tell the children stories about India. This began to plant the seed in Amy's life that would finally bring fruition in a marvelous revival ministry in the so-called sub-continent of misery, which India remains to this day. Still, she had not been truly converted.

Amy's Conversion

As Amy began to grow into maturity, David Carmichael moved his family to Belfast. He and his brother had a new mill under construction near the Dufferin rock quarry. They were a very enterprising pair and their ability as entrepreneurs was quite outstanding.

Before the family moved to Belfast, Amy had been sent off to boarding school at Harrogate in England, a Wesleyan Methodist institution. There she gained the reputation among her fellow students as "a rather wild Irish girl . . . and something of a rebel." Amy seemed to be constantly getting into some sort of mischief. By the age of fourteen she became the ringleader among all the other girls. At times the young lady even feared that she might be expelled because of the various exploits she led the other girls into doing. But Amy had a winsome way about her, and she managed to escape too severe a discipline.

Still, all the years at Harrogate were a far cry from merely frolicking and having a good time at the teachers' expense. Near the end of her three-years stay at Harrogate, the administration organized an evangelistic program at the school, conducted by the Children's Special Service Mission. Mr. Edwin Arrowsmith, one of the founders of the movement, served as the primary speaker. He faithfully unfolded the Scriptures and lifted up the Good News of Christ and His power to save.

The Bible stories and the things that Arrowsmith had to say were certainly not new to Amy. She had been brought up on them, and in her way had developed a reasonably serious religiosity. She would pray and always felt something of a sense of God's love. In the context of Mr. Arrowsmith's teaching, however, God began to speak much more directly to Amy. Arrowsmith would ask the girls to sing "Jesus Loves Me, This I Know." Then he would urge them just to sit quietly for a few minutes and think seriously about what they had just sung. During one of those times of reflection, as simple as they were, it suddenly broke in on Amy's consciousness that she was responsible to receive Christ's salvation personally. Right then and there she invited the Lord Jesus Christ to take absolute control of her life. Granted, it seems quite childlike in its simplicity, but Jesus said that one must become as a child to receive Him fully. From that moment on, Amy was transformed and began to grow and mature in her new Christian faith by leaps and bounds. More and more she came to understand the meaning of the Cross and the tremendous sacrifice that Christ had made for her, and for all people. That spirit of sacrifice, as epitomized in the Lord Jesus Christ, became the bulwark of her faith and her approach to Christian service. A new horizon opened as she began to recognize that God had definite plans for her life.

Due to the dynamics and flow of business cycles, the new venture of the Carmichael brothers in Belfast deteriorated drastically. Amy had to be brought home from Harrogate school to live at home. Financially, the family began traversing very difficult waters. Father David had lent a friend several thousand pounds, and then the friend defaulted. David refused to demand the money back. Then to compound the problems, he fell seriously ill, a victim of double pneumonia. God called him home at the early age of fifty-four on April 12, 1885. It seemed as though the very heart had been torn out of the Carmichael family.

Father was gone.

Being the oldest child in the family, Amy became her mother's confidante and comforter. Then, right in the midst of extremely difficult circumstances and heartache, God's clarion call to Amy began to resonate in her heart.

The Call

One Sunday morning as Amy and her brothers and sisters were returning home from church, they met a poor bedraggled old woman, weighed down with a heavy burden. Instantly, the children relieved her of her burden and helped her along the way. The more respected members of the congregation, when they saw this gracious Christian act, raised their eyebrows; respectable people were not supposed to do such things for bedraggled old women. One wonders about the reality of their Christianity, but Amy served the poor old lady regardless of how others reacted. She described her experience in helping the needy woman:

> Just as we passed a fountain . . . this mighty phrase was suddenly flashed . . . through the gray drizzle: "Gold, silver, precious stones, wood, hay, stubble—every man's work shall be made manifest; for the day shall declare it . . . and the fire shall try every man's work of what sort it is. If any man's work abide—" (1 Cor. 3:12). I turned to see the voice that spoke to me. . . . The blinding flash had come and gone; the ordinary was all about us. We went on. I said nothing to anyone, but I knew that something had happened that had changed life's values. Nothing could ever matter again but the things that were eternal.

The incident transformed Amy's life. Never again would she play the tomboy or the excitement-seeking teenager. She actually felt that the incident was something of a revelation of God Himself. He wanted her to meet the needs of desperately needy people. She said, "From this pool flowed the stream that is the story."

God gave Amy another marvelous touch in 1881. She was visiting Scotland at that time and went to a Christian convention in Glasgow. In one of the sessions, the person leading in prayer lifted up his voice, and said, "Oh Lord, we know you are able to keep us from falling." That may seem again a rather insignificant event, but God spoke powerfully to Amy's heart. God often uses the insignificant. She kept repeating that wonderful truth to herself throughout the day. She was safe and secure in Christ. God would see her through any difficulty or challenge that would fall across her path. The call was crystallizing clearly.

Service

These incidents of God's gracious dealings with the young lady stayed with her and gave her a security throughout the years. Amy threw herself into serving the Lord Jesus Christ. Her dedication and commitment manifested itself in many ways. She would go down the street and bring children to her home for children's meetings; then she would provide them with tea that her mother would set out, because for the Irish, as for the English, high tea highlighted the afternoon. On Monday nights Amy taught a group of boys. She would always go to the poorest and most ramshackle streets of her city on Saturday evening seeking to be a help to the needy. Another of Amy's faithful and innovative services she called "the Morning Watch," a prayer group. This particular group that she brought together had to sign a pledge that they would spend time every day in prayer and Bible study. Amy gave herself to those disciplines as her own spiritual life matured. She also spent much time in the local YWCA helping folks. One of her most effective ministries centered in her service to a class of women called the "shawlies." These were mill girls who covered their heads with shawls instead of the conventional Victorian hats. The more sophisticated of society looked down on them with suspicion and almost classified them as outcasts. But Amy gave herself to the shawlies as she ministered in Christ's name. Consequently, through the difficult times of Amy's own family's reduced circumstances and the sad death of her father, she grew by leaps and bounds in her commitment to Jesus Christ. She could say with the apostle Paul, "The things which happened unto me have fallen out rather unto the furtherance of the gospel" (Phil. 1:12 KJV). This became her philosophy of life, as shall become very evident. In many respects, this approach to Christian ministry precipitated the awakening spirit that surrounded this wonderful missionary woman of awakening.

The Work Goes Forward on Faith

Amy's faithfulness and service to her Lord developed through her earlier years. Her work with the shawlies grew and reached out more and more to those desperate women. The work expanded to the extent that she required a permanent hall. Amy felt that they needed a building that would seat at least five hundred people. But where in the world would the money come from? The family's resources had virtually evaporated, and though they were able to live reasonably well, there was certainly nothing left that would even begin to supply such a need. Yet Amy felt absolutely confident that God would provide the means. In this setting she learned one of the basic spiritual principles that guided her ministry and mission later in India: simple faith in God's provision and care.

One day while making some calls with her mother, Amy encountered two Christian ladies. They were conscious of the building need. They put Amy in touch with a Miss Kate Mitchell. Amy contacted Kate Mitchell, who donated the entire sum to construct the building. Amy had known that God would provide some way, and here it was. Then a mill owner whom Amy knew donated a prime piece of land in the city for a very nominal lease. The carpenters and builders were called in and the hall soon opened. Dr. Park, Amy's minister, dedicated the building. She had now learned first hand, as had Paul, "And my God shall supply all your needs according to His riches in glory in Christ Jesus" (Phil. 4:19).

Dedication Day

The dedication of the new hall was a festive day in the Lord. A large banner had been painted and hung across the platform. It read: "That in all things He may have the preeminence" (Col. 1:18). That verse, though Amy had read it many times, came alive in a fresh way. It became something of the hallmark of her approach to Christian ministry. Nothing, absolutely nothing, would ever stand in her way of giving Jesus Christ the preeminence and all the glory in her life and service.

The hall served as a place for study, worship, and evangelistic work. An evangelistic mission became the very first event. Two students from the Moody Bible Institute in America led the meetings. The hall was named "The Welcome." It proved true to its name; within its walls many came to faith in Christ during the days of ministry.

"The Welcome" house had a full program. Amy printed cards that outlined all the activities for a normal week. To read the card, one could hardly believe all the varied programs and organizations that Amy developed. But she threw herself into the work with her whole heart and energy. Miss Mitchell, who had given the original gift for the hall, took charge of the administration activities, which relieved Amy of any anxiety in that respect. So the work went forward as God blessed the effort.

A New Move

In 1888, a great financial crash struck the British Isles. The small amount of remaining money that Father David had left to support the family was lost in the crisis. Amy, only twenty years old at that time, retained her peace and confidence in Christ; God would supply their needs. Circumstances forced the family to move from Belfast to Manchester, England. Then two of the brothers immigrated to the United States. Later one brother moved to Canada and another to South Africa. But through it all God did provide. In Manchester, Mother Carmichael took the position as superintendent of a rescue home. There Amy started work with girls similar to those in the Welcome house in Belfast. She threw herself into the work, really working too hard and eating far too sparingly.

Amy's residence in Manchester was situated in a crime-ridden area. On one occasion a group of hoodlums mobbed Amy as she made her way to visit her mother who lived in the rescue house. All of this stress and toil and poor diet, together with several illnesses, took its toll, and Amy had to give up her beloved work. She was most reluctant to do so, but she had the assurance that God never closes one door but that He opens another.

A New Friend

Amy had come in contact with Robert Wilson in 1887 back in Ireland. He was an elderly gentlemen of Broughton Grange in Cumberland county. It had been just a chance meeting and Amy had thought nothing of it at the time; but it proved to be a very important junction in Amy's life.

From time to time Amy along with her sisters and brothers would visit Mr. Wilson. They eventually became quite close friends. Through Robert Wilson, Amy attended her first Keswick Convention. This became very foundational in the future revival ministry of Amy Carmichael. The Keswick Convention message, as seen, has fostered spiritual awakenings around the world, and an outline of Keswick teaching is found in the chapter on Bertha Smith.

The Carmichaels called Robert Wilson the "dear old man," or for short, DOM. It may appear rather strange in our culture today, but Robert Wilson asked Mrs. Carmichael if she would spare Amy to be his companion. This was not a proposal of marriage or anything in that respect; he just had a deep, platonic affection for the young lady and asked her to become his companion in his old age. The year was 1890, and Amy turned twenty-three.

Such a decision Amy herself would probably never have made, although no implications of any impropriety about such an arrangement would arise in the mindset of the Victorians. God had a hand in the situation that rebounded for Amy's good and that of the DOM as well. Later in life Amy commented, "I knew afterward it had not been easy . . . and yet looking back I can see that it fit into the Plan . . . certain great lessons not learned yet had to be learned."

Wilson served as the chairman of the Keswick Convention when Amy went to live with the family. Many Keswich speakers came to Broughton and touched Amy significantly. Wilson, born into a Quaker family, taught Amy the importance of dropping restrictive denominational labels and of thinking more of the church in its universal aspect. This became important for her when she started her work in India.

Although Amy was well taken care of by the DOM, not all proved pleasant. Wilson had two sons who were bachelors, and they lived in the house with Amy. They resented her and did not make life easy for her. Nonetheless, God worked and developed patience and understanding in the young lady, thus helping prepare her for her life's work. Perhaps above all, it gave Amy the opportunity to recover her physical strength from the exhausting time of her work in Manchester. And she was of great comfort and strength to sixty-six-year-old Robert Wilson. They really became wonderful companions. She served as his hostess and this relieved him so he could give himself to the work with Keswick and other Christian enterprises. By now the Far East began to loom on the horizon for Amy.

Answering the Call to Missions

"Go ye—to those dying in the dark—fifty thousand of them every day." Those words gripped Amy Carmichael. She sensed it as God speaking. She had thought it might be the will of her Lord to stay with the DOM until he went to heaven, but God had other plans. She had learned to love and respect Wilson as a sincere man of God; he had become like a father to her. Yet the conviction deepened more and more that she must go to the mission field to share the message of the Lord Jesus Christ. She did not find the will of God coming like a bolt of lightening, but rather just as a growing conviction; but she was utterly yielded to the Lord wherever He would lead her.

This caused real perplexity for Amy. She hated to leave Robert Wilson, and then her own mother needed her, or so it seemed. Who would care for her? But she must follow her understanding of the Spirit's leading. So Amy wrote her mother, though it cost her much inward pain. She had become convinced that God had said to her, "Go." She must answer. Her mother replied almost immediately: "Yes, dearest Amy, He has lent you to me all these years . . . so, darling, when He asks you now to go away from within my reach, can I say nea? No, no, Amy, He is yours— you are His—to take you where He pleases and to use you as He pleases, I can trust you to Him and I do." Mr. Wilson felt the same way. The road cleared for Amy to leave with a clear conscience before God and her family.

A New Decision

A new problem arose when Amy questioned as to where the Spirit of God would actually lead her. She at first had her eye on China. But Ceylon, now known as Sri Lanka, also seemed a possibility. God had shown her the needs of that country. What was the Lord's destination for Amy? Then God closed and opened a door. Amy offered herself to the China Inland Mission (CIM), the well-known faith-mission organization directed by Hudson Taylor, who happened to be a personal friend of Robert Wilson. However, the doctor refused to pass Amy as medically fit for China.

Amy had attended the Keswick Convention that year. She impressed the leadership very favorably, so they appointed Amy as the very first missionary to be supported by the Keswick Missionary Committee. What an honor. But still, where exactly would she go? Amy confessed, "Always the thought was with me, 'this is not your rest.' I knew I must go, but where?" It was a full year later that Amy began to cast her eyes on Japan. The conviction grew deeper and more profound that Japan should be her mission field. So without hesitation she set out on her journey with Keswick's blessings.

Japan

Amy sailed on the SS *Valetta*, accompanied by three other missionaries. They endured quite rough seas before finally arriving at Colombo in Ceylon. Even though the voyage had been through difficult weather, she taught a daily Bible class on the ship. The day after arriving in Colombo, she boarded another vessel and sailed for Shanghai. One of the blessings of that journey centered in Amy's leading the captain of the ship to Christ. When Amy arrived in Shanghai, a letter of confirmation from missionary leaders awaited her, which affirmed her decision. She addressed a few gatherings of the missionaries in Shanghai and then boarded a ship and arrived in Shimonoseki, Japan during a violent storm. Because of the fury of the weather, no one could come to the dock to meet her. Amy, however, had learned resiliency and tenacity of spirit many years before, and she could surely cope with this small inconvenience. She thanked God that she had reached her destination safely and immediately threw herself into evangelistic work in that needy nation.

Amy had not been in Japan long before she adopted Japanese dress, convinced that this would help her identify more closely with the Japanese. Her heart broke for their need of Christ. Later she wrote a beautiful poem concerning her life burden to win people to the Lord:

> O for a passionate passion for souls,
> O for a pity that yearns!
> O for the love that loves unto death,
> O for the fire that burns!

Amy, by the spirit of God, had developed a true passion for the lost souls. And she had no fear for the difficulties that she would face in this grand enterprise. She had chosen the high road that leads to the hilltops.

A New Field

All was not well with Amy physically during her Japanese days. As early as 1894, she had bouts with acute neuralgia. Her doctor urged her to go to China for a summer. A thorough rest would help, the doctor said. The physician urged her to go for convalescence in Cheefo, on the north China coast. There the great Shantung Revival broke out some years later. But God did not seem to be leading her in that direction, so she declined the suggestion and began to look toward Ceylon. In spite of poor health, Amy sailed to the island country. Indicative of her profound faith, she had not even received any official welcome from the Christians in Ceylon. She set her heart on working with the Heneratgoda Village Mission. When she actually arrived, they received her with open arms, much to her joy, so she decided to stay.

Amy threw herself into the work in her typical zealous style. But after the initial welcome, some of the folk did not understand her very well and she began to sense that perhaps even Ceylon would only be a stopgap measure to her ultimate ministry. She had spent but fifteen months in Japan, now Ceylon did not seem quite right, and she seriously wondered how God was dealing with her. Right at that juncture, she received news that Robert Wilson had suffered a severe stroke. Immediately Amy set off for home.

Amy's mother met her in London, but Amy was so ill she could not travel to Cumberland. Friends from Keswick days took care of her until she recovered enough strength to travel to Broughton Grange for Christmas in 1894. Through it all, the twenty-seven-year-old missionary could not but question God's dealings. Yet she realized that God has ways that go beyond our understanding. And as the future would soon demonstrate, the Lord wanted Amy to be His instrument to display His mighty, saving, awakening, reviving hand in India—a country she had never seriously considered.

Amy never doubted her original call. Although she had felt God's leading to Japan in 1893, and then to Sri Lanka for a short period, she knew that God had His hand on her for something significant.

During Amy's convalescent time back in England, she wrote her first book, *From Sunrise Land,* a small volume containing her missionary letters from Japan. Right at that time of questioning and some confusion, Amy received a letter from a friend in Bangalore, a large city in the south-central part of India. Something stirred in Amy's heart when she read the letter. She remarked, rather casually, that India might be a good place for her as the climate would be conducive to her health. This set something stirring in Amy's heart as she began to cast her eyes on that part of the world. Britain controlled India in the nineteenth century, so Amy would have no problems going there to minister.

It may seem that our heroine of revival was perhaps a little fickle in sorting out her missionary call. Nothing could be further from the truth, however. She was utterly dedicated to God and convinced that the Holy Spirit had led her, even though her brief time in Japan and Ceylon appeared strange to some. There was nothing fickle about any aspect of her life; she spent the last of her days, over fifty years, in one spot in India. A beautiful story of that half-century unfolds.

Off to India

The leaders of the Church of England's Zenana Missionary Society interviewed Amy concerning missionary work in India. She passed with flying colors and the missionary society of the Anglican Church accepted her as one of their missionaries during the Keswick Convention in July of that year. So off to India she went. Once again, Keswick formed a significant part of her life as the realization of what it means to live in spiritual revival continually deepened. How she wanted to share the message with others who had never heard!

Once again a heart-rending time of leaving loved ones thrust itself upon our missionary warrior. On September 30, she left her mother and sisters, and then on October 11 she left Robert Wilson, the dear old man. He had recovered his health as had Amy. So she left with no misgivings. She knew that God had led in it all.

When Amy arrived in India, her first three weeks were spent at Madras. She stayed in the home of the secretary of the church missionary society, Mr. Arden. His younger daughter, Maud, became very close to Amy and proved to be an able worker in Amy's mission in later years. On December 4, Amy arrived in Bangalore. Hopefully the climate would help her, for upon her arrival she was suffering from severe fever. She soon recovered, however, and was back in the harness.

Amy had a rather disquieting experience right at this time. She disagreed with the evangelistic methods that some of her fellow missionaries employed. Moreover, she did not really have anyone with whom she could confide. She felt quite alone and was not particularly happy. Nevertheless, she threw herself into the study of Urdu, one of the languages of India, but soon realized that it would be best to learn Tamil, the dialect of south India. In that way she could become something of an official hospital evangelist because the hospitals always used Tamil. But how could she be tutored in the dialect? During a brief stay in a hill resort for some rest, Amy met a missionary couple, the Reverend and Mrs. Walker, who offered to be her Tamil teachers. The couple lived some distance from Bangalore in the city of Tinnvelly. If Amy accepted the offer, it would force her to leave Bangalore, but she became convinced that God would have her do so.

The Bangalore missionaries soon approved Amy's move. The language lessons forged a close bond between Amy and her tutor and his wife. They cultivated a deep affection and profound appreciation for each other. Amy gave herself to the work with the Walkers, as well as to studying Tamil. In July 1897, the Walkers and Amy moved into a bungalow at Pannaivilai in the same general area and commenced evangelistic work among the locals. From that time on, following her previous pattern, Amy adopted Indian dress. This precipitated some criticism from other European missionaries, but she was convinced that God would have it so.

Amy soon gathered around her a group of young converts. She organized them into a small band of believers who called themselves "the Starry Cluster." One of those who came to Christ, a woman by the name of Sellamutthu, remained Amy's loyal friend and fellow worker for some forty-three years of ministry. Amy's work had begun to take lasting root.

A New Phase of the Work Begins

As Amy carried on her evangelistic ministry, two young girls ran away from their guardians seeking protection. Amy gave them refuge. Another girl, Arulai, only eleven years of age, also took leave of her relatives to join Amy's "family." They became known as the woman's band. What was God doing? What sort of ministry was beginning to take shape through this woman of awakening?

Right at this stage, a significant decision took place. The small woman's band, under Amy's leadership, felt led of God to move from Pannaivilai to Dohnavur. After they moved, the community began to grow by leaps and bounds.

For some time Amy had been concerned about a deplorable situation that persisted in most of the pagan temples of India. Young girls were taken in, many times only as children, and made temple prostitutes. The girls spent miserable, horrible lives. Amy became deeply burdened for them. After a year in Dohnavur with her women's band, Amy met the first temple child who had escaped the clutches of her "guardians." Her name was Preena. She had flown the temple scene once before, but her mother thrust her back to the temple women and they had literally branded her little hands with hot irons as punishment. But Preena could not stand the thought of being married to the god and the terrifying lifestyle that meant. So she escaped again and this time made her way to Amy. Amy immediately took her in and thus began the start of something great.

Amy was very wise in wearing Indian dress. The young girls could identify with her. Not only that, at last her brown eyes held her in good stead. Even though she wore native dress, had the girls seen blue eyes, they would not have felt nearly as secure with her as her brown eyes seemed to make them. All Indians with few exceptions have brown eyes. Amy's brown eyes were a meaningful thing for the little escaping temple girls. She appeared to them as a beautiful mother figure.

As Amy's work had begun to take shape, Amy confessed that there had always been something in her ministry that somehow seemed unfulfilled. Now the Lord was granting her that fulfillment in a wonderful, reassuring ministry to temple girls.

Of course, there were those who despised Amy's work. Her enemies described her as the "child-catching Missie Ammal." That bothered Amy very little as she saw the transformed lives of her family. A most unusual ministry had opened up for her.

It is only fair to say that everything did not automatically fall in place in this new ministry. Many obstacles had to be overcome. With the work now basically settled for the girls in Dohnavur, Amy began to reach boys for Christ. In 1901, five boys were baptized, making their public profession of faith in Jesus Christ. Amy's heart went to the little fellows in need as well as the temple girls, and she led many a lad to Christ. Tragically, within two weeks, two of the five whom Amy had won died. As can be understood, this was a great heartache for Amy; however, a settled work for them similar to the girls awaited in the future.

Up to this time, Amy had been traveling between Dohnavur and Pannaivilai, still working part-time with the Walkers. But the work was now growing to such an extent that she felt she must centralize her efforts completely in Dohnavur because the needy children kept coming. Before long a temple baby was presented to Amy's Dohnavur family. The little child, only thirteen days old, came under Amy's care. Amy named her Amethyst; and in a short time she was joined by another baby from the temple. Amy named her Sapphire. They were jewels indeed.

Building and Fellowship

Clearly, the time to start building a nursery had come and was put on the agenda. Later a boys home was built. Gifts began to come in, totally unsolicited. Amy determined that she would not solicit money for any project; she would simply trust God. Following the lead of George Müller of the Bristol Orphanage in England, she would just commit all of the needs to God; and God marvelously answered. This principle became Amy's faith commitment throughout the rest of her life. God honored Amy's trust and through the years a great complex grew up at Dohnavur, which finally became known as the Dohnavur Fellowship.

The Dohnavur Fellowship in its earlier days had no official constitution or by-laws; actually, it had very little organization. They simply lived together in a loving relationship with their eyes fixed on one goal: the meeting of needs, particularly of temple children who stood in such great moral danger. Amy's joy revolved around leading as many as possible to faith in Jesus Christ. The work increased, not with great publicity or fanfare, but with the beginning of true spiritual awakening, and that in a most unusual context: temple and needy children being brought to Jesus Christ. Yet, what could be more profound than that? It paved the way for a tremendous outpouring of the Holy Spirit.

Revival Comes to Dohnavur

During October 1905, God began to move powerfully on the Christians in the Dohnavur Fellowship. A tremendous infusion of the Holy Spirit permeated the work, which made an incredible impression on the entire neighborhood. In 1904 revival had broken out in Wales (some say it began in 1901), and by 1905 it had spread to many parts of the world, including India.

George M. Marsden, in his book, *Fundamentalism and American Culture*, makes the point that the Welsh Revival became a worldwide movement. And it essentially went forward in the spirit of what Keswick stood for. The basic Christian quest for holiness and godliness, as expressed by the Keswick Conventions, finally touched the globe. Many American scholars recognized the significance of that movement, and the Dohnavur Fellowship became one of the recipients of this move of God. It will be remembered how significantly Amy Carmichael herself had been influenced by the Keswick movement. So she was well-prepared to be a woman of awakening. Now revival had come and God had His woman of awakening, Amy Carmichael, not only ready to receive it but able to be used of the Spirit of God to deepen and develop it. Thus, multitudes were won to faith in the Lord Jesus Christ as the Christians themselves were mightily revived and moved into a quest for godliness.

Sorrow in the Midst of Blessings

The year 1905 not only saw a wonderful revival come to Dohnavur, but the sad news of Robert Wilson's death came that year also. Mrs. Carmichael was in India with her daughter at the time and was able to comfort Amy. Our woman of awakening deeply felt his home going. Also in 1905, the great J. Hudson Taylor, founder of the China Inland Mission, now known as the Overseas Missionary Fellowship, went to his reward. He had been such an inspiration to Amy at the Keswick meetings that his principle of doing mission work by faith became most influential in her whole approach to ministry. The home going of these two spiritual giants, one a missionary leader, and the other a dedicated layman, only demonstrated how vital it was that people all over the world hear the marvelous message of salvation in Jesus Christ and the victorious life of godliness that the Keswick movement emphasized.

In the midst of the revival, other disappointments and testing times also came. A serious outbreak of dysentery broke out across Amy's area of India and some of the weak little children succumbed to it. Ten children in the Fellowship died before the epidemic's grip was broken. Yet God used even this to lay upon Amy's heart the urgency of more nurseries. She started a medical work that proved most significant to the mission. In 1907, Mabel Wade, a trained nurse from Yorkshire, England, joined the staff in November. Mabel became responsible for the health care of the entire Fellowship. Needless to say, the overall work made strenuous demands on everyone, consuming everyone's energies and virtually everyone's total time.

Another need began to arise—the need for a teacher for the growing children. That responsibility had always fallen to Amy, but the numbers were getting too large for just one person. Amy described herself as a jack of all trades, master of none, though she was probably more of a master of most of the trades than she herself realized. But God would soon provide a teacher—in fact two.

The Ups and Downs of the Work

The Dohnavur Fellowship did not have the form of a full-bloomed institution in the strictest sense, regardless of its tremendous expansion. Every child was treated as an individual. Even though the numbers were now large, the workers saw every young life as precious and treated them as such. Amy, or Amma (her Tamil name) as the children always called her, stood accessible to all of the children at all times; and they loved her dearly for it. She truly gave herself to her precious family.

Moreover, Amy Carmichael stood strong when she had to defend her children. She was often dragged into court over lawsuits concerning her care of the runaway temple girls. In 1910 and 1911, the dam broke and a deluge of lawsuits were lodged against the Dohnavur Fellowship. In these difficult times and circumstances, Amy relied on Mr. Walker. He was a man of expertise in many affairs as well as being a deeply spiritual Christian missionary. His guidance saw them through many troubled waters. God continued to give them wonderful victories and lawsuit after lawsuit brought Amy permanent custody of the abused children. The lawsuits actually backfired on those who filed them.

In August 1912, a little Brahman child by the name of Lulla died before any medical help could be had. Then only six days later, Mr. Walker, who had been holding some special meetings in Masulipatam, suddenly died. Amy grieved deeply not only over the loss of the child, but for Mr. Walker, who had been such a dear friend and stronghold for her. But as God always meets needs, two sisters, Edith and Agnes Naish, who had served as missionaries in village evangelization, came to Dohnavur to offer their services. Agnes was an experienced teacher and she took over the responsibility of the education of the many children. This, of course, relieved Amy tremendously.

Not only did the Naish sisters bring much-needed help and relief, a young, dedicated Christian man by the name of Aruldasan, who had at one time worked with Mr. Walker, presented himself to supervise the work of new buildings for the compound. In 1906, the Dohnavur Fellowship had seventy members; by 1913 the number had doubled. Needless to say, they faced a constant need for expansion, not only of buildings but of personnel as well. Moreover, the demand for more funding also reared its head. At that stage, Amy received an offer from the government to aid her work financially. A problem arose with the government offer, however. Amy would be forced to accept non-Christian teachers on the staff, and the government would dictate the choice of some of the textbooks. It was a tempting offer, but Amy, not a woman to compromise, refused the government grant. Although it forced her to continue with certain hardships, she trusted God completely, and as the years unfolded, the decision she made proved a right one. The revival spirit carried on.

On August 26, 1915, Ponnammal, one of Amy's trusted fellow servants, went to be with the Lord. Amy later wrote a book under the title, *Ponnammal, Her Story* but at the time felt that she had not only lost a trusted friend but also a valuable helper who could never really be replaced. Then just a few days after Ponnammal's death, Amy's mother, Mrs. Carmichael, passed away at her home in London. Mrs. Carmichael had moved to Wimbledon, in south London, and her home had become the only official English headquarters for the Dohnavur Fellowship. Fortunately, a short time later, Mrs. Irene Streeter, who had visited Dohnavur from time to time, agreed to be Amy's official representative of the Fellowship in Britain.

By 1915, England was engulfed in the First World War. This put a heavy financial strain on the work. As the war wound down, so did the value of the British pound sterling. By 1919, it was one-half of its prewar value. Nevertheless, Amy wrote, "Yet we were able to go on . . . never once was a child left unsaved or unfed because we had no money or feared that we should not have enough in the future." Amy's faith saw them through.

The Years Move Along

As the years passed, Amy recognized her physical limitations and knew that the day would come when she would not be able to carry on the work. Contemplating the future, she prayed, *Lord, teach me how to conquer pain . . . when my day's work is done, take me straight Home, do not let me be ill or be a burden or anxiety to anyone.* Amy meant that from her heart. But when as a child she prayed that God would make her brown eyes blue and got a "no" answer, God also saw fit to answer this prayer with His gracious, "no." Little did she realize that she would endure a long illness before God would carry her home, an illness that actually became a tremendous blessing. But that waits for the future; Amy still had many years of fruitful service to perform, and the several losses that she had suffered could not but make her think of the future.

Dr. Inwood, a well-known Keswick speaker, visited the Dohnavur work on one occasion during those years. Indicative of how the spirit of revival continued on, he said, "The two days spent here have no parallel in my experience. Everything in this work has the touch of God so naturally upon it that I lived in one unbroken act of wonder and worship and adoration."[8] When God pours out His Spirit in a great awakening, after the initial excitement, the revival continues on with the empowering touch of the Spirit on kingdom work. It leaves one feeling that this is a quite natural state, and worship, adoration, and fervent service becomes the natural outflow. Such was the revival that God brought to Amy and the Dohnavur Fellowship.

By 1919, Amy Carmichael's work was beginning to be recognized for the tremendous value it afforded the people of India. In January of that year, she received a telegram from the governor of Madras, bringing her hearty congratulations; she had been included on the Royal Birthday Honors List: Amy's first official recognition by the Indian government. This put her in something of a spiritual struggle, however. Should she accept it or should she turn it down? She did not want to appear ungracious to the government, yet she did not want to bring any honor to herself; she wanted all honor to go to God. She finally decided that she would accept the award, but no one could even persuade her to go and accept the medal in person. It was actually quite incredible that from 1895, when Amy first traveled to India, in had taken just twenty-five years for this totally unknown missionary to be so respected and recognized throughout India. It can only be attributed to the grace of God working through this woman of awakening.

Prior to receiving the honor from the Madras government, in January of the previous year Amy undertook a new venture. One day a woman appeared at the Fellowship carrying a bundle. She had arrived in an oxcart with a baby bundled up in her arms. Amy quite naturally took the child thinking that another need could be met. Suddenly, however, she realized that the bundle was a boy, a little lad by the name of Arul. She had helped boys before, but never had she taken in a baby boy.

Actually, Amy had been thinking that the work should extend beyond the girls and reach out to the many boys who were likewise caught up in the temple courts. Little fellows from eight to ten years of age would be

conscripted to play musical instruments in the temples or to act as drama-
tists in temple procedures. The temple authorities would send out scouts
to look for particularly talented young boys. This often lead to tremendous moral problems for the lads, as it did for the girls. So young and
defenseless, they had little or no protection against their cruel masters.

Of course, if Amy took in the baby boy, it meant that a total program
for little fellows must be developed. Boys and girls could not be housed
together in the same compound. This necessitated the building of structures for the boys. But Amy now had Arul on her hands and something
had to be done. Land presented no problem. They had plenty of that, but
what about buildings and personnel? Amy set her mind to it and immediately drew up plans, seeking the Lord for a hundred pounds to start the
work. In short order, the first hundred pounds came in and the work among
boys commenced. The boys' work also meant that new male workers had
to be enlisted. But God met all needs.

Amy developed a network of friends throughout south India to keep a
lookout for children who were at risk of being snatched by temple authorities. Many a child, girl and boy, came to the Fellowship through that
channel. Amy set the highest standards for all her helpers. She scrupu-
lously avoided so-called problem people. Christ had to be first in the
lives of all and in every affair of the Fellowship.

As the work continued to progress, Amy singled out seven Indian girls
for special ministries. They called themselves the Sisters of Common
Life. They adopted this name from the Brotherhood of Common Life, a
great work of the Dutch pietist Gerard Grote. Grote had ministered back
in 1380, but his influence had lived on. These sisters chose voluntarily to
remain single and devote themselves completely to the Lord's work. As
can be imagined, some people misunderstood Amy's hand in this and
criticized her as being against marriage. But that was not so; she always
did her best to prepare girls for good Christian marriages. These sisters
voluntarily dedicated themselves to celibacy so they could give their complete time and life to the Dohnavur work. So Amy took the criticism in a
Christlike manner and carried on. She realized that the more one is used
by the Spirit of God, the more criticism, and even persecution, will come.
The Lord Jesus Himself said, "If the would hates you, you know that it
has hated Me before it hated you" (John 15:18). She wrote a poem that
expressed her heart when these kind of experiences occurred:

> No wound? No scar?
> Yet, as the Master shall the servant be,
> And pierced are the feet that follow Me;
> But thine are whole: can he have followed far
> Who has no wound nor scar?

An Interesting Encounter

Many exciting experiences crossed Amy's path that God used in a marvelous way. One such incident took place in 1921. Amy Carmichael's biographer, Kathleen White, tells the following story:

> Toward the end of 1921 came another curious incident completely divorced from Amy's usual activities with children. From time to time, Amy heard stories from the coolies that carried her chair, of Jambulingam, an outlaw, who called himself Red Tiger and lived in the forest rather like Robin Hood, robbing the rich to succor the poor. This proved a challenge to Amy. "I wonder if I could arrange a meeting and tell him about the Savior?" she deliberated.
>
> Incredibly, this happened. Jambulingam had spied on her with his men while she was supervising some building work in the Grey Jungle. After several days he waylaid her and, at Amy's request, poured out his sad story while Amy shared her tea with him and his followers. Although completely innocent, he had fled in great fear to Penang when falsely accused. Returning to find out about his wife and children, he found the police terrifying his wife. He fled again and his wife died of shock. Knowing there was no hope of real justice being done, he remained an outlaw in the mountain, giving his gains to the impoverished peasants.
>
> Amy promised to take care of his three children, and he in return said he would never use a gun except to defend himself. She also pleaded with him to give himself up but he refused, yet they had a few short minutes together for Amy to tell Jambulingam about the Savior and pray with him.
>
> Only just in time! Within five days he and his friend Kasi were caught, tortured, and sent to a hospital while still under guard. Amy visited Jambulingam and left him a Bible to read. After having a dream, Amy asked him if he would like to be baptized. The ceremony took place, even with the priest she had dreamed of officiating—an amazing coincidence.
>
> Visits ceased after that, except for a Tamil clergyman who instructed them once a week. Then his trial dragged on. Eventually, Jambulingam, Kasi, and two others managed to escape from the jail. Only Jambulingam and Kasi kept together in the forest. The other two deserted them when they knew they were no longer prepared to rob and steal as before.
>
> Amy sent message after message to plead with them to give themselves up to the authorities again. False rumors went flying around, although she herself felt confident that they had kept their

word. Finally, staining her face and arms and wrapping herself in a dark sari, she allowed herself to be taken to their hideout in the jungle. Jambulingam swore to Amy he had not been robbing, but he was too frightened to place himself at the mercy of the government officials. They prayed and repeated Scripture passages together, including the 23rd Psalm.

Next day they fell into an ambush. Running to get away, Kasi slipped and was shot. Jambulingam waited for his friend, threw down his gun, and then was cruelly attacked and shot by the police. Again, false rumors flew around for a long time. In the end, Amy wrote the full story in *Raj, Brigand Chief.* She herself had been the subject of much criticism because she defended these men verbally. In the book she disclosed how others had become Christians because of the testimony of the two men. She had never sent them any supplies apart from Christian literature. Although her sympathies went out to them, she did not allow her judgment to be clouded; technically they were acting outside the law. Yet she longed and fought for the law to be changed so that unfortunate people would not be falsely accused and persecuted like Jambulingam.

Such were the things that Amy not only faced but came through victoriously through her faith in God's providential care. She had learned her revival lessons well.

The Work Expands

In the ten-year period between 1920 and 1930, the work grew explosively. New nurseries were added to the compound continually. Not only that, the work of evangelization in the surrounding villages expanded dramatically. The Dohnavur Fellowship was becoming so well-known, not only in India but in other parts of the world, that many new workers from various countries dedicated themselves to the task. As pointed out, Amy always maintained the highest standard for her workers. They had to be people who had an intimate walk with Jesus Christ, compassion for needy children, and a real passion to win people to faith in Christ. Of course, she also demanded that they be qualified in the various areas of the ministry. Many dedicated Indians also responded. As the work continued to expand, new buildings became a perpetual problem. They also needed a regular fully staffed hospital. Further, Amy harbored a consuming concern for a house of prayer. Funds for the two buildings were not at hand, so what should she do? It might be thought that Amy saw the hospital as a top priority. No, she sensed that the Spirit of God would have them first build their House of Prayer. So as resources came in, they set about to build a place for the worship and praise of God. The Lord blessed in a marvelous fashion; they built by God's grace and provision. Bishop Tubbs dedicated the House of Prayer in 1927. In the goodness of the Lord, the hospital soon followed.

Amy proved very practical in her approach to the work. Through the generosity of some Syrian Christians, she purchased a small plot of ground near the seaside, some fifteen miles away. There she built a house and called it Joppa. She set it aside as a place of rest and relaxation for the Dohnavur workers. They all labored arduously and from time to time needed to get away for rest and recuperation. Amy in her practicality saw to it that they had such facilities.

During those busy days, Amy would ride around the compound on her tricycle, a little three-wheeled vehicle that the older children would push to take her to her various rounds and responsibilities. Being such an enthusiastic person, she made them push her as fast as they could. She thus acquired the nickname of "Musal Ammal," being translated, the "hare" or "rabbit." Needless to say, they had a few spills as they flew around corners.

A New Structure

About the middle of the decade, Amy began to realize that carrying on the Fellowship within the structure of the Church of England's Zenana Missionary Society just did not work well anymore. There were differences of opinion between Dohnavur and some of the leaders of the Church of England Society as to how the mission should proceed. In actuality, Dohnavur had run quite independently for some years, and several of the missionary workers who had attached themselves to the work had not been appointed by the Anglican Society anyway. So the Dohnavur Fellowship became an independent faith work. The church missionary society generously gave them some of the old buildings and the adjacent land that they had been using. Thus, in 1927, the Dohnavur Fellowship was officially registered and adopted the following constitution: "To save children in moral danger; to train them to serve others; to succor the desolate and the suffering; to do anything that may be shown to be the will of our Heavenly Father, in order to make His love known, especially to the people of India."

The constitution read rather formally, but the whole purpose centered in the principle that the Lord Jesus Christ would be the Lord of the work.

As the years slipped by, Amy faced several questions: Who would lead in an able way the boys' aspect of the work? It was expanding so rapidly. Moreover, good leadership in the hospital program became a pressing issue. Not only that, Amy, now nearly sixty, wondered how long she would be able to carry on with the vast responsibilities.

As always, God met needs. A physician by the name of Dr. Murray came to visit Dohnavur enroute to China. Amy had met Dr. Murray's grandfather who had spoken at Keswick some years earlier. Dr. Murray stayed for a period of time and helped Amy tremendously. To see him leave was not easy, yet she knew God would ultimately meet every need.

God did wonderfully provide. Dr. Murray had a very able brother by the name of Godfrey, who served in China. He became quite ill and his missionary society ordered him to break off his labor and take a long rest for convalescence. It seemed natural for him to go to Dohnavur. Of course, Amy rejoiced to welcome him. After a very short time, Godfrey also offered to join the Dohnavur Fellowship. He wrote, "I don't feel one little bit fit to join you all . . . but, I pray God may make me walk worthy of His high calling." The children shared Amy's joy as Godfrey joined the work. He and Amy threw their lives even more zealously into the task. They became partners and would serve together for more than twenty-two years. One can imagine the gratitude to God for His goodness in providing these two able brothers.

The Hospital Work

When the hospital was finally completed, after many a difficult turn of events, they named it the Place of Heavenly Healing. Prior to its construction, the medical staff had been making do with four mud huts. Now a large permanent building with many personnel greatly enhanced the work. One wonders how the funding kept coming in, yet God continually provided just as He promised. The first time that a check for a thousand pounds arrived festivities erupted. Amy never forgot it. She recounted the event by relating, "a child ran up with a yellow envelope in her hand. . . . I opened it quickly and read, 'One thousand pounds for maternity ward' . . . I stood like Rhoda, and opened not the gate for gladness." Amy had been praying for a maternity ward for the new hospital for some time, and here was the provision.

At the same time, most of the money that came arrived in very small amounts. Often the children themselves made contributions. These small sums are what really kept the work going, although the thousand pounds was most welcome.

Amy undertook a new venture when she began to sense the need for training the boys and girls for their futures. They would one day have to make a living on their own. Amy put her mind to it and reasoned that some could be trained as hospital staff, porters, cooks, and so forth. She undertook the task of training with much zeal. Moreover, Amy never lost the wider vision; as she herself said, evangelism must be their first priority. As it took time to complete the hospital, it often takes time to win people to Christ. She never gave up on people.

So the spiritual warfare raged on. Satan had no intention of letting this work flourish without doing battle.

New Spiritual Battles

In Amy's book, *The Spiritual Letters of Fire Didon*, she penned the following poem:

> Make us Thy warriors
> On whom Thou canst depend to stand the brunt
> Of any perilous charge on any front;
> Give to us skill to handle sword and spear,
> From the rising of the morning till the stars appear.

Amy knew that she, her workers, and the entire Dohnavur enterprise must put on the whole armor of God. She knew that the spiritual forces of darkness would fight the work at every turn of the road. Moreover, the multiplied demands began to take their toll on her health. She realized that she must completely rest in God's strength to give her the victory in the battles she fought. At times she felt almost too weary to carry on, yet she always found God's grace to be sufficient.

Spiritual warfare also meant winning as many people as possible to Christ. On a warm August day, during the monthly day of prayer, all the workers pledged themselves to make a fresh effort to win the thousands of Muslims and Hindus who lived in southern India. Shortly thereafter, the Spirit of God led them to target two towns to begin a new work of evangelism. Of course, the devil went to battle as well. As the work began in Eruvadi, one of the towns where the new evangelistic work was commenced, some of the townspeople actually threw rocks at the Dohnavur laborers.

Through it all, Amy kept a gracious spirit and prayed, *Do with me as Thou wilt. Do anything, Lord, that will fit me to serve Thee and help my Beloved.* Little did she understand how God would answer that prayer. Just a few hours later a seemingly insignificant incident took place that radically changed the rest of her life.

A Tragic Turn of the Road

Amy took a car journey to Kalakadu, a nearby community, to see the progress of the evangelistic work. As she and some of her helpers walked up to the small headquarters house they had established, and it being rather late in the evening, she failed to see a pit some workmen had dug and she slipped and fell into it. Her injuries were quite serious. But surely, Amy reasoned, good would come out of this seeming tragedy. In a very strange way, she called it correctly.

At the time of the accident, Amy had to wait in the mission house until help could come from Dohnavur, some forty-six miles away. She would have to be taken to Neyyoor to receive adequate medical attention. They discovered on her arrival at the hospital that her leg was broken. Dr. Howard Somervell put on a cast and reset her dislocated ankle. Amy, now sixty-four years old, found the healing much slower than when she was a young lady. But she felt confident that God would work in this situation as He had always worked in every affair of her life.

Amy continued to suffer quite serious pain from her injury. It did not seem to fade away as hoped. So in January the Dohnavur Fellowship family engaged in a nonstop chain of prayer from 6:00 A.M. to 9:00 P.M. for her healing. Still, the pain persisted and it looked like Amy's physical activity would be seriously curtailed. Such was the case. She actually became something of a semi-invalid, spending considerable time in bed. So shattered was her physical strength and health, Amy rarely left her room for nearly the next twenty years.

As the months slowly dragged on, the doctors discovered that Amy had also seriously injured her spine in the fall, and moreover, acute neuritis made one arm virtually useless. Arthritis settled in her back and she became subject to chronic infections.

But the Devil had not won a victory by any means. Although incapacitated physically from 1931 until her death, Amy still found it possible to administer much of the work. Many days the pain would virtually overcome her and she would have to retire for a period, but then she would rally and again take her leadership role even though she could not be physically present. Not only that, she wrote over thirteen books and hundreds of letters after her accident. She would write small messages to the boys and girls on their birthdays and for other important events. Many of the children did not know the actual date of their birth, so they always celebrated their birthdays on the day of the year that they had arrived at the Dohnavur Fellowship. Amy rarely forgot a single one of them. Amy not only wrote many books during this period, she reedited and republished several of her older works. The amount of work she produced during those difficult years seems incredible. Like Paul who in prison wrote so many of his letters, Amy used her "imprisonment" as a most fruitful time.

Amy's Last Years

In 1933, people far and wide sought news of the Dohnavur Fellowship. The work had gained world recognition. Amy thus produced a regular newsletter on the Fellowship's work. From 1933 to 1948, Amy herself took sole responsibility for the producing of the newsletters. She also started publication of *Dust of Gold*. This periodical presented insights to the dynamics of the Dohnavur Fellowship.

As can be appreciated, Amy's room became important to her. The furnishings and decor were one of her joys in her limited small world. She did not have any luxuries, but all were struck by the room's beauty. Above all, the presence of Christ could be found there. She had a wooden plaque put outside the room that simply read, "The Room of Peace." Actually, her room became the nerve center of Dohnavur during those last years.

Even in these rather difficult physical times for Amy, there were other battles to fight. Misunderstandings about the Fellowship's involvement in the so-called Oxford group movement permeated several evangelical circles in England and America. This movement started well, but degenerated into a rather bizarre approach to the confession of sin. It evolved into "airing one's dirty linen" to the whole world. Frowned on by most of the evangelical world, it later became known as Moral Rearmament. The accusation that the Dohnavur Fellowship had involved itself in this movement was far from the truth. They had been well-schooled in the Keswick approach to holy living, which most knew as soundly Biblical. Soon the criticism died away and the work carried on. Other anxieties arose from time to time. When the Second World War broke out in 1939, great fear gripped south India that the Japanese might launch an invasion into the area. Inflation also took its toll. Yet, as always, God saw the work through these difficult times. What was the secret of the continual victories that they experienced? The answer is very simple: The prayer support of the whole Fellowship. They prayed continually for the work, and for Amy in particular. On June 23, 1948, Amy slipped in her room, injuring her right hip and breaking her right forearm. But prayer once again saw her through.

As mentioned, Amy's literary output throughout her life amazed everyone. Despite the incredible responsibilities and the demands, from 1895 to 1950, she penned thirty-five full volumes, not counting countless other published works. Her books were translated into fifteen different languages.

Amy's personal sorrows seemed to multiply during her last years. In May 1939, God called Arulai, her beloved coworker, to her heavenly home. She and Amy had been so close through the years. Amy said, "She is perhaps the most precious thing I have on earth." Then in February 1947, Dr. Murray had to return to England—another blow. In 1950, Godfrey Murray began to suffer serious physical problems. He had a thrombosis in his right leg and in February of that year suddenly died. Amy, now eighty years of age, did not have the resilience of a young woman and she could not help but cry out, "Why am I left—I who am so useless to you all—and he, who could do so much for you, taken?" But she realized, as she put it in her own words, "Faith never wonders why. Faith trusts."

After Amy's second fall, most of the Fellowship felt that she would soon go to be with the Lord. In great frailty, however, she lingered on for almost another three years. She well recognized, with the apostle Paul, that *"to depart, and to be with Christ; which is far better"* (Phil. 1:23 KJV). She sincerely longed to go and be with the Lord. And the time did arrive. In the middle of the first month of the new year, 1951, Amy quietly sank into a coma. She slipped away almost imperceptibly as she had always wanted. In the early morning hours of January 18, she crossed over the Jordan and met the many loved ones who had preceded her, above all, her wonderful Lord and Savior, Jesus Christ.

A Last Word

There are no elaborate carved headstones to distinguish where Amy's physical remains are interred. Amy's grave can be recognized only by a simple stone birdbath beside the plot. This is the way that she would have wanted it. She had spent fifty-six wonderful years in India and had left a legacy in that land that lives to this hour. Revival had come through her faithful missionary ministry, and she would have nothing of people lingering over her grave in remorse. God's victory had come. She had filled the role of a woman of awakening. And the work carries on, as the Scripture itself promises:

> *And I heard a voice from heaven, saying, "Write, 'Blessed are the dead who die in the Lord from now on!'" "Yes," says the Spirit, "that they may rest from their labors, for their deeds follow with them" (Rev. 14:13).*

Endnotes

1. The quotes in this chapter are taken from Kathleen White, *Amy Carmichael* (Minneapolis: Bethany House Publishers, 1986).

Chapter Nine

EDITH MOULES
The African Awakening

"Who is my neighbor?" This burning query haunted the heart of Edith Moules, Christian missionary nurse in the heart of Africa. One night in a mud hut, Edith faced the most crucial question of her life since her conversion to Christ and dedication to the mission field. That very day she had met a man racked with leprosy. Although she served as a very able medical nurse, she simply could not face ministering to that malignant malady that had caught up tens of thousands of Africans in its deadly clutch. Because she was a Christian nurse, one would have thought that she would have gladly stepped in to help, yet, something of a deep aversion to the loathsome disease had caused twenty-seven-year-old Edith to refuse to address the issue. But now she had to face a real live leper: What would she do?

Edith's Early Years

Edith, a Yorkshire England lass, was born on July 31, 1900, at Redcar. Her father worked as a blacksmith. Unfortunately, Edith Moules could not remember her mother because she died when Edith was but a four-year-old girl. Shortly after her mother's passing, Edith's father married again and the parents sent the little girl to live with her grandmother in the Yorkshire village of Marske. She had a happy home with her "granny" and attended various schools in Yorkshire County in the north of England. She studied at West Dyke and Coatham schools in Redcar and then Thornton Watlas in Bedale. Edith, a strong-willed girl, had great strength of character. She did not feel that she should be a continuing burden to her grandmother, so as a teenager she took a serving position with a congregational minister's family at Ilkley in Yorkshire.

Edith had spiritual stirrings in her heart while still quite young. She herself confessed that if someone had asked her at that time if she had truly been saved, she could not say yes, even though she had a sense of God's working in her life. One of those early stirrings took a quite unusual turn.

In a church service she attended on one occasion, the congregation sang the beautiful hymn, "There Is a Fountain Filled with Blood." The beauty of the song and the sentimentality of it struck her twelve-year-old heart and she began to weep. As she stood there with tears trickling down her cheeks, the minister came up to her and asked, "Do you believe that Jesus died for you?" She immediately replied, "Yes." She had been taught so from her earliest childhood. But then the minister simply thanked God that she felt the conviction of sin. Edith realized what a great mistake the minister committed; she was crying simply because of the sad hymn. The emotional side of it all, nothing more, had moved her. But to be under genuine conviction of sin and the pressing need of repentance eluded her, even though the minister tried to convince her that she had been soundly converted.

To some extent Edith went along with the minister's words and told her grandmother that she had been saved. She tried ever so hard to convince herself. She got a hymn book and a prayer book and ardently strove to be good. She really did labor to walk a Christian pathway. She disciplined herself, reading the Scripture and praying, but she had to admit that she found the Bible rather dull. She just did not understand God's plan of salvation. She would read a chapter or a portion of the Word of God every night and then jump in bed; many times she would get out of the warm covers and finish the chapter in case she died before morning. The great Satanic deception that one finds favor with God by good works had captured her. She failed to find saving faith.

Conversion

After leaving her grandmother's house and moving to Ilkney, Edith came in contact with the local branch of the Christian Alliance of Women and Girls. There she met some genuine Christian girls her own age who had a vital experience of the living Lord. She made friends with Ethel Hulbert who influenced her tremendously. One day Edith asked Ethel why she seemed so different from herself. Ethel replied, "Well, it is because Jesus doesn't live inside you." The Spirit of God used that simple word powerfully. Edith had never realized that Christ could actually live within her. When she heard that from her Christian friend, Edith gladly invited Christ to come and live within her heart. She gave herself completely to His Lordship and trusted Him alone. That became the moment of real conversion. She had found the only way to God. What peace!

Edith reveled in her new relationship to the Lord Jesus Christ. She took part in all the various activities of the Christian club and would even go out and work on her half-days off to raise money for the mission field. She realized that God had plans for her life, and she became thoroughly convinced that our Lord would work out His plan and purpose for her future. She found herself utterly taken up with the joy of the Lord.

The Call Comes

In the context of the alliance's many activities, Edith constantly heard the challenge of the call to missions. Various missionaries would come and speak and pray for God's will to be done in the girls' lives. One day a missionary from India, serving under the Zenana's Bible and Medical Mission, spoke. God gripped Edith's heart, and it seemed to her as though the Lord himself was saying, "Come, come follow." She was only eighteen at the time, yet the call came to her so forcefully and clearly that she gave herself utterly to the Lord Jesus Christ to serve him as a missionary wherever He would lead. The other club members were thrilled with Edith's decision. They actually banded themselves together and subscribed to send her for two terms to Redcliffe House, a missionary training college for women in London.

Edith was really too young for such training. She evidently did not make a very favorable impression on the faculty and administration of Redcliffe House because she found it hard to knuckle under to the strict discipline and strenuous demands of the training college. Nonetheless, Miss Grapes, the principal, became something of an idol to Edith, even though she found her many rules not easy to take. Finally, Edith's variance with the school regulations forced her to decide to leave. She felt that she was a failure. The principal herself wrote, "Edith Patton left here out of her own accord because she was not ready to go through with the preparation. She did not take kindly to work or to being under authority. It was against my wishes that she left, as I hoped she would learn that it was worth while to go to all lengths with God and that nothing short of this would be acceptable to Him."[1]

A New Step

Edith found herself a bit at sea at this stage, so she took a job for a few months learning household and hostel work at the YWCA, which became a time of gaining experience. She also engaged in house-to-house evangelistic visitation with the Salvation Army. After those few months of practical work she enrolled at Whipps Cross Hospital, Leytonstone, London, and began training to become a registered nurse. She spent four years in training and graduated as a state-registered nurse, as the British call their medical nurses. By this time Edith had become a very disciplined young lady. She passed her course with the highest marks, even to the point that she was given special maternity training free of charge. Miss L. S. Clark, a leader in the hospital, wrote of Edith upon her graduation, "She is a very earnest little woman and well fitted for work on the mission field. We should have liked to have retained her for services here as ward sister."

Edith's spiritual life continued to grow and mature as did her medical

knowledge and obvious leadership abilities. While working at the hospital, Edith grew into an effective witness for Christ. She held a weekly
meeting for the other girls where they studied the Bible and prayed. About
ten fellow medical students and personnel would meet with her. One Sunday, on her way to church, Edith met the matron of the hospital, who
walked along with her to church. After the service, the matron mentioned
that she felt a real concern over some of the superficialities of the hospital. She asked Edith if she still conducted those Bible study and prayer
meetings in her room. Edith replied that she did. It all resulted in the
matron's giving Edith permission to start using the chapel for the Bible
study and prayer meetings. Over thirty nurses started attending a 6:50
A.M. meeting. The work continually developed, with the Matron herself
regularly attending.

The Call Comes Again

God began to speak to Edith again about her call to the mission field.
She sensed that God was saying, *To Africa,* which came as a complete
surprise. She had always directed her attention and concern toward India.
But the Lord spoke to her very definitely about Africa. Edith replied, "I
was not really at variance with God, I was simply going on planning for
India, and He brought me to a full stop. The more I thought about Africa,
the more I had a deep urge within me that that was where God wanted me
to go." So it was to be Africa.

Then out of the blue, as it were, a periodical of the Worldwide Evangelization Crusade (WEC) fell into her hands. This faith-missionary organization had been founded by the well-known C. T. Studd. He had gained
a reputation as a very fine cricketer at Cambridge University, with a wonderful heritage, having been brought up in a very wealthy aristocratic
family of England. Studd experienced a deep work of God's grace and
forsook a very promising career and a life of luxury. He turned his face to
the foreign field. In the context of his own missionary service he founded
the Worldwide Evangelization Crusade. Throughout the years, God has
used the work tremendously all around the world. When Edith investigated Studd's organization, she was fascinated. She soon applied to the
WEC and was immediately accepted by the Crusade. So off to the field
she went; and with God's blessings.

Beginning the Missionary Ministry

In 1927, Edith Patton (Patton being her maiden name) traveled to Brussels and spent six months studying French before setting sail for Africa.
With three other fellow missionaries, after their days of language study
were completed, she boarded ship and sailed for the heart of the Dark
Continent, as it was called in those days.

Edith was a very energetic and enthusiastic young missionary. As she sailed south, she said, "I was ready to knock the world over. I had great ideas of what I would do in Africa. I was full of zeal and eager to tell of the Gospel story and winning souls to Christ." Then something subtly disturbing touched her life. While on the ship she met a man who tried to tell her about the need of lepers in Africa. He said that he hoped that Edith would be able to do something for them. "I turned up my nose at his suggestion," she said. She had to confess later that that was a dangerous thing to do because she did not know what God had in store for her. In that conversation, the Lord planted a seed of what would be her life work, though she, at that moment, did not realize it and even resisted it.

After arriving on the field, Edith met the great C. T. Studd. He lived and served in Africa himself although the headquarters of the World Evangelization Crusade resided in London. He had moved his own headquarters to Ibambi in the Ituri forrest, ministering among the large Mabudu tribe. Nearing the end of his life and ministry, he had certainly "fought the good fight" if ever a man of God had. Edith found Studd as an old man battling physical weakness and living in a bamboo house with a mud floor. All he had for heat was a wood fire burning in the middle of the hut and shelves on the walls with a few little personal belongings and some books. The successor of C. T. Studd as leader of the Crusade, Norman Grubb, was C. T. Studd's son-in-law. He tells the story of Studd's daughter visiting her father in Africa. Studd, delighted to see her, wanted to give her a gift. He looked around his little bamboo hut and said, "I'm sorry my dear, but I guess I have just given everything to Jesus." Such was the spirit of this man who had been brought up in a British mansion but had forsaken all for Christ. Studd had thrown out the challenge to all of the WEC missionaries, "If Jesus Christ be God and died for me, then no sacrifice can be too great for me to make for Him." And he lived it himself.

The challenge made upon Edith during her stay with Studd was nothing short of radical. She had never witnessed such consecration and quality of Christianity such as she saw in that man. Some, of course, have criticized Studd for being too extreme. His intensity of living for Christ just seemed too much for some. But great is the reward of those who are so deeply dedicated.

Edith herself felt tempted to criticize Studd at first, but soon the criticism turned to deep and profound admiration and finally to a compelling challenge in her own life. God so spoke to her through the life of the man of God that one night she knelt down beside her camp bed and made an unconditional dedication of her body as a living sacrifice, not to criticize or admire, but to give herself to the Lord and follow the example of C. T. Studd.

Edith spent two months with Mr. Studd at Ibambi and then received an appointment to Nala in the Belgian Congo, now called Zaire. First opened by Studd himself in 1916, Nala was one of the older mission centers of WEC. The missionaries reached out to three different tribes, the Azande, the Medje, and the Mayogo. The Azande mission had a small medical work, but it had gone out of existence when the only nurse had moved to another station. There Edith settled in to restart the medical work.

Problems As the Work Begins

Many problems met Edith upon her arrival for work. The station had no hospital and no dispensary. The only course before her was to take an old tool shed and try to convert it into something of a dispensary. The shed measured about six feet by nine feet and was without a window. But there she started with some native helpers. They cut a hole in the mud wall through which she could dispense what medicines they had. Edith enlisted two African boys to serve as her assistants. They were very proud to play the role. The boys dressed in white calico shirts on which was sown a large red cross. Edith said that they were very much on duty when medicines had to be given out, but very absent when the bandages had to be washed. But they did well and patients began to come in droves.

Each morning a drum would be beaten and the crowds would begin to gather. Some days there were over two hundred people who would come seeking medical help. Edith sent home a regular quarterly report. In one such report she pointed out that 13,836 people had come, suffering from twenty-five different diseases, in the prior three months. The medical needs were all but overwhelming, but, above all, they needed Christ.

By the end of the year, two small mud buildings had been added as hospitals, though they could hardly be called that. A men's hospital equipped with ten beds and a women's with six constituted the small complex. The beds always stayed full. People traveled from miles around to be treated. It obviously opened a great opportunity to share the Gospel. Many were led to faith in the Lord Jesus Christ as a consequence. Edith never placed physical healing above spiritual needs. She kept a beautifully balanced ministry, following the New Testament pattern of her Lord.

It must be realized that the little complex was dealing with a very primitive Africa. No doctors or medical work could be found for miles around, except for Edith's meager ministry. The people therefore clung to everything she did to help them. The work grew and was going very well in Nala. Then came the crisis.

A Crisis of Faith and Ministry

"It was the biggest crisis in my missionary life." With those words, Edith described the fateful day when God did a fresh new work in her life that opened a vast field of ministry. Actually, it set the tone of her entire missionary service. True, she had made a genuine consecration of her life to Christ during the two months that she had spent with C. T. Studd. Nonetheless, she had to learn that it is not just making a decision of surrender during an immediate moment of conviction that matters in the long run. Rather, a daily discipline of obedience in the affairs of life constitute true consecration. In that setting, Edith met her crisis.

Edith felt very happy and fulfilled in her work. Hundreds were coming to her daily for their needs. "Things were going wonderfully," she said. The particular life-altering day in question started off no different from any other. Three hundred people stood waiting to have their physical and spiritual needs met. The sick people and those who had accompanied them were milling around under the trees waiting to be seen. But suddenly Edith's eyes fixed on someone in the back of the crowd. Apparently, he had been there for some time, just standing and gazing at Edith. *He was a leper.* Of course, Edith had seen lepers many times before, but this man suffered terribly, mutilated by the ravages of the disease. The man's toes and fingers had rotted off. He hobbled around on pitifully swollen feet that were hardly fit to hold up a pound, let alone a full-grown man. His face as well as his whole body were also horribly swollen. A little lad, almost naked, had accompanied him. Edith asked where they had come from, and the simple reply was, "We have come to come." When she pressed them for the exact place, she discovered that they were from Poko, more than eighty miles through the forest. It must have taken them days to travel that far because of the leper's terrible condition.

That encounter precipitated Edith's crisis. Here stood a man before her who was in desperate need of medical help. But Edith found something about leprosy terribly repugnant. Yet the man stood in such obvious need, and she knew as a Christian that she simply could not close her heart to him. Conflicting thoughts threw her into a deep moral crisis. She did not want to have anything to do with the healing of lepers. Still, she faced a dire situation. She tried to rationalize that she had come to evangelize and not just to help people medically. Then she realized that one cannot make evangelization the only goal. The perfect will of God reaches out to all needs of life. Edith brought her problem altogether with these words: "So here I was up against my problem. The little boy said, 'we have come to come,' and I had no leper hospital and no intention of building one, nor starting a leper work; I had not even thought of it. All my plans were made, and they did not include the lepers. What was I to do?"

The moral dilemma thrust Edith into a real inner struggle. Finally, she decided that she would put the man and the little boy up for the night. She thought that perhaps he would begin to realize that she could really not do much for him. She knew that if she treated this one leper, the word would spread throughout the whole area and she would have a multitude of sufferers from the dreaded disease coming for help. These facts made up her fear of treating just one poor wreck of humanity a true struggle!

Well, Edith had to do something, so she trekked up one of the nearby small hills and found an old tumbled-down shack. She had the workmen clean it up somewhat and put the boy and the leper there for the night. She told them that they could stay there if they liked. She simply did not have the courage to tell them that she would not treat them; she hoped they would get the message and leave.

But the next morning the leper and little boy were still there with the regular two or three hundred patients waiting under the palm trees for treatment. All the days previously had been days of real joy for Edith. But this morning she found no joy in her work. She knew that when one faced a moral issue in which he or she was not willing to be obedient to Christ that the joy would soon fade and the wellspring of happiness would dry up. In the final analysis, as Edith realized, whether one will do the perfect will of God becomes life's ultimate test.

The struggle went on day after day as the man would just not leave. He just stood and looked at Edith. For four long days Edith prayed for the man, telling the Lord all about him and that she felt really sorry for him but leprosy treatment was not her job. As God's Spirit kept pressing her heart, she began to realize that God did not want her prayer; He wanted her obedience. One can use a time of prayer as an opiate to dull the will of God, as paradoxical as that may seem.

Finally, after four days of struggle Edith felt utterly exhausted—spiritually and emotionally. She wilted before God and said that she would do His will no matter what. Surrender came—and with it victory. The battle ended, and God showed Edith that she must take up the role of the good Samaritan in regard to the man who had come to her in need.

The next morning Edith went to the poor leper and confessed that God had spoken to her heart deeply about his need. Of course, he did not grasp what was really going on in her life, but Edith confessed to him that at first she had shunned him but that now she would do God's will and then do all within her power to help him. He could stay permanently and she would do the best with what she had at her disposal.

Edith told the poor man that he would have to look to God because she had no medicine for leprosy, not even a place to house him. Confident that God would meet every need, she invited him to kneel down and they prayed together.

Edith was very frank in a letter she wrote concerning the situation. In her correspondence she said,

In my battle before God (and it was a battle), I was trying to tell

God that I had come out to evangelize. But that was just an excuse for not facing the situation squarely, because I have always been an evangelist and trust I ever shall be. I did not want to face up to handling leprosy, because deep down inside me I was scared lest I should contract it. That is unworthy, certainly unworthy of anybody that takes up the medical profession; but the fact remains I was scared of leprosy. . . . This was foolish, because if we belong to Jesus, it is much happier to go to Him a leper, than to go to Him with a dried up soul but without leprosy. After all, what does the body matter?

But a second fear also deepened Edith's struggle. As mentioned, she knew that as soon as the leper had been welcomed, the story would go out on the drums, or some runner would carry it to the villages, and she would be swamped with lepers. She felt that she could not quite face being inundated with more and more lepers.

A third point of controversy arose in Edith's heart; she did not want the financial responsibility of developing a full-blown leprosy ministry. True, she had gone out under a faith-mission agency and lived by faith herself, but in the case of a leprosy ministry, she simply lacked the faith for God to provide. So she wrote to C. T. Studd, outlined the possibility of a leprosy ministry, and asked if she should start a work like this. Studd wrote back a very cryptic answer, "Don't ask me, ask God!" That did not fully satisfy Edith so she wrote him again. Studd wrote back the answer, "You have got the vision, go to it!" Edith had to acknowledge that she tried to lean on Mr. Studd for an answer, but his brief pungent answers ended that false support. So by faith in God's abundant provision she launched out in the will of God; and the rest of her ministry is history—revival history.

The Ministry Expands

Edith let the needs for leprosy work be known and before long funds began to pour in. The leper ministry started and great things soon began to happen. For two-and-a-half years, from 1929 to 1931, the camp grew until it became virtually a full hospital compound. By 1931, the normal dispensary work rose to the treating of over seventeen thousand patients each quarter. In all of the labors, Edith never allowed the vital spiritual ministry to go lacking. Conversions abounded.

The number of lepers housed and cared for grew until over sixty were hospitalized in the camp. Then they started a new leper settlement. Many of the lepers joined the others and came to faith in the Lord Jesus Christ through the faithful sharing of the Gospel that always stood paramount in Edith's ministry.

Although leprosy was thought an incurable disease in earlier years, through the work of research scientists and doctors, great progress was made, and many were healed. But now the time had come for Edith to take her first furlough. In 1932, she sailed for England after five years on the field. Before leaving the Congo, a most happy event took place in Edith Patton's life; she became engaged to Percy Moules, a young missionary who had recently arrived on the field.

In many respects Percy filled the role as an ideal partner for Edith. He was a Christlike, gentle, and patient man. As one friend expressed it, where Edith came across as a forward-looking driver, Percy had the steady hand; where she might be quick and hasty and impatient, he would be very cautious; if she were brilliant, he was of the durable sort. No doubt God made the match. Percy Moules was born and reared in Chiswick, a section of London. He had the blessing of being reared in a godly home with his younger brother, Lynn, who became a pioneer missionary on the Tibetan borders.

Percy studied ten long years to make his mark in the electronic field, but before completing his full education, he felt the call of God. He set aside his own ambitions and made his way to Africa.

Married Life

Edith returned to Africa from her restful furlough in Britain and on November 6, 1934, she and Percy were married. Miss Edith Patton became Mrs. Edith Moules. Despite the joy of her new married life, to her great grief she found that the settlement at Nala had been disbanded. No one apart from herself could handle the lepers, so they had closed it down. The Crusade had gone through a crisis in 1931. That year marked the death of C. T. Studd. Also an extreme shortage of workers made it look as if the entire work rested on very precarious ground.

Yet, even in the face of severe difficulties, Edith and Percy devoted themselves to lepers. The government itself had become aware of the value and success of Edith's work. News of her labors had actually reached official circles in Brussels (the Congo was still under the dominance of Belgium). Thus, the Belgium officials stepped in and asked Edith and Percy to again begin work among the lepers. They promised to give them all the help they could concerning land, buildings, and medicines. This saw the launching of a whole new phase of leper work, and Percy and Edith rose to the occasion. So the mission went forward with great blessings.

Edith and Percy took their furlough back in England in January of 1937. While on furlough, both she and Percy traveled to Brussels, Belgium and took a special course in tropical medicine. Because Edith knew French quite well, coupled with her experience with the lepers, she came out at the top of the class. Her exams rose a clear 10 percent higher than any other student. It now became very obvious to both Edith and Percy that God had in store a large-scale leper ministry. And the One who had set them apart for this ministry never failed to meet all of their needs.

The Beginnings of Revival

The work progressed well not only from the medical perspective but also from the spiritual. Then the first harbinger of revival came. An unusual outpouring of the Spirit at one of the WEC mission stations took place. Many of the natives had set themselves apart for prayer that God would mightily move in the work. God graciously answered. The news spread to all the surrounding villages and huge crowds came to receive the Spirit's touch.

One of the native men from Edith's station, upon hearing of the outpouring of the blessings, went to see for himself. God spoke to him deeply through a verse from Hebrews: "Follow peace with all men, and holiness, without which no man shall see the Lord" (Heb. 12:14 KJV). The Word of God struck his heart as deep conviction swept over him. He kept saying to himself, *I am not holy, therefore, I shall never see God.* He had received a true vision of the holiness of God, and it caused him to cry out with Isaiah, "Woe is me, for I am undone; . . . for mine eyes have seen the King" (Isa. 6:5 KJV). The good brother, whose name was Bandangama, came through the experience in a glorious fashion. He confessed all of his sins and found the freedom of full forgiveness. His conviction went so deep that he even had to stop growing a certain plant that some natives were using as a form of tobacco. It was a source of livelihood for him, but as God spoke to his heart, he realized that he must not grow the plant, though he himself did not use it. The first fruits of revival began to trickle down to Edith's station, but would a full spiritual awakening dawn?

By now it was time for another furlough. An invitation came from the American headquarters of the World Evangelization Crusade and Edith went to the USA and Canada for a six-month tour. She had a very successful time.

At this juncture, Hitler invaded Belgium, and some good came out of the evil of Nazism. Back in the Congo, a Red Cross doctor, as a consequence of Belgium's being subjugated by Hitler's armies, had to leave Africa and return to Europe. He turned his entire camp over to Percy and Edith. It comprised a large leper colony in which some three hundred and fifty advanced cases resided. What an opportunity it afforded for the expansion of their ministry. Their lives were filled with hard, strenuous work, but God's blessing rested on them; and on the horizon loomed a great revival.

In 1943, Edith joyously reported that fifty-one lepers could be declared symptom free during the previous year and could be sent back to their homes cured. The total number of lepers who had been cared for over the years passed the one thousand mark. Blessings abounded.

But then Edith began to realize that all the institutional work and the healing of lepers could well be no more than, in Paul's words, "A fair show in the flesh." The Holy Spirit began to speak to Edith and deepened the conviction of the need for revival. She and Percy began to sense that they were slipping into a rather worldly sense of satisfaction. The conviction deepened until they began to feel terribly burdened. As Edith said,

> You can be satisfied with seeing things organized and chaos becoming order. We had seen that . . . but we were conscious that life wasn't really there, and that many of the people were defeated . . . the trouble was our own spiritual inadequacy. Our willingness was all right . . . we felt very much our own impotence, because we were not seeing victory lived out by the people. It was easy to say that, but the real fact was that we hadn't a full life of victory ourselves!

Of course, the dedicated couple was worked almost beyond belief. The work had so mushroomed that they were seeing up to five thousand people a week in the various dispensaries. Moreover, they conducted six meetings of Bible study and sharing of the Gospel every day and had to travel five days out of the week to the outlying dispensaries. In one month alone Edith and Percy vaccinated some twenty thousand people. That meant about one thousand or so a day. But still there was something lacking.

That need centered in a personal touch from heaven, a personal revival. It soon came.

The Missionaries Awakened

During these hectic days the thirst for a fresh visitation from the Spirit of God had moved Percy more profoundly than it had Edith. She confessed, "He had the burden long before I did . . . I felt that we were doing what we could. After all, we were giving our very lives. But no, he had a burden." Edith's own burden came about one morning when a problem developed among some of the natives. The lepers had to be separated from those who were not infected, but one of the women, the wife of a leprous evangelist, refused to obey the rules. She insisted on using the same water facilities as the others. Percy had an encounter with the woman over the issue and she became very angry. She took the water pot off the top of her head and smashed it at Percy's feet. Edith acknowledged that such encounters were difficult to endure, but Percy's comment about the situation struck her to the heart. He said, "We have got to be very careful we don't just get a shop window here; we have got to get down to God about this. If our Christian's behave like this, what in the world can we expect from pagans?" That simple statement from Percy moved Edith. She said that God gripped her through those words. The Holy Spirit began to reveal to her that while trying to discipline others, she lacked the acceptance of the discipline of the Holy Spirit in her own life. She admitted that it was easy to bear rebukes for what one deserves, but hard to bear things that one does not deserve. Edith knew that she must discipline the people, but she did not want the discipline of God through those folks. She came to realize that God was working in her life to make her willing to accept His discipline, even through the people's disobedience. The Holy Spirit revealed to her that she had to be holy and completely taken up by God if the ministry was to be truly life giving and become a power for the Gospel of Christ. That is revival.

The whole situation forced Edith to stay before God in prayer for long hours. The lepers would complain and be undisciplined, but every time she encountered such a situation, she would simply go to God. She came to the profound yet simple truth that Christ *died* for us. And until a person understands that, he or she will never be willing to die for the brethren. She came to the acknowledgment that Christians are supposed to be doing just that—dying for the brethren.

God showed Edith many other things as well. She had to learn that she was not a very important person. Missionaries find it so easy on the field to be paternalistic. But God loves everyone equally, and Christians are to be subject one to another regardless of race or culture or worldly position. The Spirit forms the body of Christ into a unity. Revival began to blossom in Edith's life. The cross-life was supplanting her self-life.

The secret of the cross-life began to open in Edith's spiritual comprehension. She realized that life only flows from the cross of the Lord Jesus Christ. She saw in more depth than ever before that she must sacrifice herself and die to self so that the life of Christ might live in and through her by the Holy Spirit's power. As Edith's biographer so graphically portrayed it,

> People try me, fail me, drain me, spoil my work with their carelessness, frustrate me with their stubbornness, hurt me with their thanklessness, misrepresent me in their blindness, and my only answer is to be the cross—to die, to die, to die. I kick against such a spineless way, a thousand times, but a thousand times I have to come back to it; it is the only way. It is the meekness that inherits the earth; it is the weakness in which strength is made

perfect; it is the nothingness that possesses all things, the poverty that makes many rich; it is the foolishness of God which is wiser than men. For what it does is simple. I put my little "I" out, crucified with Him; it gives His mighty "eye" all wise, all meek, all loving right of way through me; for the reverse side of the cross in action is always the resurrection in equal action. Blessed cross, where I die daily. Blessed resurrection, by which Christ the Conqueror goes out through me to His inevitable conquests over Satan and other lives. All the strain goes out of life as I learn the daily secret of this brokenness in Calvary, for no longer do I pit my wits, my energies, my impotent strivings against the contradictions and frustrations of life; I have learned where little "I" belongs, ever in the tomb of Christ that His big "I" may multiply His grace through me, as the five loaves of the five thousand. What a revelation and release!

That is true revival. The transformation of Edith's approach to the Christian experience that she learned comprises the difference between a dynamically efficient and a dynamically spiritual person. It is the difference between an ordinary ministry and a revival ministry. New revival power began to flow through Edith as she ministered to body and spirit. As God continued to enlarge the work in her life, it became clear that He was going to use her in revival. But then tragedy struck.

Dark Days

Edith and Percy both had been slavishly laboring, and Edith's health had not been too good. She had to have surgery a short time before, back in 1943. Then, a year later, illness struck again and she spent some weeks in the state hospital in Stanleyville. A vacation appeared mandatory. So Edith and Percy traveled to the lovely mountainous regions to the east. They made their way by Belgium courier van to Kisenyi, a beautiful spot on the northern shore of Lake Kivu, about four hundred miles from their station, Nebobongo. While enroute they stayed in small hostels. One night they had some doubts about the cleanliness of the hostel, but nevertheless ate a meal and then traveled on. Two weeks later Percy came down with typhoid fever. By this time, they were on the mountainside and among strangers. There seemed to be no believers for miles around, and Percy's condition worsened. What were they to do? They had never talked to each other about death, and they felt that the illness was God's way of testing them. So they stuck it out, earnestly praying that God would send them help. In a day or two, they heard a young man outside where they were staying singing "Onward Christian Soldiers." Edith said to Percy, "There must be Christians here after all." Edith went outside and found a young man ironing clothes and singing the hymn. She asked him where he had learned that. He said that he had learned it from a teacher up in the mountains. Edith asked if he could go get the teacher and the young man replied that he could. He set out and returned with the teacher.

Through the teacher, Edith learned of the Ruanda Medical Mission, a nearby branch of the Church Missionary Society (British Anglican Church). Their station was some sixty miles away, but they had missionary doctors. Edith immediately wrote a letter requesting help. Doctor Harold Adencey came at once. He found Percy slipping seriously but could not transport him because he could only be transported by lying flat, which was utterly out of the question in the old Ford that Edith and Percy had. Then right at that stage, God sent some American missionaries from the French Cammeroons, Mr. and Mrs. Cozzens, and they had a fine automobile. Percy was transported from the uncomfortable hotel where they were staying to a room at Kisenya. They had no sooner arrived when Percy's temperature soared. On a Saturday morning Percy's condition deteriorated rapidly. From the human perspective, it would seem that there was no hope at all for his recovery. Edith requested the elders of the local church to gather together and pray, anointing Percy with oil in the name of the Lord. They earnestly prayed, but God had a higher service for Percy. He deteriorated all through Saturday. In the afternoon, a small group of believers gathered around his bedside and sang Percy's favorite hymn, "Precious, Precious Blood of Jesus." Just as they were singing the last verse, the Lord called Percy into His presence. He knew that to be with Christ is far better as he quietly slipped into the arms of Jesus. The very afternoon that Percy went to be with the Lord, Mrs. Adeney came into the room and read a chapter from Amy Carmichael's book, *Gold by Moonlight*. In Miss Carmichael's fine volume, she tells of snow and desolation but also of new life that springs out of the earth beneath the snow. As Edith stood alone at Percy's grave, the Lord spoke to her: "Except a corn of wheat fall into the ground and die, it abideth alone; but if it die, it bringeth forth much fruit" (John 12:24 KJV). That brought real peace in Edith's heart and a wonderful comfort for her sorrow.

Edith felt the loss tremendously, but she knew that the providence of God is best (Rom. 8:28), as difficult as it may be to understand—and even more difficult at times to accept. But this became another step forward in Edith's absolute commitment and abandonment to Christ to be used of God in revival. And now a blessed revival was about to dawn fully on Edith.

Ruanda and the Great Awakening

The Spirit of God had been subtly moving at the station even before Percy's death. Edith, sensitive to this, felt that something new and fresh would soon come. The fellowship among the believers had deepened. Previous barriers between missionaries and Africans that seemed insurmountable were crumbling and a new spirit of oneness emerged. Soon all social barriers collapsed. Africans would go to the missionaries' homes and have fellowship in a manner that quite amazed the folk. The natives kept telling Edith that this resulted from the revival that was moving throughout the area. The missionaries, of course, had attempted to break down barriers through the years, but only as the revival began to stir did the barriers really come down.

This new fellowship with one another was predicated on a new level of fellowship with God. Small prayer meetings, informal gatherings of various sorts, as well as larger meetings, became sources of "rivers of living water" (John 7:38 KJV). Marvelous things took place. The praise and worship of God's people became as contagious as the leprosy that had invaded so many. Even the disease did not seem all that important. Open confession of sin sprang forth. Then praise to God for the cleansing blood of Christ ascended. All took place on a very sane and sensible level: thus, it brought a new sense of fellowship with God and each other.

The revival that was blessing Edith's station actually had its inception in Ruanda. The emphasis of the Ruandan revival rested on the blood of Christ to cleanse from all sin. When a believer would find cleansing, the whole group would sing a little chorus: "Glory, Glory, Hallelujah, Glory, Glory to the Lamb." This practice brought down barriers. Pretense, hypocrisy, self-righteousness, worldliness, coldness, criticism, and impure thoughts were plunged under the blood and a new freedom and exuberance of cleansing filled the air. Guilt turned to joy. This was revival. The freedom of the Spirit had come on them. At times, such an effusion of the Holy Spirit and the flood tides of blessings caused meetings to go on day and night. As a consequence, tens of thousands of native Africans came to saving faith in the Lord Jesus Christ. The church was mightily awakened. The Eastertide Conference at one of the stations saw fifteen thousand people assembled. In one area four hundred churches were established out in the bush, simply because of the testimony of those sharing Christ.

As is always the case, of course, some excesses endangered the work. But because of the strong emphasis on the Word of God, and the humble searching for the truth, most all of the problems were resolved, and the Holy Spirit kept a check and balance on the work.

As already mentioned, this work began in Ruanda, centered in the Anglican mission. Bishop Butler, a Church of England missionary from the United Kingdom, was used of God to see the work birthed. It soon began to spread throughout Uganda, and went into Kenya and Tanganyika as the wind of the Spirit blew over east Africa.

These authors first heard of the great east African revival from the lips of Norman Grubb, successor to C. T. Studd as director of the World Evangelization Crusade. In a Bible Missionary Conference at Prairie Bible Institute, Three Hills, Alberta, Canada, in the early fifties, we had the privilege of sitting at Norman Grubb's feet. He shared for four full days the glories of that revival. It became a revival for us also. Grubb later penned a little volume entitled *Continuous Revival*, relating the story of the Ruandan outpouring. A few years later it was our privilege to be in a meeting at Spurgeon's Tabernacle in London, England. There, missionary Bishop Butler and an African convert, William Nagenda of Ruanda, spoke. They were God's key instruments in starting the awakening. There were not over fifteen or twenty of us seated about in a circle. We were fellowshiping together when William Nagenda looked around at all of us with compassionate eyes and simply said, "I love you." One might think that not an unusual thing to say, and of course it was not. But the Holy Spirit descended upon that group with those simple words. It was awesome.

The revival blazed throughout east Africa for decades. It also touched many other parts of the world. For example, in 1948, at a Spiritual Life Conference in Los Angeles, one hundred and fifty ministers gathered along with Mennonite missionaries from Tanganyika. The Mennonites gave a simple testimony of how their dry bones had the wind of the Spirit blow upon them and had come to life during a visit in Ruanda. As they shared, the Spirit of God fell powerfully on the group. The next nights were spent in fervent prayer until the small hours of the morning. First came repentance and confession. Then, as God's Spirit always so graciously does, praise and glory ascended up to God. Fifty of the revived ministers met the following week to share how the revival had touched them. The spirit of revival also spread through Britain, Switzerland, and South Africa.

Norman Grubb, a keen student of the revival, gave his account of the wonderful truths that emerged in that context:

> It is no new truth. It has not centered round some special person. In fact, one of its chief characteristics has been the humbling of man and the exalting of Christ. It simply consists of individuals, the twos and threes, then groups, and larger groups, opening themselves continually to the light of God, and at any cost to themselves, walking in that light. Just as simple as that. At any moment, any hour of the day, if a motion of the heart, a thought, a word, a deed is seen in that blinding light to be less than the highest, it is squarely recognized as such, not slurred over, not excused as some infirmity or natural weakness, but faced,

acknowledged, and confessed outright as sin. Sin, in other words, takes on new meanings. It is the least thing that comes short of the glory of God, short of His perfection; nor is there any quibbling about what is merely temptation, and what is sin. Any motions in the heart of hardness towards a brother, critical thoughts, resentment, self-pity, unbelief, impurity, fear, worry, those minor attitudes of hypocrisy by which we cover up our true actions and make out we are better than we are, these and many other such things are nailed to the counter in their true colors. Such simple and continual acts of repentance for sin they often call "brokenness" or "bending the stiff neck," for on each occasion it means that self-will or self-esteem or self-seeking in some form is recognized in its true colors as claiming mastery of the heart, and is confessed and forsaken as an evil thing.

But conviction and confession are meaningless unless they take place at Calvary. Christ bore our sins. He was broken for us. His head was bowed in giving up the ghost for us. And Calvary means cleansing: "the blood of Jesus Christ His Son cleanseth us from all sin." It is there we break, and bend our necks, broken at the sight of what our sins have done to Him, broken by His brokenness, and from there we come away forgiven and cleansed. It is not merely conviction and confession, but conviction, confession and cleansing. The glory is in the Blood.

And where the Blood is applied, the Spirit abides. Jesus lives in the cleansed heart. He is both the light and the life. He is revival. Conviction, confession, cleansing is followed by cups running over with joy and victory.

This may sound altogether individualistic, but not so; no brother or sister in Christ are mere isolated believers. They are part of a body, a brotherhood, a manifestation of Christ on earth, a unified whole to serve Christ. Fellowship must be maintained within the body as well as with Jesus Christ Himself. It is often easier to be open before God than before one another. But when real revival comes, with the attending vision of the holiness of God and the brokenness of the human heart, believers find it quite easy to humble themselves before one another, lay aside their personal pride, and get perfectly and thoroughly right with the Lord Jesus Christ and with one another. The Ruanda Revival stressed that reality.

Revival had dawned and the light of Christ dispelled blindness. The greatest danger to Christian growth and maturity is simple blindness—a sinful spot in one's life that one fails to see. That dead spot must be exposed by the Spirit of God, then cleansed by the precious blood of Christ and filled with the love of the Lord. And that is exactly what Edith had to see. Edith's primary problem did not revolve around submission or failure to work; her problem centered in her own unjudged impatience and perhaps working too hard. But when the revival touched her life, she saw that dark spot in her spiritual experience, and brokenheartedly repented, confessed her sin, and found the wonderful cleansing of the blood of Christ. Then the revival fire began to run through her life and into the lives of others.

The revival that had actually started in Edith's heart was by way of the simple challenge of an African. On the very morning that Percy died, she suddenly remembered the promise of James 5:14. She immediately felt convicted that she had not earlier called for the elders of the church, had them anoint Percy, and pray for his healing. She confessed, as she reflected back on the event, that in a weak moment she probably fell victim to Satan's ploy of legalism. Physically she was worn out and at her wit's end. True, on the day of Percy's death she did call for the elders to come and had them anoint him in the name of the Lord; but why not earlier? They prayed one by one around the bed and when it came to Edith, she prayed as if her own life depended on it. After the prayer meeting, she really believed that God would heal her dear husband. Yet she could not honestly say in her heart, *Thy will be done.* Could there have been a bit of rebellion?

Immediately after the prayer, one of the African brothers who had been mightily revived and had an intimate walk with Christ said to Edith, "I have something to say to you, Mrs. Moules." He told the story of a white woman who had lost a loved one and was grief stricken. A little child came to this woman in the midst of her tears and asked, "Don't you love Jesus?" The white woman, being a dedicated Christian said, "Yes, of course I do." The little girl retorted, "Well, then, why do you cry?" That simple little story smote Edith deeply and profoundly. At first she rebelled. She thought, *This African doesn't know what I am going through; he doesn't understand that I am a missionary and understand that I love the Lord.* She confessed that she was cut to the quick. But as she stood there, God spoke to her and seemed to say, *You be careful about that spirit of yours. He is only trying to be loyal to me.* Edith had to confess that God had allowed the African to say that which hurt her deeply so that she might see the truth about herself. She saw that her resentment was a sin and that she must bring it before God and put it under the blood.

That simple incident opened Edith's spiritual understanding to what she and her beloved husband had been seeking for so long: true fellowship with Africans that only the Spirit of God can bring about. That very day, though Percy died, Edith found new victory in her heart. She gave all to Jesus Christ and His Lordship in a new depth.

The Spreading Awakening

So out of those spiritual dynamics, the life and ministry of missionary-nurse Edith Moules experienced revival. Wherever she went, she shared the truths of the awakening and the Spirit of God flowed through her until the entire area became mightily awakened.

After Percy's death, Dr. Harold Adeney accompanied Edith back to her station in Nebobongo. While Dr. Adeney lingered for a time in Nebobongo, he and two native brothers visited a Bible school at nearby Ibambi. A spirit of expectancy filled the air. They felt that God would soon do a great work among them. They were not disappointed. The Holy Spirit visited them. Hours were spent together getting things right with God and with each other. The spirit of prayer fell upon all as they imbibed the presence of God. One of the missionaries wrote, "I go to teach in the school and we all fall to pray instead. Evangelists and wives come, young men and school boys are experiencing the new life in Christ Jesus. It is wonderful. I have never been in anything like it since I have been on the field. They are seeing themselves crucified with Christ and also risen with Him."

A New Spirit in the Work

Now as Edith threw herself into the work with the lepers, her work was accompanied by real revival. Edith tells a typical story of how God worked during those awakening days:

A typical instance was the case of a man who had been fighting an issue. He had been trying to get through to peace and joy in Christ, reaching out after the revival experience, but there was sin in his life which had never been confessed. "He had been to me in tears for four days," she wrote. "He had come again to ask me to pray with him, but God wouldn't let me. 'You know the way now. You have got to get through for yourself,' I told him. It seemed a dreadful thing to say. But the man had been shown and shown that he was up against a moral issue. That night Tikima, my cook, was down with the lepers, leading the meeting. He came back at midnight and told me the story. This man got up and cried to God for cleansing, and out came the whole thing in a crowded church. I can't tell you how many people were there, I only know that that night sixty-five people hurried out of the building to go home and get right with their wives, neighbors, the missionary, and so on. One man came to me with a bit of box-wood with two or three rusty nails hanging out. He told me he had stolen it from the carpenter's shop. A person later expressed surprise that I would think anything of that. But I would take a pin back, if God the Holy Spirit was convicting somebody of sin. So God blessed us and revival came in small measure. It came first to the souls who were seeking, on stretch after a deeper work of God. He showed some of these lepers some of the principles of revival that He had been teaching me, and of the way Life could flow out of them to others. Some who were blessed at that time went out from our Leper Colony to pagan leper settlements, where we were not yet working in a medical sense. In one of these we had been seeking to found a church of Jesus Christ for years. But they were as tough as nuts. We did not seem able to make any impression. We'd go and seek to get a congregation together, and were lucky if we could get two or three to listen to us. Yet two broken African bodies with broken spirits (that is the point—with broken spirits) went up to that leper place and with their own hands built a little meeting place, and the Holy Spirit through their bodies in a few months has founded a church there with thirty-five souls."

Edith's Later Years

Edith's work certainly had not only its bright points, but also its dark days. The constant threat of closing down the leper work due to political unrest hung over her. But God kept the work growing and expanding as the revival continued to course through the countryside. But Edith was growing old in years if not in spirit.

In the wisdom and love of God, Edith's years were slowly drawing to a close. Still, even in those last years God gave this woman of awakening wonderful victories. The work expanded into the Gold Coast. Then she got a burden for the other five west African colonies. They needed leprosy work as well. God met their needs. The work began, now furlough time came around again.

On a furlough back in Britain, Edith had a small cyst removed. The biopsy showed it benign. Yet, another growth in the same place came back and was larger. Being a nurse, she had a fair idea of the nature of the problem. Yet she knew that if she did anything about it, it would probably bring an end to her next tour of duty. So she just kept quiet, made her preparations, and in December 1946 flew off to the Congo once more.

As can be imagined, when the lepers saw her, they gave her a tumultuous reception. Edith thrilled to see how God in His faithfulness had used her to bring so many to faith in Christ. She exclaimed, "The leper work is most encouraging from every point of view. More young men and women are being trained for responsible positions. The most important news is the formation of a Bible school to train young Christian lepers for evangelism. In all there are eleven settlements. We probably reach about four thousand with the Gospel in all the eleven."

She carried on until the time for her next furlough rolled around. It was to be her last farewell to those whom she loved so much in Africa. On her way home she toured throughout central and west Africa. She visited French Equatorial Africa, the Cameroons, Spanish Guinea, Nigeria, Dahomey, the Gold Coast, the Ivory Coast, Liberia, Portuguese Guinea, and Senegal. Her objective was to visit all the fields of the World Evangelization Crusade. Wherever she went, she received a warm welcome. After the two-month tour in her beloved Africa, she returned to England.

On her return to her native country, X-rays revealed that Edith must have an immediate operation. She was admitted to the Queen Elizabeth Hospital in Birmingham, and the diagnosis, as she had suspected, was cancer. The skilled surgeons removed all of the malignant growth they could, but they offered no promise of recovery. The doctors gave her an ultimatum; they said she could perhaps live another two years if she would give up her active life and take very good care of herself. If not, they prophesied that she might live no more than six months. One can well imagine the decision Edith made. She said she would not give up her work. The doctor retorted that she did not understand, and if she did not give up her work, she would only have six months to live. Edith answered, "Yes, doctor, but you see, the lepers are my life." The doctor, deeply touched, said, "Mrs. Moules, your proposal is simply crazy. But if I were in your place, I think I would do it all the same!"

The Crusade arranged a tour for Edith to travel the United States and Canada. A missionary on furlough from China drove her thousands of miles in his own car. She carried on wonderfully well despite the heavy X-ray therapy she had to endure. She traveled extensively and the blessings of revival followed her everyplace she went.

By the time the tour was over, some four months later, the cancer had spread throughout Edith's body. Not only that, they had suffered an automobile accident in their travels. All together these occurrences pretty well confined Edith to a wheelchair.

Friends wheeled Edith in her chair to an airplane and she returned to the London headquarters of WEC in July 1948. God graciously gave her more time than what the doctors predicted. She lived fourteen more months and her activity was ceaseless.

It did seem almost incredible the way Edith gave herself to service those last months. The only answer can be her absolute commitment to Christ and her unswerving faith in the goodness and grace of God. She said,

It is our inner attitude to life which makes or mars us. The glory of the cross shines out, when we understand the principle of going the way of the cross. . . . We have to choose His way of daily dying. The glory shines out, when we see the point and let the fire burn. . . . We can only reach out for the deep things, in so far as we will go the way of the Spirit. It is a vicarious way. It is the way Jesus went, and we are intercessors only when we let the same spirit of Jesus dwell within us. When we are willing to be bruised for someone else's iniquities, then we should rejoice. The bruising drives us to the place where we let the glory of the cross shine out.

With that marvelous spirit, Edith prepared to meet her Lord.

Glory

About a month before the end, Edith asked friends to come and anoint her with oil and pray over her according to James 5:14. She was laid on a wheeled couch as about sixty of her friends and fellow coworkers prayed for her and anointed her. What a marvelous spirit she exuded. She had given her body years ago to be a living sacrifice for the lepers; now she gave it to God's glory whatever His will might be. In the spirit of Paul and of the Lord Jesus Christ Himself, it was her prayer that God might be magnified in her body whether by life or by death (Phil. 1:20).

In the early morning of Tuesday, September 6, 1949, Edith sent for Dr. and Mrs. Norman Grubb. She knew that the end of her warfare and suffering had come. Heaven's gates were already opening for her. Her breathing was very heavy. The cancer had invaded her lungs, leaving her voice barely audible. Yet, with her bright smile, she welcomed them and said, "Well, the end has come." As a few friends gathered about her as her earthly life ebbed away, her voice gradually weakened until the last words that could be heard were "Jesus, Jesus." She sank into unconsciousness and with eyes closed she quietly slipped into the presence of the Lord she loved and had served so sacrificially.

A beautiful revived life left us—but did it? For the small number of those who mourned her at the private funeral, they could never concede that Edith was really gone. Her life had touched them so profoundly that she would be living in some sense of the word through them. But more than that, the hundreds and thousands of lepers whom she had impacted down through the years gave testimony that they could never be the same after having met this woman of awakening. That is what God can do with the life totally yielded to Christ and willing to follow the revival path. Edith Moules, woman of awakening, lives on.

Endnotes

1. The quotes in this chapter are taken from Norman Grubb, *Mighty Through God, The Life of Edith Moules* (London: Lutterworth Press, 1957).

Chapter Ten

BERTHA SMITH

The Chinese Awakening

The great nation of China traveled into the twentieth century on the rugged road of turbulence and upheaval. The Manchu dynasty had dominated Chinese society for two hundred years. It was an oppressive regime. Life for the peasants revolved around privation, heartache, and misery. Toiling in the rice patties day after day in knee-deep mud just to eke out a meager existence was the lot of most Chinese. The landowners and warlords dominated the economy of the country, which resulted in widespread poverty, famine, and starvation. Despite an incredible culture spanning three millennia, the common people led a mundane life of mere survival. China had not yet come to grips with the twentieth century, even though the new age pressed in on them.

If revolutions have characterized most nations generally, it particularly characterized China. The history of the largest country on earth is replete with revolutionary uprisings. The Chinese expression for revolution is *ko-ming*. It literally means to "cast the skin" or to "renew." Through the evolution of the term, it came to connote "change of mandate." This colorful term describes where China found itself as the twentieth century dawned. But little did the Chinese people realize that a new spirit of revolution, a spiritual ko-ming, would soon dawn upon them. God was preparing the way for a great revival across the giant nation.

Preparation for the Chinese Revival occurred some years earlier on a farm on the outskirts of the little town of Cowpens, South Carolina. Cowpens is hardly a place of notoriety, even though a famous battle in America's Revolutionary War took place there. Back in 1888, it was simply a little farming community with a general store and a few other businesses. In those days, America was experiencing rather troubled times as was China. As the Taiping revolution raged in China, it had only been twenty-four years since America struggled through its bloodiest conflict, the Civil War. Unrest permeated the social structure of the States. Not only that, the clouds of the impending Spanish American War of 1898 rose on the horizon. That conflict only lasted one year, but turbulence came in its wake. Those days saw deep economic depressions, not to mention the excess and exuberance of the gay nineties. But 1888 still boded to be a blessed year as well as a turbulent one, not only for China but also for America. On November 16 of that year, born into the home of John and Frances Smith, came a new little baby girl. The proud parents named her Olive Bertha. In that new life, God sent into the world a future servant who would make a far greater impact for Christ than her parents John McClellen and Frances Thorn Smith could possibly have envisioned. We met Bertha Smith in the Prologue to this book; now we must see how her life unfolds to make her a woman of awakening.

Few parents realize that those destined for greatness could be bundled up in the tiny body of their newborn child. But God wrote destiny all over the fabric of little Olive Bertha's future. Bertha—the name Olive was soon dropped—lived her first seven years as a typical nineteenth-century little girl, growing up on a farm in the deep South. In her seventh year her father moved the enlarging family from their farm into the town of Cowpens. A man of reasonable means, he built for his growing family a lovely southern-style home, which still stands. He opened a small mercantile business along with other enterprises, his entrepreneurial spirit serving the family well.

Early Years

Bertha was one of five children and proved to be most precocious. She never failed to make her school's honor roll—and she loved it. Being a proud little thing, when the teachers boasted of her accomplishments, as she herself said, she "knew no better than to believe it." But the day would come when God would break that human pride and use His humble, contrite servant to precipitate great revival. And it occurred of all places, in China. So far removed geographically, culturally, and spiritually from the "Bible Belt" of America, it seems incredible how this future missionary revivalist could be used of God so profoundly in that Far East nation.

The little school in Cowpens in the 1890s was very different from today's classrooms. Breach of etiquette, undisciplined action, and apathy toward one's studies were not tolerated. Bertha fit in that situation well; she had become a very disciplined child. Discipline has its rewards, and that discipline would one day hold her in good stead as revival came to China. The firm guidance that Bertha received in the home and her obedience at school developed in her a love of study. Being a well-mannered child, she related positively to all in her community; little Bertha was a "good girl." Moreover, she struggled to keep up the image. Through it all she created a passion to excel. Perhaps her passion to excel precipitated something of impatience, if not intolerance at times; nevertheless, it was her insistence on perfection that God used significantly. That insistence on excellence, not only for herself, but for others also got her into a strange situation in China, just as the Shantung Revival broke out.

School Days

Bertha's school opened at eight o'clock each morning with worship and singing; again a far cry from today's insistence on no religious training in public schools. The principal himself would read and explain a portion from the Word of God and then assign Scripture memory work for the students. Bertha revelled in it. She would put to memory the whole chapter of the Bible in which the required verses were found. Then she would stand up before the class and recite the entire chapter. Although there was more than a hint of pride in her, this practice did instill a deep love for the Bible. That too held her in good stead in the days that God had mapped out for her in His providence and care.

The whole Smith family was very faithful to the local church. Bertha's Sunday School teacher also required Scripture memorization. Again she excelled. In actuality, church worship, Sunday school, and the midweek prayer service became her most delightful times. She would not miss a service. Not only that, she read her Bible daily and prayed regularly. She felt that all of this would certainly make her acceptable in the eyes of the Lord. Bertha carried on in this manner throughout her early years; but then the first of several spiritual revolutions erupted in her life beginning at the tender age of ten.

Conversion

The local church where Bertha and her family attended had what was called a revival meeting. She would later learn the real meaning of *revival*. In those days, however, the term basically meant a time of preaching the Gospel, thus seeking the conversion of lost people. Many of the local churches throughout the Bible Belt would set aside a week or two for special evangelistic services. These they called revivals.

In the context of such a revival meeting Bertha Smith's journey to the Cross and salvation began. She came to a dynamic conversion experience in Jesus Christ in 1905. It seemed a long arduous journey. Her experience unfolded quite similarly to Bunyon's pilgrimage as he made his way toward "yonder wicked gate," where the burden of sin that he carried on his back fell off into the open grave made empty because of the glorious resurrection of Christ. But she should be allowed to share her journey in her own words:

> There were three classes of folk in the churches at that time: the warmhearted Christians, the backsliders, and the class who were

in those days called the "lost." Everybody went to church, the church being the social center, with nowhere else to go and nothing at home to keep one there.

The grand old man of God preacher, with tears rolling down his cheeks, pled with backsliders too [*sic*] confess their sins and come back into fellowship with Holy God. He pled with the lost to repent of their sins and flee from God's holy wrath to come, because it had been appointed unto man once to die, but after that the judgment! And while the man of God wept, preached the Word, and pled, saints prayed and the Holy Spirit moved.

Baptist churches did not have altar forms as the Methodist's did, but for two weeks in the year, we had plenty of repenting space. Those sitting on the front rows of benches across the church moved when the invitation was given, knowing that people would come. They stood in orderly lines down the aisles next to the walls and continued their share in singing to the unsaved, such as: "Come every soul by sin oppressed, there's mercy with the Lord." As more came, more benches were vacated, and sometimes half the church would be turned into a "mourner's bench!"

Mourn they did, as the Holy Spirit used the Word, to show them the exceeding sinfulness of sin, and they realized that only their life breath kept them out of an awful hell which had been made for the devil and his angels.

The backsliders were there too, like the prodigal of old, confessing to their Father their wandering away and doing as they pleased. They often wept sore as they realized what their sin had cost Holy God.

I was ten years old when, one hot July night as I sat beside the second window from the front, the Word of the Lord went to my heart! For the first time I saw myself, at least a little glimpse of what I looked like, in the eyes of Holy God. While people called me a good girl, I would not do in his sight, who saw all the pride of my heart— the selfishness and the wanting to be first in everything, just to be praised by teachers. I wanted to make a hundred on all of my examinations, but I did not want anyone else to make a hundred! I had to excel! What an awful human being, a chip off the old block, Adam, after the devil entered into him!

Praise the Lord that we had a man of God for a pastor who knew that every human being was just like that, and he knew the remedy: Jesus Christ had come and died and taken in himself the sin of the human family; and that was what he proclaimed.

I wanted to go to the altar that first night, but on the evening before, a girl my age had gone and people said that she was too small, that she did not know what she was doing. Therefore, I did not dare go, but there was no peace of heart for me during the remainder of that meeting, or any other time.

The next year when the revival meeting began, I publicly announced myself a lost sinner by going to the altar and telling the Lord about my sins. In spite of the fact that I had been silently confessing for a year, that was my first chance to let other people know that I was conscious of my being one of the Lost.

No one was trained to do personal work at the altar. Only the pastor was at the altar to help people, and there were always so many older ones there, who took first place, that he never got to me.

I had to go on another year with my burden of sin, shedding many a tear in secret. Over and over again I told the Lord about my sins and pled for his cleansing.

About the third year, I was at the altar next to a woman whom the pastor came to help. It seemed to me that he talked with her a long time. He just stuck his head over toward me and said, "Just trust the Lord and he will save you." He was right, but I did not know what he meant by trusting the Lord. So that meeting came to an end with the cry of my heart being, "The summer is ended and I am not saved" (see Jer. 8:20).

When I went fifteen miles in the country to my grandmother's in the summer and attended their Big Meeting, I would just have to go to the altar. Occasionally we went to other nearby country churches for their summer meetings, and I could not but make my distress known. I went forward so much at my home church that I was afraid people would think that I was just going for the fun of it. I could have assured them that it certainly was not fun. Sometimes I would almost hold to the bench to keep from going forward but then I went home feeling worse then than when I went; and when I did go, it did no good! Oh, the wretched girl that I was!

After our pastor had been with us for fifteen years, he resigned and pastored another church in the community. When his revival meeting came, we went. I was among those at the altar wanting to be saved from hell. I was about fourteen by that time, and I suppose the pastor felt that I was old enough to have some attention. He said, "Bertha, if you will just trust the Lord, he will save you. Are you trusting him?"

I replied, "Yes, I am trusting the Lord."

He said, "Well, you are saved then."

(Now, what about one human being telling another that he is

saved when the advisor cannot see whether or not a miracle has taken place inside?) He went back to the pulpit and asked anyone who had trusted the Lord at that service to stand. I stood, but I went home just as much in the dark as ever. I knew a good bit about the Lord, but he was away out yonder and I was here, under the burden of what I was in the sight of God, with no connection between us.

Two more summers passed, with a pastor who did no personal work. Then one last Sunday morning, after I had gone regularly to the altar as usual, the pastor asked if any at the front were ready to come to Jesus Christ and take him as Savior. For the first time, I saw that we come to the cross of Christ to be saved. Formerly I had not differentiated between God the Father and God the Son, and I did not know what was meant by "trusting God." Even though my advice had been right, all of the Godhead was God to me. I had been all those years trying to approach God the Father directly, no doubt even calling him "Father," when he is only the Father of those who believe his Son (Gal. 3:26). I learned that what the preachers meant by trusting God to save meant to trust God the Son, who settled my sin and my sinful self when he took my sins and me in his own body on the tree.

I was on the front seat, having gone forward at the first verse. I knew that I would go; there was no use to wait. It was but a step to where the pastor stood. I took it, gave him my hand to signify that I trusted in Christ's death to save me. By the time I took the second step, which was back to my seat, my years of burden of sin had rolled away, and the joy of the Lord filled my soul.

I think sometimes if the Lord could ever save one the wrong way, he would have saved me! He must really have been sorry for me. I praise him that he never let go, but made that conviction stronger and stronger until someone said enough about Christ's death, or Christ being the Savior, for me to lay hold on what he had done for me. There is no direct road from the sinful heart to God the Father. I tried to make one, but it did not work! My sin was settled at the cross, and through Christ's death I at last came, which is the only way that anyone gets to him.

I went home so thrilled, and so sorry for everyone else who was not in tune with the Lord, that I did not want any of that good Sunday dinner. My parents and two older sisters and both older brothers were church members and one brother and sister younger were old enough to be saved, so I just had to go to my place of prayer by the trunk in the walk-in closet in my room and plead with God for the family and for friends and neighbors.

But that joy wore off. Before many months I showed no more of the fruit of the Spirit in my life than the rest of my family, for whom I prayed that glorious Sunday when I passed out of death into life. I well knew to whom I belonged, even though at times I knew that I was not pleasing him. When the visiting preacher, Brother Manness, asked, "Are you girls all Christians?" I knew that Sister Jennie answered right, but I longed for something more of the Lord whom I knew![1]

A Deepening Experience

The deep longing that the Spirit of God had created in Bertha's heart for a dynamic walk with Christ after her conversion came to a head in June 1907. On a warm Sunday afternoon, Bertha, as well as her brothers, sisters, and mother were seated on the front porch of their home in Cowpens. Coming down the street they saw Father John with three other men. The quartet marched up to the front porch and John introduced them to his family. They were three Methodist evangelists. They had come to town to conduct another revival meeting.

John had previously been rather cautious about these men, but they soon proved to be very able leaders and the family joined in heartily with the revival meeting, even though they themselves were Baptists. Actually, the whole community turned out. In those days, it was the best show in town.

Night after night, the Spirit of God genuinely moved in the hearts of many people. In the context of the services, Bertha heard something that she had never heard before. At that time in Southern Baptist life, the doctrine of the Holy Spirit was virtually ignored. But the Methodist brothers had much to say about the doctrine and work of the Holy Spirit in the believer's life. It struck a responsive chord in young Bertha. Although she knew Christ in a very real way, she had never moved into the fullness of the Spirit-filled life. Here the second major step in her spiritual pilgrimage took place. She began to see that only Spirit-filled Christians could be empowered with the strength of God to achieve victory over the temptations of life and make a significant impact in the life of service for Christ. This Spirit-filled life opened a whole new vista to Bertha and her family. It began to prepare her to be used by God in becoming a woman of awakening.

As the services in the revival meeting progressed, Bertha's mother became one of the first ones down at the altar seeking "all that God had for her." She came to the place of complete surrender to the Lordship of Christ and trusted God to do in and through her all that He wished. Bertha's mother, being a quiet lady, had never given a personal testimony or even prayed in public. But after her encounter with the Spirit of God, she became a new person and simply radiated the presence of Christ.

Then sister Jenny went to the altar, then brother Lester, a third-year student at college. Lester came to the realization that he had never truly been born again. He was baptized as a twelve-year-old child, but had never known the Lord Jesus Christ personally. What an experience it became for him when he found the salvation of the Savior! All this was just simply too much for Bertha. When the preacher gave the invitation one night, Bertha immediately went to the front, fell on her knees, and as she herself expressed it, did "a business transaction with my Lord." She surrendered her entire life to Christ. She found herself willing to serve Him wherever He might lead, into whatever avenue of service He wished her to engage. Suddenly everything began to change. At first, Bertha thought her old sinful nature had actually been eradicated. The Methodist brothers did believe and taught such perfectionism, but Bertha soon learned differently. Still, her experience of Christ was profoundly deepened and the old worldly pleasures, even her besetting sin of pride, lost all of its attractiveness. She actually took off her jewelry and pretty clothes and ribbons and wore the plainest of clothes.

The Bible became a new book for Bertha, more than just for memorization. She started a correspondence course in Bible study and thoroughly enjoyed it. Even though she had learned many passages of Scripture, the Bible came alive to her in a way she had never known up to that point. The key to it all can be summed up in her own words, "prayer became communion with God."

Bertha immediately found herself gifted in personal evangelism. All the kids would say, "Bertha has religion." She was anything but reticent to share her faith and to let the world know that she belonged to the Lord Jesus Christ—totally and completely. She had come into the fullness of the Spirit.

Bertha completed her high school days and went for higher education first at Lynwood College near Gastonia, North Carolina; then after one year, she transferred to Winthrop College in Rockhill, South Carolina. There God began an even deeper work in her heart. She met with a group of students who called themselves the Student Volunteer Band. These consecrated young people had dedicated their lives to the mission field and met regularly for prayer and study. They wanted Bertha to join their organization, but she could not be admitted unless she dedicated her own life to the mission field. Consequently, she could not join until she had settled in her heart whether or not God had actually called her to the foreign field. The quest to discover God's will began.

The Call Comes

On a Sunday afternoon, January 9, 1910, the climax of God's call to Bertha came. It had been a long, hard struggle, but it at last became clear that God truly did want her to become a missionary. She joined the Volunteer Band and began preparing for the mission field. She at first thought that she would be going to Africa, but God had other plans. God set her eyes on China.

After graduation at Winthrop College in 1913 and a one-year stint of teaching public school in Blackburn, South Carolina, Bertha moved on to Louisville, Kentucky, to attend the Woman's Missionary Union Training School, an auxiliary of the Southern Baptist Theological Seminary. An appointment under the Baptist Mission Board required this level of education. Bertha's years in Louisville were delightful and fruitful. After two years, she graduated and presented herself to the Foreign Mission Board for appointment.

Her tentative appointment came in 1916, but it was only tentative. America struggled in the grips of World War I and she could not travel to the field in such a turbulent time. Consequently, she taught school for another year in Spartenburg, South Carolina. This gave her experience in education that held her in good stead when she arrived in China. Then on July 3, 1917, Bertha received her formal appointment to China, and she was on her way to share the Gospel with that great nation.

Off to China

Bertha sailed to the Far East on the steamship *Little Empress of Japan*. She made her way after arrival in Shanghai to Peking (now Beijing), for language study. As she had always excelled in all of her studies, she excelled in language study. She became very proficient in Mandarin Chinese and studied it throughout the many years of her missionary service. She could actually speak the language with little or no accent. All the Chinese marveled at her adeptness in their native tongue.

After a year of language study in Peking, Miss Bertha, as all who knew her affectionately called her, went to her first assignment in Laichowfu, in Shantung province. She fit into the situation remarkably well. Of course, there were cultural adjustments to make; China is a long way from Cowpens, but Bertha's self-discipline as a child now came to the fore. With her determination and self-discipline and her intimate walk with the Lord, she became a very happy missionary.

In this new setting, God began to deepen Bertha's spiritual experience even more. Summer missionary conferences were held in various places in Shantung province through the beneficiaries of a wealthy Christian American layman. There God began to do a deep work in her heart.

The realization that Bertha came to, through the study of the Scripture in the context of the missionary conferences, centered around what is commonly called the deeper-life message. It derives its name from spiritual conferences held in Keswick, England, a town in Britain's lake district.

The message is sometimes even called the Keswick message. It had a very dynamic affect on Miss Bertha. The essential truths that she came to understand unfolded on several vital principles:

- the serious problem of sin in the believer's life and subsequent rupture of a dynamic fellowship with Christ (1 John 1:8, 10);
- the necessity of brokenness over sin, honest confession, and the restitution required (1 John 1:9; Matt. 5:23–26)—and all of this is precipitated because of a consciousness of the holiness of God;
- the necessity of absolute surrender and obedience to Christ in all things—service, life, relationships—wherever life is lived, Christ is to be Lord (Rom. 12:1–2);
- the in-filling of the Holy Spirit (Eph. 5:18)—no believer can be used of God significantly unless they are Spirit-filled, even as the Methodist brothers taught Miss Bertha so many years before;
- identity with the Lord Jesus Christ—one of the key issues that Miss Bertha had to learn was her "identification" with the Lord Jesus Christ in His death and resurrection (Rom. 6:1–12; Gal. 2:20); (Keswick makes it very clear that because the believer is "in Christ," he or she shares in His crucifiction and in His glorious resurrection. This constitutes the basis of victory over temptation and sin);
- commitment to evangelism and missions and ministry wherever the Spirit of God may lead; in a word, the fulfilling of the Great Commission stands as essential (Matt. 28:18–20; Acts 1:8).

This basic message of the Keswick movement richly blessed Bertha, especially the truth of her identification with Christ. Although she understood the Spirit-filled life, the truth of being in Christ had eluded her. But now she moved into a rich experience of Christ's fullness. Moreover, the rich realities became the biblical basis for the truths that precipitated the great Shantung Revival in which Miss Bertha played a key role—as we have already seen.

The Need

As Miss Bertha's own spiritual life continually matured, she developed a deep burden and concern for the Chinese Christians to whom she was attempting to minister, not to mention the multiplied millions who had not yet come to faith in Jesus Christ. A general apathy pervaded the churches in Shantung province, which disturbed our woman of awakening. Many of the believers were what was called rice-bowl Christians. That is to say, they would make some profession of faith in Christ, hoping for a handout or perhaps acquiring a job through the missionaries. Therefore, their Christian experience was often quite superficial.

It was not long before once again, China began to be racked with serious unrest. Because of the activity of Communists and others, a time of upheaval surfaced that caused all the Shantung missionaries to retreat to the seaport city of Chefoo. There some two dozen missionaries gathered. It was there that the prayer meeting took place that brought about the marvelous Shantung awakening.

In light of the fact that it was Mrs. Culpepper who experienced a wonderful healing, it is only fair that Dr. Culpepper, who wrote about the event, should give the full account in his own words.

As Miss Monsen gave her testimony, Ola began to be impressed with the fact that she should go and talk to her about the eye damage. We made an appointment and went to her apartment. As she met us at the door, Miss Monsen's first question was, "Brother Culpepper, have you been filled with the Holy Spirit?" I stammered out something less than a definite reply. Then, recognizing my uncertainty, she carefully related a personal experience fifteen years earlier when she had prayed for and received the promise of the Holy Spirit as recorded in Galatians 3:14. After visiting with her for two hours, we urged her to come to our home to pray for Ola's eyes.

That night we were deeply troubled. Prayer for healing seemed unorthodox for Baptist people. But in private we read James 5:14–16 and were greatly encouraged. The words "confess your faults" particularly pierced my heart. A consuming realization that our hearts must be completely open to God pervaded all our senses. I began to feel the Lord was going to undertake a great thing for us.

The next morning about twenty people came to our home for prayer. We felt an electric excitement, a feeling that God was preparing us for something we had never known before. After praying for several hours, we all seemed in a complete spirit of communion. Suddenly Ola took off her glasses and laid them on the mantle. Following the instructions in the Book of James, I anointed her with oil. Then we all knelt and continued praying. It was as though God had walked into the room. Everyone prayed aloud. We felt that Heaven came down and Glory filled our souls.

As we prayed, the male Chinese cooks from both missionary residences in Chefoo walked into the room. Their hatred for each other was common knowledge. But, as the power of God's Holy Spirit worked, they went to each other, confessed their hatred, sought forgiveness, and accepted Christ as personal Savior.

In the midst of our joy for the cooks' salvation, we had completely forgotten Ola's eyes. Then someone remembered and asked her, "What about your eyes?" She replied, "They feel all right and the pain is gone."

It never returned. This was the most wonderful experience in our lives. We had never known such spiritual joy. The events surrounding those days in Chefoo were the prelude to the great Shantung Revival.[2]

After they had all come to the mountaintop experience of Ola's healing, and the previous spiritual deepening that had precipitated the significant event, Miss Bertha, in her typical outspoken fashion, broke into the moment of ecstasy.

"What kind of missionaries are we?" I asked. "We have gone through a week of heart searching, humbling ourselves before each other and before the Lord, in order that we might be altogether right with Him, so that He could hear our prayers and heal the physical eye of one of our own number. Yet we have never gone to this much self-negation for preparation to pray for the opening of the spiritual eyes of the Chinese to whom we have been sent." Our mountaintop of ecstasy suddenly became a valley of humiliation. We all went to our knees in contrite confession for having been so careless as to have gone along supposing that we were right with the Lord, while holding all kinds of attitudes which could have kept the Lord's living water from flowing through us to the Chinese."[3]

Needless to say, as the missionaries returned to their respective stations when the political unrest had settled they were different people with a different message. They were now ready spiritually to minister in power, and the Lord was about to come down in real revival upon China.

Revival Breaks

The great Shantung Revival began in 1927, and went on for some nine years until the invasion of the Japanese in 1936. The stories that emerged in the life of Miss Bertha, our woman of awakening, in the revival context are fascinating and captivating.

Many of Bertha's experiences during the revival read almost like a page out of the book of Acts. First, the Christians themselves were profoundly and radically transformed. The Spirit of God touched many lives. One of those was the Chinese cook of the Larsons, Baptist missionaries. The cook had formerly been an apparently warm-hearted church member, actually conducting Bible classes for other Chinese servants. But during the meeting at Bertha's station in Laichowfu, he became deeply convicted of his own personal sins. He could find no rest or peace. One morning at six o'clock he came to Miss Bertha. The burden of his sins robbed him of sleep; he had not been to bed the entire night. He first sought Miss Bertha's forgiveness for having said untrue and unkind things about her. Miss Bertha said he should go to others and tell them that the things he had said about her were not true. He did so. Then he went to the Larsons and confessed that he had stolen money by buying food for them in the market. He had been pocketing the difference between the market price quoted to the Larsons and the price that he had actually paid. He offered to work for two months without wages, believing that would put the matter square. The Larsons let him work without wages; they knew the Holy Spirit was doing a convicting work in his heart and he would have no peace otherwise. Miss Bertha said when she saw the cook for the first time after his reviving experience that "his face looked like that of an angel."

In the Chinese churches in Bertha's days, a dividing screen to separate the men from the women was put in place when the church gathered for worship. Miss Bertha confessed that she was often guilty of peeping over the screen to see how many men were in church—a little technique that she employed to be able to say what she felt would be relevant for the folk. She would see the face of the cook that looked like an angel. At a prayer meeting Miss Marie Monsen, who was speaking at the time, asked someone thoroughly right with God to pray. The cook immediately arose and began his prayer: "Lord, I thank You that I am no longer I."

After the meeting Misses Bertha and Marie Monsen traveled together to Laiyang, the hometown of the revived cook. Traveling with the women were several other missionaries and the cook. The missionary group went by car to Laiyang. There was no room in the car for the cook, however, so he rode his bicycle and arrived the next day. In a prayer meeting that night, Miss Monsen once again asked for any brother who was right with God to lead in prayer. The cook rose and prayed. As Bertha expressed it, such a volume of praise to the Lord poured forth that his old friends around him wanted to know how such a change had come over him. The cook's new commitment became typical of what God did in multiplied ways as the revival spread. In a true awakening the Holy Spirit profoundly probes God's own people and transforms them.

One could hardly count the numbers who were saved in the revival. Even some preachers came to saving faith in Christ during the awakening. Bertha tells of a Mr. Chow, a Chinese preacher. Mr. Chow, an evangelist in the area, became uneasy about his own relationship with the Lord. After every service he would seek out Miss Bertha. He wanted some evidence that he had truly been born again. At last Miss Bertha asked, "Mr. Chow, what are you trusting in for salvation?" He straightened himself up and immediately replied, "You need not tell me that after I have walked for twenty-five years over this country telling people about the Savior, the Lord is going to turn me away from heaven's gate!" Miss Bertha immediately replied, "If that is what you are trusting in, you most certainly will be turned away!" Bertha never hesitated in frankly telling the bare truth. The evangelist immediately came to Christ alone for his salvation! Works never save. There were actual, verified physical healings as well. Real revival produces incredible experiences. The awakening spread and deepened. Thousands found Christ as Savior through a revived church as the movement engulfed the land. But that is what revival is all about. Bertha really did become a woman of awakening.

The Work Continues

The awakening began to permeate Bertha's entire work. It must be recognized that it would be three or four years after Ola's healing before the full impact of the movement would be generally felt; nevertheless, the revival moved with real power. The revival especially permeated the Chinese preachers' and Bible-teaching women's lives. One evening Miss Bertha walked out into the school yard where she was teaching when one of the Chinese women teachers came up and asked to see her. They went into Bertha's study, and as Bertha started to light a lamp, the Chinese lady said, "Please do not make a light. I cannot look into your face and make this confession!" So they simply sat in the darkness as the Chinese Bible teacher said that she should surrender her high-school diploma to Miss Bertha because she had cheated on one of her examinations. Miss Bertha, always sensitive to the probing of the Holy Spirit, realized that the woman was under deep conviction. Bertha told her to return the diploma which Bertha had signed in good faith thinking that the Chinese lady had completed all of her studies honestly. The brokenhearted teacher surrendered it. Then, through confession and cleansing, the Holy Spirit filled her with great joy. The diploma meant very little compared to God's peace and power in her life. For years Miss Bertha kept the diploma among her "precious things." She always saw it as something of a token of the probing of the Spirit in revival, for spiritual awakenings always begin with a consciousness of the holiness of God and human sinfulness. Then confession and restitution follows, climaxed by joy. This we have often seen.

A pastor in one of the city churches where Miss Bertha served recounted that he had been as a fireplace with the wood all laid out but with no one to strike the match. After his encounter with this woman of awakening he got his sins "confessed up to date," and the Lord revealed Himself in a marvelous way in the pastor's life. Then "the fire blazed."[14] Moreover, the revival flames spread all over the land. The missionaries themselves were deeply touched. Miss Pearl Caldwell, a Southern Baptist missionary, was led by the Spirit of God into deep heart searching and humiliation as she sought the fullness of the Holy Spirit in her life. When she came to the Lord in real surrender and confession, the "rivers of living water" (John 7:38) flowed from her life. Bertha said that if anything characterized the revival it was what Nehemiah called "the joy of the LORD" (Neh. 8:10).

In all of this marvelous work, Marie Monsen played a significant role as did Bertha Smith. We shall see her full story in the next chapter.

New Life

One of the amazing things that took place during the awakening centered in the conversions of the many rice-bowl Christians. The spirit of evangelism even reached some of the Chinese preachers as seen in the case of the Reverend Chow. One year later, one of the missionaries, the Reverend Larson, came to the mission station to lead the annual workers' conference, a gathering for the preachers and Bible women from the surrounding villages. They would assemble for an entire week to plan their work and receive inspiration and Bible instruction. In that setting, Mr. Larson shared with his fellow believers the wonderful theme of the Spirit-filled life. The spirit of the revival soon created an insatiable hunger in all. On Wednesday night, the closing evening of the sessions, Larson urged all those who desired God's best to remain in the church and join him for prayer that they might experience "all the fullness of God" (Eph. 3:19). Several lingered.

One of those who remained to pray with the Reverend Larson was Brother Lai, a Chinese pastor of the local church. He had been unable to sing for several days, suffering from a serious case of laryngitis. He could hardly speak above a whisper. But about midnight the Spirit of God fell upon them, and Brother Lai rose from his knees to his feet and began to sing with a beautiful clear voice. Mr. Larson jumped up and exclaimed, "the Spirit has come!" Suddenly both men were virtually prostrate on the floor as though struck by an electric bolt. Miss Bertha related the story:

> In a few minutes they were loudly praising the Lord while others were crying to him for mercy. The sleeping ones were aroused and rushed to the church, falling upon their knees in confession of their sins, coldness, and lack of power of the Holy Spirit in their lives. Loud hallelujahs and cries for mercy rang out through the rest of the night.
>
> Some were convinced of not having been saved, but by daylight they had entered into the joy of the Lord. Among these was

Mr. Chow, the evangelist, for whom many had been praying. He refused to take a salary for further preaching, saying that he had already accepted too much for preaching without having known the Lord or the power of the Spirit. Now and then after that he had to sell a few acres of land to get money to support his family.

Mr. Larson went back to his home in Laichowfu just in time for the workers' conference of that section. His burning testimony so moved the people that they continued in meetings through Christmas. Chinese leaders as well as missionaries so died to themselves that the Holy Spirit gloriously filled them.

In January during the Chinese New Year's vacation time, a small group of church workers and missionaries in Hwanghsien invited Mr. Larson to lead a week's prayer meeting. One by one, those attending were brought low before the Lord as the Spirit revealed what he wanted to prune from their hearts and lives. He could not fill them until they were emptied of self, and that act had to be performed by each one.

What joy the filling of the Holy Spirit brought! Martha Li, wife of one of the evangelists, walked up on the platform to give a testimony. She stood there for about two hours with the light of heaven on her face, pouring out praise to the Lord, using the words of the Psalms.

It was a humbling experience when missionaries had to confess to Chinese their lack of love and patience. When missionary and Chinese were brought low together, there was no longer any East or West.

Dr. Glass, Dr. Culpepper, Dr. Lide, and Dr. Abernathy were set on fire by the Holy Spirit. They, with Mr. Larson, were invited to church after church in Shantung, where the Lord worked mightily. They then moved into Honan Province, where a great reviving began in the churches.

China Touched

The revival continued to broaden until it spread throughout many areas of China. One fascinating story centers around Dr. Charles Culpepper. While still a student at Baylor University in Waco, Texas, he worked in the college cafeteria as the cashier. On a certain Sunday, a man and his family came in for lunch. As they filed out to pay, Dr. Culpepper did not have proper change to give to the man for the ten-dollar bill that the man offered. The gentleman said that it was all right and that he would pick up the change later. So Charles kept the money thinking the man would come back. Not long after this seemingly innocent incident, Charles' sister became critically ill, which necessitated his traveling to her home. Charles had no money of his own, so he spent the stranger's money for the train fare home. He had fully intended to give it back to the man but had completely forgotten about the incident.

Years later, when the revival came and Charles began to realize the necessity of confession of sin and restitution, that whole incident loomed large before his eyes. He knew that he must make it right with God, but it threw him into a real struggle. He argued with himself: He was too old and well-respected to bring up something that had been a mere oversight as a college student. It would surely cause criticism, he reasoned. What would people think? Yet, the Spirit of God continued to impress his heart with the necessity of making restitution. Finally, he wrote the president of Baylor University enclosing a check. He felt that he would surely be disgraced and lose the confidence of the Baylor family. Several months passed before a letter finally arrived from the president of Baylor. In the letter the president wrote, "Dear Charlie, I think more of you than ever. I wish Baylor had more graduates like you." God vindicates His servants, especially in the context of real revival.

It is important to realize that all this emphasis on confession and restitution did not degenerate into morbid, introspective, psychological exercises. The Holy Spirit generated confession in the light of God's utter holiness. Moreover, the missionaries were careful to keep confession under control and to make sure that public confession was only made for public sins. The principle that sin is confessed only in the area of the offense became their guiding principle. This kept the whole movement wholesome. The pruning process proved necessary and God blessed profoundly.

Perhaps the most significant impact of the revival revolved around the Chinese preachers themselves. One revived preacher said,

> I want to tell you that I have been preaching for thirty years and have not been worth my salt. I was so lazy I could not walk a mile and a half to tell people about Jesus. Since the revival, I go to prayer meeting at five o'clock in the mornings, go home and eat breakfast, take a little bread for lunch, and walk twenty five miles witnessing in villages, then go home and go to prayer meeting at night. The next morning I am ready to go again. When the revival began, we had about fifty members in our little church. Now we have at least one Christian in each of the one thousand homes in this town. Dozens of villages surround us and we have witnessed in all of them. There are hundreds of Christians in them.

What marvelous days!

War Erupts

Fascinating is Bertha's story of how she survived the events leading up to and during the first days of World War II as the Japanese invaded China. In Tsinging, Bertha's station at the time, pandemonium and panic pervaded as the Japanese approached. Children screamed in terror, but Bertha kept right on working. She immediately increased the number of church services, and at times the church could not hold the crowds. The revival actually continued, even in very difficult circumstances. For weeks Bertha carried on, trying to make every moment count for eternity, as she expressed it. One Saturday afternoon a Chinese man by the name of Mr. Wang asked to see her. He had been attending the Bible classes and had decided that he wanted to be saved. So on his knees, before an open Bible, Bertha walked him through the promises of the Scriptures on forgiveness of sins and how in Jesus Christ he could have new life. Bertha wanted to be sure that the man understood what sin was, so she asked Mr. Wang, "What is the greatest sin you have ever committed?" To her utter astonishment he replied, "Murder." Miss Bertha said, "What a glorious message I had for a murderer." She showed him that according to God's holy law he should have forfeited his life, but that the Lord Jesus Christ had done that in his place. In a short time Mr. Wang was rejoicing in Christ as he experienced God's wonderful forgiveness. Miss Bertha explained, "That one trophy would have been sufficient reward for all that I endured during the war, had I been looking for rewards."

As the war continued, the mission complex filled with refugees. Christmas time drew near, and the victorious Japanese armies were approaching the station. The missionaries had taken in several women refugees. The women would bring flour or millet and little mud cook stoves and pots for their meals. At night they rolled out their pallets all over the mission yard; each had an assigned place. The church basement was reserved for the men of the church. Soon the city fell under siege. As the Japanese armies came closer and closer, the roar of the cannons became louder and louder. The people, panic-stricken, began fleeing to the west to escape the encroachment of the overwhelming Japanese forces. Shops were closed most of the day and air raids became a regular occurrence.

Upon returning from visiting the local hospital one afternoon, Miss Bertha discovered that a Japanese bomb had exploded just across the street from the mission grounds. Even the Christians were in panic. Bertha kept quoting to them, "God is our refuge and strength. . . . Therefore will not we fear, though the earth be removed" (Ps. 46:1–2 KJV). Bertha said, "My own favorite verse was John 14:20: 'I am in my Father, and ye in me, and I in you' (KJV). How safe! Anything touching me would have to pass by God the Father, then it would have to get by Jesus Christ the Son, before it could reach me; and if it did, there would be the Lord inside of me. There would be no problem." Bertha readily confessed that what the Chinese friends called courage and boldness was really Christ Himself living His life through her. She said, "Now you may be sure that I had my sins forgiven up-to-date at such a time! I was not only keeping clean enough inside for him to dwell, but I was choosing his will in advance, daily and moment by moment." Therefore, she lived a victorious life, even in the midst of the tragedy.

Bertha, filled with the Spirit, made each day count during those hectic times. She never thought of personal danger or what might happen. She said, "I was completely possessed with the desire to do all that I could, for all the people that I could, while I could, *for the night would surely come. What kind of a night no one knew!*"

As Christmas Day approached, there was scarcely any money to hold the traditional holiday dinner. Just as the missionaries decided not to celebrate with dinner, however, God again interposed with His grace and $25.00 came from an unexpected source. The missionaries had a great time. "It was thrilling to see the joy of those who were having their first Christmas and to hear their testimonies as to the change that had come to them," said Miss Bertha.

Disease ravaged many in those days of privation, and Miss Bertha did not escape Chinese amoebic dysentery. Earlier, while in the port city of Tsingtau, she had contracted this disease—her first in China. She spent ten days in a hospital that had been built by Germans, and upon her release was advised to have a checkup every two months. But on Christmas Eve, just before the two months were up, the dysentery returned as an unwelcome visitor.

Bertha felt that it had been nothing short of a miracle that enabled her to do all she had done as a well woman, but now that she fell ill, what would she do? She prayed, "Lord, I am the only one you have to use here. With what is already on, and the Japanese army only a few days from the city, I cannot afford to be sick! In the Name of my Lord and Savior Jesus Christ, I command this dysentery to leave me!" Not another symptom of dysentery did she experience!

On Christmas Day, Miss Bertha shared in a time of celebration and singing of hymns with fellow Presbyterian missionaries who lived in one of the suburbs of the city. Some Americans argue that different denominations on the same mission field confuse the Christian message. This was not true in China. The Chinese people were very accustomed to "denominations" because Buddhism was riddled with various divisions and sects.

The Japanese army was now closing in quickly. A large silk store selling beautiful Chinese silk, located near the mission compound, received a bomb on the morning of January 10, 1938. The invading army was only one day's march to the east of Tsinging. Early the next morning many callers came to Miss Bertha with multiplied problems. By about 9:00 A.M. she managed to get away for her quiet time; she never neglected that discipline. While before the Lord in prayer she heard the roar of planes— she had failed to hear the signal warning of an air raid. Her heart began to beat more rapidly, but as she said, "I had spiritual sense enough to know that the only way to be acceptable in God's presence was by identifying myself with Christ and his death." She had no doubt that the Mighty Creator, the Sustainer of the Universe, would hear her cry. She prayed, *Lord, there come those instruments of torture flying out of the pit of hell.* (I did not mean from Japan—I meant from the Devil himself!) *Now, for the sake of these helpless people who have no way of escape, will you take charge of those planes? Hold the hands of the bombers and do not let those bombs fall anywhere on this city today except where you permit them to fall.* A sweet peace and assurance came over her. She knew that the Lord had heard. She left the attacking planes with Him and went on praying for those who would be attending the daily meetings.

Praying

When praying for people, Bertha would intercede for them individually by name before the Lord. At times, if she did not know their names, she would pray for the man with "the gray scarf, the one with the red button on the black silk hat, the stooped one, or the student." Bertha was so involved in intercession that she not only did not even hear the planes, she forgot all about them. When she finished praying, she went to her study to help her Chinese secretary finish preparing the noon Bible class. They absorbed themselves in the task. Miss Bertha said, "The message from the Lord must be just what the Lord wanted that day, for the next day we might not be living." Suddenly, their two-story brick house began to shake. The window panes flew out. A bomb had struck. But so great was the peace of Christ in their hearts that Bertha said she did not utter one sound; she had perfect peace and did not even have "one irregular heart beat." She knew in her heart that God had some purpose in permitting the bomb to fall. When they got to the basement where people were screaming and yelling, someone pointed out the damage. Bertha replied, "The house does not matter now. I only came to see if anyone is hurt." No one had suffered any injury, so she went out into the yard.

When Bertha looked up, she saw that the whole sky was black from the gray brick and tile that had been blown into powder. Her little Chinese home was in ruins, obliterated. Other buildings suffered damage along with trees. Mr. Tai, a Christian brother walked up to Miss Bertha with his mother who, with some cuts on her face, was holding one of the Tai babies in her arms. They were not seriously hurt. Bertha was about to go outside, but poor Mr. Tai, standing by his mother with the other scream-ing baby, cried, "Teacher Ming [Bertha's Chinese name], do not go out now." Bertha replied that she was going out to see if anyone was hurt. But he pleaded again for her not to go. But she replied, "A moment's delay might mean the loss of a life!" Mr. Tai begged, "For Jesus' sake I ask you not to go out there now." Stepping back, Bertha replied that if it were for Jesus' sake, she would not go. A second bomb screamed down right at that moment in the yard just where she would have been standing had she gone out. She said she was glad that she was not a "hard headed old maid that did not take suggestions." When she finally got to the girls school she found them on their knees praying. No one was hurt. God had pro-tected them all.

The war cut off Bertha from the missionary secretary in Shanghai, but she did manage to get a telegram to the American consulate in Hankow to report the bombing. She also communicated with the Presbyterian mis-sion in the other part of their city.

The bombing of the mission compound confused the more immature Christian Chinese. They questioned why God, in whom they felt they were trusting, permitted their buildings to be bombed. Bertha replied, "We never ask 'Why' about anything that God permits. He knew that we were here and He knew that we were trusting Him. We may not under-stand in this life, but this is not evil. The Lord permitted this for some purpose. He, the mighty God, does not have to explain himself to human beings—at least not now." Some packed up and left the mission com-pound, others were invited to stay at the Presbyterian mission. It seemed wise to move out of harm's way.

God's Leading

Bertha herself began to pack and select what she would take with her on the evacuation trek she felt she would be compelled to make. But she did not know whether to look west to keep ahead of the Japanese army or to go into a port city or even perhaps to America.

Although the approaching armies were extremely close now, none heard any artillery barrages. So Bertha and the others made their way to the Presbyterian mission until they could find the mind of the Lord. Just as they arrived, the firing began. The artillery barrage grew louder and louder until about two o'clock in the afternoon when it became deafening. Sud-denly, about five o'clock, everything grew deathly still. They knew that the city had fallen into the hands of the Japanese.

The next morning, Dr. Walter and Mr. D'Olive, the Presbyterian missionaries, went with Miss Bertha into the city hopefully to communicate to Dr. Rankin, the Southern Baptist missionary secretary in Shanghai, that she was safe. But all the wires had been cut by the Japanese. Unable to send her message, she took some Japanese soldiers to her own mission compound where they looked over the damage that had been done. Considerable more havoc had fallen on the buildings after they had all left. Bertha said, "I thrilled over the fact that the mighty God hears our prayers. He had guided the hands of those pilots and allowed those bombs to be dropped into our mission grounds in order to scatter us all out from there, that perhaps he might save the lives of some and protect the nerves of all." By God's gracious providence, only one life, that of the gatekeeper, had been lost in the bombing the day before. God controlled the whole affair and, after all, the buildings were only brick and mortar. "This was the Lord's doing, and it is marvelous in our eyes" (Mark 12:11 KJV).

So the city fell, and Miss Bertha made her decision: She would stay with her Chinese friends until God led otherwise. Bertha labored under Japanese domination until 1942. And as difficult as it may seem, she had a marvelous, fruitful ministry, even under the most trying circumstances. Then God began to work in a marvelous way, and Bertha was repatriated to the States because for the Japanese authorities to grant repatriation was indeed a miracle. Thus on July 15, 1942, the Italian Steamer, the *Conte Verde* of the Lloyd Triestine Line, took Bertha and several other missionaries on board and they sailed out of Shanghai harbor, one happy group of missionaries along with other Americans. They were homeward bound.

Back to the Field

Miss Bertha stayed in the States throughout the war and for three more years caring for family needs in Cowpens. Then in 1949, she made her way back to China. One can imagine what greeted her there. All rejoiced.

By this time, however, the armies of General Chiang Kai-shek were being virtually routed by the invading communist armies of Mao-Tse-tung. Could it be that after all of the years in China and the great Shantung Revival that Bertha's mission to the Chinese people could not be fulfilled? Hardly! God still had wonderful things in store.

Bertha had to leave China in 1949 due to the communist takeover. She really had no choice in the matter. But now, what would she do? Did God want her to go back to America or did the Lord still have a place for her among the Chinese whom she loved so deeply? Once again the providence of God stepped in and a quite marvelous happening took place.

Opening a New Field

The Island of Formosa off China's coast had become the retreat where the followers of Chiang Kai-shek had gone for refuge. Being a free country, the Gospel could be fully proclaimed. Could God use her there? But the Baptists had no work in Formosa (now called Taiwan); therefore, Bertha could not receive an appointment from her mission board to work on the island. But as God always provides for His will to be accomplished, the Baptists of Hong Kong, which had remained free from the communist takeover, appointed her as a missionary and the Baptist board in America paid her salary through the Hong Kong mission. So to that island nation she went and started Baptist work. In many senses of the word, it became a continuation of the Shantung Revival. The story of Miss Bertha's days in Taipei are fascinating indeed.

The work was not easily launched. No one in Formosa seemed able to help Miss Bertha. She had no place to start a mission; she even found it extremely difficult to find a place to live. Slowly, with the assuredness of God's provision (Phil. 4:19), she went forward. Doors began to open. Before long, she did find a permanent place to live and also a small building where she could start a church. One or two helpers came to her from her days on the mainland and the work was underway. Much of her labor was organizational at first, but she never lost the zeal of her personal witness, and she won many to Christ personally.

Bertha started Bible studies and before long several people were attending and many became open to the Gospel. One of the men who had been attending the Bible study came to her one day and asked how he could be saved. She later recounted the intriguing story:

> The next morning at nine o'clock he was there. Handing him a Chinese Bible, I had him read passage after passage showing something of the sinfulness of his own heart in contrast to the holiness of God. After an hour or two he asked, "How can I, this terrible sinner, ever get right enough to have fellowship with such a holy God?" He was then prepared to hear what Christ had done for him. When he was ready to surrender his will to the Lord, he knelt by my sofa and started confessing his sins one by one. Before he had half finished his sin account, there was a knock at the door. I tiptoed out into the hall and said to the newcomer, "You just take this chair here. The man inside wants to be saved. When I get through with him, I will see you."
> He said, "I want to be saved."
> I answered, "Come inside and get on your knees."
> After a little while there was another knock and I tiptoed out again and said to another man, "The two men inside want to be saved. Please sit here until I get through with them."
> He replied, "I want to be saved."
> I answered, "Come inside and get on your knees." So three men were seeking the Lord, instead of the one who had come by appointment.

That was the way God's work proved to be on the island of Formosa. There were always three opportunities to the one which I had on the mainland. And I had thought back there that I was doing the greatest work in the world!

Another fascinating account began early one morning about nine o'clock when an attractive young lady knocked on Bertha's door. She asked, "What time do you have church service?" Bertha said, "Come in and we will have it now!" Bertha handed her a Chinese Bible and attempted, as was her custom, to help her see herself as God saw her. She wanted the young lady to realize that she had failed God miserably and that no one could attain righteousness in himself or herself. The young woman, Miss Wang, was a teacher from Peking. She had graduated from Peking Normal College after having been reared in the capital city. She had also studied in Japan. But never in all of that time had she heard the name of Jesus until one day on her way from Peking to Formosa, fleeing the communist takeover. On her journey, she had spent one night in Nanking near a small Baptist chapel. Being tremendously disturbed and distraught about leaving home, she felt a desperate loneliness. The singing at the chapel had attracted her, so she went in. She saw the word "Baptist" on Miss Bertha's sign and she said to herself, "That is the same word that is on the chapel in Nanking. I will go in and hear some more."

Miss Wang had just arrived in Taipei. She had no place to live or work. She was sharing a very small room with others, and the little bit of money she did have was soon gone for food. But Miss Bertha did not compromise the Gospel in her compassion for the needy girl. She made it very plain that if Miss Wang desired to receive Christ, she must utterly die to herself. Bertha sensed that Miss Wang was not quite at that place, so she frankly said, "It is not the Lord you want. You just want His blessings . . . a job so that you can have your own money and a place to live." That shocked the young lady and cut her to the heart. After a long, thoughtful pause she looked up at Miss Bertha and said, "I must have the Lord at any cost." That was all Miss Bertha needed to hear. They fell on their knees by the sofa and tears stained the upholstery—but it was well worth it. Miss Wang truly repented and gave herself completely to Christ, the true cost of discipleship. That is a lesson in evangelism that many in the West need to hear and understand. When they rose from their knees, Miss Wang was filled with "joy unspeakable and full of glory." She had now come into the family of God, linked up with the great God of creation Himself. What joy!

Miss Bertha always recorded the date and name of all whom she had had the privilege of leading to Christ. When she recorded Miss Wang's conversion, she remarked that that was the day on which Columbus had discovered America. Miss Wang said, "I have made a bigger discovery than Columbus! He only found a continent. I have discovered the kingdom of heaven!" Miss Wang often came to Miss Bertha's little mission for Bible study and prayer. Bertha found her prayers wonderfully refreshing. She did not know the typical "language of Zion" or the so-called orthodox prayer language. She just talked to the Lord Jesus freely about everything that concerned her. She always closed her prayer with, "Lord, I am just delighted to talk to you!" That is real praying.

Such instances became so common that an interesting aspect of the continuing revival spirit relates to Miss Bertha's sofa. She loved her sofa and had much pride in it. Whenever someone came to her or she was able to bring someone home to tell them about the Lord Jesus Christ and they were ready to open their heart to the Lord and receive His salvation, she would always have them kneel beside her sofa. So many people came and shed so many tears that she called the beautiful material on her sofa, brocaded. It was so spotted with the tears of the many penitents that it looked like an entirely different piece of material. What a token of God's grace to this woman of awakening.

Expansion

The work continued to grow and expand in Formosa. In February 1956, Billy Graham went to the island nation to conduct an evangelistic crusade. This proved a great treat for not only the Formosans, but for Miss Bertha as well. She received a worker's badge and did personal counseling during the crusade. She said, "Billy Graham seems to be just as sweet and unspoiled as if he had never been invited to dine with the queen."[4]

Miss Bertha labored on, but now her seventieth birthday rapidly approached. The Southern Baptist Foreign Mission Board, her sponsor, had a policy that when any appointed missionary reached age seventy, they had to retire and return to America. What a wrench it was for her to think of leaving her Chinese people. She confessed:

Becoming of age! What pain! I never dreamed that anything in this life could ever hurt like giving up work with the Chinese and returning home. I was still doing about fifteen hours of work a day, and I never became too tired to get up rested the next morning. . . . I felt that I was just then qualified from experience for missionary work. The forty-one-and-a-half years had been very short, interesting indeed, at times thrilling, and always rewarding. Every trial along the way had been forgotten as soon as the next person was saved.[5]

Miss Bertha had to go home. But she received a fresh word from the

Lord in the prospect of her returning to America in retirement. The Holy Spirit seemed to impress her that she should go home and tell. Tell what? She was to tell the story of the great revival that ultimately touched virtually all of China and sparked the work in Taiwan. What a message it was! When she returned to America, she wrote a book *Go Home and Tell*. It became the best-selling work for her publisher for ten years and has just been reprinted. Retirement had come, but what would her last years hold? Here again an incredible surprise opened before her.

A New Work—at Seventy

Seventy years of age and still in good health, Bertha decided that she should not only write about her experiences, but she should tell all that God had done in the great Shantung Revival. Invitations began to flood in as churches and Christian organizations invited her to come and share. Her burden was not just to relate the message of the revival in China, but to trust the Spirit of God to use her messages to spark revival in America also. In that context, God used her significantly. As incredible as it may seem, she lived another thirty years, and it was only in the last very few months of her life that she became unable to keep an unbelievably busy schedule. She traveled all over the United States and to many other parts of the world as well. Every place that she went, there was one message: God revives His people. She would share the stories of Shantung, but above all the biblical principles of what true revival is. God used her powerfully for thirty more years.

During Miss Bertha's American years these authors first heard her, and we shared many conferences on spiritual awakening! The lives that she touched in the States are too many to count. The way she impacted churches is another tale of revival in itself.

Miss Bertha, great woman of awakening, had wanted to live to be one hundred. But on June 12, 1988, just five months before her one-hundredth birthday, God called her home to her reward. Disappointment? Not really. The Chinese count one's age not by birth but by the year of conception. So Chinese style, Miss Bertha made one hundred. That would have pleased her well.

Endnotes

1. Bertha Smith, *How the Spirit Filled My Life* (Nashville: Broadman Press, 1973), 14–19.
2. C. L. Culpepper, *The Shantung Revival* (Dallas: Crescendo Publications, Inc., 1976), 13–14.
3. The following quotes are taken from Bertha Smith, *Go Home and Tell* (Nashville: Broadman Press, 1965).

4. Personal files of Bertha Smith.
5. Smith, *Go Home and Tell*, 153–54.

Chapter Eleven

MARIE MONSEN

The Missionary of Awakening

For many years, the Christian movement languished in China. Its historic culture, its suspicion of the West, its pantheistic religions, and a thousand other impediments made the work of Christs' ambassadors, the missionaries, hard sledding indeed. Then, quite suddenly God began a deep work of grace; and it all began largely through the testimony of a Norwegian Lutheran missionary woman, Marie Monsen, whom we met in the Prologue to this book.

In 1932, a Mr. Louis Gaussen penned the following letter from Honan province in China:

> The Lord has been reviving the work here even during the last few weeks, largely through the visit of Marie Monsen for special meetings. In these, two men school teachers and one of the two evangelists were brought to real life and blessing. Since then the blessing has spread and several others have been saved. Quite a revival broke out in the school just before we arrived, work having to be suspended for a few days since so many children were under deep conviction of sin. Since then, a large proportion have been brightly saved and have testified to their salvation in public.
>
> It seems possible to have a strong mental belief in the facts of the gospel, without any conception of the fundamental moral demands of it, and so for church members to be still involved in the toils of the appalling sin of a heathen land without sense of sin. The Lord seems to have given Marie Monsen a special ministry to such.
>
> China desperately needed a touch from God in true revival. The land cried out for it. The Gospel of Christ had made little headway and the entire country suffered terribly. Right in the midst of all the misery, God sent this lovely Norwegian, Lutheran lady; and the rest is history.[1]

The Marie Monsen Story

Marie Monsen was a student at a Norwegian teacher-training college when God placed His hand on her for mission work. Her call to the mission field came at a most difficult time in Norway, at least psychologically, because strong nationalistic spirit pervaded the country. A negative attitude arose against anyone who would leave his or her native land. Much of society was caught up in that spirit. The so-called Bjornson's days, a pervasive nationalism, ran hot. What brought it all about centered in the fact that many Norwegians had left their country, immigrating to America. Consequently, a reaction against anyone's moving to any country set in. Early on, Marie shared these nationalistic feelings herself, at least to some extent. She did not want to leave her own land; she was willing to go wherever God led her as long as it did not mean leaving Norway. At the time, she lacked the spiritual maturity to understand that her citizenship did not reside on earth but in the kingdom of Heaven.

A gospel preacher by the name of Tormod Rettedal, a friend of Marie's family, influenced Marie's life tremendously at that time. He reminded her of the story of Jonah and of God's call to the prophet to go to Ninevah. He stressed the prophet's refusal to surrender and its consequences. Rettedal said to her, "At first he [Jonah] was allowed to go his own way, but God did not go with him on his self-chosen path. Don't be a Jonah!"

Marie confessed that for three days the word of the preacher haunted her. Finally, she yielded to God's will and responded with, "Yes, Lord, I will go." Then God put China on her heart. She had known of the Norwegian China mission since a child; that was to be her spiritual destiny. She never "repented" of the commitment, and God had an incredible ministry in store for the young woman.

Miss Monsen completed a year of nurse's training at the Lovisenberg Hospital, spent some time in England, then a winter teaching at Framnes School in Norway. She had intended to go to China immediately after teaching school, but the Chinese Boxer uprising of the early 1900s prevented her from sailing for China. God used the delay in a most significant way. She said, "The most memorable experience of those days was seeing Brandtzaeg [an acquaintance] go to his study every morning to take time with God and the Bible before breakfast." The Holy Spirit brought home to her heart that nothing less would do for a missionary. A disciplined devotional life with Christ became her life's pattern. Then off to China she sailed.

A Testing Time

Scarcely a month after arriving in China, Marie's first testing came. She fell down an iron staircase and lay unconscious for several days with a severe concussion. The missionary doctor gave the orders: "No language study for two years." All she could do as she recovered would be to listen as Chinese people spoke and hope to pick up something of the dialect. She suffered with severe headaches for six years. It became a depressing time. Then one day the promise of James 5:14–15 came to her: "Is any one of you sick? He should call the elders of the church to pray over him and anoint him with oil in the name of the Lord. And the prayer offered in faith will make the sick person well; the Lord will raise him up. If he has sinned, he will be forgiven" (NIV). She called the elders of the church, they anointed her with oil, and after prayer she experienced instantaneous healing. But because of ignorance in such matters, she got the idea that healing could only happen once in a person's life. She soon learned differently.

Not long after Marie's fall down the staircase, she fell victim to malaria. This illness brought her close to the gates of death. She feared that this would end her career on the mission field. The anguish of her own soul about having come all that distance for such a short time seemed worse than the anguish of the fever. She said, "My heart rebelled. The thing was incomprehensible."

Finally, however, heart weary and plagued beyond endurance, she submitted herself totally to the Lord and cried out, "Oh, Lord, if it was only this that was Thy will, Thy will be done." That very day, her temperature dropped. From that time forward Marie knew that her call, her life, her health, and all that she could ever be came by the grace of God alone. She was now ready to go forward to serve Him in the power of that fathomless grace.

Her physical suffering, however, did not cease. She suffered constantly from attacks of malaria and dysentery. It wore her down until she again bordered on the point of despair. Then once again God delivered her from those sicknesses in answer to prayer. It became evident that the Lord was preparing her for great things in missionary service. She could probably hear the words of the apostle Paul resounding in her heart and mind: "We also rejoice in our sufferings, because we know that suffering produces perseverance; perseverance, character; and character, hope" (Rom. 5:3–4 NIV).

One Door Closes, Another Opens

Marie thought her primary work on the mission field would be educational, which would be the fulfillment of a childhood dream. She felt well-equipped to do educational work, much like Bertha Smith. It seemed, however, that each time she received an assignment in school work, chronic malaria would again put her in bed, and the work would have to be postponed. This happened time and time again. Finally, she came to realize that the Lord had simply closed the door to education. It proved a heavy blow, but soon thereafter she saw God's wisdom in it all.

Marie moved to the neighboring province of Honan where the climate was drier. Ignorance, superstition, suspicion, and hatred of foreigners greeted her, almost shutting out the hearing of the Gospel. She felt the constant harassment of satanic temptations. The Devil would try to tell her that the work was futile—just throwing one's life away. But she encouraged herself with the Scripture: "For God did not give us a spirit of timidity, but a spirit of power, of love and of self-discipline" (2 Tim. 1:7 NIV). God permitted her to go through severe testing. But she did the wise thing; she would start each day with the assurance that God had called her to declare the Gospel no matter how cold or resistant the people might be. She knew that the Lord had put her where she was, so she must be faithful. Gradually, a handful of folks became more friendly. As time passed, they opened their hearts to the Word of God and came to faith in Christ. With a foothold thus secured, the work grew.

Marie learned to pray more effectively and began seeing significant changes take place. In turn, she taught the Chinese people to pray and claim God's promises. One native woman set a wonderful example, and would pray for the most incredible things. Even Marie thought her requests would never be answered, yet they were. The dear woman had a simple childlike faith that got her exactly what she requested of God. Marie confessed that, at the time, she had more doubts about her prayer requests than faith. But she, too, soon learned the way of faith.

In those days, Miss Monsen learned not only to pray in faith, but to live the life of faith, just as she had read about in George Müeller's faith work in his orphanage. Hudson Taylor's founding of the China Inland Mission by simple faith influenced her significantly as well. She turned daily to the book of Acts and claimed the promise of God's provision, care, leadership, and power to evangelize. God met her at every juncture.

Revival in Korea

At this time (1907), the first great revival in Korea broke out. The awakening grew into one of many mighty movings of the Holy Spirit in that land, all coming about through the fervent prayers of missionaries and Korean Christians. Marie, deeply inspired by the movement, prayed for money to travel to Korea to imbibe something of the spirit of revival. God responded to her prayers by saying, *What you want through that journey you may be given here, where you are, in answer to prayer.* In light of that tremendous challenge of the Holy Spirit, she made the solemn promise that she would pray until a revival came to her life and ministry. God heard her and did a beautiful work. She related:

> Having pledged myself, I set out to cross the floor of my room to my place of prayer, in order to pray this prayer for revival for the

first time. I had not taken more than two or three steps before I was halted. What then happened can only be described as follows: it was as though a boa constrictor had wound its coils round my body and was squeezing the life out of me. I was terrified. Finally, while gasping for breath, I managed to utter the one word: Jesus! Jesus! Jesus! Each time I groaned out the precious Name, it grew easier to breathe, and in the end the serpent left me. I stood there dazed. The first conscious thought was: Then prayer means as much as that, and that my promise should be kept means as much as that.

That experience helped me to endure through the almost twenty years which were to pass before the first small beginnings of revival were visible. Truly, God works unhurriedly.

Marie's concern and vision for revival expanded. She studied reports of revival on other mission fields of the world. The results of these studies gave her patience because she learned that often long periods of waiting with much fervent prayer comes before a real awakening occurs. But revivals do come, regardless of circumstance; as Marie said, "In answer to prayers borne in deep anguish." And, it may be added, in God's sovereign time. His divine timetable is not always ours, but God is never late.

Preparing for Revival

Through these and other experiences, Marie learned how to prepare for revival. She realized first and foremost that she must take the long view and along with much prayer share God's Word. The Word of God must be understood and applied to one's life. She said, "The Spirit uses the Word." She repeated that phrase countless times during her ministry. And she waited on God.

Marie Monsen's third term of service in China began in a time of serious social change. Pervasive political unrest settled across the country. The old religious institutions began to be questioned. Bandits roamed the countryside. All this drove Marie to more prayer and Bible study for revival. And certain sections of society seemed to become more open— especially the women of China. Prayer became more and more vital. Marie said:

One day I was reading Matthew 18:19–20: "If two of you shall agree on earth as touching anything that they shall ask, it shall be done for them of my Father which is in heaven. For where two or three are gathered together in my name, there am I in the midst of them." This promise, which I had known and believed so long, was suddenly and vitally made near and searching. It was new. It came as a fresh prayer-stimulant. I saw a new path to the goal of revival: "it shall be done for them." Faith clung to that. A prayer-stimulant, working among missionaries and all believers at home and abroad, was the vision given that day.

Thus Marie continued to take the long look. The Word of God was read, learned, and experienced. Prayer deepened. The mission work continued to expand. Through it all, God constantly gave Marie tokens of grace, glimpses of what would come when the awakening finally arrived. For example, she described what she called the greatest day in her missionary life. It happened in the context of a prayer meeting.

The first day that we prayed together, in deliberate reliance on the promises of God, was the greatest day in my missionary life. It was an hour truly in the Lord's presence, when the little room became a holy sanctuary.

When we rose from our knees we clasped each other's hands spontaneously and in silence. Then, in holy fear, words broke from us:

"The Lord has been here with us."

"Yes."

"His ear was bowed down to hear."

"Yes. He heard it all."

"And He will answer."

"Yes. He will bring it to pass."

"Something is going to happen here."

It had been an hour at the throne of grace, and each day following was the same.

We had been holding classes for three days. On the fourth I was to have a session with the group of heathen women again. There were sixteen of them. We dealt with infanticide. Suddenly, in extreme amazement, one of the women said:

"Can't we do what we like with our own children?"

We talked about it for a little longer. Then they broke down:

"Oh, and I have killed three."

"And I five . . ."

"I took the lives of eight of my children."

"And I of thirteen, but they were all girls."

(All the others had probably been girls too.) Only two of them did not confess themselves guilty of this sin.

It was the first time in over twenty years on the mission field, that I heard women, who knew we regarded the killing of infants as sin, confess that they themselves had committed this particular sin. They all knew, of course, of many others who had done it. This was the first time I had seen the Holy Spirit deal with a whole group—a miracle indeed.

The experience left me speechless. Then one of them suddenly asked:

"Why can't we sleep here?"

"Don't you sleep? What do you do at night?"

"We weep, we only weep."

"Why do you weep?"

"We remember so much."

"Do you remember all the wrong things you have done?" They nodded in silent admission. Then I knew that He, who had come to convict the world of sin, had been doing it in this group of ignorant heathen women from the very first day they came to us.

As far as that class was concerned, school was at an end for the day.

"Now you may come in and talk to me one by one."

The whole group was at my heels immediately, one stood with her hand on the door handle.

"I must come first, I have such pain, I cannot wait."

Once behind the closed door, she threw herself down on her knees with her head on the floor and her confession gushed from her like a black flood. I was not used to this happening, and felt perplexed and a little desperate. How was I to help a whole group of women, who had practically no knowledge of God, to get saved? The word about asking for wisdom came as a salutary reminder and did me good in my utter helplessness. But there was hardly time to pray, I only sighed to the Lord out of deep anguish and a God given compassion for this woman who had grown up in heathendom.

When she had finished her confession she rose, and then I saw eternal life and light shining in her eyes, and the peace of God radiated from the face that had looked so weary and worn before. She was saved—without human help.

"Do you know what I feel like?" she asked. "It is just as if I were a great bandit and after hot pursuit the soldiers caught me and dragged me before the Mandarin; and instead of denying everything, I confessed everything, and the Mandarin did not say, 'Take her away and execute her,' but he said, 'She has confessed, it is no longer held to her account. Go home in peace.'"

What a life Marie lived! God truly was preparing her to be one of His key instruments in a great awakening.

The Revival Begins

In the context of Marie's ministry, at this time, the continuing unrest caused her to retreat to Chefoo along with the Baptist missionaries. The story of her impact on the Baptists in the healing of Ola Culpepper has been recorded earlier. What led up to that event for Marie, and the event itself, is best described in her own words.

In Chefoo

After my first brief visit to Manchuria, where I was so unexpectedly led into evangelistic work, the summer months found me at Chefoo, by the sea in north-east China. I stayed with some English missionary friends from the interior of the country. The China Inland Mission had three schools for the children of missionaries there as well as a hospital and sanatorium. This led to Chefoo becoming a natural holiday resort for missionaries. The whole summer was a wonderful experience, for I met numbers of missionaries carrying the same burden of longing for revival as I had myself, and who were praying for, and expecting, the same kind of revival for which I was looking. Whether we met in large gatherings or small groups or in personal conversation, we always spoke of the spiritual condition of the churches, and of the spiritual renewal that was so greatly needed.

In Chefoo I heard too of many missionaries I had not met, who were walking a lonely road with the same great problem: a Spirit-wrought revival in China. And they were praying steadfastly for it. One of these "solitaries" had come to China only for two years to relieve a missionary who needed to go home. He had to work with the help of an interpreter. Although he had indeed felt the need of spiritual revival, the work he had come out to do filled his time. Then he was stricken down by one of the infectious diseases of the Far East—either cholera or smallpox—and lay at death's door. The doctor allowed the other missionaries to stand outside an open window for a last look at their dying friend. As they stood there, they heard him pray: "Lord, if my life is spared, I will spend much time in prayer in accordance with Thy will." From that moment there was a change for the better. He was true to his promise and used to spend hours in prayer several times a day. The burden of his prayers was for revival.

It was an indescribable joy to discover these burden-bearers in prayer scattered throughout the whole of China. This was God's plan, the method of His choice. He needed to have all these fellow-workers with Him rightly related to Himself, before He could send, or we receive, the revival that was a work of the Holy Spirit. The period of waiting and praying brought us to the maturity that was necessary before we could receive God's answer to our prayers.

Laura Moller, in writing of that summer in Chefoo in her book *By Faith in God*, used the only appropriate words to describe it: "A prayer-revival in Chefoo."

While there, I was present at the first little revival among missionaries. Some American missionaries had invited me to attend a small gathering. One of their number was losing her eyesight and had asked to be anointed and that her own husband should anoint her. The eleven or twelve friends who met took ample time for prayer after the service of anointing. We were kneeling in a ring. After some time had passed, I felt that something was happening behind me, and on looking round, I saw two or three talking to each other in whispers. They were putting things right between themselves. The Holy Spirit of God was so really present among us that we felt His presence.

When we finally broke up the meeting, we found that out in the kitchen, which was separated from the room in which we had been praying by a corridor, the Chinese brethren who were there had been visited by the Spirit of God too, and were under conviction of sin. It made an overwhelming impression on us all. That was the first small beginning of a revival which, a few years later, grew into the largest revival any one mission in China experienced—as far as I have been able to follow the spiritual movements. The eyesight was restored, I heard later.

Early in the autumn, the various consular authorities allowed the missionaries to return to their stations. The many who had experienced a prayer-revival, went back firmly purposed to begin prayer groups among leaders and others at whatever hour of the day suited the majority best. Even itinerant evangelism was set aside, both by missionaries and Chinese evangelists, in order to make room for this ministry which had been so neglected and was so essential: prayer in oneness of mind for a revival wrought by the Holy Spirit.

A little later it was off to Hwanghsien for more renewal ministry among the Baptists.

Hwanghsien: A Fantastic Adventure

After Marie received the invitation to go to the Chinese churches in the Hwanghsien area, she immediately began to pack. She had to travel by train from Peking to Tientsin, then travel by boat to Hwanghsien, about a day and a night journey overall. As Marie began packing and making arrangements to embark by boat from Tientsin, the Holy Spirit impressed her to buy some apples. Since the voyage was only a one night's journey, this impression left her somewhat confused. But the Holy Spirit kept laying this upon her heart. So inescapable was His leading that she finally bought an entire basket of apples. She reasoned, *Perhaps some sick person on the other side of the Gulf of Chihli needs them.* She also took four boxes of chocolates she had received for Christmas from friends in Norway.

The Baptist meeting in Hwanghsien, Shantung province, had been scheduled to start on April 22, 1929. But the boat Marie needed to take to meet the schedule had all its berths booked. It looked, humanly speaking, as though it would be impossible for her to make the journey as planned. But she claimed the promise of God and said to herself, *If I am to travel by that boat, my Heavenly Father will see to my being given a berth, and if not, He must have some reason for my spending a few days in Tientsin.* [2] God did provide. She received a message stating that the second mate would willingly give up his cabin to her for a certain amount of money in addition to the price of her ticket. She saw this as God's providence and paid the price. With apples, chocolates, and a few biscuits in hand, she prepared to embark.

At eleven o'clock on the morning of the nineteenth, accompanied by an English missionary, Miss Monsen boarded the boat, ready to sail at noon. When an English missionary saw the second mate's cabin, she said to Marie, "It is a good thing you will have to spend only one night in there." Little did she realize it would be twenty-seven nights; an amazing adventure waited in the wings.

Marie had not taken the normal bedding roll with her on the voyage, thinking she would only have one night to spend on board. She could surely manage one night on the hard wooden planks of the second mate's bunk. She said, "It is undeniable that it felt hard that first night, but I had plenty of sound sleep on it later, and in the end it even felt fairly comfortable."

As the ship maneuvered out of the harbor, Marie pulled out a duster from her case and cleaned the room. She dusted the wooden bunk and the little table that made up the furniture of the tiny cabin. A small cabin it was; an American friend who saw it afterward said, "It looked like an old piano case."

Marie went out on deck, talking with passengers and handing out tracts. She could not help noticing some passengers who looked as though they might be thieves. Yet, she thought, surely in the midst of civilized Tientsin that could not be the case.

As they prepared to set sail, they were delayed in the harbor for a short time because of stormy weather but soon made their way to open waters, sailing along at good speed. They fully expected to see the Shantung coast the next morning. However, as soon as they had put to sea, two bandits with loaded guns burst in upon the helmsman shouting orders. Pirates took over and were in command of the vessel. It was frightening. Twenty pirates had secretly boarded the boat in Tientsin. Pistol shots, shrieks, and pandemonium broke out all over the ship. Marie knew at once that they had fallen into evil hands. At that moment the Spirit of God spoke to her heart: *This is the trial of your faith,* and she became conscious of the "peace that passeth understanding" (Phil. 4:7). Her prayer was, *Oh, that He may succeed in keeping me close to Himself.*

About the time the first shots rang out, more pirates came on board— sixty altogether. They forced the cabin doors open and ordered all personnel out on deck. They instructed the passengers to leave their possessions in their cabins. The pirates wrenched open Marie's door and commanded her to leave the cabin. She refused and just stood there. She knew that she had been given that cabin in answer to prayer and trusted God to leave her in it.

Since Marie had not taken her bed roll with her, she was fully dressed. The pirates recognized her as a foreigner and a Christian at that. Every time they ordered her out of the cabin, the promises of God came to her "gently and refreshingly, like spring showers." She thanked God for His promises and rested on Him and stayed put. And the pirates accepted it.

In the evening of the first full day at sea, a junk came alongside the ship, loaded with guns and ammunition. These were taken on board along with plunder that the pirates had gained from pirating other boats. The pirates offered Marie all kinds of food: lobster, crayfish, tin goods of every kind, fish, and chicken. But they were stolen goods, so she adamantly refused them. She would not eat what had been stolen from others. She began to realize why God had had her bring the apples, chocolates, and biscuits aboard. Incredibly these lasted nine days. Not once in all the time she was holed up in the little cabin did the pirates ask for any of her apples or chocolates; they only asked if she had pears or oranges. God's providence prevailed.

On the tenth day at sea there came a gentle scratching on her door. She jumped from her bunk remembering the Elijah story; her heart sang, *This is the raven!* The second mate stood there and asked Marie if she had any food. When she replied that she had none, he said, "Let me come in. I have a full box of eggs and a tin of cakes. You can have it all." He had bought them in Tientsin with honestly earned money. God continued His wonderful provision. The second mate had hidden the boxes of food under buckets of paint and old shoes. From that day on, when the guard patrolled the other side of the ship, the second mate would take two or three eggs from the boxes, put them in his pocket and go away. Later he would come back to Marie's cabin with them boiled. Her daily ration was one egg for breakfast, one or two for dinner, one for supper. She had a sweet cake in the forenoon and afternoon. The supply of food that God provided lasted for the exact amount of time she was on board the ill-fated ship. She said that she asked the Lord to transform this simple menu into all the nutrients her body required. She testified that when she had eaten the small ration, she felt so satisfied that she could not have eaten more had it been available. God kept His promise to "supply all your need according to His riches in glory in Christ Jesus" (Phil. 4:19).

Miss Monsen had not taken any warm clothing with her because she thought that she would soon be in a warmer area, but the weather grew quite bitter. As she left Peking on the morning of April 18, a parcel came to her from Norway—a belated Christmas gift that should have reached her before Christmas. She would have to take it along. She stored it in her baggage with a bit of complaint; she did not want to carry it everywhere. But it contained a heavy sweater and a pair of woolen stockings that, of course, proved tremendously helpful on the cold and stormy days on the Gulf of Chihli where the pirates had steered the ship.

Every night one of the pirates stood outside the door to prevent Marie from escaping. In one sense of the word, that protected her, and she slept peacefully in the midst of all the difficulties.

The Rescue

After many miserable days on the Gulf, they sailed up an inlet on the Yellow River. On Sunday, at three o'clock in the afternoon, they heard the sound of guns. A great deal of running about the ship erupted and soon most of the pirates evacuated posthaste. All hoped that this meant that they had been found by the authorities. They were right; a race up the river began, a gunboat pursuing. Before long the pirates who had remained on board saw the gunboat gaining. Then a cannon shot screamed across the bow. The pirates, in something of a panic, decided they should abandon the ship and take the foreigner, Marie, with them. They thought a hostage would help them escape. But one of the pirates said, "Under these circumstances, there's no use taking the foreigner. She has eaten nothing for days, she can't walk much less run, as we must now." They fled the ship leaving Marie on board.

Immediately Marie went out on deck. The captain turned the ship and went downstream toward the gunboat. The pirates, some of whom had made shore, were running across the sand bank for their lives. Others in junks were sailing away at full speed. The pirates did take twenty hostages with them, most of whom were women, but returned them before dark. All were rescued.

After twenty-seven long days, the ordeal came to an end, and Marie made her way to serve the missionaries in their conferences. Needless to say, the Baptist missionaries were delighted and relieved to see her. In the conference, God blessed in a marvelous fashion. Hwangshien felt a touch of the spreading revival.

Marie's Approach

Miss Monsen employed a unique method powerfully used by the Holy Spirit to extend the revival. She would stand at the door greeting everyone leaving the church after each service, take each hand, look straight into the person's eyes and ask, "Have you been born of the Spirit?" If the person answered "yes," she would immediately ask, "What evidence do you have of the new birth?" If the person had less than a ringing testimony, she would say, "I'm uneasy about you. Ask the Lord to show you your position before Him." Of course, if the person answered "no" she would share the Gospel. This approach impacted the lives of many and became the means of the conversion of multitudes. All the missionaries made it clear that they never gave comfort to anyone who felt the slightest uneasiness about their relationship to Christ. They would urge each person to make a full confession of his or her sins and make restitution when necessary and possible. They then encouraged the believer to keep constantly before God so that the Holy Spirit could continue to reveal needs. Actually, the question Marie always asked, "Have you been born again?" became a key to the revival. A fascinating story emerges on how she learned the principle.

Personally I have no doubt at all that it was the Spirit of God who guided me into it. It consisted of questioning the church members who were spiritually alive to find out how they had been brought into life. This study was pursued on every occasion and in many places.

It had shaken me to realize how seldom we used the words, "saved" and "born again." The expression used oftenest was, "to believe in God" or "to believe in Jesus." "Do you believe in Jesus?" was a question which members and regular attenders of our churches always answered in the affirmative.

Here is an example . . . of this most interesting work:

H. had been an Evangelist for several years. Not for a moment did I question his soul's salvation.

"Do you believe in Jesus?" I asked him. He looked at me in astonishment.

"Yes, you know I do."

"Have you been born again?"

"Born again, born again? No, I do not know that I have."

"Think about it and we can talk it over another time."

The next day he came to me with a radiant face and said:
"Yes, I am born again."
"How do you know?"
"The Catechism says that when you are born again, you hate what you used to love and love what you used to hate. I used to hate foreigners and their doctrine, and most of all I hated the name Jesus, from the very first time I heard it. Now I love Jesus and the Bible and the missionaries and all the believers."

He was obviously happy about the clear understanding that had come to him.
"When did the change come?"
"I don't know at all."
"If you ever find out, will you tell me?"
Early the next morning he was there again and his face shone.
"I know now. It may sound strange, but the change came after a little thing that happened one day. There was a conference in our station. I was sitting well to the front in the meeting, but that day I seemed to want to weep all the time. What would the people say if they saw me cry? Finally it was impossible to keep back the tears, so I ran out of the meeting. I was walking up and down the courtyard outside with tears running down my cheeks, when an unsaved man who had come late, stopped to look at the strange sight: an Evangelist in tears."
"Why are you weeping?"
"The question drew forth an answer in which I said a thing I had not realized until the words were spoken: Because I am such a great sinner."
"But that isn't a thing to weep about. Don't you always say that Jesus saves sinners?"
"In a flash the truth became a living reality, and peace and rest and joy filled me."
"It must have been on that very day you were saved."
"Yes, I understand that now. I am glad I shall be able to tell others how I was saved, it may be a help to someone. I wanted to go back into the meeting that day and cry aloud to them all: 'Jesus died to save sinners.'"

So the hallmark of the revival: "Have you been born again?" was set, and how mightily God did use it.

General Revival Methods

During the early days of revival, people were not invited to go forward and confess Christ in a public invitation—the custom in much American evangelism. Chinese culture would force them to go forward to keep the speaker from losing face. And that could precipitate superficial decisions, though later as the revival spread, people were invited to come to the front of the church for prayer. By and large, inquirers were dealt with individually, and dealt with until they became absolutely clear about their conversion experience. They would then be assigned to a study group that considered the meaning of the Christian life, church membership, and all that is involved in walking as a true disciple of the Lord Jesus Christ. Every person would share his or her testimony before the church; only then could they be received into full membership by Christian baptism. The missionaries gave real care to see that their evangelism was an evangelism for discipleship, which is the heart of New Testament principles for bringing people into a true born-again experience. Marie would stress, for example, that it is not so much our receiving Christ as it is His receiving us as we truly repent and believe. Their evangelism became an evangelism of biblical integrity.

The revival spirit continually deepened until many people could neither eat, nor sleep, nor hold their heads up because of the burden of sin. Peace, restoration, and joy only came when they learned to put all of their sins upon Christ, then make peace with everyone to whom confession and restitution became necessary. When they trusted and enthroned Christ, abounding joy flooded their hearts and they knew what it was to be born again.

The Work Goes Forward

Thus, the revival had its born-again motif and the work spread far and wide. At that time, Marie and Bertha Smith held a series of services in Laichowfu. The Spirit of God probed many there.

After the Laichowfu meeting Miss Bertha and Marie Monsen traveled together to Laiyang. Great blessings were had in that city.

One of the central motifs of the great revival that swept all through China was confession and forgiveness of sins. Sin always stands as the persistent obstacle to revival, but when God's people are willing to get thoroughly right with God through the confession and the forsaking of their known sins, then the Spirit of God has freedom to move through them into the community and bring people to faith in Christ. A purified church becomes an evangelizing church. Marie Monsen was very conscious of this principle, and her experiences proved it time and time again.

On one occasion, Marie was ministering to a school for the blind outside Peking. It was a part of a large college. The school had been praying for, as they expressed it, the gift of eternal life. As Marie ministered the Word of God and emphasized the truths of being born again, the Holy Spirit began a wonderful work. One of the senior teachers became the very first to be saved, and he thus became a spiritual resource for the students.

One of the pupils, Marie said, was not easy to forget. He honestly confessed, "I have a heart of a thief and I steal and steal." This shocked most everyone there. He was asked, "From whom do you steal?" He quickly replied, "From everyone here in the school." This sounded almost incomprehensible because he was blind. They asked him, "How can you steal and you cannot even see?" He quickly retorted, "Hearing takes the place of seeing with me." But they all wanted to know why he wanted to steal when he was blind and the things he pilfered were of no use to him. He replied, as strangely as it may sound, "No, that is just it. There is a deep pool nearby, just outside the school compound. It is all there. I have to throw the things away almost at once." He just loved to steal for its own sake. That is how sin so often works, exploiting the psychological foibles of people.

The honest, broken young man was deeply distressed over his evil heart. But he soon came to genuine faith in the Lord Jesus Christ as the forgiveness of God swept over him. Not only was he forgiven, but he was completely delivered from his kleptomania.

During Marie's ministry at the blind school, one of the senior teachers came to faith in the Lord Jesus Christ. She related the following story:

> Last night, I was leading evening prayers with the boys, and I said that salvation is like a lifeline hanging down from heaven, and that it is for us to hold it fast. As the Spirit of God does strange and unusual and marvelous works, when the teacher went back to his room, he felt terribly uneasy about what he had said. He actually began to groan aloud but could find no help. He finally went to bed and fell into a deep sleep and it was there that his problem was resolved. In the dream he saw a great hand coming down from heaven and in His hand was one of the boys who had been saved. He wrote from his own slate by his own voice shouting Hallelujah, Hallelujah. The next morning he spoke to the boys again and corrected the message that he had communicated to them the night before. He read the wonderful promise of the Lord Jesus Christ, "No one shall snatch them out of my hand. . . ."

The understanding Christian teacher had learned a great lesson in a most unusual fashion as God met his needs.

The principal of the blind school was a professing Christian who held a doctor of divinity degree. He deeply desired to see revival permeate the entire school and impact every life. In his burden he said, "If we cannot have revival here, we may as well close this blind school and go home, the students are a wild set." The principal went on to declare that hardly anyone there believed in the Lord Jesus Christ. Marie asked whether or not they had any regular prayer times. The principal replied that they did have a weekly prayer meeting but that they were quite lifeless. Marie asked permission to attend one of the prayer meetings before anything was settled concerning the school as a whole.

Marie joined the next prayer meeting, but only three came, the principal and two elderly women missionaries. Marie described the prayer meeting as unspeakably dry. Marie stressed to the principal that there must be dynamic prayer before God will do anything great and unusual.

Marie had left the prayer group somewhat discouraged, when suddenly it seemed as though God spoke clearly to her heart, *Do you have any intercessors?* Immediately Marie thought of her nearby missionary friends who were earnestly praying for her. She contacted them and urged them to give themselves to fervent intercession for the school.

Marie then decided that the school itself should begin meeting together to strive in prayer for the students. The principal, of course, was thrilled that prayer meetings would be held. Marie joined them once a day as they gave themselves over to intercession for revival.

Many of the students of the college thought that the entire affair was just ludicrous; they were very proud and condescending to all that Marie suggested. They had been ordered to go to the chapel and listen to what Marie had to say, but after the first meeting, they all literally stormed out shouting and laughing. Some even went so far as to ridicule the text that Marie had used. As the principal had said, they truly were a wild set. Marie immediately made her way to where the missionary friends had gathered for prayer. They began to intercede for the students individually by name. One of the students was known as the Scorner. God gave them the burden of intercession and Marie herself said that she had never experienced such a prayer meeting. The Scorner was something of the ring leader of the group and they pleaded before God for his salvation, by getting down to the hard business of real prayer. Marie tells the story in the following words:

> "Lord, Thou hast said in Thy Word, that Thou canst turn the heart of a king like watercourses, we commit this heart to Thee tonight to be turned by Thee. Thou are able to do it, and we praise Thee. We confidently expect something to happen to him these days."

> "Lord, if Thou canst not turn his heart by any other means, hold him over the mouth of the abyss, till he sees it yawning beneath him."

> That prayer looks cold in print, but the spirit of the prayer was

beautiful, it was uttered from the depths of a soul agonizing for the salvation of "the Scorner."

"The Doubter" was specially prayed for too. His was the only serious face among the twenty students.

"May Jesus become all to 'the Doubter,' let the name of Jesus be the dearest name he knows. May Jesus be his message to his people."

The Principal and the other members of the lecturing staff were all mentioned in prayer. Great transactions were carried out behind the closed door of that box room. Although we did not speak of it to one another, we had a strong sense of the Holy Spirit's work going on among the students and great confidence that something would happen.

The next day as Marie spoke to the students, they were all quite amazed. Almost the entire group listened intently. After the meeting, there was no noisiness and scorn from the students.

The next evening, there were no scornful smiles or smart remarks at all. One of the students had been sick in bed all day; nevertheless, he attended the meeting, drawn by the Holy Spirit. A new earnestness had invaded the student body. As God's Spirit began to move, suddenly the Scorner stood up and said, "You call me the Scorner and not without cause, the name suits me. I have been sick these days of a strange disease. God summoned me to His judgment seat. You know all about me, but I must say it myself now, I must make a clean breast of it all."[3] The brokenhearted young man addressed each of the students by name and confessed how he had wronged them. Sometimes they were small and insignificant things in the eyes of people, but they were great in the eyes of God. He was deeply broken over it all.

Suddenly, to the amazement of the few believers who were there, others began to rise and silently came forward and stood around the Scorner in a ring. They were there to give him comfort and their forgiveness. Needless to say, that young man came to faith in Christ that very hour. The evening closed with songs of praise among the prayer group.

A young Swedish missionary, who was filling a vacant teaching position on the staff of the college, went the next morning to his lecture room to give his lecture. When he entered the room, to his amazement no one was there. The students were all out getting right with God. A whole new atmosphere began to pervade the college. Deep impressions, that only the Spirit of God can give, swept across the campus. One of the newly converted said, "I was blind and have received my sight. I have found a Savior from all my sins. A conscience that was burdened with guilt has been cleansed, my sins have been blotted out."

Needless to say, Marie found the following days very busy ones. Student after student saw their lives wonderfully transformed. One of the first who came to real faith in the Lord Jesus Christ was known as the Doubter. He said that he found it impossible to believe that Jesus was any more than a good man. But when asked the question, "Do you believe that God is God?" He replied, "Yes, I have never doubted that." Further queried as to whether or not he believed that what the Bible said was true, he said that he had no difficulties believing the Bible to be true. So then the wonderful words of Scripture did its work in making him very well-aware that Jesus Christ was God's Son and had died for his sins. The Spirit made the Word come alive to him; it even became visible on his face. He sat with his eyes closed for a long period of time. Suddenly, someone knocked on the door. The young man immediately said, "Don't let anyone come in and disturb me, I am sitting in the presence of my heavenly Father." That young man had found peace in the Lord Jesus Christ.

The stories go on and on. The entire college experienced a radical transformation. A multitude of the students were born again. God had used his servant Marie Monsen in a marvelous fashion. And that is just typical of the revival.

An Expanded Ministry

Marie's ministry expanded over large areas of China. In the province of Shansi, God used her in a most wonderful fashion. Manchuria felt the touch of the revival spirit from the ministry of this woman of awakening. In 1929, she went to Peitaiho, a well-known health resort in northeast China—not far from the Great Wall. Hundreds of missionaries would gather there in the summer to hear outstanding speakers from England, America, and other countries. Marie spoke and shared revival blessings. In that context, God used her powerfully as the revival spread all over China.

A short time after Marie's experience with the pirate episode, she went back to Shantung province. She tells the following story:

A far longer time than expected had elapsed before the journey which had been broken by the pirate episode was accomplished. In the autumn of 1929, however, I set out again to visit the missionaries it had been such a joy to meet in Chefoo two years earlier. They belonged to an American mission, the Southern Baptist. They were a group of steady, well-trained, godly, warm-hearted missionaries and they had prayed for revival for years. It was like coming to a vast field fully ripe for harvesting. It was the harvesting work we were now to do together.

After the first few days' meetings, one of the missionaries "fell sick." Though none of us knew till afterwards, there had been a night of getting right with God and of being brought through to salvation quite alone in her room. After the forenoon meeting, she asked to be allowed to give her testimony to the large audience. It was not till then that we learned what had happened during the night. Her testimony was deeply moving. Many missionaries were present, and when the meeting was over and the people had dispersed, they gathered round and asked for an explanation of what looked an incredible situation. That same missionary had been regarded as the best in the whole mission, how was it that she had not experienced salvation until now?

They were told that she herself could answer that question alone and she did it quite simply. Raising her hand in response to an appeal at an evangelistic meeting had led her to believe that this was the great decision, without having received life. But now life had been given, after thorough transactions with God and man. Letters had been written to her home in U.S.A., and then, by faith, she had received Jesus, God's unspeakable gift, relying on John 1:12 (As many as received him, to them gave he power to become the sons of God, even to them that believe on his name).

An elderly missionary then said, deeply moved: "I remember the experiences of student days were just like this. We had revival then. Perhaps this is the beginning?" I realized he meant that he had not seen revival since. His deep emotion touched all his fellow-workers, and the sense of strain that had come passed in a moment.

One of the missionaries, M. Crawford, published a book in 1933 entitled *The Revival in Shantung,* and writing of this time she says: "The revival was born in prayer groups; some of them began as far back as 1925. The unrest in the country had shown up some of our work in the churches as 'hay and stubble.' Blessing came to the workers and to the churches, a blessing that could be seen. There was nothing sensational or emotional in the meetings, just a definite confidence in the promises of God and particularly reliance on John 16:8 (margin), 'And when he (the Holy Spirit) is come, he will convince the world of sin, and of righteousness, and of judgment.' Many had a terrible experience of conviction of sin."

The same book quotes from a worker's letter about the continuation of the revival in 1932: "The old provincial capital had never known anything like it. The power of God was specially manifest in prayer meetings. Distress and weeping over sin preceded great joy. Later there were wonderful results among university students, through one of the professors saved in 1929. Missionaries, pastors and others grew discontented and were renewed and filled with the Spirit."

Visiting the different stations of this mission was a wonderful experience. In each place one felt everything had been prepared in definite, believing, unceasing prayer. It was marvelously open everywhere and there was a unity in the work between us missionaries.

Another passage from this book says: "In the theological seminary in Hwanghsien there was great blessing as in the Bible School. Every member of the faculty received special help. They became entirely new schools. In the hospital many of the staff were saved and some filled with the Spirit. In Tsining station and district we have become one mind as never before. This year we have been led to new spiritual heights. In Laichow and district this year has been the best we have ever had. It is absolutely impossible for human tongue to describe the new and wonderful fellowship into which we have entered. In Pingtu and district souls are continually being added to the church. It is generally believed that about three thousand have been so added in this one year, and it is the same in other stations and districts. Only time will show how much of this is of abiding value, but it is clear that something new has come into the life of the churches. Lives have been transformed, opium broken off, idols put away, enmities that have lasted for years have been put right, hopeless individuals have become humble men and women of prayer and soul-winners. Many, many have left their homes and their farms to seek the lost around them."

The attentive crowds that filled the large chapels are unforgettable. It was wonderful to watch so many being gathered in like ripe fruit, and to see the experience of sin and of the grace of God becoming like new capital immediately put into circulation.

There was the cook who stood in the kitchen with tears pouring down his face while he confessed to his employer all the ways in which he had cheated her, and the missionary herself asking his forgiveness for the snares she had left in his path by not being more careful. They were apparently equally convicted and equally happy afterwards.

There was the upright Chinese pastor with a fine American education and naturally noble character, who discovered that he had never been really saved. He became a new miracle of grace and was henceforth what he had never been before—a fisher of men.

There was the clever but very proud Chinese doctor who had been the subject of our prayers for a long time. He had two patients who were very seriously ill and had been bedridden for twenty years. He said he would be saved if they were healed. The Christians accepted the challenge and met to pray for them. Both patients were healed within two days of each other. The doctor also was saved, and so delivered from his pride that he became a humble witness for the Lord; and, from that time on, was often to be found in the poorest homes.

There was the fine scholarly teacher, a church member, but unsaved. Late one evening he crept in the dark down to the goatherd's home. The goatherd was not exactly the most intellectual of believers, but he knew how to help the teacher to have a meeting with the Savior of sinners.

There was the pastor, who stood banging the floor with his stick for rage, and who really looked as though he very much wished he could chastise the person who had dared to say that even a pastor might be unsaved. One day while he was walking along a muddy street, he was so overpowered by the Spirit of God that he fell down on his hands and knees in the road, crying out for mercy.

A number of women, too, and others, who dreaded the revival meetings because of the transaction which would have to be faced, were as ripe harvest ready for reaping.

The results of the revival were simply phenomenal. Years passed as the revival continued its spreading impact across the great nation. In 1936, Dr. G. Carlberg, principal of the Lutheran Theological Seminary in the province of Hupeh, wrote a fascinating book on the revival in which he enumerated the results. He wrote:

What has been written of the revival up to this point is what a few of us experienced personally, but the revival spread widely, from Fukien in the southeast to Kansu in the northwest before 1936. Later it spread further. In 1936 a book was published in America, written by Dr. G. Carlberg, Principal of the Lutheran Theological Seminary in the province of Hupeh. There had been a true, deep revival there. The book is reliable and reveals a fine grasp of a vast theme. In it are mentioned the results of the revival, which, in brief, are these:

1. The Church in China gained a large number of native spiritual leaders, men and women.

2. A large number of church members began to enjoy a personal experience of God as Savior.
3. A considerable harvest was reaped among former scholars in mission schools.
4. The churches no longer felt they were dependent on foreign aid: they had become independent national churches.
5. Joy in the Lord brought more singing, especially choruses, which were thoroughly Chinese in tune and literary expression.
6. The number of church members greatly increased.
7. The foreign missionaries who were used of God in the revival were few in comparison with the large number of Chinese whom the Lord raised up as the instruments of His grace.
8. The Chinese leaders became more conscious of their responsibility and manifested a new gratitude to the missionaries for their work in laying foundations.
9. Self support, which had been a distant goal, was now known to be attainable.
10. It has been amazing to witness the tact and ability which even young Christians were given in their care of awakened souls. They were taught of God and used by Him.
11. Preaching is alive with a note of authority; and there is more dependence on prayer in preparation for preaching, with the consequence that consciences are more readily roused.
12. There is a new insight into the nature of sin and God's thoughts about it. Conviction of sin has been overwhelming.
13. There is a new note of victory over sin where before there was only powerlessness.
14. The Bible has a new significance for the Chinese Christians: it is a light and a guide.
15. New power and new gifts have been given to the churches. Newly saved and renewed Christians seem to have been appointed their special functions. It is wonderful to see the great, once grey mass vitalized, individualized and activated by the Spirit of God.
16. In the background there have been many cases of healing; but foremost have been the many and greater miracles of salvation.

Marie was very conscious of the fact of what actually precipitates revival. She enumerated three things that bring about a genuine awakening. First, definite prayer. This has always been the case. Second, the reality and power of a call. God must call people to prayer and to the ministry of intercession if it is to be effectual. Third, the absolute necessity of the power of the Holy Spirit. In the final analysis, He is the author of revival.

True, there are dangers in revival. Marie, very sensitive to these things, saw the possibility of people's being led astray in wrong interpretations and perversions of the Scriptures. Then the danger of excessive emotionalism lurks about. Spiritual pride and arrogance can subtly slip in as well. But through much prayer and the leading and the instruction of the Holy Spirit, through the Word of God, the revival was kept well-balanced, and the vision never lost it charm.

The great Shantung Chinese Revival became one of the epochal moments in God's dealings in spiritual awakening. Perhaps the key figure, along with Bertha Smith whose story is told in this book, was this simple, lovely, Norwegian Lutheran woman, Miss Marie Monsen. Truly, a missionary of awakening.

Endnotes

1. The following quotes are taken from Marie Monsen, *The Awakening: Revival in China* (China Inland Mission, 1986).
2. The following quotes are taken from Marie Monsen, *A Present Help* (China Inland Mission, 1959).
3. Monsen, *The Awakening*, 62–63.

Chapter Twelve

RUTH BELL GRAHAM

The Evangelist's Wife of Awakening

It may seem somewhat strange, perhaps even straining the point, to call the wife of the great evangelist Billy Graham a "wife of awakening." Many historians are prone to say that there has not been, at least in America, a sweeping spiritual awakening in the twentieth century. From a purely historical perspective, that may well be true. America experienced great revivals in the eighteenth and nineteenth centuries, but the twentieth has been rather bereft of a movement similar to the First and Second Great Awakenings.

At the same time, however, never has there been an evangelist who has preached to more people and seen more come to faith in the Lord Jesus Christ in the entire history of the Christian movement than has Dr. Billy Graham. And if the final fruit of revival centers in the glory of God in the salvation of souls, then certainly at the heart of Billy Graham's ministry there has been something of a genuine awakening. And Billy Graham will be the first to say that his ministry was undergirded, strengthened, and, in many respects, carried on by the faithfulness of his dear wife, Ruth. Therefore, it is altogether appropriate to end this book on great women of awakening with our contemporary, Ruth Bell Graham: wife of the world's greatest evangelist, woman of God, woman of awakening.

Ruth's Roots

Ruth Graham came from sturdy stock. Her father, Dr. L. Nelson Bell, served as a missionary medical doctor in China. His first name, "Lemuel," literally means in Hebrew "belonging to God." This also typified his dedicated life. Dr. L. Nelson Bell was born July 30, 1894, in the beautiful Allegheny Mountains near Clifton Forge, Virginia. His father, James Bell, headed the commissary at the Longdale Mining Company. Nelson's earlier ancestors were Scotch-Irish immigrants, having arrived in America to settle in the Shennendoah valley in the early 1700s. There they became farmers of an eight-hundred-acre plot of land in that lovely part of the eastern United States.

At the age of six, Nelson Bell and his family moved to Waynesboro, Virginia, where he began school. Young Nelson, even at an early age, cultivated a deep reverence and faith in the Lord Jesus Christ. Moreover, he fostered an unshakable loyalty to the Presbyterian church that had been the family's spiritual roots for many years. Nelson excelled in athletics and as well possessed an unusually high I.Q. Actually, athletics consumed him, dominating his intellectual life. At the age of sixteen, he became captain of the high school championship baseball team. An excellent pitcher, he became noted for his unique version of the knuckleball. Virginia Leftwich, a fellow student, greatly admired Nelson. She would sit in the stands at every game, watching her idol throw his famous knuckleball.

Virginia was born on April 12, 1892, in Richmond, the eldest of four children. Her father, Douglas Lee Leftwich, worked as a traveling salesman. He possessed a beautiful baritone voice. As a baby, Virginia's family moved to Waynesboro where she lived just five blocks from the Bell's home. Inevitably, Nelson and Virginia were attracted to each other. God saw to that.

Although Virginia and Nelson had been acquainted in their early years, when they reached high school they fell in love. After graduation, Nelson Bell entered Washington and Lee University. Virginia went on to study nursing in Richmond. Nelson had fully intended to study law, but God in His providence worked through a seemingly insignificant event to change his mind radically. In the winter of 1911, Nelson and a friend were strolling across the campus when the friend suddenly slowed down and said to Nelson, "Did you ever think of becoming a medical missionary?" This chance remark struck home. Nelson immediately began to question if the practice of law was God's will for his life. The very next morning he changed his major from law to premed. The student Volunteer Movement for Foreign Missions, launched by the famous evangelist, Dwight L. Moody, had already impacted his life. But this crisis point brought him to dedicate his life to medical missions.

The question immediately arose as to where God would have him serve. In Nelson's background he remembered his mother's missionary friends tell of their experiences in China. A deep attraction to that needy land gripped his heart. Soon he became a student at the Medical College of Virginia in Richmond, with an eye focused on China.

At that stage Nelson faced a dilemma. He had signed a baseball contract with a professional Virginia league. Two years after signing the contract, the team was sold to the Baltimore Orioles, a major-league team. It had always been Nelson Bell's dream to play in the majors and now it appeared right at hand (that had also been Billy Graham's dream as a young man). The situation threw Nelson into an immediate struggle. To God's praise, the Holy Spirit prevailed as the will of God ascended as the most important issue for Nelson; he resigned from the league. In May 1916, the Southern Presbyterian Foreign Mission Committee contacted him and asked if he would be willing to go to China immediately. The situation was critical because two American doctors at the Tsingkiang General Hospital in North Kiangsu had died and there was a great need in the hospital. Nelson accepted the offer. He saw God as being in it all. But what about his love, Virginia?

Virginia was a Baptist. She realized that if she were to marry Nelson and serve as a missionary nurse, she must become a Presbyterian. So she forsook her Baptist background and joined the Presbyterian church as Nelson received his medical license. On June 30, 1916, they were married. Nelson completed a short three-month residency and they packed the few belongings they had, shipped them to Seattle Washington, and sailed to the Far East.

Difficult Days

Difficult days confronted most missionaries in the early decades of the twentieth century, especially in China. Virginia had not been particularly strong of body and when some of the fellow Presbyterian missionaries saw her they said quietly to one another, "She will not last a year." It was not unusual for missionaries to spend a relatively short time on the field and then fall into the grip of some native illness and see their life of service come to an abrupt end. This is what coworkers prophesied for Virginia. God had other plans.

The Tsingkiang General Hospital had been instituted only two years prior to the Bells arrival. The hospital boasted of 170 beds, and rested on a six-acre tract of land. Absalom Sydenstricker, father of the Nobel prize-winning novelist, Pearl Buck, had founded the mission station in 1887. So the Bells settled in, ready for a long and fruitful ministry of meeting the needs of both the body and the spirit of the desperate Chinese.

China was in a state of turmoil in the early part of the twentieth century, as has previously been described, so the Bells went into a very uncomfortable political situation. Regardless of the difficulties, however, the Bells stood ready to serve Christ and serve Him faithfully, even if it meant death. Into this wonderful, dedicated, sacrificial missionary family Ruth was born.

Ruth's Early Years

On Thursday, June 10, 1920, Dr. Bell scrubbed for the delivery of a baby. This was not going to be just another delivery for the good missionary doctor; his own child struggled to be born. A beautiful baby girl cried her first cry that day. The happy mother and father named her Ruth McCue

Bell for her paternal grandmother. Seeing such a healthy baby, the missionary doctor and his wife gave praise for the Lord's mercy in giving them such a lovely little girl. The year 1920 was the Year of the Monkey in Chinese culture, and tradition said that those who were born in that year were destined to be very talented, adventuresome, and witty people. It certainly proved prophetically correct for little Ruth. Her life has been a constant testimony of those so-called prophesies.

Ruth was the second of the children to be born into the Bell family, her older sister Rosa having been born two years earlier. As the family grew, the need for more space arose and the Lord provided a beautiful home. In 1922, the Bells built a two-story brick house on the mission compound. They did their best to make their home comfortable. After the hospital acquired a generator, Dr. Bell wired the house so that they might have electric lights and even a refrigerator. He installed a small circuit telephone system in all the missionaries' homes within a mile radius of their headquarters. Theirs was a wonderful, happy, and Christ-centered home. Ruth inherited a great legacy.

Little Ruth not only had a deep loving relationship with her immediate family, but Dr. Bell also had hired a Chinese nanny for the girls. Her name was Wang Nainia and she was barely five-feet tall and only weighed ninety-six pounds. She lived in a small room in the Bell's home. She was a marvelous Christian lady, and Ruth and Rosa loved her dearly.

Although Dr. Bell was a very skilled surgeon and physician, the family still suffered their periodic illnesses. That seemed to be the norm for China, especially for the missionaries. Hardly a month would pass without one of the family members contracting the flu or a cold or some unexplainable infection. Mrs. Bell had her problem with daily headaches, but through it all, they were a happy family as God met their many needs.

In December 1924, the Bell's first son came into the world. They named him after his father; but tragically, ten months later he died of amoebic dysentery. The missionaries realized that this was the fate that many of them would have to face. Dying in China for the cause of Christ actually became almost routine. Clayton, a second son, was born and today serves as pastor of a great Presbyterian church. There were difficult days indeed, yet God saw them through them all.

Ruth's Spirituality

Ruth proved to be an unusually spiritually minded little girl. One of the missionaries said of her, "Ruth was a very normal child but above average in spirituality. I'd say she was rather deep in her feelings. She was a very thoughtful little girl, and she was pretty, with curly hair and big hazel eyes."[1] Ruth early on found joy in her faith.

The Bell girls had playmates who lightened their day. William Talbot and his family, fellow missionaries, lived just a half mile from their home. Their children became very dear to Ruth and Rosa. Ruth also loved her pets. She had almost a small zoo with canaries, pigeons, ducks, turtles, and even a goat. And, of course, she had a dog. She named it Tar Baby. Her love for animals carried on throughout her life.

In 1927, war broke out between the Communists and the Nationalist Forces under Chiang Kai-shek. That was the same year, as we have seen in a previous chapter, the great Shantung Revival experienced its birth. Little Ruth was only seven years old at the time, but she would ultimately be the recipient of the blessings that spread over China as a result of the awakening.

The Bells were situated right on the path of the fighting between Chiang Kai-shek's Nationalist's Forces and the Communists. As a consequence, the American Consul in Shanghai insisted that the missionaries leave, so they sailed to America on a United States naval ship. Upon arriving in the United States, they settled once again in Waynesboro where a third daughter, Virginia, was born. From there they moved on to Holden, West Virginia. Dr. Bell became head of the surgical department of a local hospital, and then one year later the family moved to Houston, Texas. In Houston, Dr. Bell, in addition to practicing medicine, served as a lay minister at the First Presbyterian Church.

Approximately a year after the disruption of the Bell's Chinese ministry, the great nation once again opened up and on December 15, 1928, the family set sail on the SS *President Cleveland*. When they returned to their mission compound, they discovered that the soldiers had ransacked the hospital and had even smashed much of the expensive equipment. But the Bells soon put things reasonably in order and settled down again to their work.

A New Venture

The time came when Dr. Bell realized that his children had to receive a better and more thorough education than they were able to receive at their particular station. In June 1930, Dr. Bell set out for Shanghai to meet Lucy Fletcher, a young school teacher who had been hired by the Presbyterian Mission Board to teach the missionary children.

Dr. Bell was pleased with his interview with Lucy Fletcher and they made their way back from Shanghai to the station where she began to instruct the children. She introduced the family to great literature, and in particular to the works of Amy Carmichael, whose life we have explored earlier. Amy Carmichael's writings influenced Ruth more than any other author; thus, Ruth became well-schooled in the meaning of true revival.

Ruth reveled in her new educational adventure. By the age of twelve, she had dedicated her life to becoming a missionary herself. She had seen much suffering and sacrifice, even martyrdom, and in one sense coveted that for herself. She realized that she must give herself totally to Christ in a life of service, even to death if it be God's will. She dedicated herself to become a spinster missionary to the nomads in Tibet. The Spartan life and the difficulties that such a ministry would demand reflected the depth of young Ruth's dedication.

Ruth had an innate artistic flair, and because of her sense of humor and happy spirit, she would often sketch cartoon figures along with her flowers and landscapes. Her father, who was quite practical said, "Ruth has real artistic talent. For a long time we knew that she was clever with drawing, but recently, she shows remarkable talent. . . . It has never been a talent I have especially desired for a child of mine." Actually, Dr. Bell made something of a mistake on that score because later Ruth's creativity aided her tremendously in Christian service.

Leaving Home

Ruth loved her family and the security of her home. Yet she knew the time would come when she would have to leave for further education. In 1932, Ruth and Rosa left home for Pyeng Yang Foreign School, some fifteen hundred miles away. The city in which the school was located later became known as Pyongyang, North Korea. The school, thoroughly Christian, enrolled one hundred and forty students, the Bible being a central part of the curriculum. In September 1932, the Bell sisters, along with several other missionary children, made their way to Shanghai where they boarded a boat to sail to Japan. They landed in Nagasaki after crossing the Yellow Sea, where they boarded a train. After traveling across Japan, they boarded another ship and sailed to the Korean port of Pusan. From there they made their way to their destination where their education would continue. Those days in the Korean high school were not easy. Ruth, however, settled in, after some struggle, and soon began to enjoy her education. She became the cartoonist and poet for "The Kulsi," the school yearbook.

In America Again

After Ruth's junior year in Pyeng Yang, the Bell family once again traveled to the United States on furlough. They settled in a small rented home in Montreat, North Carolina. There Rosa and Ruth finished their senior year of high school. They were graduated from the Montreat school in the spring of 1936. Rosa left immediately for Wheaton College in Illinois, but Ruth, just sixteen years old, returned to Korea for a year of postgraduate study. Her parents felt that she was just too young for college at the age of sixteen; so back to the Far East they sailed.

War and Return to America

The year 1937 became a very decisive year for China. That year witnessed the Japanese invasion of the giant nation. Even though Japanese armies had invaded Manchuria earlier in 1932, the new aggressive incursion in 1937 of the island nation rocked all of China. On August 19, 1937, Ruth was sent to America. She boarded the *Empress of Asia* and set sail for Vancouver. From there Ruth traveled to Wheaton, Illinois, where she joined Rosa and began her freshman year of college. Her mother wrote, "Ruth is a precious child and still a child, and going home will be hard for her. It is certainly one hard thing missionaries have to do—have their children so far away during their important years." Wheaton certainly was a long way from China—in every sense of the word.

Ruth did not feel any real compulsion about going to college; and leaving the Far East did not thrill her at all. She had already made up her mind what her life would be. One day she would give herself to the spreading of the Gospel of Jesus Christ in the Himalayan Mountains of Tibet. She felt that she could get a good working knowledge of the Tibetan language and the Bible right where she had been, and she did not need to go to America. Her parents simply smiled, and so it was off to America at the age of seventeen.

Not long after Ruth's departure for the States, an urgent call went out to all the missionaries from the American ambassador: They were to leave China as soon as possible. The general upheaval grew to such proportions that the State Department feared for their well-being. Dr. Bell wired back to inquire if there could be a later evacuation. He wanted to stay in China as long as possible. On September 8, a voice came over the radio with the message, "Foreigners have been invited *for the last time to leave*." So the Bells immediately began to make their plans for travel back to the United States. Little did they realize all that was in store for the family, especially for Ruth at Wheaton College.

College Days

By the time Ruth had enrolled at Wheaton College, she had lost all her teenage awkwardness, not that she had ever had very much. She had grown into a very attractive and popular young lady. Several upperclassmen sought her attention. She found herself invited to dinners and ice shows and was fast becoming very popular on campus. On more than one occasion she was late returning from one of her dates and had to crawl through the window of the dormitory. Once her absence was discovered by the housemother and she accosted Ruth, demanding, "Where have you been and how did you get in?" Ruth very innocently, but honestly, said, "I've been on a date and I climbed through my window." She received an immediate "appointment" with the dean of students to face the consequences.

Ruth was a dedicated and spiritually minded young lady with a high moral code, qualities the college recognized; still, the dean said to her, "You have disgraced the school, you have disgraced your parents. You have disgraced yourself. You can choose between expulsion first semester or an indefinite campusing." She knew that she could hardly return to China and she had no intention of moving to Waynesboro where her parents now lived. She simply said, "I prefer to be campused, sir." That ended that little episode.

Of course, all that this meant was that Ruth could have no more campus dates until her probationary period had expired. A fellow classmate, Harold Lindsell, later to become very close to the family and to work with Billy, took the opportunity to court Ruth. He escorted her to classes and even enrolled in one of her courses. It proved a positive thing for Ruth, because she felt almost disgraced by her antics of the previous date. By the next spring, the faculty realized that Ruth's "waywardness" was just something that she had done out of innocence. They released her from her campus sentence and regular college life became the norm. Needless to say, most colleges then were quite different in their discipline than they are today.

A Spiritual Battle

During college Ruth entered into a real spiritual struggle. In the spring of 1938, a student friend from the University of Chicago who had attended high school with her in Korea, came to visit. He had utterly repudiated his Christian faith. He tried to convince Ruth that if she would give up her commitment to Christ, it would be her liberation. He told her, "It could be the best thing that ever happened to you." Thus, along with the rigid intellectual exercises that she had been experiencing, she began to entertain some serious doubts concerning the Christian faith. Such a struggle often becomes the fate of college students, even in the context of a dedicated Christian institution. Ruth actually began to be shaken loose from her spiritual roots. She never slipped into absolute atheism, though. The old cosmological argument for the existence of God proved too much for her. She knew that the ordered universe could not just have happened; there must be an intelligent Mind behind it all. The pressing question, however, was centered on this Man called Jesus Christ. Was He a great philosopher, a great teacher? Just who was He?

Ruth began to delve deeply into the life, ministry, and teachings of the Lord Jesus. One day she said to Harold Lindsell, who had now become a very close friend, "Jesus was either God or He was a liar or crazy." Lindsell immediately replied, "Well, we should really pray about this." Ruth retorted, "I don't want prayers, I want proof."

For days and weeks Harold Lindsell and Ruth debated these issues.

Lindsell would always point to the Bible and Ruth would always point to her skeptical attitude that was seemingly getting a real grip on her mind. She finally got to the place where she said, "I can't be sure that God loves me, for who am I amongst so many." Clearly, she was putting her intellect above the clear revelation of God in Christ as revealed in the Scriptures. She ceased walking by faith and demanded rational proof. Harold kept reminding her of the absolute necessity of the leap of faith. Actually, Ruth's faith had never really been severely tested before this trauma, and she found herself in the midst of a serious struggle.

In the summer of 1938, Ruth went to visit her grandmother, and she invited Lindsell down for a few days. Delighted, he accepted; he wanted to marry her, but she was only eighteen. She told him then that she never planned to marry anyone. So, she struggled on.

Finally, through the rigors of a long, hard spiritual battle, Ruth came to the important realization that all human questions simply cannot be answered. God is infinite; therefore, there will always be a pervasive element of mystery concerning His nature and acts. The unanswerable rational questions must thus be committed to Christ in faith. The mind must be subjected to Christ as well as the heart and will. As she realized this most important principle and thus took a firm, biblical stance, her problems began to dissipate and the presence of Christ flooded her heart once again. It had been a severe testing time as well as a deepening and a strengthening experience that she would never forget.

But what about her ever getting married? Did God want her never to marry? What about going back to Tibet? Was this truly God's plan for her life? All these questions flooded Ruth's mind. Little did she realize that in a very short time she would have her answer. She would soon meet Billy Graham, the man who would make her a "wife of awakening."

Meeting Billy Frank

William Franklin Graham, Billy Frank to his parents and Billy Graham to the world, was born November 7, 1918, just outside of Charlotte, North Carolina, where the family dairy farm was situated. Four days before the end of World War I, God gave to the world another soldier; only this time he was destined to be a soldier of the Cross.

Billy came to Christ under the preaching of Mordecai Ham, a Baptist evangelist from Kentucky. Several laymen in the Charlotte area had banded together to invite evangelist Ham to hold a tent meeting in their locale. Billy, though he lived in a dedicated Christian home, had no desire whatsoever to visit the old-fashioned tent-meeting revival. One night, however, friends persuaded him to go and hear the Baptist evangelist.

Billy Frank came to Christ in Ham's revival meeting during those dynamic days. It was almost symbolic that Billy should be converted in the context of mass evangelism under an itinerant evangelist. It became a prophesy of his own future ministry. Ham's preaching was a model of revivalism. It certainly touched Billy; he fell under deep conviction. Realizing that he had not fully repented of all of his sins and had not placed his faith solely and completely in the atoning work of Jesus Christ, one night, as the evangelist finished his searching message and the choir began to sing the invitational hymn, "Almost Persuaded," Billy Frank and his close friend Grady Wilson went forward to render openly their decision of "repentance toward God, and faith in our Lord Jesus Christ" (Acts 20:21). Billy confessed, "I didn't have any tears, I didn't have any emotion, I didn't hear any thunder, there was no lightning. I saw a lady standing next to me and she had tears in her eyes and I thought there was something wrong with me because I didn't feel all worked up. But right there, I made my decision for Christ. It was as simple as that, and as conclusive."[2]

Billy burst into the house that evening and announced to his parents, "I am a changed boy." As he went upstairs to his bedroom, however, he privately wondered what the next day would bring. In the swirl of all of his conflicting ideas and emotions, he dropped to his knees and cried out, "Oh God, I don't understand all of this. I don't know what's happening to me. But as best I can figure it, I have given myself to You." And what he said was absolutely true. He gave himself to Christ unreservedly and that was enough. After graduation from high school in 1936, Billy Frank made his way for a short time to Bob Jones University and then later for a three-year course at the Tampa Bible Institute where he graduated. He entered Wheaton College in the fall of 1940.

Billy had become a Baptist in Florida, thus leaving his Presbyterian roots. Yet, he fit in very well with the interdenominational atmosphere of Wheaton College, as did Ruth. College life went well. He did need to work, however, so he joined up with a fellow student by the name of Johnny Streater. Johnny had acquired an old, beat up, yellow pickup truck and had painted on the side of the doors, "Wheaton College Student Trucking Service." He and Billy went around freelancing, moving what equipment people would hire them to transport.

One day Billy was carrying some packages to a house when he saw Ruth for the first time. Although Ruth claims not to remember very much about that first meeting, Billy fell in love with her immediately. It took him some time to work up enough courage to ask her for a date, but cupid's arrow had pierced his heart—soon Ruth would feel the delightful arrow also.

Courtship

The first real impression that Billy made on Ruth was at a prayer meeting. By the end of the fall semester of 1940, Billy had already been dubbed by his fellow students "the preacher." What really impressed Ruth, however, was his prayer life. Ruth said, "I had never heard anyone pray like that before, I sensed that here was a man that knew God in a very unusual way." When Billy finally found courage to ask her for the date, they went to a performance of Handel's Messiah. After the concert, they walked in the snow to a professor's home for tea. Clearly, the backgrounds of Billy Frank and Ruth were dramatically different. Yet, a kindred spirit of love for Christ and later for one another began to blossom.

Billy wrote home immediately that he planned to marry this new girl who reminded him so much of his mother. The Graham's did not give a great deal of stock to his statement, because as Billy's younger sister Jean recalled, "He had fallen in love so many times, we didn't pay much attention to him." Ruth, however, had a much more spiritual approach to the relationship. She actually prayed, "If you let me serve you with that man, I would consider it the greatest privilege of my life."

Billy felt quite uncertain that he could win Ruth's hand in marriage. Little did he know how she had been praying. After their first date, they actually did not date again for six weeks. At the end of that protracted period of uncertainty, Ruth finally invited Billy to a party at her boarding house. Then a week later he asked her for another date and confessed one of the problems that precipitated his apparent reluctance to pursue a serious relationship. He told Ruth that he did not feel a definite call to the mission field as she did. He sensed God's call to evangelism. But he asked her out again. The courtship then began to grow. Finally, Billy opened his heart to Ruth and told her he had been praying that if it were God's will he would be delighted if the Lord would give her to him. Ruth was impressed even though it hardly constituted a formal proposal. She wrote to her parents that this young man was "humble, thoughtful, unpretentious, courteous." Above all, she said, he was determined to do God's will, and that meant everything to her. But Ruth wanted to be sure that God was in it all; Tibet still stood in need. So Billy precipitated something of a minicrisis. He gave Ruth an ultimatum: "Either you date me, or you can date everybody but me!" Ruth responded with a big "Yes." The relationship immediately deepened and it became clear to both that God was bringing them together.

A Problem

A rather difficult situation began to develop as Billy and Ruth's relationship developed. As Billy became assured of God's will for their lives together, he began to mimic his parents in a rather patriarchal sense. He told Ruth what to eat and advised her to get more exercise and to do all sorts of things. She finally had to confide in her parents that "Bill [she always calls him Bill and never Billy] isn't often easy to love because of his sternness and unwavering stand on certain issues." But the relationship grew in spite of the minor problems, and finally at the end of the spring semester of 1941, Billy formally asked Ruth to marry him. Ruth did not immediately give an affirmative answer. But to Billy's delight, a few weeks later, while he was preaching in Tampa, Ruth wrote him that she felt led of the Lord to be his wife. The issue was settled. On July 7, she wrote to her parents, "To be with Bill in evangelistic work won't be easy. There will be little financial backing, lots of obstacles and criticism, and no earthly glory whatsoever. I knew I wouldn't have peace 'til I yielded my will to the Lord and decided to marry Bill." As strange as it may seem to people today, up to that point, Billy had never kissed Ruth.

The summer of 1941 saw Billy at the Bell's home in Montreat, North Carolina, where they had moved. Billy traveled to Montreat to present Ruth with an engagement ring and to meet his future in-laws. The bond was sealed and the happy couple looked forward to their wedding.

Ruth did not return to Wheaton College that fall, however. She had become quite ill late that summer, and Dr. Bell feared that perhaps she had earlier on contracted malaria in China. The disease was rampant in the Far East, and he was very concerned for his daughter. Consequently, Ruth and her sister Rosa, who suffered from tuberculosis, were sent to a Presbyterian sanitarium in New Mexico. It would mean separation from Billy, but a time of complete rest and rehabilitation seemed important for both the sisters. And in the good grace of God, Ruth and Rosa regained their health.

A New Crisis

The long separation from Billy began to raise doubts in Ruth's mind. She wrote Billy that she had grown unsure of her love for him and thought that it might be best for both if they called off their engagement. Needless to say, Billy was deeply disturbed. But in the wisdom of the Lord he did not react hastily, as his disposition often dictated.

Ruth went back to Wheaton in January 1942, and Billy offered to take the ring back. Ruth confessed that the real problem centered in the fact that for years she had long held a conviction that she should be a missionary. The old conflict had reasserted itself. Billy immediately responded that what one wants to do is not necessarily what God desires. He asked her, "Do you, or do you not think the Lord brought us together?" Ruth had to confess that she really did feel this was the case. Billy immediately, in a rather authoritarian way, said, "Then I'll do the leading and you do the following." So Ruth gave up her missionary dreams and dedicated herself to become Billy's wife. Clearly, as the years have shown, God had His way.

The happy couple announced the wedding date for August 1943, some eighteen months away. In the meantime, they both graduated from Wheaton College. Billy had majored in anthropology and Ruth had studied art with a minor in biblical studies. All their friends said that she was the student and Billy was the charismatic communicator. God certainly led in the match and set the stage for the unfolding of a great evangelistic revival.

The Wedding

On Friday, August 13, 1943, at 8:00 P.M., in the Montreat Presbyterian Church, Billy and Ruth joined hands in matrimony. Some two hundred and fifty people had gathered to celebrate the wedding. The Reverend John Minder, a close friend of Billy's from the Florida Bible Institute days, and the Reverend Kerr Taylor, a former missionary to China, officiated at the ceremony. Rosa served as the maid of honor and Ruth's other sister, Virginia, and Ruth's childhood friend, Sandy Yates, were bridesmaids. Billy's sister, Jeannie, was the junior bridesmaid. Ruth, beautiful in her homemade gown of white satin and a long lace veil, brought smiles to every face. She wore a white satin cap quilted in pearls. She carried a bouquet of colorful daisies and tuberoses. Billy stood tall and proud, attired in a white jacket and black trousers. They made a handsome couple to say the very least. Billy was attended by his brother, Melvin, who served as best man. The groomsmen were evangelists Jimmy Johnson, Grady Wilson, and Roy Gustaphson. These men later became significant associates in the Billy Graham Evangelistic Association. Ruth's brother, Clayton, now a prominent Presbyterian minister, served as the junior groomsman. The vows were said and a thin gold band was slipped on Ruth's finger by her now-beloved husband. The marriage was sealed in heaven.

A Strange Start

The family gave a reception after the ceremony, and the Graham's drove off for their honeymoon. It was a delightful time, but a minor problem arose. Billy had saved some seventy-five dollars for their honeymoon trip. That sum soon evaporated and the happy couple had to return to Charlotte and then to Montreat to visit their parents before driving the seven hundred and fifty miles to Hinsdale, Illinois, their future home. Billy had been called to become pastor of a small Baptist church in Western Springs, Illinois. Ruth would now be a pastor's wife.

On the way to Illinois, Ruth got a chill and by the time they arrived at their apartment in Hinsdale, she had a high fever. Billy was scheduled for a preaching engagement in Elmira, Ohio, that weekend and felt that he should keep it. Of course, he felt very uneasy about leaving a sick wife, so he checked her into the local hospital and left. He sent her a telegram and a box of candy, but that did not help too much. Ruth joked about an incident that occurred that weekend. When the collection was being passed in the Elmira Baptist Church where Billy was preaching, he reached into his pocket and pulled out a bill and dropped it into the plate. He intended to give only five dollars, but realized he had inadvertently dropped in a twenty-dollar bill. Ruth told him when he returned home, "That's all [$5] God gave you credit for." She felt that she had been somewhat vindicated by Billy's absence, but through the years she realized this would be part and parcel of their life together. She soon learned that Billy would rarely cancel a preaching engagement regardless of how ill either one of them happened to be. (Recently, much against the doctor's advice, Billy was speaking to a luncheon group in Toronto, Canada, during his crusade in that city. He was so ill that he collapsed in the pulpit. Yet, that is something of the dedication of the man to the preaching of the Gospel.) Ruth never found it easy with Billy to be gone so much, but as she said so often, "I'd rather have a little of Bill, than a lot of any other man." There was good reason for Ruth to feel that way about her Bill; he was a great soul winner and that was close to her heart. On one occasion early in their ministry, Billy led a man to Christ who simply broke down in tears of repentance. Ruth said, "I had never heard a broken down sinner pleading for forgiveness." As one author has said, "She would spend the rest of her life hearing just that."[3]

A Faithful Preacher's Wife

Billy, though a pastor, still traveled considerably as invitations to preach came in. Ruth bore Billy's absences with real spiritual fortitude and bravery. Often while Billy was on the road, she would do research for him to aid his sermon preparation. She would spend hours studying the Bible and going through magazines and newspapers looking for illustrations. Billy himself is the first to admit that many of his sermon illustrations and sections of his better books really can be attributed to Ruth's faithful studies.

Ruth and Billy are both strong personalities. One biographer relates the following story. It gives something of an insight to their independence but yet their wonderful forbearance one for the other:

The first phase of their marriage was peppered with the usual adjustments and oversights. He draped his wet towels over the top of the bathroom door. She depended on serendipity instead of recipes for her cooking, and the results—like a yellowish batch of pickled peach jello—were not always palatable. Nor did he appreciate her quick tongue.

"I have never taken your advice," he told her bluntly one day, "and I don't intend to begin now."

"I'd be ashamed to admit," she replied, "that I had married a woman whose advice I couldn't take."

Like many new husbands, he wasn't always a paragon of sensitivity. One day several of Billy's bachelor friends visited unannounced and suggested that they all go into Chicago.

"That would be fine," Ruth said happily, eager to escape the monotony of the apartment. "I have some shopping I can do. I'll go get my coat."

"No," Billy said. "We guys just want to be alone. No women today."

No amount of begging would change his mind. Through tears she watched the car drive away, and she prayed, "God, if You'll forgive me for marrying him, I'll never do it again."

Ruth often said that if there are no disagreements in families, then one of the two is not necessary.

Billy received, at times, criticism from some members of the Western Springs church because of his continual traveling and absences. They wanted him at their beck and call. Yet, by early 1944, the attendance had doubled and the offerings had increased to the point that they were able to burn the mortgage contract. Further, Billy became something of a local celebrity when Torrey Johnson invited him to take over the well-known radio broadcast, *Songs in the Night*. The program consisted of forty-five minutes of preaching and singing. It came on the air Sunday night at 10:15 and was broadcast live from the church. Billy persuaded George Beverly Shea to sing on the program, which skyrocketed the broadcast into a great success.

The program became so popular that it was soon broadcast twice on Sunday. Ruth would sit in the studio, and while George Beverly Shea sang, she would jot down little notes and give them to Billy to help him with the comments to make between the songs. She served as Billy's helpmate in the most profound sense of the word. Billy's popularity soared until he became known as "that hustling Baptist preacher."

The grumbling of some of the deacons continued to grow until finally one suggested that if Billy did not curtail his travels they would cut his salary. Ruth remarked, "If they think they can run Bill, they've got another think coming." As always, she stood by her husband.

Of course, the issue had come up whether or not Ruth would become a Baptist and leave her Presbyterian background now that she had become a Baptist pastor's wife. In their earlier relationship, this question almost broke up their engagement. They both had strong convictions, with Billy's being an ordained Baptist and she a Presbyterian medical missionary's daughter. Ruth adamantly refused to give up her Presbyterian affiliation. One day while they were driving along, Billy thoughtlessly remarked that if Dr. Bell remained a Presbyterian, he really could not be a man of God. That did not sit well at all with Ruth—she knew better. Denominationalism reigned strong in those days. But they weathered the storm and Ruth continued on as a Presbyterian and Billy a Baptist, mutually respecting each other for their convictions.

Criticism continued to mount, and it became evident that the situation was shaping up for Billy and Ruth to leave Western Springs. Billy had received numerous opportunities for ministry in other areas. Having been the pastor and wife of a local church was to hold them in good stead through the years of itinerant evangelistic ministry. They could empathize with the thousands of pastors whose lives they would later touch in such a profound manner.

The undercurrent of criticism began to grow until one Sunday night during the sermon Billy said, "Some of you need to confess the sin of trouble-making. A person tries to build a testimony for God in this town and all you do is tear it down. You had better confess before God has to remove some people. As for me, I'm here to do this job for God and with His help, I'll get it done, regardless." Of course, as can be imagined, the troublemakers resented what he said, but Ruth said that it was all worthwhile when they saw so many people being saved. Still, it did seem that their days at the Western Springs church would be a long-term ministry. What did God have for their future?

The Future?

The United States Army accepted Billy in August 1944 to serve as a chaplain. World War II still raged on and the Graham's saw this as an opportunity for great ministry. They felt that God had surely worked all this out, because twice before Billy had applied for the chaplaincy and had been turned down because of being underweight. He still fell three pounds underweight in relation to his height, but he was accepted nonetheless. Then suddenly an illness intervened and changed the entire course of Billy's and Ruth's lives of service. Billy began to suffer from a stress-related paralysis of the throat. Further, in October of that year he fell victim to a dangerous strain of mumps on both sides of his neck. All he could eat was strained baby food and liquids as Ruth graciously sat by his bedside and fed him. She stood by him "in sickness as in health." And her beloved was really sick. There were no antibiotics available; the pharmacist's coffers were empty because of the military needs overseas. At times Billy's temperature rose so high that he became virtually delirious. One night he began describing angels on the ceiling. "Can't you see them?" he asked. Ruth felt that perhaps he was actually dying, and she knelt by his bedside pouring out her heart before God with tears. God heard her cry. Six weeks later, he, at last, could get out of bed, but he had fallen to just 130 pounds. Being well over six feet tall, he looked like a virtual beanpole of a man and was white as a corpse. God in His graciousness always provides, and a $100 check came in the mail from a woman who had heard him on the radio. The letter urged him to go to Florida and take a vacation. So the Grahams jumped in their little car, drove down to Miami, and rented a small room several miles from the ocean, not realizing that Torrey Johnson, leader of the Youth for Christ organization, was vacationing in a hotel just three blocks away.

Johnson and Billy got together, and they went fishing one day. While out on the water, Torrey asked Billy if he would become a full-time evangelist with Youth for Christ. Billy would have the responsibility of organizing rallies and crusades and would travel throughout the United States and Canada.

What a challenge this presented to the young pastor/evangelist. He discussed it thoroughly with Ruth and with her concurrence accepted the offer. He resigned his position at the Western Springs church along with his army commission, believing that he could reach more servicemen through his rallies than he could as a chaplain. So now the restraints and relative curtailment of pastoral responsibilities were laid aside, and Billy felt totally free to pursue that which God was leading him to do: evangelism. With the full support of his dear wife Ruth, he launched out. Robert Van Kampen, one of the members of the Western Springs Baptist Church, said, "God has given him a special gift—he's going to be another Billy Sunday or Dwight L. Moody." Van Kampen was a prophet indeed.

The Evangelistic Ministry Begins—As Does the Family

As 1945 unfolded, Billy and Ruth moved to Montreat, North Carolina, and occupied an upstairs bedroom in Ruth's parents' home. The ministry developed rapidly as Billy traveled to virtually every large metropolitan area in America. A wealthy businessman from Kenosha, Wisconsin, gave Billy and Torrey Johnson airline credit cards. This, of course, meant that Ruth had to spend most of her time in Montreat alone while Billy traveled in his itinerant evangelistic ministry with Youth for Christ.

In the summer of 1945 Ruth was getting ready to welcome into the world their first child. She found a plain straw bassinet and painted it blue. She lined it with quilted blue satin and trimmed it with the material of her own wedding veil. The happy day, September 21, arrived and Ruth gave birth to Virginia Leftwich, whom they affectionately called GiGi, which in old English means "Sister." Billy was away preaching when GiGi came into this world and she became a great comfort to Ruth. After the birth of GiGi, Ruth confessed that she really felt at home for the first time since she had left Tsingkiang for Korea in 1933.

As the ministry grew, the next year (1946) Billy acquired a new song leader, Cliff Barrows. They held rallies in twenty-six cities and made their first trip to the British Isles. As Youth for Christ expanded and the impact of the ministry enlarged, the budget also grew, and Billy found it possible to take Ruth with him on his trips from time to time. She accompanied Billy on his first British trip. They were to meet in New York and go overseas together, but by the time Ruth had paid the taxi drivers and the airline agent who penalized her for overweight baggage, she boarded an old DC-4 with only two cents in her purse.

The British trip proved a rich blessing. But Ruth had a problem. At that time in Britain, evangelical Christian women did not wear makeup, so Ruth had to get rid of hers. However, she did put on a little transparent lipstick that the people used in China. It was virtually undetectable, but one very pious woman came up to Billy and said, "We had a great blessing from your sermons, but we lost it all when your wife was wearing makeup." Obviously, times have changed since those days.

In the fall of 1947, Ruth discovered that she was again to have a child. So, they bought a two-story partly furnished summer house on the same street as her parents; not a large place at all, the payments were only forty-five dollars a month. Ruth and her mother traveled all through the mountain villages looking for junk shops where they could perhaps find some antiques and second-hand furniture. Ruth's sister, Virginia, who was home from nursing school at Johns Hopkins University at the time, helped her paint some of the old furniture that she found. The family had a great time together. In May, Ruth and Billy's second daughter, Anne, was born. Through the years, though very shy as a growing child and teenager, Anne has become a tremendous Bible teacher and speaker. In demand all around the world, she has been given, by the Holy Spirit, a powerful ministry of her own. Someone a little factiously said, "If Billy has a successor, it ought to be his daughter, Anne." There is a real element of truth there. Anne is a great Christian, a prayer warrior, a genuine power for Christ, and is deeply admired by these authors.

An Academic Venture

In the summer of 1947, a very unusual opportunity came to Billy and Ruth. William Bell Riley, the president of Northwestern Schools in Minneapolis, Minnesota, asked Billy to become president. Riley, getting up in years, was eagerly seeking his successor in the leadership role at the school. A very forceful individual, he absolutely insisted that Billy must follow him as president. Billy was very hesitant, but Riley insisted. Graham acquiesced and said that he would take the place of leadership in academia. On December 6, 1947, William Bell Riley died and at the young age of twenty-nine, Billy became president of a school with more than seven hundred and fifty students. He immediately gave the school a new vision, capsulized in the motto he penned, "Knowledge on Fire."

The entire situation did not really settle well with Ruth. She could not see herself at all in the role of a "first lady" of a Bible institution. One day, one of the administrators telephoned her in Montreat and asked when she was going to move to Minneapolis to take up residency in the president's mansion. Ruth, well aware of the fact that Billy would not be spending much time on campus and would be continuing his itinerant evangelism, immediately replied, "Never." Ruth was deeply concerned that this new position, like the interim at Western Springs Baptist Church, would tend to sidetrack Billy from the ministry in which he was most gifted: namely, evangelism. Thus she never moved to Minneapolis. Billy's ministry at Northwestern schools did not last long, and Ruth's sensitivity and prophecy of the possibility of being sidetracked proved on target. A new phase of ministry was about to open up on the Youth for Christ circuit for the devoted couple.

The Ministry Explodes

Many are quite familiar with the story of Billy Graham's intellectual struggles at this stage of his life, similar to Ruth's days of doubt. The struggles unfolded dramatically in 1949, while Billy labored in the Youth for Christ ministry. In those days, another fellow evangelist, Charles Templeton, decided he needed to further his theological education. He enrolled at Princeton Theological Seminary and urged Billy to do the same. They both felt that theological education plays a vital role in a minister's life, and that they should therefore get all the training possible. Yet Billy simply could not bring himself to believe it was the will of God for him to follow his good friend and fellow evangelist to Princeton. While at seminary Charles began to doubt seriously the verities of the evangelical Christian faith. He virtually gave up preaching, and try as he might, Billy could not help him. However, some of the questions that Charles Templeton raised began to disturb Billy. He too began to question certain aspects of what the Bible clearly declares. In the midst of these struggles, Billy faced a major crisis: was the Bible totally true? In the heat of the struggle, and through deep prayer and searching, he came to the important decision that though he could not understand everything in the Bible, he accepted it as the inspired Word of God, and he would preach it as the authoritative truth from the Lord Himself. He would let the problems worry for themselves. That might seem a simplistic answer to an intellectual, spiritual struggle; but because of its depth and in its profundity, that is the approach one must take when such testing times come. The human intellect as well as the human heart must be yielded to God's revelation. Ruth had learned that some years earlier. Billy rose from his knees, got back into his car and traveled south. The rest is history. In 1949, the great Los Angeles Crusade burst on the scene.

Los Angeles and the Revival

Something of a spiritual awakening had already been touching parts of America by 1949. The Youth for Christ movement and the similar Southern Baptist Youth Revival movement saw tens of thousands brought to faith in the Lord Jesus Christ. A deep moving of the Holy Spirit among college and seminary students, probably sparked by the returning servicemen who had gone through the riggers of World War II, blessed many lives. The atmosphere blossomed, ripe for a profound "prophet" to arise on the scene. That man was Billy Graham. As he came to the fore, back of him stood his wonderful wife, Ruth, lending her support.

In downtown Los Angeles, a group of concerned California laymen pitched a tent on the corner of Washington Boulevard and Hill Street and asked Billy to preach. The canvas cathedral covered almost an entire city block. Six thousand people could be crammed under its stretched awnings. There Billy held forth the Gospel. Billboards read, Dynamic Preaching—Heavenly Music—Six Thousand Free Seats. As the crusade began, Ruth joined Billy for what she thought would be just a three-week crusade. She left GiGi who was now four years old with her parents and fifteen-month old Anne with her sister Rosa in New Mexico. What a surprise God had in store for them.

The first few weeks of the Crusade went rather typically. Good crowds attended and a fair number of people came to Christ. Then two or three very significant things happened. First of all, William Randolph Hearst, of the Hearst newspaper chain, focused his eye on Billy Graham. The story is told that he had a maid in his mansion who was a very devout Christian. She drew Hearst's attention to Billy, although he had known something about Graham's ministry prior to the maid's insistence that he should give his attention to the tent meeting. Hearst apparently did some investigation and wrote a memo to his reporters. The tale has it that Hearst wrote a simple two word memo: "Puff Graham." William Randolph Hearst Jr. denies that this really happened. Hearst Jr. said, "Pop would have never sent a memorandum to an editor of his papers with the words, 'Puff Graham.' He was not given to talking or writing in cryptic style, and I never heard him use the word, 'puff.'" It was not a word used in the journalism profession except by press agents. Don Goodenow, the picture editor of the old Los Angeles *Examiner,* said that he received a message to "Give attention to Billy Graham's meetings." That is probably the gist of what Randolph Hearst Sr. actually said. So reporters and photographers from the *Examiner* and several other of Hearst's thirteen papers went to the services each night. In that setting some tremendously significant conversions took place.

A man deeply involved in syndicated crime, Jim Vaus, came to faith in Jesus Christ during that crusade. Jim Vaus was a notorious criminal, yet at the same time a genius. His father was a minister of the Gospel and he himself a professing Christian. But even while in Bible school, serving as editor of the yearbook, Jim Vaus absconded with the funds. He went into the military, became an officer, and confiscated for his own use untold amounts of army equipment. He received a court marshal and a dishonorable discharge. President Harry Truman, however, gave him a pardon. At the time that the Graham crusade opened, Jim Vaus had involved himself in syndicated crime in the Los Angeles area; he worked for the godfather, Mickey Cohen. Vaus had developed electronic equipment that could tap any telephone conversation in the entire Los Angeles area without even cutting into the lines. All he had to know was the telephone number and he could break into any conversation. Not only that, he had invented an electronic instrument that would interrupt the teletype reports coming from the East Coast to the West Coast, read them, interpret them, and then send the message back into the line completely unknown by the wire operators. The purpose of this was to interrupt the teletype reports of horse races on the East Coast, place a large bet on the winning horse, and then feed the message back into the wires. It was a sure-fire way of making millions.

Jimmy Vaus' wife, a dedicated Christian, had prayed for her husband for many years. One night, very reluctantly, Jimmy Vaus went to hear young Billy Graham preach. There is only one way to describe what happened that night: God spoke powerfully to his heart and he was gloriously converted on the spot. So deep and profound was his conversion experience that he made restitution to everyone from whom he had stolen as long as he had resources to do so. He even changed his testimony in a court case where he had committed perjury to get one of his fellow henchmen off the hook. He finally gave away everything until he was absolutely penniless. But God gave him a great ministry thereafter. At his conversion, the headlines of the Los Angeles papers read, "Jim Vaus Hits Sawdust Trail." That began to draw incredible attention to the crusade.

Another miracle had also occurred. The most popular radio star on the West Coast at that time was Stuart Hamlin, a western-style singer. His program was sponsored by one of the large tobacco companies of America. He lived a notorious life and spent hours at the race track. Hamlin had a dedicated Christian wife, and one night she persuaded him to go hear Graham preach. The Holy Spirit struck his heart profoundly and he went home deeply under conviction. He called Billy to come and see him, which of course Billy gladly did. He had a life-changing experience with Christ and the very next day, on his radio program, he startled the country. He said that he had sold all his race horses except for one or two that he was very fond of; he wanted to keep them for his own personal use. He went on to say that though he did not now believe in smoking cigarettes since he got right with God, if someone just had to smoke, they should smoke the brand sponsoring his program. Needless to say, the sponsor soon canceled. But it caused an incredible impact in the whole of California. Multitudes began to come to the services. Then a great Olympic, gold medalist came to faith in Christ. He made headlines as well. By this time the three weeks were up, but it just had to be extended. The crusade actually went on for two months. Ruth stayed in California longer than she had ever anticipated. What days those were. Billy completely ran out of sermons and one night even preached the heart of Jonathan Edward's classic sermon, "Sinners in the Hand of An Angry God." That was a disaster, and Billy learned that he must be himself and preach his own messages regardless.

The Country Is Alerted

The news of the crusade spread all over the country. A new young revivalist had ascended onto the national scene. The very next year the authors of this book were in seminary in Fort Worth, Texas. Billy was holding a crusade in Dallas, Texas, and came to Southwestern Baptist Theological Seminary's ten o'clock chapel service. The campus crackled with electric anticipation of Graham's visit. When the nine o'clock class ended, the buildings literally exploded as students ran headlong toward the chapel, we among them. Never shall we forget sitting in chapel and hearing God's man. He was still very young and had the flamboyancy of youth. Being the young man he was, he lifted up his trousers' leg and showing his bright argyle socks to us he said, "Young men and women, don't dress down or be drab. Let the world know that you stand for Christ and that you're really with them and thus dress accordingly." It was a good lesson.

As a result of the great Los Angeles Crusade, the nation, and before very long the entire world, fixed its eyes on Billy. Again, standing beside him was his faithful wife Ruth, not only praying for him but also giving him counsel and advice that he greatly appreciated and cherished. If ever there has been a wife of awakening, it has been Ruth Bell Graham. After Ruth saw what God was doing through her husband, she said, "This was without a doubt what God had called Bill to do." But the saga was only beginning.

Ruth's message got through to Billy; he must be relieved from his responsibilities at Northwestern. He approached the trustees, and they too recognized that he should go into full-time itinerant evangelism.

The next year Billy traveled to Portland, Oregon. During the Portland Crusade, he was offered a contract to go on network radio. He telephoned George Wilson, the business manager of Northwestern and the proprietor of a Christian bookstore, asking him if he would handle the mail and some of the details relative to the broadcast. Wilson very happily agreed and suggested that they set up a nonprofit corporation so that incoming funds would be tax deductible. A lawyer in Minneapolis drew up the papers and the organization became known as the Billy Graham Evangelistic Association. George Wilson became the business manager of the infant association.

In November of that year, Graham launched the *Hour of Decision* radio broadcast. He started by channeling the message through 223 stations of the American Broadcasting Company. In just five years that number exceeded one thousand stations, not including many short-wave broadcasts around the world.

On December 19, 1950, the Graham's third daughter was born. They named her Ruth Bell, but her mother gave her the nickname Bunnie. Ruth said that she looked like a rabbit. By December 22, the family was home and Ruth spent what she recalls as one of the most blissful of all their Christmases.

A New Life

With the children now looking to their mother for care, and with Billy being gone so much, Ruth realized she would have to make the decision of staying home the bulk of the time to raise the family. They had apparently learned a lesson from the life of Billy Sunday's family. "Ma" Sunday, as she was affectionately known, traveled with Billy Sunday during much of his itinerant evangelism ministry. As a consequence, the children suffered. Mrs. Sunday urged the Grahams not to make that mistake, so Ruth made the sacrifice of being just the wife of the revivalist and the mother of their children. It was not an easy thing to do or an easy lesson to learn, but Ruth stood tall in it all and was quite content.

This lesson came home to Ruth very forcefully on a rainy day in March 1950. Billy was holding a crusade in Columbia, South Carolina. In that setting she wrote,

> The clouds were hanging low on the surrounding mountains. The whole outdoors was sodden and gray and gloomy. Then in the middle of it all, I looked up from my kitchen sink and through the window up on the side of the mountain, was a bright patch of sunlight where the clouds had broken. The only patch of brightness in all that dismal scene. I thought how if I were free, I'd love to

climb up and sit in that patch of sunlight awhile . . . but God is not limited to Columbia. The same God so marvelously working there is in the house with me. I shall have a little revival of my own."

That was the wonderful spirit of this wife of awakening. Actually, that is revival in itself.

Writings and a Growing Family

In 1952, Billy wrote his first book, *Peace with God*. Ruth had a significant hand in it. As close friends recognize, her ability with the pen greatly aided her husband. Since those early days she has penned several volumes of her own—and they have enjoyed wide circulation. She is really a gifted woman.

In July of the same year, 1952, Ruth gave birth to their fourth child, William Franklin Graham, III. Billy was delighted. He said, "I would have loved another girl, but every man needs a son." Although Franklin had his rebellious days, he has now become the future director and CEO of the Billy Graham Evangelistic Association as Billy approaches older age. He has become a true man of God himself, leading two great benevolent agencies: The Samaritan's Purse and a ministry of sending medical personnel overseas to needy areas. Moreover, Franklin has grown into a very able evangelist himself. His crusades are beginning to draw large numbers as did his father's.

The Great Harringay Crusade

In 1953, Billy spoke at the Church House in Westminster, London. This is the headquarters of the worldwide Anglican Church. He so impressed the English clergy and laity that they invited him to come and hold a major London crusade, which came to fruition in 1954 in the now demolished Harringay Arena. What a crusade it proved to be. London was all astir, reminiscent of the great Wesley-Whitefield crusades of the eighteenth century. When the subway trains left the Harringay Arena, they would be filled with people singing hymns. The crusade became the talk of London. Headlines of it filled all of the papers day after day. It moved London to its foundations. One would have to live in London to grasp fully the profundity of the Graham's ministry.

London is an exceedingly secular city. Very few people go to church. Something about the devastating effects of World War I and World War II virtually emptied the churches. Moreover, Billy and Ruth were not well-known in England, though Billy had been there in 1946. For the city to be so moved spiritually became one of the incredible phenomenons of the last half of the twentieth century. The crusade went on for three months.

Ruth stayed with Billy the entire time, that being the longest period of separation from the children that Billy and Ruth had ever experienced. Both parents missed them dearly, as the children did them. But a real touch of revival came to London through this dedicated man and woman of God.

Billy and Ruth had sailed to London on the SS *United States*. They were given a handsome stateroom and the "Revival Widow," as Ruth had been dubbed by the press, thoroughly enjoyed the voyage. However, opposition brewed. One newspaper article recorded:

> London: A labor member of Parliament announced today he would challenge in Commons, the admission of Billy Graham to England on the grounds the American evangelist was interfering in British politics under the guise of religion.

A bad mistake had been made in the publicity. The Graham Association had sent calendars to London to generate prayer and financial assistance for the crusade. The caption beneath one of the photographs on the calendar read, "What Hitler's bombs could not do, Socialism, with its accompanying evils shortly accomplish." Jerry Bevin, who at that time served as the Director of Crusade Planning and Organization had written the phrase. He had not realized that Socialism with a capital "S" was synonymous with the British Labor Party. What he really tried to say was that *Communism* had been a devastating thing in European life. That unfortunate choice of words put a serious question mark on the Grahams when they landed at the docks in Southampton. Several Britishers accused the team of meddling in their politics. Fortunately, they caught the mistake early before the bulk of the calendars had been mailed. Nevertheless, some had slipped through and found their way to Fleet Street, the street upon which all of the British newspapers have their offices. A minifuror erupted. Ruth said, "For awhile there, the wireless was kept buzzing with accusations, explanations and apologies. It kept us busy praying too, that the Lord would override this inadvertent mistake to His glory." But the storm passed, and before long Billy and Ruth had completely won the hearts of the Londoners.

Of course, Billy was often accused of flamboyance. Someone made the curt remark, "If Jesus were here today, would He wear a hundred dollar suit, eat steak, fly in a jet or stay in the Holiday Inn?" One reporter sarcastically remarked to Grady Wilson, Billy's associate, "When Jesus was on earth, he rode a lowly donkey. I cannot imagine Jesus arriving in England aboard the Queen Mary." Grady, always ready with a quick reply, said, "Listen, if you can find me a donkey that can swim the Atlantic, I'll buy it." Those were just some of the things that Billy and Ruth had to face, not only in London, but throughout all of their ministry. But as Ruth often said, "I knew that they were after Bill's scalp, and there was nothing we could do but pray for wisdom and be as courteous and gracious as we could." That is what a woman of revival will do.

All was not negative, however. As Billy and Ruth passed through customs in Southampton, one of the custom agents said, "God bless you, sir. We need you here." A soldier passing by said, "I'll be praying for you, sir." They were needed in secular Britain, and prayers were answered.

Billy and Ruth were housed at the Stratford Court, a very modest small hotel just off Oxford Street. On the way to the arena the first night, in a dark green sedan compliments of the Ford Motor Company, Ruth confided, "There are butterflies in my stomach." They rumbled through the streets of London until they arrived at Harringay in the northern part of the city. As they pulled into the lot, Willis Haymaker, crusade director, got hold of the Grahams quickly and said, "The building is filled to capacity!" He was in a state of excitement if not ecstasy. Moreover, two American senators were there waiting for Billy in the office to share in the crusade.

The crusade began and the rest of the story is once again history. Night after night the crowds were overwhelming. People had to be turned away. One journalist wrote, "Not since the Dwight L. Moody revival of the late nineteenth century has Britain been so deeply stirred."

All the publicity, the television cameras constantly being poked in their faces, the indescribable attention they received, though necessary for the propagation of the crusade, just did not appeal to Ruth. She shrank from it. Ruth had been reared on the mission field. It would never be her way of life to be in the limelight. Yet she graciously accepted the inevitable and went along with the flow, realizing that God worked in it all and that this was a necessary part of being the wife of a great revivalist. But after the first month, Ruth was close to distraction. She had served as a counselor in the crusade but felt that she had not really seen one single person come to faith in Christ, although no doubt her testimony and witness moved many. At the end of March she instructed one of the team members to get her a ticket home. Billy immediately canceled it, even giving a severe warning to the team members, "If you get her the ticket, you're fired." Billy needed her. She was his most reliable, trusted, and understanding confidante. He depended on her. One year later, when Billy evangelized in Glasgow, he wrote to his beloved:

> I don't have to tell you that you are in my mind every moment and that I love you with all my heart, and miss you so much that it hurts. . . . Naturally I think of you a thousand times a day and each little experience I wish I could share with you. Last night I

told Lorne Sanny and Charlie Riggs to gather all the stories for me daily. I said, "Last year every evening Ruth would bring me a number of stories of conversions of people who had come to Christ. I don't have her this year to report to me every night; therefore I am depending on you fellows." You see what an important place you had on the team. Your letters have been a balm in Gilead. They have given me inspiration, quieted my nerves. They bring me so close to you. Be assured that my love grows for you every day and I miss you more than I ever thought I could miss any person.

Still, the thought of remaining in London for two more months really depressed Ruth. So Billy relented and said that she could go home. Joyously she started making plans to leave. Before she left, she strolled down to Hyde Park and found a crowd assembled at Speakers' Corner. A regular at that interesting tourist attraction for many years was Donald Soper, a Methodist pastor and a well-known soapbox orator. She walked up to listen to what he had to say. Soper began to expound, "I have no patience with those who preach sudden conversion. To think an entire life can be changed in half an hour's time is a diversion of Christian truth!" This obviously upset Ruth and she did not appreciate at all a Christian minister's siding with the unbelieving multitudes as they reveled in his ridicule of evangelical Christians. She hurried back to her hotel as rain began to come down. As she walked along, a young Englishman had fallen in step with her. He said, "It's a pity the rain had to break up Soper's speaking. Where are you going?" Ruth replied that she was going back to her hotel. The young Englishman immediately recognized that she was an American and he said, "Would you have time for a cup of coffee?" Ruth declined, of course. He pressed on, "But what about tomorrow night—are you busy?" Ruth replied, "Yes, I'll be going to Harringay." Then she looked at him and said, "Could you come?" "I suppose I could, but how about Tuesday night?" he asked. Ruth told him she would be going to Harringay again. Again he asked, "You won't be going to Harringay every night next week, will you?" "Every night," she assured him. The young man began to sense that she must be connected with the Billy Graham Association, so he asked her if that were the case, and Ruth replied that she was Billy's wife. She went on to say that she did hope that he would come to the crusade.

That encounter put Ruth right in the midst of indecision about whether or not she should go home. The next day she received a letter from a retired missionary who reminded her that God would certainly take care of the children back in America. What was she to do? The answer came to Ruth that very night in the arena. As she sat there and saw the multitudes who so desperately needed the Lord Jesus Christ (so many of them that did not even realize their peril without the Lord), she made her decision. She canceled her reservation to go home and stayed through the crusade.

In the middle of April, on Good Friday, Billy took his place in Hyde Park at Speakers' Corner. More than forty thousand people assembled. Soper never drew a crowd like that. Ruth did not sit on the platform that had been built for the event, but wandered through the crowd to see the reaction. It was great.

The last month of the crusade unfolded and was even more hectic than the previous two. Billy had lost fourteen pounds. He and Ruth were absolutely exhausted. The two final services were held on Saturday, May 29. The rain pelted down. The first service was held at the White City Stadium. Seventy thousand people jammed into the stands and onto the playing field. The second convened at Wimbley Stadium. There, many people had actually camped overnight in the inclement weather hoping to get in. More than one hundred and twenty thousand people packed the stadium. Ruth was seated in the royal box, situated in back of the platform with eleven members of the House of Commons, the mayor of London and his wife, along with the archbishop of Canterbury and his wife. Billy's sermons at both of the closing meetings were once again the simple message of salvation. He realized that people who would want to come forward would be unable to do so, therefore he asked them to make their decisions for Christ and wave their handkerchiefs. It seemed as though the whole stadium became a sea of waving white handkerchiefs. London, in a very real sense of the word, could never be quite the same again. The Gospel had triumphed, and Ruth played no small part in that victory of the Cross.

The World before Them

After Harringay, Ruth and Billy belonged to the world. Tourists came from all over just to see their little house in Montreat. Of course, the children greatly enjoyed all the attention, but it was not easy for Billy and especially for Ruth who had to stay home most of the time while Billy preached crusades.

Other temptations came along as well. In the 1950s Billy was offered a million dollars a year to host a two-hour Sunday morning talk show on NBC. Paramount Pictures Corporation wanted to make a movie star out of him. In the same period, ABC offered him a starting salary of one hundred and fifty thousand dollars if he would just serve as a consultant. He constantly had to refuse such appeals as well as many other offers. For example, someone offered him a year's lease of a jet and a pilot. Things that were left to him in wills, beyond his control, he donated to either the Billy Graham Evangelistic Association or to Wheaton College.

He gave half of his own family inheritance to various Christian organizations. Fame and fortune were his at the bidding, but he refused them all in the name of Christ. Behind him in every one of these decisions his supporting and loving wife Ruth prayed, counseled, and guided him.

A New Home

The Grahams moved from their little house in Montreat; it had become almost a thoroughfare. They found a one-hundred-and-fifty-acre plot located two miles from their house in a cove between two ridges in the beautiful Smokies just outside Montreat. While they were contemplating buying, Ruth felt that the place had great potential. Billy was skeptical, but said, "I will leave it up to you to decide." He then left for the West Coast for another crusade. Ruth borrowed money from the bank and bought the beautiful cove property.

Ruth's first project was to remodel one of the old cabins on the land so they could escape tourists on weekends until a permanent house could be built. Then a few weeks later, Ruth, with the help of an architect, designed a new home. It would be a U-shaped, story-and-a-half house. It afforded a beautiful view of Black Mountain and the Swannanoa valley.

Whatever Ruth threw herself into, she did with all her heart; the house being no exception. She studied books on architecture and did everything in the world to make the house all that she and Billy would want it to be. Ruth wanted their home to have character and to look as if it had existed for years. Ruth said Billy felt more at home in a Holiday Inn or a hotel because of his constant travels, but that he would have a comfortable "old" country house when he came home. So she went ahead and hired a team of mountain men who had remodeled her parents home to build hers. It turned out to be a beautiful place. It is rustic, much like an old log house, and Ruth filled it with large Victorian furniture. She is a great homemaker. The Grahams live in that house to this day.

New York Next?

In 1955, John Sutherland Bonnell, well-known pastor of New York's fifth Avenue Presbyterian Church, approached Billy and asked him if he was ever going to hold a crusade in the Big Apple. Billy, in typical humility, replied that he felt not yet ready for that. Regardless, the Protestant Council of the city of New York representing seventeen hundred churches of thirty-one different denominations, invited him to hold a crusade in Madison Square Garden. Billy sensed the leadership of the Lord and finally accepted the invitation. Immediately his organization began the preparations.

The work of the preparation committee was quite amazing. They prepared six hundred and fifty billboards, forty thousand telephone dials reading "pray for Billy Graham," thirty-five thousand window posters and forty thousand bumper stickers, two hundred and fifty thousand crusade song books, and one hundred thousand gospels of John. It actually took the better part of two years to put all the preparations in place. The crusade began in 1957, and Vice President Nixon promised to attend the crusade on behalf of the president and speak to one hundred thousand in Yankee Stadium. It was the longest and most expensive of all the Graham crusades up to that time. The six weeks of scheduled services stretched into sixteen. When the final benediction was said, over 2.3 million people had attended. Not only that, one hundred and sixty thousand jammed into Times Square for the final meeting on September 1, 1957. In that context Billy Graham began his television ministry.

Billy's and Ruth's Sensitivity

Turbulent time faced America in 1957. Three years earlier the Supreme Court had ruled that racial segregation in the United States was unconstitutional. That touched off the many well-known riots and protest movements. Ruth and Billy took a strong Christian stand on those issues. Billy refused to hold any crusades that were not fully integrated, and he stuck to his guns. These authors were involved in the Birmingham, Alabama, rally. Betty had worked in the Billy Graham office in London while Lewis was working on his Ph.D. degree at Kings College, University of London. When that London stint was accomplished and we came back to America, Betty worked in the Graham office in preparation for the Birmingham rally. Birmingham had been the scene of tremendous racial upheaval. FBI personnel guarded the Graham office where Betty worked. The "Bessemer bombers," those who had been responsible for the infamous bombing of the Sixth Avenue Baptist Church that killed six precious African-American children, had threatened to blow up the Billy Graham office. Billy and all the team tenaciously held up the principle of Christian openness and unity. Many of the churches refused to cooperate. On the day of the big rally, the Legion Field municipal stadium was a sight to behold. The place was filled with blacks and whites and Hispanics and people of all ethnic origins. Billy faithfully preached the Gospel and many came to faith in Christ. What a triumph for the cause of Christ, not to mention the testimony it left to those who fully understand that in Christ there are no human barriers that keep people from being one in the Lord.

The TV Ministry

The New York Crusade gave birth to Billy's television career. Not following the pattern of the traditional televangelists, Mr. Graham, as his team members call him, simply telecasts three or four nights a week at prime time on a major network—usually NBC. The programs are edited presentations of a crusade meeting. The viewer thus feels that he or she is right in the crusade itself. The crusade television ministry of Billy Graham has been seen by literally millions upon millions of people. Telephone counselors are available for those who wish to call in. Multitudes have come to Christ as a result of that effective methodology. The television ministry reached a great height in 1995, through the marvels of modern technology. Billy broadcast from Puerto Rico via satellite around the world. It is estimated that one-billion people heard the simple Gospel of Christ through hundreds of interpreters in over one hundred and fifty nations. It is certainly true that seeds were sown where few before had ever heard the name of Jesus. In the spring of 1996, a similar program was telecast that had the potential to reach over 2.5 billion viewers. What a triumph, not only of technology, but of kingdom progress above all.

Along with Billy's crusades, schools of evangelism were launched. A dedicated Christian layman from California endowed the schools. In the earlier years, they were held in conjunction with the crusades themselves and ministers were invited from all over the surrounding area to come to hear messages and seminars on effective evangelism. The ministers' way were paid and their housing and food was taken care of through the endowment. Some have said that that program is perhaps the longest-lasting contribution of the Graham crusades. Now conferences are held in various venues. Although millions have heard the Gospel through the crusade ministry, pastors and evangelists who have been inspired and challenged by the schools of evangelism have fanned out all over the world. The multitudes who have come to Christ as a consequence of that fruitful ministry have perhaps even exceeded the crusades themselves.

A Life of Service for Ruth

Through the years, Ruth has been deeply involved in the ministry of the Presbyterian church in Montreat. The pastor, Calvin Thielman, just recently retired, has been a friend of the family for some time. It will be remembered that Ruth remained a Presbyterian. She found great satisfaction in serving the Lord in that setting. God gave Ruth a special ministry to the college students at a nearby Christian college in Montreat. Ruth had special appeal to those who were caught up in the generation gap of the so-called rebellious sixties. She would take time with these young people, and though they were unattractive and something of a problem to the older generation, she gave of herself to them to draw them closer to Christ. She had learned early in life to cross cultural barriers. In one sense of the word, she was like a Tsingkiang missionary in Montreat. Dr. Thielman would direct Ruth to students who seemed to have the greatest need, and she always rose to the occasion. She found it a deep source of satisfaction to reach people who others were not concerned about. Ruth has remained a faithful member and servant of the Montreat Presbyterian Church throughout her life.

Ruth's father, Nelson Bell, retired from his surgical practice in the mid-fifties. He had had a very successful medical ministry in America. Being the exemplary Christian gentleman that he was, his life counted for Christ in the United States, even though he left much of his heart in China. In Ruth's parents' later years, Mrs. Bell became a partial invalid. Dr. Bell cared for her as lovingly and as graciously as anyone possibly could, and he did not see it as a burden. He said, "My greatest delight is to care for my wife." She had been such a faithful mother and wife and fellow servant of Christ for so many years that Dr. Bell saw a real part of his ministry as giving loving care to the one whom he loved so much and who had meant so much to him.

The Ministry Grows

Throughout the decades, Billy Graham's ministry continued and expanded. For years he has been voted as one of the most-admired men in the world. Virtually every award: religious, humanitarian, and every other category have been heaped on him. Despite it all, Ruth kept an even keel and a beautifully balanced approach to life. She stands as a great token of the grace of Jesus Christ. Their last child, Ned, topped off the family. With three girls and two boys, the Graham legacy is bound to carry on.

Throughout it all, Ruth never lost the human touch. One December, just before Christmas, word went around the community that a nearby family was virtually starving to death. They lived in an abandoned toolshed in Black Mountain, the next little town beside Montreat. Calvin Thielman and two deacons investigated and found a mother and five small children eking out an existence. The father, who had been a carpenter, was dying of cancer in the hospital. It was going to be a very difficult Christmas. Calvin visited the man in the hospital and told him that some people wanted to do something for the children and find a decent place for them to live. Yet, he said, he would not do it without the husband's permission. The dear man's eyes filled with tears and said, "I reckon they would appreciate that." When Billy heard the story, he went to the Presbyterian pastor. He handed Calvin Thielman a very generous check saying that there was more where that had come from.

Ruth, of course, had already risen to the occasion. She found out the ages of the children and bought clothing and toys for them. Just before Christmas they were able to move the family into an old house. It left something to be desired, but it was infinitely better than the abandoned shabby toolshed.

The father, in the hospital, was receiving very little attention. His pain mounted as the days went by. When Calvin visited him, he asked if some oxygen could be given to make him more comfortable. The attendant said, "Well, we'll have to get clearance from the head doctor and I don't know where to get him." The pastor, outraged, telephoned Ruth and told her the whole situation. "You let me handle it," Ruth said. She knew when to throw her weight around, as one biographer put it. In no time the situation was radically altered. A doctor came and a private nurse was stationed by the dying man's side. That is real Christianity.

Strange Problems

In those days Billy had a very difficult time whenever he went out in public. He would literally be mobbed by crowds wherever he went. Often he would resort to going out in something of a disguise. He would wear large sunglasses and a cap pulled low over his face. On one occasion in Mexico he wore a large brimmed hat. An autograph hound came up to him thinking he was James Arness, the Matt Dillon character of television's *Gunsmoke* fame. Only when Billy would go off to Europe where people are far more restrained in such matters, could he find some peace. These authors had dinner with the Grahams one night in London, and even though people would look over at his table, realizing who he was, no one ever came up to him. Perhaps this is the reason that Billy and Ruth have always had such a fond affection for Europe—not to mention wonderful memories of the crusades.

The problem of popularity and fame also affected the children. In November 1961, the *Indianapolis Times* printed the following: "The handsome lad nightclubbing in New York with Gayle Horn, Lena's daughter, was Billy Graham, Jr., son of the evangelist." What was so ridiculous about the report was that Franklin was only nine years old at the time. "But the sobering fact," Ruth declared, "is that it shows none of our children can ever live privately."

Christianity in Action

Billy's and Ruth's involvement in social action as well as evangelism is an unheralded story. Both are deeply touched by the needs of people and do far more than most people ever realize to help people in their need. Billy and Ruth have never lost the personal touch or the importance of the individual. As a simple case in point, on one occasion we were together at a banquet in Billy's honor at Southern Seminary in Louisville, Kentucky. Seated at the head table with him, we suddenly missed him. He was gone for some ten or fifteen minutes. We wondered the reason for his absence, but did not ask. Later we found that he had gone to the kitchen of the hotel where the banquet was being held and thanked all of the cooks and the waiters for making the evening and the meal such a delightful experience. That is Christian sensitivity as it ought to be. Ruth too exemplified that spirit constantly as has been illustrated by her touching the couple in the little deserted toolshed in Black Mountain. Ruth and Billy also uphold the highest moral standards. Billy himself takes very literally Paul's admission to "flee from all appearance of evil." He will never enter a hotel room first, but will always have someone walk in before him lest there be some trap laid for him. Such has been the case in the past. Moral purity of the biblical kind is always upheld in the Graham home. Ruth, who has had such a central role in raising the children, certainly has instilled morality deeply in the Graham clan. Then again, that is real revival. May God give us more men and women of awakening like that.

Critics

The Grahams, of course, have not been without critics. Billy receives it especially from theological circles. It is exceedingly easy for theologians to become very abstract in their theologizing, and thus miss something of the simplicity of the Gospel. Dr. Karl Barth, a well-known theologian and something of the father of the neo-orthodox movement, did not feel too kindly toward the Graham ministry. In a long conversation they had one time, Barth pointed out to Billy that it was very easy for people to see the idea of becoming a Christian in a far too simplistic way. Billy asked him what he would say to a person who came to him seeking help to find a right relationship to God. Barth replied, "I would say to him, friend, you are in great danger . . . but then so am I." Ruth reacted to that and said, "One could not help but feel that was a rather dreary outlook—nothing of hope and certainty in it." She went on to say, "Trying to follow their profound reasoning, I felt myself getting thoroughly confused." As the conversation went on, Karl Barth finally suggested to Billy that he should come to his school and teach theology for six months, and that he would go out and hold Billy's evangelistic meetings for six months. Ruth did not rise to that suggestion. Barth smiled a bit as he said, "And anyway, I should love to have lunch with the Queen and meet President Eisenhower and people like that."

Not only were the more liberal theologians critical of Billy, but many of the ultraconservative fundamentalists in America were unhappy with Graham's evangelism. For example, Dr. Bob Jones grew extremely critical. For Billy to allow Roman Catholics, or those of more liberal persuasions, to cooperate with him in his crusades, was in his thinking abominable. One of the strange switches in this context was in the approach of the late evangelist John R. Rice. During the great Harringay crusade, Billy had invited John R. Rice to come and participate. He went, and in his periodical, *The Sword of the Lord*, he eulogized Billy's ministry in London. But then, seemingly, someone got hold of him and he had a complete switch. *The Sword of the Lord* began to criticize Billy severely for his broad-based approach in developing the crusades. All this put Billy in virtually the same position as the Lord Jesus Himself. Our Lord received barbs from both sides of the theological spectrum, from the Sadducees on one side and the Pharisees on the other. The two extremes of Judaism could not stand our Lord's approach to the faith. Such became the case with Billy. The Left attacked him as did the extreme Right. But that put him in a good stance, because he stood by his Lord. And Ruth stood right there by his side to encourage him.

Meeting Celebrities

True, as Barth said, the Grahams did have the opportunity to meet many world leaders. Ruth, never awed by all the glamour and fame that attended such meetings, has remained a disciplined, devout, well-balanced Christian throughout her life.

Billy Graham has almost become the personal confidant and chaplain to president after president, although his first encounter with Harry Truman proved anything but a happy one—he was a very young man at that time and made some blunders. Down through the years, up until the present time, presidents have always looked to him. Billy was with President Bush for prayer and encouragement on the night he ordered the commencement of Dessert Storm in the Persian Gulf War. One of the great disappointments of the Grahams' lives centered on the Watergate incident when President Nixon resigned as the leader of America. When Billy heard some of the tapes and the language that Nixon used, it made him literally sick. Later the breach was healed, and when President Nixon died, Billy preached his funeral, as he had done when Mrs. Nixon passed on. In the significant tragedy of the bombing in Oklahoma City in 1995, Billy and President Clinton were the main speakers at a memorial service for the two-hundred-and-sixty-plus lives that had been snuffed out in that tragic and inexplicable crime. Ruth always appreciated such opportunities that came their way, but once again, always kept it in good perspective. Simply put, she loved the Lord Jesus Christ supremely and was concerned primarily for His kingdom and for His glory, not for Billy's or hers.

A Trying Time

In August 1973, Ruth experienced a severe blow. On Wednesday, August 1, she had telephoned her parents to come and have supper with her. They refused, saying that they were really not hungry, so she did not see them that day. The very next morning when Mrs. Bell woke up at 7:30, she was rather surprised not to hear the television. Dr. Bell normally rose early to get the morning news on TV. She rolled out of bed and getting hold of her aluminum walker, went looking for him. She found him sitting with his right arm comfortably tucked around his neck, but he was gone. She was able to reach the telephone and simply said, "Nelson, dead." T. W. Wilson, Billy's personal associate, was the first to arrive and then Ruth, still in her bathrobe. She gently kissed her mother and said, "He is in heaven now—with Nelson Jr."

As the seventies and eighties unfolded, Billy and Ruth's ministry continued to expand if that was possible. Hardly a person in the world had not heard their names, at least in places where mass communication is possible. Their ministry (for it truly is a joint ministry) has become the most widespread ministry of evangelism in the history of the church. Ruth always expressed gratitude to God for being a vital part of the reviving movement.

Health Problems

In the 1970s Ruth's health began to deteriorate somewhat. Suffering from severe arthritis, a hip replacement became necessary. Her pain was very difficult at times, more acute than most people realized. Yet, in the Christian spirit that she always exuded, she bore up bravely and carried on in an amazing fashion. While these authors served as president and wife of Southeastern Baptist Theological Seminary in North Carolina (Billy had preached the inauguration ceremony), Ruth was hospitalized in Raleigh for more surgery on her hip. One of the professor's wives became her nurse and it was touch and go for a period of time. Yet God saw her through the surgery and restored strength and vitality. Billy was off at that time doing a crusade and could not be there for the actual day of surgery. This always grieved him, but Christ came first in both their lives. That too makes up the real spirit of revival. As these pages were being written, Ruth was once again stricken with a serious illness, but God saw her through another crisis. She is a strong lady.

The devoted couple, with their lovely children and their many grandchildren, eased into the 1990s. By the middle of the decade, it became evident that the ministry was beginning to taper off somewhat. Billy, suffering from Parkinson's disease and battling his old enemies of high-blood pressure and phlebitis, does not have the strength that he once had. The same is true for his dear wife Ruth. Yet it absolutely amazes all how they continue and how well they carry on. When Billy walks into the pulpit, the Spirit of God comes powerfully on him, to the point that he is much like his old self. He preaches with a zest and a dynamic that captivates the masses who come to hear him. The marvel is, his crusades are greater than ever. He probably does not make front-page news of the paper every day as during his earlier ministry, but statistically, the crusades are the greatest ever. The percentage of people who make decisions for Christ are higher than ever before, the actual attendance reaches all-time records, and the Graham name is revered and respected as never before. All the criticisms have now basically fallen away and Billy and his dear wife shine forth as examples of what revivalism in the evangelistic sense truly is. In back of it all that woman of revival, that wife of awakening, has been an incalculable strength and stabilizing force in the entire ministry.

A Positive Spirit

Throughout the years, Ruth has learned to laugh at almost anything.

One day the Grahams were expecting guests for dinner and Ruth asked Billy, "What would you like to have on the menu?"

"Uh-huh," came the reply.

Deciding to have some fun, Ruth began rattling off a rather unusual bill of fare.

"I thought we'd start off with tadpole soup," she began.

"Uh-huh," he replied.

"And there is some lovely poison ivy growing in the next cove which would make a delightful salad."

"Uh-huh."

"For the main dish, I could try roasting some of those wharf rats we've been seeing around the smokehouse lately, and serve them with boiled crabgrass and baked birdseed."

"Uh-huh."

"And for dessert we could have a mud souffle and . . ." her voice trailed off as his eyes finally focused.

"What were you saying about wharf rats?" he asked.

As can be imagined, Ruth was a marvelous mother to the children. It would have been very easy for the children to be superficially caught up in the fame and popularity of their father, but Ruth modeled her home after her childhood in China. They were, therefore, disciplined children and were expected to be normal like all the other kids. Ruth did discover considerable differences among her children, but she knew how to handle each one very well. What a relief to Billy to have such a wife at home taking care of the children while he carried on his itinerant ministry.

Moreover, Ruth strove to be diligent in bringing up the children in the nurture and admonition of the Lord. One Sunday while the family was still young, the following incident occurred:

That afternoon she gathered GiGi, Anne, and Bunny into the Jeep and drove them up to the cabin below the then unfinished house. They sunned, read, picked cherries, hunted turtles. Then GiGi and Anne performed skits based on nursery rhymes. Ruth hung a blue and white bedspread from the loft for the curtain. She and Bunny were the audience.

When Anne began acting out "Little Miss Muffet" GiGi climbed a ladder, ostensibly to drop the "spider" beside her. The spider turned out to be a lump of manure. GiGi hurled it with the cheek of a mockingbird dive-bombing a squirrel.

"It's the only thing I could find that was brown and we could pretend was a spider," GiGi explained as her mother scrubbed a teary Anne.

One unfortunate scene led to another, and Ruth ended GiGi's tantrum with a spanking.

After a supper of hot dogs roasted over the fire she read the children a Bible story and GiGi began asking questions.

"Mommy," she asked, "if I die, will I go to Heaven?"

"You tell me," she replied.

"I don't know."

"Want me to tell you how you can know?" Ruth asked.

"I don't think you can know for sure."

"I do," Ruth said.

"O.K., how?"

"First," she explained, "you know you are a sinner, don't you?"

"Oh, I know that," GiGi assured her enthusiastically.

"Then you confess your sins to Him," Ruth said.

"I do that. You know when I got so mad at you this afternoon I told Him I was sorry three times just to make sure, in case He didn't hear me the first time."

"He heard you the first time," Ruth said. "Listen, 'If we confess our sins, He is faithful and just to forgive us our sins and cleanse us from all unrighteousness' [1 John 1:9]."

"Are you sure He heard me?"

"I know He did," Ruth said.

"But it doesn't say 'GiGi.'"

"It says 'whosoever,'" Ruth said.

GiGi said nothing and her mother continued. "Now you have done the first two. You have become a child of God. You are born into God's family, just as eight years ago you were born into our family. Your body was born then, your soul is born again now."

"But I still am not sure," GiGi said.

"GiGi, would you call God a liar?"

"Of course not!"

"But you are. He said if you confess He will forgive; if you believe, you have eternal life. You have done both, but you don't think He will keep His promise. That is the same as calling Him a liar."

Ruth held up a piece of paper and said, "Whoever wants it can have it."

GiGi snatched it from her fingers.

"What makes you think I said you?" Ruth demanded.

"You said 'whoever,'" she replied.

"Exactly."

They knelt beside the cabin's bed and prayed.

"Mommy," GiGi said breathlessly as they drove away, "I feel like a new person."

All of that notwithstanding, the Graham children were children. They had their sibling rivalries; they had their spats; they were disobedient and rebellious at times; they were typical children. They were not the sterling examples of what children ought to be all the time. But Ruth, a good disciplinarian, saw them all grow up to be marvelous dedicated Christians.

Separations

It was not easy for Billy to leave home as he often is still compelled to do. There would be no teary farewells when Billy left for a crusade, at least not an open display of emotions. There would be a hug and a kiss and Billy would be on his way to the airport. Yet, Billy said, "Many a time I've driven down that driveway with tears coming down my cheeks not wanting to leave." No matter where he was, from anywhere in the world, if it were at all possible, he would telephone Ruth every night. His deep feelings and love and appreciation for Ruth are beautifully expressed in a letter that he wrote many years ago:

How can I find words to express my appreciation for all you have meant to me. Your love and patience with me in my ups and downs . . . have meant more to me than you will ever know. Your counsel, advice, encouragement and prayer have been my mainstay—and at times I have almost clung to you in my weakness, in hours of obsession, problems and difficulties. "Whoso findeth a wife findeth a good thing, and obtaineth favor of the Lord." One reason that in spite of my own lack of spirituality, discipline and consecration I have found favor of the Lord is *because of you*. I found a good wife and as a result have found favor with God. . . . It seems that in the recent months my capacity to love you has

been increased—I did not think that age would bring greater and
deeper love—but it has and is. I *love* the wife of my youth more
every day! When we are apart, I miss you so much more than I
used to. A week seems like a month. Yes, I am thankful to God
for you. What a wonderful helpmeet He provided—certainly our
marriage was planned in heaven. I am thankful for the five
precious children you bore me—each one a bundle of joy. And
what a wonderful mother you have been to them! No child ever
had a greater mother than our children. You may compare yourself
to Susanna Wesley and think you are a failure—but she did not
rear her family in a modern, secular society. For our generation
you are near perfection.

Ruth's emotions are revealed in her poetry:

> We live a time
> secure;
> sure
> It cannot last
> for long
> then—
> the goodbyes come
> again—again—
> like a small death,
> the closing of a door.
> One learns to live
> with pain.
> One looks ahead,
> not back,
> . . . never back,
> only before.
> And joy will come again
> warm and secure,
> if only for the now,
> laughing,
> we endure.

That expresses it all.

Blessed Events Still Come

Many wonderful things still take place in Ruth's life despite the problems of health and aging. The world still looks to them, as does the White
House, Buckingham Palace, and dignitaries around the globe. Even the

U.S. government recognized Ruth's and Billy's contributions. In the *Birmingham* (Alabama) *News*, the following article appeared on January 24, 1996:

> House to Give Graham Medal—Washington—The House voted to commission a Congressional Gold Medal for evangelist Billy Graham and Ruth Graham, his wife of 52 years.
>
> The bill, passed 403–2 and sent to the Senate on Tuesday, also authorizes the sale of collectible bronze duplicates of the medal, all at no taxpayer expense.

What an honor to Billy and Ruth! The ceremony took place in the nation's capital on Thursday, April 25, 1996. The award was presented in the rotunda of the Capitol. Many dignitaries were there. In the evening, a lovely dinner was hosted by commentator Paul Harvey. The President of the United States spoke as did Billy and others. These authors had the privilege of being there. It was a great event and a wonderful tribute to our woman of awakening and her famous husband.

Ruth has been a great strength to her husband; but perhaps above all, she is a constant inspiration to countless women as being the kind of a wife and mother that the Scriptures lift up, taking her role as wife and mother from what God intends for the Christian family. Throughout the years of countless crusades, world travel, difficulties, not everything always going right with the children, and a thousand other obstacles, not the least of which was to give up her hope of being a missionary in Tibet, Ruth Bell Graham has arisen as a mighty woman of God. To repeat one more word of appreciation for this spiritual giant, the question is legitimately raised again: What would Billy be without Ruth? She has been a helpmate, companion, counselor, strength, prayer warrior, and all that a man of Billy's stature and ministry so desperately needed. If ever there was a wife of revival, Ruth Graham is that wife. When the crowns are handed out, there will be many a star in hers, as many as in Billy's because she has taken her place by his side and has been mightily used of God in making him and their shared ministry what it has become.

A Fitting Tribute

It is fitting that this volume, *Women of Awakenings,* ends with one of our own contemporaries, Ruth Bell Graham. The Graham's youngest daughter, Bunnie, in a recent article in *Decision* magazine (May 1996) wrote: "How do I see my mother? As a woman of joy—like the living water that 'Shall be in her a well of water springing up into everlasting life.'" Well said. We all say thank God for Ruth Graham and all the great women who have seen revival come to nations and to the world and have witnessed multitudes who have placed their faith in the Lord Jesus Christ. That is the goal of revival for "the Lord is . . . not willing that any should perish, but that all should come to repentance" (2 Peter 3:9 KJV). It must never be forgotten that our Lord goes after that one lost sheep who desperately needs His rescuing touch. In that role Ruth Graham, and the many more great women of awakening, take their place in history and in the annals of spiritual greatness. May God give us more!

Endnotes

1. The following quotes are taken from Patricia Daniels, *A Time for Remembering* (San Francisco: Harper and Row Publishing Co., 1923).
2. The following quotes are taken from William Martin, *A Prophet with Honor* (William Morrow and Co., 1991).
3. The following quotes are taken from Daniels, *Remembering*.

EPILOGUE

A Plea for Prayer for Revival

God alone sends revival; and God uses women in great awakenings as this book has attempted to show. These foundational facts have hopefully become quite clear. Moreover, the Church of Jesus Christ always stands in need of a reviving move of the Holy Spirit. Today, this issue appears more pressing than perhaps ever before. It does not seem an exaggeration to say that unless we do experience a fresh awakening touch from God, the future for Christianity in the Western World does not glisten too brightly. What can we do?

In answer to the preceding question, let it be understood that in one sense, we can do nothing to generate a revival from the standpoint of mere human activity, sincere as that effort may be. It must be stressed again and again that *God sends revival;* and He sends it in His way, in His place, and in His time. Our great God is absolutely sovereign in all true revival movements.

Yet God never works in a vacuum; He uses people to accomplish His purposes. These "mini-biographies" of women of revival have surely demonstrated that reality. What, therefore, constitutes the human factors in the dawn of a great awakening? Several factors emerge, such as the faithful sharing of God's Word, openness to the Holy Spirit, a hungry heart, etc. Still, one factor ascends above all others: *Prevailing Prayer.* If revival has its birth in any one context, it is conceived, generated, born, and sustained in fervent intercession. History attests to that reality over and over again.

Therefore, this brief epilogue really becomes a plea for prayer for revival; a plea for personal private prayer, corporate prayer, the organizing of prayer cells and groups, prayer on every level. Thus it seems altogether appropriate to urge you, the reader, to seek God's leadership in becoming a prayer leader for a new reviving from heaven.

Will you be such a person— woman or man? Will you permit God to move and use you in prayer? Will you pay the price? Will you become a channel through whom our gracious God will once again revive His church to the glory of Jesus Christ? *The world waits for those who will answer YES!*

365